D0154560

Understanding Hospital Billing and Coding: A Worksheet

Marsha S. Diamond, CPC, CPC-H

**Program Director/Instructor
Coding and Health Information
Central Florida College (Orlando)**

THOMSON

DELMAR LEARNING

Australia   Canada   Mexico   Singapore   Spain   United Kingdom   United States

THOMSON

DELMAR LEARNING

Understanding Hospital Coding and Billing: A Worktext
by Marsha S. Diamond, CPC, CPC-H

Vice President, Health Care Business Unit:
William Brottmiller

Director of Learning Solutions:
Matthew Kane

Managing Editor:
Marah Bellegarde

Senior Acquisitions Editor:
Rhonda Dearborn

Product Manager:
Jadin Babin-Kavanaugh

Editorial Assistant:
Debra Gorgos

Marketing Director:
Jennifer McAvey

Marketing Coordinator:
Kimberly Duffy

Production Director:
Carolyn Miller

Production Manager:
Barbara A. Bullock

Senior Content Project Manager:
James Zayicek

COPYRIGHT © 2007 by Thomson Delmar Learning, a part of the Thomson Corporation. Thomson, the Star Logo, and Delmar Learning are trademarks used herein under license.

Printed in Canada
1 2 3 4 5 6 7 8 XXX 08 07 06

For more information contact Thomson Delmar Learning, 5 Maxwell Drive, Clifton Park, NY 12065-2919
Or you can visit our Internet site at
http://www.delmarlearning.com

ALL RIGHTS RESERVED. No part of this work covered by the copyright hereon may be reproduced or used in any form or by any means—graphic, electronic, or mechanical, including photocopying, recording, taping, Web distribution, or information storage and retrieval systems—without the written permission of the publisher.

For permission to use material from this text or product, contact us by
Tel (800) 730-2214
Fax (800) 730-2215
www.thomsonrights.com

Library of Congress Cataloging-in-Publication Data
Diamond, Marsha S.
  Understanding hospital billing and coding / Marsha Diamond.
    p. ; cm.
  Includes bibliographical references and index.
  ISBN 1-4018-7943-8
  1. Hospitals--Business management.
  2. Hospitals—Accounting. 3. Health insurance claims—Code numbers. 4. Medical fees.
  I. Title.
  [DNLM: 1. International classification of diseases. 2. Hospital Charges. 3. Fees and Charges. 4. Insurance, Health—economics. 5. Patient Credit and Collection—methods. WX 157 D537u 2007]
  RA971.3.D53 2007
    362.11068—dc22   2006013143

NOTICE TO THE READER

Publisher does not warrant or guarantee any of the products described herein or perform any independent analysis in connection with any of the product information contained herein. Publisher does not assume, and expressly disclaims, any obligation to obtain and include information other than that provided to it by the manufacturer.

The reader is expressly warned to consider and adopt all safety precautions that might be indicated by the activities described herein and to avoid all potential hazards. By following the instructions contained herein, the reader willingly assumes all risks in connection with such instructions.

The publisher makes no representations or warranties of any kind, including but not limited to, the warranties of fitness for particular purpose or merchantability, nor are any such representations implied with respect to the material set forth herein, and the publisher takes no responsibility with respect to such material. The publisher shall not be liable for any special, consequential, or exemplary damages resulting, in whole or part, from the readers' use of, or reliance upon, this material.

Dedication

Writing about and teaching medical coding are my opportunity to share with others the world of coding that I love and have dedicated my professional life to. For these opportunities, I thank Thomson Delmar Learning and Central Florida College.

My special thanks go to the many students who have entered the world of coding, and who have helped me refine my teaching skills and the materials utilized in this text. They are the reason teachers continue to teach!

Many individuals in my life have supported me in my writing over the past several years, and to them I extend warm and sincere thanks:

> To my four-legged companions, Charlotte and Cassie, who are always at my side during my writing, and to those who have been at my side and passed, Charles and Oreo.
>
> To my grandchildren, Tavious and Jaylen, who serve as my new inspirations. I hope my work and diligence leave you a legacy to remember.
>
> To my loving daughter Jennifer, whom I hope has been inspired by my perseverance, hard work and dedication to my profession.
>
> To Stan, for his assistance in improving the finished product and assuring the clinical accuracy of the medical information.
>
> And of course, to Mom and Dad, for always encouraging and supporting my endeavors.

A special thanks also to the staff at Thomson Delmar Learning who worked diligently on this first edition:

> To Rhonda Dearborn, Acquisitions Editor, whose vision saw the need for a textbook that combined the skills of hospital inpatient and outpatient coding and billing.
>
> To Developmental Editors Sherry Connors and Jadin Babin-Kavanaugh and Editorial Assistant Debra Gorgos, for working diligently toward the publication of this text.

Marsha S. Diamond

Contents

SECTION I   HOSPITAL CODING AND BILLING OVERVIEW   1

CHAPTER 1   HOSPITAL CODING OVERVIEW   3

CHAPTER 2   HOSPITAL BILLING PROCESS   37

Preface

INTRODUCTION

Understanding Hospital Coding and Billing offers a comprehensive look at the world of hospital and facility coding and billing in a textbook format. It is designed to assist the student in comprehending the inpatient and outpatient facility as well as both the coding and billing aspects of the facility. This textbook provides the tools for a student to be successful in the fields of Health Information Technology, Health Information Management, Health Science Administration, Medical Assisting, Medical Coding, Medical Billing, Patient Business Representative, Insurance Representative, or Consultant. This success is based on an understanding of the entire facility process from patient intake through the billing process. Knowledge of the total process is imperative to successful comprehension of both coding and billing in the facility setting.

The majority of textbooks covering this topic include only a portion of the hospital coding or billing instruction necessary to succeed in the hospital medical field today. *Understanding Hospital Coding and Billing* is one of the only comprehensive hospital facility coding AND billing text work book on the market to date. After successfully completing this material, students should be capable of sitting for the hospital coding certification examinations offered by the American Health Information Management Association (AHIMA) or the American Academy of Professional Coders (AAPC).

This textbook has been designed so that the student or instructor may utilize only those portions of the text necessary to their specific needs or curriculum. It is assumed that the student utilizing this textbook has had some training in medical terminology and/or anatomy and physiology; while these are imperative to the comprehension of the medical coding process, they are topics usually covered in other classes. As for the curriculum needs of instructors, all sections of the book can be used independently of one another, so essentially the book can be adapted to fit a given curriculum. For example, if a particular curriculum only encompasses coding, the coding sections of the book may be utilized independent of the other sections.

Extensive exercises are placed throughout each chapter, with space provided in the text for the student to make notes and work exercises as needed. Depending upon the length of the curriculum, the instructor may choose to utilize all or a portion of the exercises included. In addition to the chapter exercises, extensive billing (UB-92 completion) and coding exercises (including the assignment of DRGs or APCs) are included in an appendix as well as on the CD-ROM provided with the text.

ORGANIZATION OF TEXT

The format of this text makes it easy to utilize only those portions covered in a specific curriculum. Section I provides an overview of the hospital coding and billing processes. Since many students will have already completed studies on ICD-9-CM, CPT-4 and perhaps medical billing processes, this section serves as review of the processes involved in the facility environment as opposed to the physician perspective. It can also serve as a review for those already versed in billing and coding, and as an introduction to the new student not previously exposed to these areas of study.

Section II encompasses the details of the inpatient facility processes. Inpatient coding is covered in Chapter 4, while Chapter 5 covers the details of inpatient billing, including specifics on completion of the UB-92 for inpatient purposes. Section III covers the outpatient facility processes, again incorporating the coding process in Chapter 6 and the billing process in Chapter 7.

CLAIMS UPDATES

Due to the evolving nature of the coding and billing field, updates to the claims format and coding conventions inevitably become necessary before publication of the next edition of this text. A website has been established by Thomson Delmar Learning to keep you informed regarding any updates, changes, corrections, or revisions that are integral to claims and coding of hospital/facility services. Go to www.delmarhealthcare.com for more information.

As this book went to press, the UB-92 form was under revision. The new billing form, to be known as the UB-04, will include a number of changes, including new fields, deletion of some existing fields, and expansion of the character field for other fields. Proposed changes, deletions and revisions, as well as handy crosswalk information mapping the changes from the UB-92 to the UB-04, are provided in an appendix of this text. Please note that the information given in the appendix was correct at the time of publication; additional changes may made be made to the UB-04 before its adoption in 2007.

Proposed Changes to the UB-04

Some of the most significant changes being proposed for the UB-04 claim are as follows:

FL2: Pay-to Information

- Line 1: Name
- Line 2: Address
- Line 3: City, State, ZIP
- Line 4: ID number (when applicable)

FL29: Condition Code/Accident State

- Two-Letter Abbreviation of the State Where Accident Occurred (when applicable)

FL43: Line 23 Only/Page Numbers/Creation Date

- When claim is multiple pages, "Page ____ of ____" will be inserted
- Creation Date

FL72: External Cause Codes

Two additional fields for External Cause (E Codes) have been added when more than one E code is necessary to adequately describe factors influencing the cause of the injury or reason for encounter.

FL 82: Qual/Code/Value

A complete definition for this field had not been provided at the time of publication.

FL79: Procedure Coding Method Used

In addition, several fields will be updated with expandable character fields, many to accommodate the upcoming changes in ICD-10 with additional digits for diagnostic codes. Other revisions are being made to make the UB-04 compliant with HIPAA guidelines, such as the Patient Address Information.

FEATURES OF THIS TEXT

- The format provides space for note-taking and answers
- Practice exercises throughout encourage "as you go" reinforcement of learned concepts
- The ALERT feature draws attention to additional information or resources available relevant to chapter content
- The tables contain key reference information in one convenient location, such as those covering UB-92 Completion Details in Chapters 3, 5, and 7
- The CD-ROM in the back of the book contains case studies specific to hospital billing and coding, with field-by-field block help information provided to aid understanding
- Case studies from the CD-ROM are also provided as appendices in the book for handy reference and for manual competition

Instructor's Manual ISBN 1-4018-7944-6

The *Instructor's Manual to Accompany Understanding Hospital Coding and Billing* is an invaluable resource that provides instructors with the answers and rationales for all practice exercises in the text, as well as the answers to the case studies that appear in the appendices and on the CD-ROM. It also contains suggestions for classroom activities and lecture materials such as sample syllabi and lesson plans.

ACKNOWLEDGEMENTS

Thomson Delmar Learning and the author wish to thank the following reviewers for their input and suggestions, which greatly contributed to the development of this text:

Karen R. Fisk, CBCS, RHE
Medical Instructor
Indiana Business College
Terre Haute, IN

Pat King, MA, RHIA
Baker College
Cass City, MI

Margaret A. Stackhouse, CPC, RHIA, MCSE
Pittsburgh Technical Institute
Pittsburgh, PA

Lori A. Warren, MA, RN, CPC, CCP, CLNC
Medical Department Co-Director
Medical Coding/Health Care Reimbursement Program Director
Spencerian College
Louisville, KY

Introduction

The Flow of the Hospital Organization

KEY TERMS

Admitting Diagnosis
Appeal
Charge Capturing

Health Information
   Management (HIM)
Hospital-Based Physicians

Physician Employees
Physician Order
Third-Party Contract

LEARNING OBJECTIVES

- Discuss the hospital revenue cycle
- Understand and explain the hospital billing process
- Recognize services performed in the facility setting
- Discuss career opportunities in the hospital setting

INTRODUCTION

The world of hospital coding and billing is indeed complex. When one considers the complexity of the hospital environment and that hundreds, sometimes thousands of individuals are employed at a hospital facility, it is a monumental challenge to ensure that the patient billing process is complete, and that successful reimbursement is obtained on a timely basis.

With continued increases in the cost of quality medical care, a competitive market, an aging population that is living longer and therefore requires more years of health care, and the complexity of the reimbursement process, the demands on the hospital employee are great.

THE HOSPITAL REVENUE CYCLE

There are many individuals within the hospital network that assist in the patient process, and there are few that are not involved in securing accurate information for the billing process. From scheduling at the beginning of the hospital revenue cycle to the end of the cycle when payment occurs, many individuals provide key information to the billing and coding process essential for correct reimbursement.

As a result of this complex environment, knowledgeable employees in the billing and coding areas are essential to the successful operation of the hospital.

A view of the departments involved in the hospital revenue cycle is demonstrated in Figure I-1.

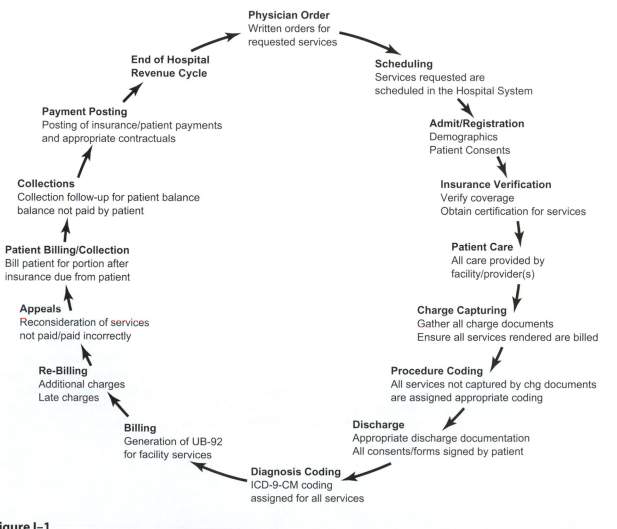

Figure I-1

Let's discuss how each of these departments within the hospital organization plays a key role in securing proper reimbursement.

Physician (Physician's Order)

Physicians who are employed by the hospital are known as **physician employees,** while others who provide services only in the hospital setting are called **hospital-based physicians.** The majority of the physicians providing care in the facility are private physicians who are a part of a group of physician organizations.

Before a patient may be admitted to an inpatient facility or receive any services, the physician must request specific services with a **physician order.** This document is key to the entire process, as the order must contain:

- Status of patient services (inpatient, outpatient, observation)
- What services are ordered
- Diagnosis (medically necessary documentation)

Scheduling/Appointments

The facility's scheduling/appointment area will arrange an appropriate time and setting for requested services to be performed. This area must be familiar with the areas where services may be performed (inpatient, outpatient, ancillary) and be able to communicate appropriate patient instructions as well as acquire key billing/coding data such as:

- Patient name and demographic information
- Insurance information to determine whether services may be performed
- Contact information in the event the patient needs to be recontacted for further information or instructions

Admit/Registration

All patients will be registered into the hospital system through the admit/registration department. This department will generate a patient account number for this encounter or admission as well as gather additional information needed for insurance and patient billing and collections. As a result of this process, a patient registration/admit sheet will be generated and posted to the patient's chart. Copies of this sheet are often utilized by providers of service during the encounter or admission for capturing needed billing and insurance data.

Appropriate Consents for Treatment, Release of Information and Insurance Verification

The information obtained during the admit/registration process usually will be verified with the insurance carriers(s) within two to three days, including any additional authorizations or information that may be needed at the conclusion of that admission or encounter to procure payment. The patient's registration form will be updated with corrected or additional information obtained during this process. Medical necessity must be met with the information obtained from the physician for patient status (inpatient, outpatient, observation), as well as services provided through the assignment of appropriate diagnostic codes. These serve as the **admitting diagnosis** and are included on the billing form sent to the insurance carrier.

> **!** ***ALERT:*** Under the Health Insurance Portability and Accountability Act (HIPAA) of 1996, patient confidentiality issues became paramount in the medical field. Details regarding what patient information is governed under HIPAA is available on their website at www.hipaa.org.

> **!** ***ALERT:*** Additional resources on registration forms and consent forms utilized in the hospital setting are available from the American Hospital Association Resource Center on their website at www.aha.org.

Patient Care

While the patient is being treated, care must be taken to ensure that length of stay, services and patient status approved during the insurance verification process have not changed. If they have, the carrier must be contacted.

Charge Capturing

Charge collection or **charge capturing** is the gathering of charge documents from all departments within the facility that have provided services to patients. Making certain that all charges are coded and entered into the billing system is paramount to receiving payment for all services performed.

Procedure Coding

The process of reviewing documentation for services provided and assigning the appropriate ICD-9-CM and CPT-4 codes as applicable is typically performed in the coding department of the **Health Information Management (HIM)** area. Inaccurate or missed procedure or diagnosis codes can result in nonpayment, incorrect payment, or partial payment for services.

Discharge

When the patient is discharged from the facility, whether inpatient or outpatient, it is important that all information gathered has been verified, all consents have been signed and all payment policies have been explained to the patient and signed by them. This will ensure prompt payment from the insurance carriers as well as the patient.

Diagnosis Coding

All services must have medically necessary diagnoses assigned, without regard to whether the services are coded or input from an encounter form. Inappropriate diagnosis coding will result in denial of payment, reduced payment, or requests for additional information that will delay payment.

Billing

All information gathered and input into the billing system will be processed and an appropriate claim form generated (CMS 1450 or UB-92 for facility services, CMS-1500 for professional/physician services). Claims will be sent electronically or manually processed to insurance carriers with the information necessary for reimbursement.

As mentioned in the preface of this book, the UB-92 is currently under revision. Implementation of the revised UB-92, which will be known as the UB-04 (because it was created in 2004), is expected sometime in 2007. Additional information regarding the proposed changes to the form is listed in the Appendix of this text.

Re-Billing

Lost or late charges or corrections to previously processed claims will generate a corrected or additional claim and will be submitted to the insurance carrier on the appropriate form. Re-billing results in delays in payment, denials, and considerable additional time in researching and reprocessing for reconsideration for payment.

Appeals

When payment resulting from a claim is received, a review will take place to determine whether that payment was as expected. When payment does not appear to agree with contractual guidelines with the insurance carrier, an **appeal** or request for additional consideration and payment will be made.

Patient Billing

When final payment has been made by all third-party carriers, the account will be handled by the patient account representative assigned to the account. The patient must be notified of their responsibility and arrangements made for payment.

Collections

When patient payment is not received in a timely manner, collection activity on the balance of the patient account will begin. A series of collection letters may be sent in an attempt to receive patient payment. If payment is still not received, the account may be placed with an inside or outside collection agency and/or credit bureau.

Payment Posting

When payments are received, the appropriate payment(s) and insurance carrier contractual(s) will be posted to the patient account along with any patient payments until the balance has been satisfied. The term *third party* derives from the three parties who are involved in the contract for services. The first party is the facility or provider, the second is the patient, and the third is the insurance carrier. Thus, the term **third-party contract** refers to an agreement between the three parties mentioned.

UNDERSTANDING THE PATIENT BILLING PROCESS

Just as complex as the number of employees who contribute to the functioning of the hospital revenue cycle are the many types of facilities and services rendered. The determination of what services should be coded and billed by which entities and the coding nomenclature and billing guidelines to be utilized are quite involved. Perhaps this can be best illustrated by an example of a typical hospital admission (See Table I-1).

TABLE I–1   Represents Services Typically Provided during a Hospital Admission Delineates Services Billed by Facility vs. Physician.

Date/Service Provided	Facility Services	Professional Services
01/01 Admitted to Acute Care	Room/Board Charge	Admit History/Attending
01/01 Electrocardiogram	Technical Portion	Professional-Cardiologist
Chest X-Ray	Technical Portion	Professional Portion-Radiologist
Pathology (Lab Work)	Technical Portion	Professional Portion-Pathologist
01/02 Inpatient Hospital Care	Room/Board Charge	Hospital Visit-Attending Consultation-Cardiologist Consultation-Pulmonary
01/03 Coronary Artery Bypass Graft	OR Room Charge OR Supplies/Drugs Recovery Room Charge	Surgeon Charge Anesthesiologist Charge Hospital Visit-Attending
01/04 Transferred to CCU (Coronary Care Unit) Respiratory Therapy	CCU Room Charge CCU Supplies/Drugs Respiratory-Technical	Critical Care Cardiologist Hospital Visit-Attending Respiratory-Professional
01/05 Transferred to Acute Care Chest X-Ray Electrocardiogram Pathology (Lab)	Room Board Charge Technical Portion Technical Portion Technical Portion	Hospital Visit-Attending Professional Portion-Radiologist Professional Portion-Cardiology Professional-Pathologist
01/06 Continued Inpatient	Room/Board Chg	Hospital Visit-Attending
01/07 Continued Inpatient	Room/Board Chg	Hospital Visit-Attending
01/08 Patient Discharge	Room/Board Chg	Discharge Visit-Attending

SERVICES PROVIDED IN THE FACILITY SETTING

Table I-2 outlines services provided in a facility setting as well as professional services provided in conjunction with the facility. In some instances, the hospital may agree to bill and code for the professional component on behalf of the physicians or providers, in which case the facility will code and bill for both facility and provider services. This table also illustrates the differing billing forms, reimbursement methodologies and coding nomenclatures involved in the various types of billing that evolve from the hospital admission or encounter.

TABLE I–2   Services Provided in a Facility.

Facility Types

Inpatient	Outpatient	Professional
Acute Care	Outpatient Hospital	All services provided inpatient provided in a facility
Acute Condition/Illness	Length of stay less than 24 hours	
Continuous Medical/Nursing	Hospital-Based Departments (e.g., Radiology, ER)	
Skilled Nursing Facility		
Care/Rehabilitation	Ambulatory Surgery Center (ASC)	
Intermediate Care Facilities	Same Day Surgery Center	
Inpatients Not Requiring Acute Facility	Outpatient Clinic	
Skilled Nursing (Disabled)	Outpatient Facility	
Hospice	Home Health Agency (HHA)	
Care of Terminally Ill	Visiting Nurses	
	Home-Based Programs/Care	

TABLE I–2   continued

Billed Services

Inpatient	Outpatient	Professional
Room/Board	Room/Board	Surgeon/Assistant Surgeon
Operating Room Charge	Operating Room	Attending Physician
Drugs/Supplies	Drugs/Supplies	Anesthesiologist
Ancillary Technical (e.g., Radiology/Pathology)	Ancillary Technical (e.g., Radiology/Pathology)	Ancillary Professional (e.g., Radiology/Pathology)
	Emergency Department	Consultants
	Observation Care	Specialists

Billing Forms

Inpatient	Outpatient	Professional
UB-92 or CMS 1450 (Uniform Billing Form 92)	UB-92 or CMS 1450 (Uniform Billing Form 92)	CMS 1500 (formerly HCFA 1500)

Reimbursement
   Methodology

Inpatient	Outpatient	Professional
Prospective Payment System (e.g., Diagnosis Related Groups (DRG) Cost-Based Reimbursement Per Diem	Outpatient Prospective Payment System (e.g., Ambulatory Payment Classifications)	Cost-Based Reimbursement
	Cost-Based Reimbursement	

TABLE I–2   continued

Coding Methodology

Inpatient	Outpatient	Professional
ICD-9-CM (Diagnosis)	ICD-9-CM (Diagnosis)	ICD-9-CM (Diagnosis)
ICD-9-CM (Procedures)	ICD-9-CM (Procedures)	CPT-4 (Procedures)
	CPT-4 (Procedures)	

CAREER OPPORTUNITIES IN THE HOSPITAL SETTING

Qualified, trained individuals are vital to the successful procurement of reimbursement on a timely basis. There are many types of jobs available. To some degree, all of the facility processes we have discussed require some knowledge of the billing and coding process. There are many entry-level positions available, as well as positions for experienced individuals and those who have acquired certification for their skills.

! ALERT: Sample job descriptions for many hospital facility positions are available from the American Hospital Association on their website, www.aha.org, or through the Medical Group Management Association at www.mgma.com.

Scheduling/Appointments

Working in scheduling/appointments requires a knowledge of scheduling as well as insurance coverage information that must be obtained at the time of the appointment. Job descriptions typically list these positions under the title "Appointment Secretary" or "Scheduler."

Admit/Registration

The admit/registration process is the beginning of the billing process, as these individuals secure insurance information as well as diagnostic data. This position often serves as an entry-level position into the hospital employee network.

The individual performing this job function should have a minimum knowledge of diagnostic coding, in order to code the chief complaint or admitting diagnosis, as well as a basic knowledge of insurance coverage, requirements for authorizations, and so on. Jobs in this area are typically referred to as "Admissions Representatives."

Coding

Unlike the physician or professional billing side, the facility side typically has a number of coding career opportunities available. In many instances, the facility will provide diagnostic coding, ICD-9-CM procedural coding as well as CPT-4 coding on the facility side and may also provide physician coding for any physician employees who have a contractual agreement with the facility. As a result, the facility may employ coders with various qualifications or skill requirements.

Inpatient DRG Coder

This senior level coder assigns ICD-9-CM diagnostic and procedural codes for inpatient charts. This individual must have prior coding knowledge—preferably, inpatient coding experience—as well as an understanding of inpatient reimbursement methodology. Often the facility will recruit an experienced inpatient coder or an individual with coding training with a clinical background due to the large volume of medical and clinical documentation that must be reviewed by this individual. This individual will often be certified as a Certified Coding Specialist (CCS) through the American Health Information Management Association (AHIMA). Typically, the facility will refer to these Inpatient Coders as "Senior Coders" or "Inpatient Coders."

Outpatient APC Coder

The outpatient coder assigns ICD-9-CM diagnostic and procedural codes as well as CPT-4 procedural codes to chart documentation. As services for the outpatient are often provided in a number of locations throughout the facility, some of these services will be captured by encounter forms or charge tickets, while others will be forwarded to the outpatient coding area for code assignment. The outpatient coder should have prior coding knowledge and an understanding of outpatient reimbursement methodology. As outpatient coding utilizes both ICD-9-CM and CPT-4, this individual should have knowledge of both nomenclatures. The qualified applicant may also possess a coding certification, preferably the CPC-H (Certified Professional Hospital Coder) from the American Academy of Professional Coders (AAPC) or CCS (Certified Coding Specialist/Hospital). Facilities usually refer to these outpatient coders as "APC Coders" or "Outpatient APC Coders."

Diagnostic Coder

Many services (especially those performed on an outpatient basis) may be captured and their codes assigned through the use of charge documents. These services may still need diagnostic codes to be assigned appropriately and reviewed to make certain that medical necessity has been met. Some larger facilities employ individuals in the coding department at an entry level as "Diagnostic Coders" who assign diagnostic (ICD-9-CM) codes only to these services.

Physician-Facility Coder

Many large facilities have physicians hired by the facility to provide health-care services. Part of their agreement with the facility requires the facility to provide the coding and billing expertise for these services. In such instances, the facility will employ coders typically known as "Physician Coders" or "Physician/Professional Coders." These individuals will have a physician/professional background in coding, and will be familiar with ICD-9-CM diagnostic and CPT-4 procedural coding. As these services are coded and billed on a separate form utilizing independent coding and billing methodologies, this coder is often a separate, independent coder from the other coders in the department. This individual may be required to be certified, often as a Certified Professional Coder (CPC) or Certified Coding Specialist-Physician (CCS-P).

> **! ALERT:** Additional information regarding membership and certification through AAPC and AHIMA can be obtained from AAPC's website at www.aapc.com or AHIMA at www.ahima.org.

Table I-3 illustrates the four coding certifications available to the coder to demonstrate their mastery of coding skills.

TABLE I–3   Coding Certifications Available for Coders to Demonstrate Their Mastery of Coding.

Certification	Full Name	Accrediting Body	Concentration	Competencies
CPC-H	Certified Professional Coder/Hospital	AAPC	Outpatient Hospital	ASC Facility CPT-4 and HCPCS Codes ICD-9-CM Volumes I, II, III
CCS	Certified Coding Specialist	AHIMA	Hospital	ICD-9-CM Volumes I, II, III Regulatory Guidelines

CPC	Certified Professional Coder	AAPC	Professional/ Physician	CPT-4 and HCPCS Codes ICD-9-CM Volumes I, II
CCS-P	Certified Coding Specialist Physician	AHIMA	Professional/ Physician	CPT-4 and HCPCS Codes ICD-9-CM Volumes I, II

Billing/Patient Business

Several individuals are employed in the patient business area of the facility. Their titles differ from facility to facility, but these are some of the services they perform:

- Claims Processing: Responsible for ensuring that claims are processed and submitted to third-party carriers on a timely basis. This includes both electronic and paper claims within the guidelines of each third-party carrier contract.
- Electronic Claims Submission: Responsible for tracking electronic claims to carriers or clearinghouses.
- Claims Reviewer: Reviews claims, both electronic and paper, before submission to third-party carriers. Ensures coding and billing guidelines meet requirements for specific third-party carrier.
- Reimbursement Specialist: Ensures that reimbursement has been made by third-party carrier according to contractual guidelines. Also ensures that appropriate contractual write-offs have been taken and patients billed the appropriate amounts.
- Reimbursement Analyst: Determines whether coding and billing have provided the maximum reimbursement under third-party guidelines. Determines whether an appeal or additional reimbursement should be requested. Provides feedback to the appropriate departments when coding and billing issues prevent maximum reimbursement.
- Appeals: Responsible for handling all claim appeals to third-party carriers if appropriate reimbursement has not been made.
- Patient Collections: Responsible for collecting patient balances on self-pay accounts as well as patient portions after insurance.

Compliance/Administration

In addition to the coding and billing functions performed in specific departments within the facility, there are individuals outside of those departments who must have knowledge of the coding and billing fields. These individuals typically work in the administrative areas and are involved with compliance and ensuring that appropriate coding and billing guidelines are being followed throughout the facility.

These individuals usually assume the title of Compliance Specialists or Auditors within the facility organizational structure and report directly to administration. They review claims and coding and billing processes and ensure that contractual obligations with third-party carriers and governmental agencies are being enforced.

Individuals assuming these positions typically have been involved in the facility coding and billing process, have knowledge of reimbursement methodologies and are usually certified.

! **ALERT:** Certification in the compliance fields can be through several different organizations. One certification is the CHC (Certification in Healthcare Compliance), available through the Health Care Compliance Association (HCCA) at www.hcca-info.org.

Training

Due to the vast size of many facilities, it is necessary to employ individuals who perform training functions. While the individuals employed in the coding and billing positions within the facility have typically received prior instruction, each facility will have specific coding and billing guidelines, policies and procedures that must be adhered to. With facilities of size, it is imperative that practices be consistent and follow third-party and governmental guidelines as well as adhere to internal policies and procedures. This usually requires a specific individual or individuals to provide training, continuing education and consistency to facility billing.

CONCLUSION

The complexities of the hospital billing and coding field and the multitude of individuals who contribute to the successful completion of this process should now be apparent. It is vital that all these individuals understand the significance of their roles, as well as the importance of working in unison to accomplish their common purpose of ensuring appropriate reimbursement to the facility on a timely basis.

Section I

Hospital Billing and Coding Overview

Current Procedural Terminology (CPT) © 2005 American Medical Association. All Rights Reserved.

Chapter 1
Hospital Coding Overview

KEY TERMS

CMS 1450/UB (Uniform Billing)-92 claim form

CPT-4 (Current Procedure Terminology, 4th edition)

E & M (Evaluation and Management)

E Codes

HCPCS (Healthcare Common Procedure Coding System)

ICD-9-CM (International Classification of Diseases, 9th edition, Clinical Modification)

Modifier Codes

NEC (Not Elsewhere Classified)

Neoplasms

NOS (Not Otherwise Specified)

Principal Diagnosis

Table of Drugs and Chemicals

V codes

Volume 3 ICD-9-CM Procedural Codes

LEARNING OBJECTIVES

- Demonstrate an understanding of the basic principles of ICD-9-CM diagnostic coding
- Apply additional coding guidelines for assigning ICD-9-CM codes
- Discuss the concepts of ICD-9-CM procedural coding
- Demonstrate the basic concepts of CPT-4/HCPCS procedure coding
- Communicate the importance of documentation to the coding/billing process
- Apply all appropriate coding principles to coding documentation

INTRODUCTION

The basis of reimbursement for both inpatient and outpatient facilities is coding. The vehicle by which reimbursement is considered is the claim form: specifically, the **CMS 1450/UB(Uniform Billing)-92 claim form.**

This form lends itself to the assignment of code numbers to describe both the services that have been rendered, **CPT-4 (Current Procedure Terminology, 4th edition)** or **ICD-9-CM (International Classification of Diseases, 9th edition, Clinical Modification)** Procedures, and the medically necessary reason services were furnished, ICD-9-CM codes. Inappropriate or incorrect assignment of these codes results in denial or delay in payment for services rendered.

3

Current Procedural Terminology (CPT) © 2005 American Medical Association. All Rights Reserved.

While many students may have already discovered ICD-9-CM and CPT-4 coding on the professional side, a brief review of coding assignment and the proper use of the ICD-9-CM and CPT-4 books is appropriate.

ICD-9-CM DIAGNOSTIC CODING GUIDELINES

While specific guidelines vary for inpatient versus outpatient diagnostic coding, the general principles remain the same. Specific guidelines for inpatient and outpatient coding are included in corresponding sections of this textbook. This section is intended only for a general overview of coding principles.

1. The primary diagnosis should be the diagnosis, sign or symptom that resulted in the encounter.

    Inpatient: **Principal Diagnosis**
                    Chief reason for admission following services.

    Outpatient: Chief reason for encounter or primary diagnosis.
                    Specific diagnosis, sign or symptom responsible for a
                    specific service.

2. Conditions, signs or symptoms should always be coded to the highest level of specificity.

3. Signs and symptoms need not be coded if they are an integral part of a diagnostic statement.

4. Chronic conditions contributing to the diagnosis, evaluation and/or treatment during the encounter should be coded.

5. When previous conditions are part of the evaluation and treatment process, they should be coded as "history of."

6. Diagnoses that are not listed or clearly stated by the physician cannot be used. The coder may query the physician to clarify the information; however, the coder may not utilize information that is clinically unclear.

7. Always use both the alphabetic and numeric indexes when determining appropriate diagnosis codes for assignment.

8. Utilize combination codes when appropriate. Do not utilize multiple diagnostic codes when one combination code would be appropriate.

9. Conditions listed as "acute" should be coded first as they are assumed to be the chief reason for the encounter when more than one diagnosis meets the chief reason for the encounter rules.

10. Always determine the diagnosis or condition, as this represents the main term under which the diagnostic statement will be located.

    e.g. Upper Respiratory Infection will be found under:
    Infection, Respiratory, Upper

    Coronary Artery Disease will be found under:
    Disease, Artery, Coronary

Current Procedural Terminology (CPT) © 2005 American Medical Association. All Rights Reserved.

Notes

Once the coder has utilized these basic coding concepts, along with any specific guidelines for inpatient or outpatient facility, the coder should begin the process locating the appropriate codes in the ICD-9-CM coding manual.

Coding Conventions

The coding conventions contained in the ICD-9-CM (International Classification of 9th Edition) manual should be utilized as follows:

- **NEC (Not Elsewhere Classified)**
  No specific diagnosis code for the condition, even though the physician may have been very specific in his diagnostic statement.

- **NOS (Not Otherwise Specified)**
  Physician documentation does not include any specific information about the condition.

- **Inclusion/Exclusion Notes**

  At beginning of chapter/section: Includes/excludes applies to all codes in that section.

  Following the code descriptor: Includes/excludes applies only to the code(s) in that category.

- **Code First Underlying Condition**
  Used for a condition that is a manifestation of an underlying disease. This notation indicates that the underlying condition should be coded first, followed by the manifestation.

- **Use Additional Code**
  An additional code may need to be added in order to correctly assign the diagnostic statement for the chart.

- **See**
  Alternative terms may be necessary in order to correctly assign diagnostic codes for the condition.

- **See Also**
  Indicates there is another location in the alphabetic index where the condition may be more completely defined.

- **See Category**
  Refers the coder to another category for identifying the appropriate code for the condition.

- **Parentheses ( )**
  Enclose additional words that may be present or absent from the diagnostic statement. The statements or words enclosed in the parentheses do not have to be included, but are included to assist the coder when other terms may be utilized for referring to the condition.

Current Procedural Terminology (CPT) © 2005 American Medical Association. All Rights Reserved.

- **Brackets [ ]**
  May indicate either synonyms or alternative words for a condition, or indicate that the code(s) listed in brackets must be utilized in combination with the code listed below the code in brackets.
- **Colon :**
  Utilized to abbreviate the term or meaning. Rather than repeating a term that applies to all of the diagnoses listed, it is listed once, with the colon, but applies to all conditions listed after the colon.
- **And**
  For the purposes of ICD-9-CM, the term "and" is interpreted as "and" or "or."
- **With**
  When utilized to tie words or diagnostic phrases together, both statements must be present in order to assign the code.

It is imperative that the facility coder be capable of reviewing the chart documentation and determining which conditions were present and contributed to the complexity of the encounter.

PRACTICE EXERCISE 1–1

Assign ICD-9-CM diagnostic codes to the following exercises, placing them in the correct diagnostic code order.

Diagnosis	Code
1. Bronchitis	_____
2. Acute Bronchitis	_____
3. Gastroenteritis, suspect food poisoning	_____
4. Infectious mononucleosis	_____
5. Acute asthmatic bronchitis	_____
6. Acute exacerbation of COPD	_____
7. Acute serous otitis media	_____
8. Streptococcal Pneumonia	_____
9. Salmonella due to food poisoning	_____

Current Procedural Terminology (CPT) © 2005 American Medical Association. All Rights Reserved.

Notes

10. Nausea and Vomiting due to
    Viral Gastroenteritis   _____

11. Syncope, probably vasovagal response   _____

12. Chest pain due to myocardial infarction _____

13. Dysuria with possible UTI   _____

14. Urinary Tract Infection with
    Dysuria and Polyuria   _____

15. Abnormal Glucose Tolerance Test   _____

16. Dehydration due to either
    Polyuria or Influenza   _____

17. Painful hematuria as the result of UTI _____

18. Acute and chronic appendicitis   _____

19. Acute and chronic bronchitis   _____

20. Chest Pain, R/O MI   _____

PRACTICE EXERCISE 1–2

Review the following case scenarios. Determine which diagnostic statements, signs and/or symptoms would be appropriate to be reported, and assign ICD-9-CM code(s) to each.

1. Patient presented to the emergency room complaining of right upper quadrant abdominal pain. Tests were performed, and the pain was determined to be the result of acute pancreatitis.

   Condition Coded: _____ Code: _____

   Condition Coded: _____ Code: _____

2. Patient presented with history of breast carcinoma. Patient complained of lump in breast. Biopsy of breast lesion was taken to rule out recurrent breast carcinoma.

   Condition Coded: _____ Code: _____

   Condition Coded: _____ Code: _____

3. Patient was admitted to hospital with complaints of fever, hematuria and lower back pain for the past several days. Upon examination, the patient presented with a fever of 103.1, frank hematuria. A urinalysis was performed, which revealed UTI. A subsequent kidney ultrasound indicated that the patient was suffering from pyelonephritis.

   Condition Coded: _____ Code: _____

   Condition Coded: _____ Code: _____

4. Patient presented to the emergency room with a pain in the left calf. Examination revealed an area of swelling in the left calf with a slight fever. Venous Doppler was performed, which revealed the presence of a thrombus in the left calf. The patient was admitted and placed on Coumadin therapy and discharged on the third day of hospitalization with the diagnosis of deep venous thrombosis.

   Condition Coded: _____ Code: _____

   Condition Coded: _____ Code: _____

5. Patient was seen in the emergency room with complaints of abdominal pain. Patient had a history of alcohol dependency and appears to be intoxicated. The abdominal pain resolved over a 2–4 hour period of time with the assistance of a GI cocktail and IV fluids.

   Condition Coded: _____ Code: _____

   Condition Coded: _____ Code: _____

6. Patient was seen in the emergency room due to a fall from stairs at her home. She reported pain in the right wrist and was unable to use her wrist. On examination, the wrist appeared to be swollen, tender and obviously displaced. Wrist x-ray indicated a closed fracture of the radius and ulna, which was treated with the application of cast. Surgery did not appear to be necessary.

   Condition Coded: _____ Code: _____

   Condition Coded: _____ Code: _____

7. Patient presented to the emergency room with lower abdominal pain accompanied by nausea and vomiting. WBC was elevated; the patient had a recorded fever of 103.1. Diagnosis of acute cholecystitis was made and the patient was scheduled for a cholecystectomy on an urgent basis.

   Condition Coded: _____ Code: _____

   Condition Coded: _____ Code: _____

Current Procedural Terminology (CPT) © 2005 American Medical Association. All Rights Reserved.

Notes

8. Patient who has been diagnosed with prostatic cancer presented for chemotherapy regimen on an outpatient basis. Patient developed shortness of breath and became diaphoretic. The patient was admitted to the hospital.

Condition Coded: _____ Code: _____

Condition Coded: _____ Code: _____

9. Patient presented for chemotherapy treatment for uterine cancer, which has metastasized from the breast.

Condition Coded: _____ Code: _____

Condition Coded: _____ Code: _____

10. Patient presented to the emergency room as the result of a laceration to the occipital area as the result of an auto accident. The laceration was cleaned and sutured and the patient was released following treatment.

Condition Coded: _____ Code: _____

Condition Coded: _____ Code: _____

Additional ICD-9-CM Diagnostic Coding Considerations

In addition to the general coding guidelines listed above, special coding situations require specific coding guidelines.

V Codes

V codes are utilized for circumstances other than signs, symptoms, illness or diagnosis of a condition. These codes are utilized as primary diagnosis when they are the chief reason for the encounter.
Examples of V codes may include:

-   Exposure to, contact with, or need for prophylactic treatment for diseases.
-   Family or personal history of diseases.
-   Observation of newborns/infants.
-   Procedure or procedure aftercare.
-   Persons without reported diagnoses.

Current Procedural Terminology (CPT) © 2005 American Medical Association. All Rights Reserved.

E Codes

E codes, or codes for External Causes, are never utilized as a primary diagnosis, but only to provide additional information regarding the cause for the injury, illness or condition that precipitated the encounter.

Typically, the E code would be the last diagnosis code listed for the encounter or service. Examples of E codes may include:

- Railway/auto accidents.
- Place of occurrence.
- Accidental poisonings.
- Surgical/medical procedure problems.
- Accidental falls.
- Accidents from fire or flame.
- Submersion accidents.
- Biologically adverse effects of drugs or medicinals.
- Injuries from attempted suicide or homicide.
- Injuries undetermined whether accidental or purposeful

Table of Drugs and Chemicals

The **Table of Drugs and Chemicals** found in the ICD-9-CM diagnosis code book is utilized for locating codes relating to encounters that are the result of adverse effects from drugs and chemicals. These individuals will typically be demonstrating signs, symptoms and/or illnesses as a result of accidental poisoning, such as an accidental overdose, or drugs taken in error. These circumstances would necessitate the use of a code that indicates the condition that resulted in the encounter, a poisoning code as well as an E code from the Accidental Poisoning section of the Drugs/Chemicals table.

Adverse effects may also result when prescribed medications are taken exactly as prescribed yet still result in a condition that necessitates a medical encounter. These circumstances require the assignment of a condition code as described above, a poisoning code, as well as an E code from the Therapeutic Use section of the Drugs/Chemicals table. This set of codes can only be utilized when no other drugs, medications or alcohol are taken in conjunction with the prescribed medication.

When a suicide is attempted, whether successfully or not, a condition code for the chief reason for encounter, poisoning code and E code from the Suicide section of the Drugs/Chemicals table would be utilized. Assaults, or injuries or poisonings inflicted by another for the purpose of bodily harm, are coded with a condition code, poisoning code and E code from the Assault section of the table.

In many instances, it is unclear whether any or all of the above conditions apply. For instance, the presentation to the emergency room of a patient who

Current Procedural Terminology (CPT) © 2005 American Medical Association. All Rights Reserved.

Notes

has ingested a large number of pills cannot always be construed as a suicide attempt. Therefore, the proper assignment of an E code for this encounter would be taken from the "undetermined" section of the Table of Drugs/Chemicals.

Hypertension Table

The hypertension table represents conditions resulting or arising from the diagnosis of hypertension. In instances where the physician has not made such a diagnosis but simply recorded an elevated blood pressure, the use of a hypertension code would be inappropriate. Instead, code 796.2 (high blood pressure reading without a diagnosis of hypertension) would be appropriate.

When hypertension is simply stated as such, it should not be assigned as either benign or malignant hypertension. Code 401.9 (hypertension unspecified) would be appropriate in this instance.

There are a number of combination codes that combine one or more diagnoses into one diagnosis code applicable in the hypertension table. However, a causal relationship between any condition and hypertension cannot be assumed, with the exception of chronic renal failure. In that instance, codes from the 403 category would be assigned for both chronic renal failure and hypertension.

Neoplasms

Neoplasms, or "new growths," can be either benign or malignant in nature. As a result, there are a number of coding possibilities for neoplasms that need to be discussed. In the event a neoplasm has been defined as malignant, codes from the primary, secondary or in situ sections of the neoplasm table should be utilized. If the malignant neoplasm is not specifically stated as primary, secondary or in situ, it is assumed to be primary. In situ neoplasms must be stated as such in order to assign codes from the in situ category.

Care should be taken in the assignment of primary and secondary codes, as they are often stated in a number of different ways. "Metastatic from" indicates the neoplasm spread from the site specified, while "metastatic to" indicates the neoplasm spread from an original site to the site stated.

The general principle of "assigning the chief reason for the encounter" should be followed closely in the assignment of neoplasm codes for proper sequencing.

Pregnancy Coding

Pregnancy codes typically require the use of 5-digit ICD-9-CM codes, the fifth digit typically indicating the episode of care—e.g., "delivered," "not delivered," "postpartum," "unspecified episode of care."

Current Procedural Terminology (CPT) © 2005 American Medical Association. All Rights Reserved.

Notes

Code V22.2 (Pregnancy State, Incidental) is utilized when it is the chief reason for the encounter with no other indication, or, when it is coincidental to the chief reason for the encounter.

Typically, however, a condition that is chiefly responsible for the encounter occurs during pregnancy, requiring the use of a code from the 600 series of ICD-9-CM codes. A patient with hypertension prior to pregnancy, for instance, would be assigned a 600 series code for "hypertension during pregnancy."

Unlike other ICD-9-CM codes and coding rules, pregnancy codes indicate conditions arising during pregnancy that are assumed to be complications of the pregnancy, unless stated otherwise.

When coding for normal deliveries, code 650 should be utilized only when the admission and subsequent delivery of the infant is completely normal without any complications.

Injuries/Trauma

Due to the fact that many injuries, such as fractures, contusions, abrasions and lacerations, can occur during the same encounter, it is necessary to determine which code(s) would be assigned as the chief reason for the encounter. Whenever multiple injuries necessitate the encounter, the most severe injury is always coded as the primary diagnosis.

Burns

Burns are typically categorized as first-degree (erythema), second-degree (blistering), or third-degree (full thickness). The most severe, significant burn is the one that should be coded as the chief reason for the encounter.

!   **ALERT:** Additional information regarding additions, deletions or revisions to ICD-9-CM diagnostic or procedural codes may be obtained from the Department of Health and Human Resources website at www.dhhs.org.

PRACTICE EXERCISE 1–3

Assign ICD-9-CM diagnostic codes to the following, based on the specific coding guidelines outlined above:

1. Coronary artery disease.
   Hypertensive heart disease.

Current Procedural Terminology (CPT) © 2005 American Medical Association. All Rights Reserved.

Notes _____

_____

_____

_____

_____

_____

_____

_____

_____

_____

_____

_____

_____

_____

_____

_____

_____

_____

_____

_____

_____

_____

Diagnosis: _____ Code: _____

Diagnosis: _____ Code: _____

2. Hypertension due to Cushing's disease.

Diagnosis: _____ Code: _____

Diagnosis: _____ Code: _____

3. Essential hypertension.
   Headache.

Diagnosis: _____ Code: _____

Diagnosis: _____ Code: _____

4. Patient presents for tetanus immunization due to dog-bite wound of arm.

Diagnosis: _____ Code: _____

Diagnosis: _____ Code: _____

5. Patient presents for routine immunization of MMR (mumps, measles, rubella).

Diagnosis: _____ Code: _____

Diagnosis: _____ Code: _____

6. Congestive heart failure.
   Essential hypertension.

Diagnosis: _____ Code: _____

Diagnosis: _____ Code: _____

7. Breast carcinoma.
   History of GI cancer.

Diagnosis: _____ Code: _____

Diagnosis: _____ Code: _____

Current Procedural Terminology (CPT) © 2005 American Medical Association. All Rights Reserved.

Notes

8. Metastatic malignant neoplasm from chest wall to axillary lymph node.

Diagnosis: _____ Code: _____

Diagnosis: _____ Code: _____

9. Open wound, hand.
Contusion, knee.
Abrasion, foot.

Diagnosis: _____ Code: _____

Diagnosis: _____ Code: _____

10. Fitting and adjustment of leg prosthesis.

Diagnosis: _____ Code: _____

Diagnosis: _____ Code: _____

> **!** **ALERT:** Additional ICD-9-CM guidelines and specifications can be obtained from the American Hospital Association *Coding Clinic*, a newsletter with updates, deletions, revisions and clarification of ICD-9-CM coding issues. Subscription or back issues may be obtained on the AHA website at www.aha.org.

ICD-9-CM PROCEDURAL CODING GUIDELINES

In addition to diagnostic coding, **Volume 3 ICD-9-CM Procedural Codes** describe what services were performed during the encounter.

Volume 3 ICD-9-CM procedural codes should be assigned under the following conditions:

- **The procedure is surgical in nature.**

  Procedures that involve excision, incision, destruction, amputation, repair and manipulation would be considered surgical in nature.
- **The procedure carries an anesthetic risk.**

  Any procedure performed other than with topical anesthesia is considered an anesthetic risk for procedural coding purposes.

Current Procedural Terminology (CPT) © 2005 American Medical Association. All Rights Reserved.

- **The procedure carries a procedural risk.**

  Any procedure that has an inherent risk of loss of physiological function or life would be considered a procedural risk.

- **The procedure requires specialized training**.

  Training over and above the usual nursing or physician training would be considered specialized training.

  Table 1–1 represents an index of the ICD-9 procedural codes:

TABLE 1–1   ICD-9-CM PROCEDURE INDEX.

Procedures on the Nervous System (01-05)

01	Incision/Excision Skull, Brain, Cerebral Meninges
02	Other Procedures Skull, Brain, Cerebral Meninges
03	Procedures on Spinal Cord, Spinal Canal Structures
04	Procedures Cranial, Peripheral Nerves
05	Procedures Sympathetic Nerves, Ganglia

Procedures on the Endocrine System (06-07)

06	Thyroid, Parathyroid Glands
07	Other Endocrine System

Procedures of the Eye (08-16)

08	Eyelids
09	Lacrimal System
10	Conjunctiva
11	Cornea
12	Iris, Ciliary Body, Sclera, Anterior Chamber
13	Lens
14	Retina, Choroids, Vitreous, Posterior Chamber
15	Extraocular Muscles
16	Orbit, Eyeballs

Procedures of the Ear (18-20)

18	External Ear
19	Reconstructive Procedures, Middle Ear
20	Other Procedures Middle, Inner Ear

(continued)

Current Procedural Terminology (CPT) © 2005 American Medical Association. All Rights Reserved.

Notes
_____

_____

_____

_____

_____

_____

_____

_____

_____

_____

_____

_____

_____

_____

_____

_____

_____

_____

_____

_____

_____

TABLE 1–1 *continued*

Procedures of the Nose, Mouth and Pharynx (21-29)

21	Nose
22	Nasal Sinuses
23	Removal or Restoration of Teeth
24	Other Procedures Teeth, Gums and Alveoli
25	Tongue
26	Salivary Glands and Ducts
27	Mouth and Face
28	Tonsils and Adenoids
29	Pharynx

Procedures of the Respiratory System (30-34)

30	Excision of Larynx
31	Other Procedures Larynx and Trachea
32	Excision of Lungs, Bronchus
33	Other Procedures Lungs, Bronchus
34	Procedures Chest Wall, Pleura, Mediastinum, Diaphragm

Procedures of Cardiovascular System (35-39)

35	Valves, Septum of Heart
36	Vessels of Heart
37	Other Procedures Heart, Pericardium
38	Incision, Excision, Occlusion of Vessels
39	Other Procedures Vessels

Procedures of Hemic and Lymphatic System (40-41)

40	Lymphatic System
41	Bone Marrow and Spleen

Procedures of Digestive System (42-54)

42	Esophagus
43	Incision, Excision Stomach
44	Other Procedures Stomach
45	Incision, Excision, Anastomosis Intestine
46	Other Procedures Intestine
47	Appendix

Current Procedural Terminology (CPT) © 2005 American Medical Association. All Rights Reserved.

Notes

48 Rectum, Rectosigmoid, Perirectal Tissue

49 Anus

50 Liver

51 Gallbladder, Biliary Tract

52 Pancreas

53 Hernia Repairs

54 Other Procedures Abdominal Area

Procedures on Urinary System (55-59)

55 Kidney

56 Ureter

57 Urinary Bladder

58 Urethra

59 Other Procedures Urinary Tract

Procedures on Male Genital System (60-64)

60 Prostate, Seminal Vesicles

61 Scrotum, Tunica Vaginalis

62 Testes

63 Spermatic Cord, Epididymis, Vas Deferens

64 Penis

Procedures on Female Genital System (65-71)

65 Ovary

66 Fallopian Tube(s)

67 Cervix

68 Incision, Excision Uterus

69 Uterus, Support Structures

70 Vagina, Cul-de-Sac

71 Vulva, Perineum

Obstetrical Procedures (72-75)

72 Forceps, Vacuum, Breech Delivery

73 Other Procedures Inducting, Assisting Delivery

74 Cesarean Section, Removal of Fetus

75 Other Obstetrics

(continued)

Current Procedural Terminology (CPT) © 2005 American Medical Association. All Rights Reserved.

TABLE 1–1 _continued_

Procedures on Musculoskeletal System (76-84)

76	Facial Bones, Joints
77	Incision, Excision, Division, Other Bones
78	Other Procedures, Bones, Except Face
79	Fracture, Dislocation Reduction
80	Incision, Excision Joints
81	Repair, Plastic Procedures Joints
82	Muscle, Tendon, Fascia, Hand
83	Procedures Muscle, Tendon, Fascia, Bursa, other than Hand
84	Other Procedures Musculoskeletal

Procedures of the Integumentary System (85-86)

85	Breast
86	Skin, Subcutaneous Tissue

Miscellaneous Procedures (87-99)

87	Diagnostic Radiology
88	Other Diagnostic Radiology, Related Techniques
89	Interview, Evaluation, Consultations
90	Microscopic Exams - I
91	Microscopic Exams - II
92	Nuclear Medicine
93	Physical, Respiratory, Rehabilitative Therapy
94	Psychiatric
95	Ophthalmological, Otological Diagnosis and Treatment
96	Nonoperative Intubation, Irrigation
97	Replacement, Removal Therapeutic Appliances
98	Nonoperative Removal of Foreign Body, Calculus
99	Other Nonoperative Procedures

Additional Coding Considerations for ICD-9-CM Procedural Coding

A number of the guidelines that apply for ICD-9-CM diagnostic coding for hospital outpatient also apply for ICD-9-CM procedural coding. In addition to the general ICD-9-CM guidelines listed above, the following guidelines are specific to ICD-9-CM procedural code selection:

- If the procedure code description does not specify "bilateral," the service should be coded twice if performed on both the right and left sides of the body.

Current Procedural Terminology (CPT) © 2005 American Medical Association. All Rights Reserved.

Notes

- When procedures are started but not completed, code them only to the extent they are completed.
- Biopsy codes are utilized when only a portion of the lesion is removed, whereas excision codes should be utilized if the entire lesion is removed.
- When procedures are converted from laparoscopic to open, only the open procedure is assigned an ICD-9-CM procedural code.
- When endoscopic procedures are performed, only the most significant procedure in the body region is coded.

PRACTICE EXERCISE 1–4

Assign ICD-9-CM procedural code(s) to the following:

1. Open reduction, fracture, ankle. ICD-9-CM Procedure Code: _____
2. Hemorrhoidectomy. ICD-9-CM Procedure Code: _____
3. Cholecystectomy. ICD-9-CM Procedure Code: _____
4. ORIF, left humerus. ICD-9-CM Procedure Code: _____
5. Infusion therapy. ICD-9-CM Procedure Code: _____
6. Exploratory laparotomy with appendectomy. ICD-9-CM Procedure Code: _____
7. Open biopsy of breast followed by lumpectomy. ICD-9-CM Procedure Code: _____
8. Needle breast biopsy. ICD-9-CM Procedure Code: _____
9. Bronchoscopy with biopsy. ICD-9-CM Procedure Code: _____
10. D & C. ICD-9-CM Procedure Code: _____
11. Esophagogastroduodenoscopy. ICD-9-CM Procedure Code: _____
12. Laparoscopic cholecystectomy. ICD-9-CM Procedure Code: _____
13. Knee arthroscopy. ICD-9-CM Procedure Code: _____
14. Arthroscopic meniscectomy. ICD-9-CM Procedure Code: _____
15. Laceration repair, arm. ICD-9-CM Procedure Code: _____

Current Procedural Terminology (CPT) © 2005 American Medical Association. All Rights Reserved.

16. Vaginal hysterectomy.   ICD-9-CM Procedure Code: _____

17. Prostatectomy.   ICD-9-CM Procedure Code: _____

18. Cataract extraction.   ICD-9-CM Procedure Code: _____

19. Blood administration.   ICD-9-CM Procedure Code: _____

20. Chemotherapy infusion.   ICD-9-CM Procedure Code: _____

CPT-4/HCPCS PROCEDURE CODING GUIDELINES

In addition to the ICD-9-CM diagnostic and procedural coding, codes must be assigned for the specific services provided in hospital outpatient coding. This is accomplished through the use of CPT-4 and HCPCS Level II codes.

Under the **HCPCS (Healthcare Common Procedure Coding System),** codes are assigned from the following:

> Level I—CPT-4 Codes
> Level II—HCPCS Codes
> Level III—Local Carrier Codes

CPT-4 Coding

Unlike the ICD-9-CM coding book, where codes are looked up in the alphabetic index and cross-referenced in the numeric, the CPT-4 book is arranged in a distinctly different manner.

The CPT-4 manual is divided into six major categories or chapters:

- Evaluation and Management
- Anesthesia
- Surgery
- Radiology
- Pathology
- Medicine

The Evaluation and Management section is utilized for services provided during a patient visit or encounter. These encounters may occur in many settings, such as office, outpatient or nursing home, as well as others.

Anesthesia Services are located in Section Two. This section is utilized primarily by professional or physician coders. As anesthesia services are usually included in the reimbursement under the APC for the surgical procedure, the assignment of anesthesia codes is usually not necessary. Therefore, this section will not expand on coding for these services.

Current Procedural Terminology (CPT) © 2005 American Medical Association. All Rights Reserved.

Notes

The Surgery section is the most extensive section of the CPT-4 manual. Due to its scope, it is subsectioned into procedures performed by anatomical system (such as integumentary, musculoskeletal, etc.). Procedures in this section are primarily invasive or definitive in nature. "Invasive" can be defined as requiring entry into the body, while "definitive" can be defined for these purposes as any procedure that results in resolution or containment of the problem or diagnosis. Here is the order in which the coder should proceed:

- Identify the anatomical system (e.g., Musculoskeletal).
- Identify the anatomical part (e.g., Radius, Distal).
- Identify the specific procedure information (e.g., Open Reduction, Fracture).

In the above example, the coder would begin in the Surgery section; look in the Musculoskeletal area; then determine the specific anatomical part on which the invasive or definitive procedure was performed—in this case, distal radius. This will locate a small range of codes for Fracture Repairs of the Distal Radius. The coder will then ascertain from the operative report additional specific information regarding the fracture repair (such as open or closed, with or without manipulation, and with or without internal or external fixation) and assign the appropriate code accordingly.

The Radiology section of the CPT-4 manual identifies images that are taken under radiographic imaging such as x-ray, MRI, CT scan, ultrasound, nuclear medicine, fluoroscopy and radiologic oncology. It is divided into four sections:

- Diagnostic X-Ray
- Ultrasound
- Radialogic Oncology
- Nuclear Medicine

The Pathology section encompasses the study of living things, such as bacteria, blood, cells, body fluids and other substances found within the body. In order to code these services correctly, the coder must identify the type of service performed (such as microbiology, hematology or chemistry), and then the specific test(s) performed.

Codes in the Medicine section include services of a diagnostic and/or therapeutic nature. While services typically located in the Surgery section are usually definitive and/or invasive in nature, medicine procedures are typically performed to identify or diagnose a problem, identify the extent of a problem, or treat the problem. The coder must determine the specialty of the service (such as ophthalmology, pulmonary, gastroenterology or cardiology) and then determine the specific testing performed.

(A more detailed look at the CPT-4 coding guidelines will be discussed in the Outpatient Coding section, as these codes are utilized only in the outpatient coding arena.)

The index of CPT-4 is intended only for the purpose of locating the general section services may be in. It should not be utilized for assigning CPT-4 codes and, if utilized for such, will often result in incorrect code assignments.

Current Procedural Terminology (CPT) © 2005 American Medical Association. All Rights Reserved.

Notes

> **! ALERT:** Additional guidelines, revisions, additions and deletions can be obtained from the American Medical Association website at www.ama-assn.org. Also available from the AMA is the publication *CPT Assistant*, which has clarifications, feature articles and information about changes to CPT-4 codes throughout the year.

PRACTICE EXERCISE 1–5

Use what you have learned about CPT-4 to determine which section the following services would be located in:

1. Office visit, outpatient.   Section:
2. Bronchoscopy with biopsy.   Section:
3. Vasectomy.   Section:
4. Laceration repair.   Section:
5. CT scan.   Section:
6. Chest x-ray.   Section:
7. Hemoglobin.   Section:
8. CBC.   Section:
9. Pap smear.   Section:
10. Nursing home visit.   Section:

Further CPT-4 Breakdown

Within each of the major sections of CPT-4, the codes are broken down further:

Evaluation and Management Section
• Type/Location of Service
• New/Established
• Level of Service

Anesthesia Section
• Anatomical Region
• Anatomical Body Part

Current Procedural Terminology (CPT) © 2005 American Medical Association. All Rights Reserved.

Notes

Surgery Section
- Anatomical System
- Anatomical Part
- Surgical Procedure

Radiology Section
- Category
- Anatomical Part

Pathology Section
- Category
- Alphabetical

Medicine Section
- Specialty
- Procedure

Using these section breakdowns will facilitate locating the correct code.

PRACTICE EXERCISE 1–6

Use the section breakdowns to locate the appropriate code(s):

1. Arthroscopic repair of meniscus tear, knee.

   Section: _____

   Next Breakdown: _____

   Next Breakdown: _____

   Next Breakdown: _____

   Code Assignment: _____

2. 2.5 cm laceration repair of the knee, simple.

   Section: _____

   Next Breakdown: _____

   Next Breakdown: _____

   Next Breakdown: _____

   Code Assignment: _____

3. Radical modified mastectomy.

Section: _____

Next Breakdown: _____

Next Breakdown: _____

Next Breakdown: _____

Code Assignment: _____

4. Fracture repair, closed, distal radius.

Section: _____

Next Breakdown: _____

Next Breakdown: _____

Next Breakdown: _____

Code Assignment: _____

5. Esophagogastroduodenosocopy (upper GI) with biopsy.

Section: _____

Next Breakdown: _____

Next Breakdown: _____

Next Breakdown: _____

Code Assignment: _____

6. Bronchoscopy with removal of foreign body.

Section: _____

Next Breakdown: _____

Next Breakdown: _____

Next Breakdown: _____

Code Assignment: _____

7. Colonoscopy with polypectomy by hot biopsy forceps.

Section: _____

Next Breakdown: _____

Next Breakdown: _____

Next Breakdown: _____

Code Assignment: _____

Current Procedural Terminology (CPT) © 2005 American Medical Association. All Rights Reserved.

Notes

8. Upper GI endoscopy with esophageal dilation.

    Section: _____

    Next Breakdown: _____

    Next Breakdown: _____

    Next Breakdown: _____

    Code Assignment: _____

9. Abdominal hysterectomy with colpocystourethropexy.

    Section: _____

    Next Breakdown: _____

    Next Breakdown: _____

    Next Breakdown: _____

    Code Assignment: _____

10. Laparoscopic tubal ligation.

    Section: _____

    Next Breakdown: _____

    Next Breakdown: _____

    Next Breakdown: _____

    Code Assignment: _____

Modifier Codes

Under the CPT-4 coding system, services assigned a CPT-4 code that need descriptors for unusual circumstances are also assigned a modifier code. **Modifier codes** are two-digit codes that are appended to the CPT-4 code.

EXAMPLE

CPT-4 Code 99285-25

CPT-4 Descriptor 99285: Emergency Room Visit, Level 5

Modifier 25—Significantly Separately Identifiable Evaluation and Management Service

Modifier codes utilized for outpatient hospital services differ in some instances from those utilized for physician or professional code assignment. For instance, the modifier 51, multiple services, is not appropriate for outpatient

Current Procedural Terminology (CPT) © 2005 American Medical Association. All Rights Reserved.

Notes

services. Similarly, modifier 27 is not appropriate for physician/professional coding.

Outpatient CPT-4 Modifiers are as follows:

27	Two Evaluation and Mgt. Services Same Day Same Location
50	Bilateral Services
52	Reduced Services
58	Staged/Related Services
59	Distinct Services
73	Discontinued Outpatient/ASC Procedure Before Anesthesia
74	Discontinued Outpatient/ASC Procedure After Anesthesia
76	Repeat Procedure Same Physician
77	Repeat Procedure Different Physician
78	Return to the Operating Room for Related Procedure
79	Unrelated Procedure

A complete discussion of appropriate usage of outpatient CPT-4 modifier codes will be held during our discussion of Outpatient Coding.

HCPCS Coding

Under Level II of HCPCS, additional codes were established for the purpose of reporting services not included in CPT-4—usually drugs, supplies and miscellaneous services. The Level II HCPCS code book is organized differently.

! ALERT: Updates, including revisions of, deletions from and additions to the HCPCS Level II, are available from the Department of Health and Human Services website at www.dhhs.org.

These codes are arranged according to the product or types of supplies. For example, J codes are drugs; D codes are dental codes. Within these categories, the codes are assigned alphanumeric codes.

The HCPCS Index is as follows:

A9990-A0999	Ambulance and Transporation
A4000-A8999	Med/Surg Supplies
A9000-A9999	Administrative/Miscellaneous Supplies
B4000-B9999	Enteral/Parenteral Therapy
D0000-D9999	Dental Codes
E0100-E9999	Durable Medical Equipment
G0000-G9999	Temporary
J0000-J8999	Drugs Other Than Oral
J9000-J9999	Chemotherapy Drugs

Current Procedural Terminology (CPT) © 2005 American Medical Association. All Rights Reserved.

Notes

L0000-L4999	Orthotics
L5000-L9999	Prosthetics
M000-M0302	Medical Services
P0000-P9999	Pathology
R0000-R9999	Radiology
V0000-V2999	Vision Services
V5000-V5999	Hearing Services

We will take a look at additional coding guidelines for HCPCS Level II codes in our review of Outpatient Coding.

PRACTICE EXERCISE 1–7

Identify which sections in HCPCS Level II the following codes should be selected from:

1. Hospital bed, NOS.   Section: _____
2. Wheelchair, electric.   Section: _____
3. Methotrexate, 50 mg, IM.   Section: _____
4. Spectacles, single vision.   Section: _____
5. Hearing aid battery.   Section: _____
6. Pap smear.   Section: _____
7. Full foot orthotic.   Section: _____
8. Nebulizer.   Section: _____
9. Lasix, 20 mg, IV.   Section: _____
10. Rocephin, 1 gm, IV.   Section: _____

REVIEW OF APPROPRIATE CODING ASSIGNMENTS

It is imperative that the facility coder identify the location of service (inpatient versus outpatient) in order to determine which codes need to be assigned and from what sources those codes should be selected.

Later we will study specific coding guidelines for specific coding specialities. The purpose of this chapter and the following exercises is only to properly identify the types of codes needed and apply general coding principles.

Current Procedural Terminology (CPT) © 2005 American Medical Association. All Rights Reserved.

PRACTICE EXERCISE 1–8

Identify the place of service (inpatient/outpatient), the types of codes needed (ICD-9-CM diagnostic and/or procedural, CPT-4, HCPCS codes) and assign code(s) accordingly.

1. Outpatient diagnostic knee arthroscopy performed for knee pain.

   Location of Service: _____

   ICD-9-CM Diagnostic Code(s) Needed: ____Y ____N   Code(s): _____

   ICD-9-CM Procedural Code(s) Needed: ____Y ____N   Code(s): _____

   CPT-4 Procedural Code(s) Needed: ____Y ____N   Code(s): _____

   HCPCS Procedural Code(s) Needed: ____Y ____N   Code(s): _____

2. Patient S/P breast cancer who has become dehydrated and is admitted to the hospital for IV rehydration. Chemotherapy also completed during hospitalization.

   Location of Service: _____

   ICD-9-CM Diagnostic Code(s) Needed: ____Y ____N   Code(s): _____

   ICD-9-CM Procedural Code(s) Needed: ____Y ____N   Code(s): _____

   CPT-4 Procedural Code(s) Needed: ____Y ____N   Code(s): _____

   HCPCS Procedural Code(s) Needed: ____Y ____N   Code(s): _____

3. Patient admitted for abdominal pain and swelling of the abdominal region. Admitted for exploratory laparotomy and an ovarian tumor was diagnosed.

   Oophorectomy was performed and chemotherapy treatment was begun while the patient was still hospitalized.

   Location of Service: _____

   ICD-9-CM Diagnostic Code(s) Needed: ____Y ____N   Code(s): _____

   ICD-9-CM Procedural Code(s) Needed: ____Y ____N   Code(s): _____

   CPT-4 Procedural Code(s) Needed: ____Y ____N   Code(s): _____

   HCPCS Procedural Code(s) Needed: ____Y ____N   Code(s): _____

4. Patient admitted outpatient for upper GI due to blood in stools, weight loss and diarrhea. Procedure is performed with biopsy of two polyps by hot biopsy forceps, polypectomy by snare of 1 polyp.

Current Procedural Terminology (CPT) © 2005 American Medical Association. All Rights Reserved.

Notes

_____

_____

_____

_____

_____

_____

_____

_____

_____

_____

_____

_____

_____

_____

_____

_____

_____

_____

_____

_____

_____

_____

_____

_____

Location of Service: _____

ICD-9-CM Diagnostic Code(s) Needed: ____Y ____N Code(s): _____

ICD-9-CM Procedural Code(s) Needed: ____Y ____N Code(s): _____

CPT-4 Procedural Code(s) Needed: ____Y ____N Code(s): _____

HCPCS Procedural Code(s) Needed: ____Y ____N Code(s): _____

5. Patient with previous history of hemophilia is admitted due to abnormal white blood count. Patient has packed red blood cell transfusion and diagnosis is exacerbation of sickle cell.

Location of Service: _____

ICD-9-CM Diagnostic Code(s) Needed: ____Y ____N Code(s): _____

ICD-9-CM Procedural Code(s) Needed: ____Y ____N Code(s): _____

CPT-4 Procedural Code(s) Needed: ____Y ____N Code(s): _____

HCPCS Procedural Code(s) Needed: ____Y ____N Code(s): _____

6. Six-year-old patient admitted on an outpatient basis for tonsillectomy and adenoidectomy.

Location of Service: _____

ICD-9-CM Diagnostic Code(s) Needed: ____Y ____N Code(s): _____

ICD-9-CM Procedural Code(s) Needed: ____Y ____N Code(s): _____

CPT-4 Procedural Code(s) Needed: ____Y ____N Code(s): _____

HCPCS Procedural Code(s) Needed: ____Y ____N Code(s): _____

7. Patient seen in emergency room for migraine headache. Treated with IM Demerol and Vistaril and released.

Location of Service: _____

ICD-9-CM Diagnostic Code(s) Needed: ____Y ____N Code(s): _____

ICD-9-CM Procedural Code(s) Needed: ____Y ____N Code(s): _____

CPT-4 Procedural Code(s) Needed: ____Y ____N Code(s): _____

HCPCS Procedural Code(s) Needed: ____Y ____N Code(s): _____

8. Patient was admitted as the result of an open fracture of the shaft of the right tibia as a result of an auto accident where driver, who is the patient, collided on the highway with another vehicle.

Location of Service: _____

ICD-9-CM Diagnostic Code(s) Needed: ____Y ____N Code(s): _____

Current Procedural Terminology (CPT) © 2005 American Medical Association. All Rights Reserved.

Notes

_____

_____

_____

_____

_____

_____

_____

_____

_____

_____

_____

_____

_____

_____

_____

_____

_____

_____

_____

_____

ICD-9-CM Procedural Code(s) Needed: ____Y ____N Code(s): _____

CPT-4 Procedural Code(s) Needed: ____Y ____N Code(s): _____

HCPCS Procedural Code(s) Needed: ____Y ____N Code(s): _____

9. Patient was admitted to the hospital for uncontrolled hypertension. Patient was admitted approximately five weeks ago for myocardial infarction. Patient received hypertensive medication and an EKG and CXR will be ordered to assess their cardiovascular status.

Location of Service: _____

ICD-9-CM Diagnostic Code(s) Needed: ____Y ____N Code(s): _____

ICD-9-CM Procedural Code(s) Needed: ____Y ____N Code(s): _____

CPT-4 Procedural Code(s) Needed: ____Y ____N Code(s): _____

HCPCS Procedural Code(s) Needed: ____Y ____N Code(s): _____

10. Patient admitted to the hospital with acute hip pain, no history of trauma, just began experiencing hip pain after walking in the garden. She also has a history of diabetes, CHF and COPD. X-ray was performed that revealed fractured femur shaft. Cast applied and the patient will attend physical therapy on an outpatient basis.

Location of Service: _____

ICD-9-CM Diagnostic Code(s) Needed: ____Y ____N Code(s): _____

ICD-9-CM Procedural Code(s) Needed: ____Y ____N Code(s): _____

CPT-4 Procedural Code(s) Needed: ____Y ____N Code(s): _____

HCPCS Procedural Code(s) Needed: ____Y ____N Code(s): _____

DOCUMENTATION REVIEW

Another integral component of the coding process is the ability to review the documentation for specific information needed for coding purposes. The needed information will differ somewhat for outpatient and inpatient coding; however, the basic review would include capturing the following data:

	Outpatient	**Inpatient**
ICD-9-CM Diagnosis:	Chief reason for encounter	Chief reason for admission
Secondary Diagnosis:		Complications/ comorbidities

Current Procedural Terminology (CPT) © 2005 American Medical Association. All Rights Reserved.

Notes

	Contributing dx to complexity of encounter	Contributing diagnosises to complexity of admission
ICD-9-CM Procedures:	Significant procedures	Significant procedures
CPT-4 Procedures:	All services performed	Not applicable
HCPCS Codes:	All services performed	Not applicable

The most basic of coding and documentation principles—that information not documented cannot be coded and billed—is applicable to both the inpatient and outpatient coding arenas.

We will look at this process in more depth during our discussion of Inpatient Coding and Outpatient Coding once we have looked at additional in-depth coding concepts for these settings.

We will be taking these same coding charts, applying the billing process principles in Chapter 2, to complete the UB-92 claim forms in later chapters. Again, these are basic principles intended only to follow the process through from services provided, identified, coded and billed appropriately. The assignment of the correct ICD-9-CM diagnostic and procedural codes and CPT-4/HCPCS codes in the correct order is integral to correct and timely reimbursement. In addition, their correct placement on the UB-92 along with other essential information is imperative to receiving reimbursement for services provided.

PRACTICE EXERCISE 1–9

These exercises present some basic coding scenarios. Look at the documentation and determine what information is integral to applying inpatient or outpatient coding principles in assigned code(s) as appropriate.

1. Chart #1—Operative Report
   Outpatient diagnostic arthroscopy of the right shoulder with mini-open rotator cuff repair.
   Postoperative Diagnosis: Right rotator cuff tear.

   Patient was taken to the operating room and, after general anesthesia was administered, her shoulder was examined. She was placed in the beach-chair position and her shoulder was prepped and draped in sterile fashion. Scope was inserted and a diagnostic arthroscopy was performed. There were no significant findings other than a small rotator cuff tear at the anteriormost aspect of the supraspinatus tendon. Cuff edges were debrided and the area of insertion was roughened at the humeral head. A suture anchor was used to the fix the cuff back down to the bone; however, this ripped through the tendon. After this complication, it was decided to perform a mini-open approach to

Current Procedural Terminology (CPT) © 2005 American Medical Association. All Rights Reserved.

Notes

further evaluate. A small 4–5 cm incision was made with sharp dissection through the deltoid. The cuff tear was identified and it was indeed about a centimeter in size and was easily repaired. The suture anchor that had been used with the tendon was unable to be retrieved, so another suture anchor was placed.

The shoulder was able to be placed through a full range of motion with no obvious extension or impingement noted. Sterile dressing was applied. Patient was taken to the recovery room in stable condition.

Location of Service: _____

ICD-9-CM Diagnostic Code(s) Needed: ____Y ____N Code(s): _____

ICD-9-CM Procedural Code(s) Needed: ____Y ____N Code(s): _____

CPT-4 Procedural Code(s) Needed: ____Y ____N Code(s): _____

HCPCS Procedural Code(s) Needed: ____Y ____N Code(s): _____

2. Chart #2—Operative Report
   Excision of mass, right arm.
   Diagnosis: Mass, right arm.

   Patient's right arm was prepped and draped in standard fashion. A tourniquet was placed about the right arm and was elevated to 250 mm of mercury.

   The area of the skin incision was infiltrated with 1% lidocaine with epinephrine. An incision was made slightly lateral to the biceps tendon.

   Blunt dissection was then carried out and the firm mass encountered. It was removed without difficulty and sent for pathology.

   The wound was irrigated; skin was closed using 5-0 nylon in horizontal mattress fashion. Dressing applied, tourniquet was released and the patient tolerated the procedure well. The patient was released to home in satisfactory condition.

   Location of Service: _____

   ICD-9-CM Diagnostic Code(s) Needed: ____Y ____N Code(s): _____

   ICD-9-CM Procedural Code(s) Needed: ____Y ____N Code(s): _____

   CPT-4 Procedural Code(s) Needed: ____Y ____N Code(s): _____

   HCPCS Procedural Code(s) Needed: ____Y ____N Code(s): _____

3. Chart #3—Operative Report
   Operative arthroscopy of the left knee with chrondroplasty of the patellofemoral joint and partial medial meniscectomy.
   Diagnosis: Chondromalacia patellofemoral joint, left knee.

Current Procedural Terminology (CPT) © 2005 American Medical Association. All Rights Reserved.

Notes

Degenerative tear medial meniscus left knee.

Patient given satisfactory spinal anesthetic and placed in the supine position in the OR. Tourniquet placed and area was prepped and draped in usual sterile manner. Scope was placed inferolaterally and instrumentation portal was inferomedial. Examination showed Grade II chondromalacia that was smoothed off with a shaver. Lateral compartment showed minimal chondromalacia. Lateral meniscus was intact. Medial compartment showed large area of 3 cm of Grade IV chondromalacia and other areas of Grade III chondromalacia. There was a complex tear of the anterior horn of the medial meniscus, which was shaved off with a shaver down to the stable rim. Posterior horn was intact.

Portals were closed with interrupted nylon sutures. Patient was taken to the recovery room in stable condition where he was discharged the same day.

Location of Service: _____

ICD-9-CM Diagnostic Code(s) Needed: ____Y ____N   Code(s): _____

ICD-9-CM Procedural Code(s) Needed: ____Y ____N   Code(s): _____

CPT-4 Procedural Code(s) Needed: ____Y ____N   Code(s): _____

HCPCS Procedural Code(s) Needed: ____Y ____N   Code(s): _____

4. Chart #4—Operative Report
Closed reduction of distal tibia, casting with fluoroscopic guidance. Diagnosis: Refracture left distal tibia, delayed union.

Patient underwent open reduction internal fixation of a distal tibia fracture approximately six months ago. In a subsequent follow-up, it was determined that the fracture had not healed appropriately, and therefore, she was taken to the operating room for closed reduction of distal tibia fracture on an outpatient basis.

Posteromedial angulation was corrected with manipulation and the fracture was placed in a cast. The patient tolerated the procedure well with no complications.

Location of Service: _____

ICD-9-CM Diagnostic Code(s) Needed: ____Y ____N   Code(s): _____

ICD-9-CM Procedural Code(s) Needed: ____Y ____N   Code(s): _____

CPT-4 Procedural Code(s) Needed: ____Y ____N   Code(s): _____

HCPCS Procedural Code(s) Needed: ____Y ____N   Code(s): _____

5. Chart #5—Operative Report
Trigger point injections.
Diagnosis: Chronic low back pain, mostly myofascial in origin.

Current Procedural Terminology (CPT) © 2005 American Medical Association. All Rights Reserved.

A total of three trigger points were identified and marked on either side of the spine at the L1-L2 levels in the erector spinae muscles. The skin overlying these trigger points was prepped and draped in the usual sterile fashion and each of these trigger points was infiltrated with .5 to 1 cc of solution containing .25% Marcaine with 4 mg per cc of Kenalog. Patient tolerated the procedure well in the outpatient clinic and was discharged.

Location of Service: _____

ICD-9-CM Diagnostic Code(s) Needed: ____Y ____N Code(s): _____

ICD-9-CM Procedural Code(s) Needed: ____Y ____N Code(s): _____

CPT-4 Procedural Code(s) Needed: ____Y ____N Code(s): _____

HCPCS Procedural Code(s) Needed: ____Y ____N Code(s): _____

6. Chart #6—Operative Report
Paracentesis under ultrasound.
History of ascites.

During her third day of stay, an area of ascites was seen in the midline anterior abdomen. The area was cleansed and appropriately anesthetized. A 16-gauge paracentesis catheter was placed in this area, removing 2,400 cc of milky, turbid fluid. The vital signs were stable throughout the procedure. The patient was returned to their room for further treatment.

Location of Service: _____

ICD-9-CM Diagnostic Code(s) Needed: ____Y ____N Code(s): _____

ICD-9-CM Procedural Code(s) Needed: ____Y ____N Code(s): _____

CPT-4 Procedural Code(s) Needed: ____Y ____N Code(s): _____

HCPCS Procedural Code(s) Needed: ____Y ____N Code(s): _____

7. Chart #7—Operative Report
Declotted ASH catheter.
The examination was initially done through the venous port, which was occluded.

Wires were inserted through the catheter and a 4 French glide catheter was also inserted over the wire. This did not resolve the occlusion. Two mg of TPA was inserted into the venous side of the catheter and left in position for 20 minutes. This improved the flow somewhat, but not adequately. At this point, the right groin was cleansed and anesthetized appropriately. A gooseneck snare was inserted and the end of the ash catheter was snared. The catheter was stripped with reestablishment of excellent flow through the catheter. The patient was released to home.

Location of Service: _____

ICD-9-CM Diagnostic Code(s) Needed: ____Y ____N Code(s): _____

ICD-9-CM Procedural Code(s) Needed: ____Y ____N Code(s): _____

Current Procedural Terminology (CPT) © 2005 American Medical Association. All Rights Reserved.

Notes
_____
_____
_____
_____
_____
_____
_____
_____
_____
_____
_____
_____
_____
_____
_____
_____
_____
_____
_____
_____
_____
_____

CPT-4 Procedural Code(s) Needed: ____Y ____N Code(s): _____

HCPCS Procedural Code(s) Needed: ____Y ____N Code(s): _____

8. Chart #8—Operative Report
Left heart catheterization due to angina.

Right groin was prepped and draped in the usual sterile fashion. Right femoral vein was entered via percutaneous technique. 8 French sheath inserted into vein. Right femoral artery was entered and the LCA selected and assessed via angiography. Catheter was exchanged and RCA selected and assessed via angiography. LV was next selected and assessed via angiography. Catheter removed over wire. Perclose device was deployed and hemostasis obtained.

Location of Service: _____

ICD-9-CM Diagnostic Code(s) Needed: ____Y ____N Code(s): _____

ICD-9-CM Procedural Code(s) Needed: ____Y ____N Code(s): _____

CPT-4 Procedural Code(s) Needed: ____Y ____N Code(s): _____

HCPCS Procedural Code(s) Needed: ____Y ____N Code(s): _____

9. Chart #9—Operative Report
Colonoscopy with pedicle cauterization of AV malformations; upper GI with CLOtest biopsy.
Diagnosis: Hematochezia and chronic pyrosis with history of gastric resection.

First colonoscopy was performed and the scope was advanced all the way to the cecum. There were several AV malformations which were identified, and I electrocauterized at least six lesions. The rest of the colon mucosa appears normal. The scope was straightened and pulled out.

The upper endoscopy was performed. Mouth sprayed with Cetacaine, and EGD scope introduced into the esophagus. Esophagus appeared normal, and the scope was advanced into the stomach. Pylorus normal, but duodenal bulb appeared severely erythematous. Scope was advanced further and a CLOtest biopsy was performed. Scope was dropped down into the fundus, which also appeared normal. Scope was taken out and patient tolerated procedure well and was discharged home.

Location of Service: _____

ICD-9-CM Diagnostic Code(s) Needed: ____Y ____N Code(s): _____

ICD-9-CM Procedural Code(s) Needed: ____Y ____N Code(s): _____

CPT-4 Procedural Code(s) Needed: ____Y ____N Code(s): _____

HCPCS Procedural Code(s) Needed: ____Y ____N Code(s): _____

Current Procedural Terminology (CPT) © 2005 American Medical Association. All Rights Reserved.

10. Chart #10—Operative Report
Esophagogastroduodenoscopy with biopsy and esophageal dilation.
Gastritis performed in outpatient endoscopy suite.

Gastroscope was introduced into the patient's mouth and passed through the pharynx and into the esophagus. Mucosa was normal in appearance. The endoscope was then passed through the EG junction into the stomach. The endoscope was then passed through the pylorus into the duodenum. The endoscope was brought back into the stomach and a wire was deployed in the antrum. She was then dilated with a 60 French savory dilator. The wire and dilator were removed. Biopsies were obtained from the distal esophagus to assess esophagitis. Biopsies were also obtained from the gastric body from the area of the gastritis.

Impression: Nonerosive gastritis in the stomach.

Location of Service: _____

ICD-9-CM Diagnostic Code(s) Needed: ___Y ___N Code(s): _____

ICD-9-CM Procedural Code(s) Needed: ___Y ___N Code(s): _____

CPT-4 Procedural Code(s) Needed: ___Y ___N Code(s): _____

HCPCS Procedural Code(s) Needed: ___Y ___N Code(s): _____

CONCLUSION

At the conclusion of this chapter, the student should understand the basic coding principles of both ICD-9-CM diagnostic and procedural coding and where they should be utilized, as well as the basic concepts of CPT-4 and HCPCS coding. In addition to understanding the basic coding concepts, the student should be able to apply the appropriate ICD-9-CM, CPT-4 and HCPCS codes to facility documentation. The student should have successfully completed the coding exercises contained in Practice Exercises 1-1 through 1-9, applying the coding principles discussed in this chapter.

Current Procedural Terminology (CPT) © 2005 American Medical Association. All Rights Reserved.

Chapter 2
Hospital Billing Process

Accounts Receivable (A/R)
Adjudication
Advance Beneficiary Notice (ABN)
Allowance
Appeal
Assignment of Benefits
Authorization Number
Capitation Plan
CHAMPUS/CHAMPVA
Charge Capturing
Charge Description Master (CDM)/Chargemaster
Charge Ticket
CMS 1450
Coinsurance
Collection Agency
Collections

Commercial Insurance
Consent to Treat
Contractual Write-off
Co-payment
Deductible
Encounter Form
Exclusive Provider Organization (EPO)
Explanation of Benefits (EOB)
Guarantor
Health Maintenance Organization (HMO)
Managed Care Plan
Medicaid
Medically Indigent
Medicare
Medicare HMO Replacement
Medigap

Nonavailability Statement (NAS)
Nonparticipating
Participating
Per Member Per Month (PMPM)
Point of Service (POS)
Preadmission Certification
Preferred Provider Organization (PPO)
Primary Care Physician (PCP)
Revenue Codes
Share of Cost
TRICARE
TRICARE Extra
TRICARE Prime
TRICARE Standard
Workers' Compensation

LEARNING OBJECTIVES

- Demonstrate understanding that the billing process involves a number of departments and completion of forms to successfully receive reimbursement
- Describe the many types of insurance carriers
- Discuss the necessity of capturing all patient services through the use of charge forms and various departments within the facility
- Discuss the reimbursement process of third-party carriers
- Describe the collection process for patient balances

Notes

GENERAL OVERVIEW OF THE BILLING PROCESS

The coding process within the facility organization is only one of the components necessary for the billing process to take place.

As mentioned in the overview of the hospital organization, not all billing is accomplished through the coding or health information department. Later, when we discuss the process of outpatient and inpatient coding and billing, it will become apparent how intricate the facility coding and billing process is.

Part of the billing process is the capturing of all essential information and services performed. This information is captured through a series of forms housed in the departments within the hospital facility.

ADMISSION/PREADMISSION PROCESS

As part of the admission process, the patient may be contacted prior to admission for registration and insurance information. In the case of an urgent or emergency admission, however, the information will probably be obtained during the admission process. A series of forms is utilized for capturing this information in the hospital/facility setting.

Admission Forms

The admission form, an example of which is shown in Figure 2–1, is utilized for capturing all insurance/third-party information as well as billing information. During the admission/preadmission process, authorization for services is obtained from the third-party carrier when necessary. This process is known as **preadmission certification**. The carrier will review the medical necessity of the admission and the services to be performed and issue an **authorization number**, a preassigned number that designates that the procedure(s) and admission were preapproved. Additional services or additional length of stays typically will need additional authorization.

Consent Forms

As part of the admission/preadmission process, a **consent to treat**—an authorization for the provider and facility to provide those services that are considered medically necessary—will be obtained as well as an **assignment of benefits**. The assignment of benefits indicates the patient has "assigned" the right of payment directly to the facility, rather than monies for services being sent to the patient. The patient, or the **guarantor**—the individual responsible for paying for services—will typically sign a financial agreement

CODING REGIONAL HOSPITAL
123 MAIN STREET, ANYWHERE, USA

HOSPITAL ADMISSION FORM

PATIENT INFORMATION

PATIENT LAST NAME	FIRST NAME	MI	DOB	ADMIT DATE/TIME

STREET ADDRESS	CITY/STATE/ZIP	AREA CODE/PHONE

SEX M ☐ F ☐	RACE	AGE	RELIGIOUS PREFERENCE

PATIENT'S EMPLOYER	OCCUPATION

STREET ADDRESS	CITY/STATE/ZIP	AREA CODE/PHONE

EMERGENCY CONTACT

#1 LAST NAME	FIRST NAME	MI	AREA CODE/PHONE	RELATIONSHIP
#2 LAST NAME	FIRST NAME	MI	AREA CODE/PHONE	RELATIONSHIP

GUARANTOR

#1 LAST NAME	FIRST NAME	MI	AREA CODE/PHONE	RELATIONSHIP
#2 LAST NAME	FIRST NAME	MI	AREA CODE/PHONE	RELATIONSHIP

ADMISSION INFORMATION

ADMISSION STATUS	PATIENT TYPE	UNIT	ROOM	ATTENDING MD

ADMITTING DIAGNOSIS

INSURANCE INFORMATION

#1 PAYOR NAME	STREET ADDRESS	CITY/STATE/ZIP	AREA CODE/PHONE
POLICY #	GROUP #	GROUP NAME	
SUBSCRIBER NAME	DOB	AUTHORIZATION #	

#2 PAYOR NAME	STREET ADDRESS	CITY/STATE/ZIP	AREA CODE/PHONE
POLICY #	GROUP #	GROUP NAME	
SUBSCRIBER NAME	DOB	AUTHORIZATION #	

#3 PAYOR NAME	STREET ADDRESS	CITY/STATE/ZIP	AREA CODE/PHONE
POLICY #	GROUP #	GROUP NAME	
SUBSCRIBER NAME	DOB	AUTHORIZATION #	

Figure 2–1 Example of a hospital admission form.

Notes

indicating they will be responsible for payment for services not covered by third-party carriers.

In the case of Medicare, if services are believed not covered prior to provision, the patient will be requested to sign an **Advance Beneficiary Notice (ABN)**. This form must be completed only for those services possibly not

Patient's Name: Medicare # (HICN):

ADVANCE BENEFICIARY NOTICE (ABN)

NOTE: You need to make a choice about receiving these laboratory tests.

We expect that Medicare will not pay for the laboratory test(s) that are described below. Medicare does not pay for all of your health care costs. Medicare only pays for covered items and services when Medicare rules are met. The fact that Medicare may not pay for a particular item or service does not mean that you should not receive it. There may be a good reason your doctor recommended it. Right now, in your case, **Medicare probably will not pay for the laboratory test(s) indicated below for the following reasons:**

Medicare does not pay for these tests for your condition	Medicare does not pay for these tests as often as this (denied as too frequent)	Medicare does not pay for experimental or research use tests

The purpose of this form is to help you make an informed choice about whether or not you want to receive these laboratory tests, knowing that you might have to pay for them yourself. Before you make a decision about your options, you should **read this entire notice carefully.**
- Ask us to explain, if you don't understand why Medicare probably won't pay.
- Ask us how much these laboratory tests will cost you (**Estimated Cost: $**_____), in case you have to pay for them yourself or through other insurance.

PLEASE CHOOSE **ONE** OPTION. CHECK **ONE** BOX. **SIGN & DATE** YOUR CHOICE.

☐ **Option 1. YES. I want to receive these laboratory tests.**
I understand that Medicare will not decide whether to pay unless I receive these laboratory tests. Please submit my claim to Medicare. I understand that you may bill me for laboratory tests and that I may have to pay the bill while Medicare is making its decision. If Medicare does pay, you will refund to me any payments I made to you that are due to me. If Medicare denies payment, I agree to be personally and fully responsible for payment. That is, I will pay personally, either out of pocket or through any other insurance that I have. I understand I can appeal Medicare's decision.

☐ **Option 2. NO. I have decided not to receive these laboratory tests.**
I will not receive these laboratory tests. I understand that you will not be able to submit a claim to Medicare and that I will not be able to appeal your opinion that Medicare won't pay. I will notify my doctor who ordered these laboratory tests that I did not receive them.

_____   _____
     Date   **Signature of patient or person acting on patient's behalf**

NOTE: **Your health information will be kept confidential.** Any information that we collect about you on this form will be kept confidential in our offices. If a claim is submitted to Medicare, your health information on this form may be shared with Medicare. Your health information which Medicare sees will be kept confidential by Medicare.

OMB Approval No. 0938-0566   Form No. CMS-R-131-L   (June 2002)

Figure 2–2 Medicare Advanced Beneficiary Notice.

covered, and for a specific date. This form is not intended as a universal noncoverage form. An example of an ABN is shown in Figure 2–2.

With many carriers, a **co-payment**—a set amount required to be paid by the patient—may be collected from the patient. In other instances, the patient will be required to pay a certain percentage of the services known as the **coinsurance**. In some cases, the patient may be unable to make the required co-payment or coinsurance. Payment arrangements or a payment plan may be arranged at this time or at the time of discharge, based on the carrier facility requirements.

Notes

Because each carrier has specific admission, payment, and billing requirements, it is imperative that the correct insurance carrier is captured during the admission/preadmission process.

INSURANCE CARRIERS

Table 2–1 provides a brief outline of the types of carriers the facility's billing department will deal with.

TABLE 2–1   Carrier Type Summary.

Carrier	Primary Care Physician	Authorization Required (Yes) / (No)	Co-pay/Coinsurance Deductible, Varies
Medicare	No	No	Deductible Coinsurance
Medicare HMO Replacement	Yes	Yes	Varies
HMO	Yes	Yes	Co-pay Coinsurance Hospital
PPO	No	No	Coinsurance
		Yes/Hospital	Deductible
EPO	Varies	Varies	Varies
POS	HMO/Yes	HMO/Yes	HMO/Yes Co-pay
	PPO/No	PPO/No Hospital/Yes	PPO/Varies
Commercial Indemnity	No	No Deductible	Coinsurance
Tricare Prime (HMO)	Yes	Yes	Co-pay
Tricare Extra (PPO)	No	No	Coinsurance
		Yes/Hospital	Deductible
Tricare Standard	No	No	Coinsurance
		Yes/Hospital	Deductible
Workers' Compensation	No	Yes by Workers' Comp	None if fully covered

Medicare

Medicare, federal health insurance for patients over the age of 65 or the disabled, is available to all United States citizens who have paid into the Social Security program during their lifetimes. Under the program, all qualified individuals are eligible for benefits under Medicare Part A, facility services, without a monthly premium (Part B, for professional services, is available at an additional cost). Many Medicare patients do not understand that professional services rendered in the hospital or facility are covered under Part B provisions, not Part A, and that therefore, patients who have only Part A coverage will be responsible for all physician/professional services rendered during their hospitalization. Medicare recipients are responsible for an annual **deductible**, an amount that must be paid before the carrier begins payment for services, as well as a coinsurance amount.

! ALERT: Additional guidelines as well as official CMS (Center for Medicare Services) memorandums are available on the CMS website: www.cms.hhs.gov.

Because the patient deductible and coinsurance can be substantial in the case of a complex medical condition or prolonged hospital stay, many patients elect to replace their regular Medicare product with a **Medicare HMO Replacement**. This product is available in lieu of federal Medicare and typically costs the patient about the same, but it may cover additional services not covered by the federal Medicare program, such as prescriptions and eyeglasses. The Medicare HMO Replacement functions as a **Health Maintenance Organization (HMO)**, a managed care plan that controls health insurance costs by assigning each participant a **primary care physician (PCP)** who must approve all health care in advance.

Some Medicare patients elect to keep their regular Medicare but also carry a supplemental policy that pays in addition to Medicare. Obviously, an additional premium through an insurance carrier other than Medicare is required for such coverage. Some of these carriers or plans are **Medigap** carriers, indicated by the Medigap insignia or verbage on the insurance card. These carriers supplement Medicare, usually covering the coinsurance amount not covered by Medicare. Typically these carriers have an agreement under which Medicare automatically sends claims to them electronically for secondary processing.

Medicaid

Under the federal Medicaid program, each individual state administers funds from the U.S. government. Some states choose to cover a large number of individuals with their funds, thus reducing the reimbursement to each, while others elect to cover a more limited group of individuals. Patients eligible for **Medicaid** are typically low-income, indigent and/or disabled.

! **ALERT:** Medicaid guidelines are available on the CMS website: www.cms.hhs.gov. Additional information may also be available on your state government website as well.

Medicaid recipients may be eligible for one of three types of Medicaid:

Medicaid HMO	Functions as an HMO with a primary care physician. All services must be authorized by the primary care physician in advance.
Traditional Medicaid	Does not function as a managed care insurance, therefore no prior approvals or primary care physicians are involved. In some instances, a minimal co-payment may be required from the patient.
Share of Cost Medicaid	Medicaid recipient is required to pay a deductible or **share of cost** (an amount the patient must pay before Medicaid will pay for services).

Managed Care Plans

Due to the rising cost of insurance in the United States, many carriers have implemented **managed care plans** that implement methods for controlling health costs, such as co-payments, primary care physicians and insurance carrier networks.

Some types of managed care plans are discussed below:

Health Maintenance Organizations (HMOs)

Third-party insurance carriers offer HMO plans that require all services to be authorized by a primary care physician (PCP), also referred to as a "gate-keeper." Under such plans, services may be reimbursed under a contractual fee schedule, or under a **capitation plan**, in which the patient is covered under a **per member per month (PMPM)**, a set fee covering all services on a monthly basis regardless of the amount of services provided or not provided.

Preferred Provider Organizations (PPOs)

Unlike HMOs, **Preferred Provider Organization (PPO)** carriers do not require authorization by a primary care physician. Instead, they typically require that the participant only remain within the PPO's network of providers. However, in the case of surgical procedures or inpatient admission, the PPO sometimes will require preauthorization for services. Such preauthorization may be obtained directly from the carrier, since the patient does not have a primary care physician.

Exclusive Provider Organization (EPO)

In an **Exclusive Provider Organization (EPO)**, the provider typically performs services only for a specific third-party carrier. In other words, these providers and facilities are "exclusive" to that insurance carrier network and typically do not provide services outside the network.

Point of Service Organization (POS)

Point of Service (POS) networks function in some instances as an HMO, with co-payments and primary care physicians; in other instances they function under the guidelines of a PPO. The determination is usually based on the "point of service." Point of Service networks are often referred to as "hybrid" because they function both as an HMO and a PPO.

Commercial Insurance/Indemnity Insurance

Unlike the managed care plans listed above, **commercial insurance** carriers do not restrict their enrollees as to where their services may be provided. However, should the patient receive services in a **nonparticipating** facility, or one not contracted with the insurance carrier, the patient will be responsible for the difference between the charges for service and the amount the carrier allows and pays for the services authorized. On the other hand, should the facility be **participating**—meaning that they have previously contracted with the carrier to perform services for a predetermined fee—the patient will only be responsible for a percentage of the amount allowed by the carrier, as outlined in their individual insurance plan.

EXAMPLE

Let's take an example of a service performed in both a participating and nonparticipating environment to demonstrate the corresponding difference in patient responsibility:

Participating or Contracted Facility   80%

	Charge	Allowance	Insurance	Patient
Chest X-Ray	$100.00	$80.00	$64.00	$36.00

Nonparticipating or Noncontracted Facility   80%

	Charge	Allowance	Insurance	Patient
Chest X-Ray	$100.00	$80.00	$64.00	$16.00

Facility Contractually Obligated to Write Off $20.00

Notes

This concept also applies for each of the managed care plans as well. When the provider or facility does not participate, the provider of service is not obligated to accept the allowance as payment in full.

PRACTICE EXERCISE 2–1

Let's try some exercises to determine the appropriate amount that the facility would expect from a carrier, the amount the patient would be responsible for, and the amount that the facility agrees to write off in the event they participate.

	Charge	80% Allowance	Insurance	Patient
1. Participating Clinic Visit	$110.00			
2. Nonparticipating Clinic Visit, Level 3	$ 90.00			
3. Nonparticipating Cardiac Stress Test	$200.00			
4. Participating Electrocardiogram	$150.00			
5. Nonparticipating Electro-encephalogram	$175.00			
6. Participating Office Visit, Level 2	$ 80.00			
7. Nonparticipating Laceration Repair	$250.00			
8. Participating Incision/Drainage	$100.00			
9. Participating Immunization	$ 50.00			
10. Nonparticipating Thallium Stress Test	$120.00			

CHAMPUS and CHAMPVA

Active and retired military and their families are eligible for benefits under **CHAMPUS** (active) or **CHAMPVA** (retired). CHAMPUS (Civilian Health and Medical Program of the Uniformed Services) was created to help military personnel pay for medical costs. However, with those costs continuing to escalate, CHAMPUS became known as **TRICARE**, offering three products to military and their families and dependents:

- **TRICARE Standard** (formerly CHAMPUS, commercial/indemnity)
- **TRICARE Prime** (HMO Product)
- **TRICARE Extra** (PPO Product)

In order for military personnel with TRICARE benefits to receive inpatient care outside of a military treatment facility, the services must be preauthorized. A **Nonavailability Statement (NAS)** will be issued, usually electronically, indicating approval for these services. Such a statement is not necessary for outpatient procedures, nor for inpatient services in the following circumstances:

- A medical emergency that could result in death or threat to health.
- Other primary insurance exists.

! ALERT: Additional information and guidelines regarding TRICARE coverage and benefits are available on the TRICARE website: www.tricare.osd.mil.

Workers' Compensation

Insurance covering an employee's injury or illness resulting from their job is known as **Workers' Compensation.** For an injury or work-related illness to be covered, the event must be reported within a specified period of time. That time differs on a state-to-state basis, so it is necessary to know what your individual state requires.

! ALERT: Workers' Compensation funds are administered by the specific state in which the injury or illness occurred. Consult your State Workers' Compensation website by going to your state government website and accessing the Workers' Compensation division.

Medically Indigent

Some patients will not be eligible for any third-party coverage, and not eligible for Medicaid as well. The facility will screen such patients to determine their ability to pay for services rendered. Depending on their funding, some facilities will receive county or state funding to care for these patients, who are known as **medically indigent**.

Notes

CAPTURING PATIENT SERVICES

Once the patient is registered and the appropriate forms have been completed and signed, the patient will receive those services that are considered medically necessary. These services may occur in a number of locations throughout the facility, therefore presenting a challenge to **charge capturing**—the process by which the facility ensures all services performed have been coded and billed appropriately.

Chargemaster and Charge Ticket Forms

A number of areas within the hospital facility capture their services through the use of a **charge ticket** or **encounter form**. An example is shown in Figure 2–3. This document is completed by the department personnel, who will record the patient information as well as the services performed and a diagnosis. All services, codes and charges provided by the facility are maintained in the facility's computerized billing system in the **charge description master (CDM)** or **chargemaster** (see Figure 2–4). Because departmental personnel typically are not trained in coding, many of these charge documents will be forwarded to the coding or health information department for assignment of ICD-9-CM diagnostic codes.

Chargemaster

The charge description master or chargemaster is the computerized billing system's summary of services provided, with the appropriate charges, HCPCS/CPT-4 codes and revenue codes. It allows a significant number of outpatient services to be entered by facility personnel who do not have the expertise of a coding professional. However, diagnostic coding and more involved procedures require code assignment by a member of the Health Information or Coding staff.

Since the chargemaster includes all services the hospital or facility provides, the typical CDM contains thousands of entries, usually including the following information:

- Department number
- Inventory/control number
- Revenue code
- CPT/HCPCS code
- Fee or charge for service
- Description of service

It is imperative that the chargemaster be reviewed and updated on a regular basis. New codes should be added, old ones deleted and an analysis of charge to cost for services should be made for all services contained in the chargemaster.

CODING REGIONAL HOSPITAL
123 MAIN STREET, ANYWHERE, USA

FACILITY ENCOUNTER FORM

RADIOLOGY

Code	Descriptor	Diagnosis (enter Below)
200001	Chest X-Ray, PA	_____
200002	Chest X-Ray, PA/Lateral	_____
200003	X-Ray, Finger, 2 Views	_____
200004	X-Ray, Radius, 2 Views	_____
200005	X-Ray, Abdomen, Flat/Upright	_____
200006	Abdominal Ultrasound	_____

PATIENT INFORMATION

PATIENT LAST NAME	FIRST NAME	MI	DOB	ADMIT DATE/TIME

STREET ADDRESS	CITY/STATE/ZIP	AREA CODE/PHONE

SEX M ☐ F ☐	RACE	AGE	RELIGIOUS PREFERENCE

PATIENT'S EMPLOYER	OCCUPATION

STREET ADDRESS	CITY/STATE/ZIP	AREA CODE/PHONE

EMERGENCY CONTACT

#1 LAST NAME	FIRST NAME	MI	AREA CODE/PHONE	RELATIONSHIP
#2 LAST NAME	FIRST NAME	MI	AREA CODE/PHONE	RELATIONSHIP

GUARANTOR

#1 LAST NAME	FIRST NAME	MI	AREA CODE/PHONE	RELATIONSHIP
#2 LAST NAME	FIRST NAME	MI	AREA CODE/PHONE	RELATIONSHIP

ADMISSION INFORMATION

ADMISSION STATUS	PATIENT TYPE	UNIT	ROOM	ATTENDING MD

ADMITTING DIAGNOSIS

INSURANCE INFORMATION

#1 PAYOR NAME	STREET ADDRESS	CITY/STATE/ZIP	AREA CODE/PHONE
POLICY #	GROUP #	GROUP NAME	
SUBSCRIBER NAME	DOB	AUTHORIZATION #	
#2 PAYOR NAME	STREET ADDRESS	CITY/STATE/ZIP	AREA CODE/PHONE
POLICY #	GROUP #	GROUP NAME	
SUBSCRIBER NAME	DOB	AUTHORIZATION #	

Figure 2–3 Facility Encounter form.

CODING REGIONAL HOSPITAL
123 MAIN STREET, ANYWHERE, USA

CHARGE DESCRIPTION MASTER

DEPARTMENT NUMBER	SERVICE CODE	HCPCS CODE	DESCRIPTION	REVENUE CODE	CHARGE
100	001	99281	ER Visit Level I	450	$100
100	002	99282	ER Visit Level II	450	$125
100	003	99283	ER Visit Level III	450	$150
100	004	99284	ER Visit Level IV	450	$200
100	005	99285	ER Visit Level V	450	$250
100	006		ROOM–BOARD/PVT	110	$500
100	007		INTENSIVE CARE	190	$750
200	001	71010	Chest X-Ray, PA	324	$100
200	002	71020	Chest X-Ray, PA & Lat	324	$125
200	003	73140	X-Ray, Finger, 2V	320	$100
200	004	73100	X-Ray, Radius	320	$100
200	005	74020	X-Ray, Abdomen Flat/Upright	320	$100
200	006	76705	Abdominal Ultrasound	320	$275
300	001	Q0081	IV Therapy	260	$350
400	001	93005	EKG	730	$250

Figure 2–4 Chargemaster.

Notes

This involves an extensive amount of time and effort on the part of the hospital; therefore, often an individual or individuals will be assigned to maintain the chargemaster.

Revenue Codes

Revenue codes—three-digit codes that identify the department and/or subdepartment services are supplied from—assist the facility in allocating costs and revenues by helping determine the profitability of each department and subdepartment. A revenue code must be assigned for each line item assigned in Form Locator 47. The codes are entered in the chargemaster based on the service provided. As mentioned earlier, while some services can be data-entered into the billing system to generate appropriate charges and revenue codes, others will require the expertise of the coding professional. However, even in such instances, revenue codes and CPT-4 codes must already be available in the billing system in order for the coding professional to be able to utilize them.

General guidelines for revenue code assignment were discussed previously. However, remember the following:

- All revenue codes should be listed in ascending order.
- Do not assign duplicate revenue codes unless required by the specific FI, or unless more than one HCPCS code is needed on the same claim.
- Revenue codes must be valid for the type of claim billed.
- All outpatient hospital claims must have HCPCS codes except drugs, supplies and end-stage renal disease services.

Revenue codes appropriate for facility use are listed in Figure 2–5.

PRACTICE EXERCISE 2–2

Let's determine the appropriate revenue codes for the following services:

Revenue Code

1. Clinic Visit, Level 2 _____
2. Electrocardiogram _____
3. Electroencephalogram _____
4. Chest X-Ray, PA & Lat _____
5. CT Brain, with and w/o Contrast _____
6. Spirometry _____
7. IV Infusion _____
8. ER Visit, Level 3 _____
9. Urinalysis _____
10. IV Supplies _____
11. ER Visit, Level 1 _____
12. Complete Blood Count _____
13. X-Ray, Abdomen, Flat and Upright _____
14. Clinic Visit, Level 4 _____
15. Arterial Blood Gas _____

Notes

42 Revenue Code	43 Revenue Description
01X Reserved	
02X Health Insurance PPS	
0 Reserved	
1 Reserved	
2 SNF PPS System	SNF PPS (RUG)
3 Rehab Facility PPS	HH PPS
4 Inpatient Rehab Facility	IRF PPS
5-9 Reserved	
03X - 09X Reserved	

Accomodation Codes

10X All-Inclusive Rate	
0 All-Inclusive R & B Plus Ancillary	ALL INC R&B/ANC
1 All-inclusive R & B	ALL INCL R&B
11X R & B (Private/Med/Gen)	
0 General	ROOM-BOARD/PVT
1 Med/Surg/Gyn	MED-SUR-GY/PVT
2 Obstetrics (OB)	OB/PVT
3 Pediatric	PEDS/PVT
4 Psychiatric	PSYCH/PVT
5 Hospice	HOSPICE/PVT
6 Detoxification	DETOX/PVT
7 Oncology	ONCOLOGY/PVT
8 Rehabilitation	REHAB/PVT
9 Other	OTHER/PVT
12X R & B (2 Bed/Med/Gen)	
0 General	ROOM-BOARD/SEMI
1 Med/Surg/Gyn	MED-SUR-GY/2BED
2 Obstetrics (OB)	OB/2BED
3 Pediatric	PEDS/2BED
4 Psychiatric	PSYCH/2BED
5 Hospice	HOSPICE/2BED
6 Detoxification	DETOX/2BED
7 Oncology	ONCOLOGY/2BED
8 Rehabilitation	REHAB/2BED
9 Other	OTHER/2BED
13X R & B (3-4 Beds)	
0 General	ROOM-BOARD/3&4 BED
1 Med/Surg/Gyn	MED-SUR-GY/3&4 BED
2 Obstetrics (OB)	OB/3 & 4BED
3 Pediatric	PEDS/3 & 4BED
4 Psychiatric	PSYCH/3 & 4BED
5 Hospice	HOSPICE/3 & 4BED
6 Detoxification	DETOX/3 & 4BED

(continues)

Figure 2–5 Complete listing of revenue codes for use on the CMS 1450/UB-92 form.

Notes

7 Oncology	ONCOLOGY/3&4BED
8 Rehabilitation	REHAB/3&4 BED
0 General	ROOM-BOARD/PVT/DLX
1 Med/Surg/Gyn	MED-SUR-GY/DLX
2 Obstetrics (OB)	OB/DLX
3 Pediatric	PEDS/DLX
4 Psychiatric	PSYCH/DLX
5 Hospice	HOSPICE/DLX
6 Detoxification	DETOX/DLX
7 Oncology	ONCOLOGY/DLX
8 Rehabilitation	REHAB/DLX
9 Other	OTHER/DLX
15X R & B (Ward/Med/Gen)	
0 General	ROOM-BOARD/WARD
1 Med/Surg/Gyn	MED-SUR-GY/WARD
2 Obstetrics (OB)	OB/WARD
3 Pediatric	PEDS/WARD
4 Psychiatric	PSYCH/WARD
5 Hospice	HOSPICE/WARD
6 Detoxification	DETOX/WARD
7 Oncology	ONCOLOGY/WARD
8 Rehabilitation	REHAB/WARD
9 Other	OTHER/WARD
16X Other R & B	
0 General	R&B
4 Sterile Environment	R&B/STERILE
7 Self-Care	R&B/SELF
9 Other	R&B/OTHER
17X Nursing	
0 General	NURSERY
1 Newborn Level I Routine Newborn Care	NURSERY/LEVEL I
2 Newborn Level II Low birthweight neonates	NURSERY/LEVEL II
3 Newborn Level III Sick neonates/Not NICU	NURSERY/LEVEL III
4 Newborn Level IV Sick neonates/NICU	NURSERY/LEVEL IV
18X Leave of Absence (LOA)	
0 General	LOA OR LEAVE OF ABSENCE
1 Reserved	
2 Pt Convenience-Billable	LOA/PT CONV CHGS BILLABLE
3 Therapeutic Leave	LOA/THERAP
4 ICF Mentally Retarded	LOA/ICF/MR
5 Nursing Home (Hosp)	LOA/NURS HOME
9 Other LOA	LOA/OTHER

Figure 2–5 Continued

Notes

19X Subacute Care	
0 General	SUBACUTE
2 Subacute Level II Moderate Nursing Care	SUBACUTE/LEVEL II
3 Subacute Level III Mod/Extensive Nursing	SUBACUTE/LEVEL III
4 Subacute Level IV Extensive Nurs/Tech	SUBACUTE/LEVEL IV
20X Intensive Care	
0 General	INTENSIVE CARE OR ICU
1 Surgical	ICU/SURGICAL
2 Medical	ICU/MEDICAL
3 Pediatric	ICU/PEDS
4 Psychiatric	ICU/PSTAY
6 Intermed ICU	ICU/INTERMEDIATE
7 Burn Care	ICU/BURN CARE
8 Trauma	ICU/TRAUMA
9 Other ICU	ICU/OTHER
21X Coronary Care	
0 General	CORONARY CARE OR CCU
1 Myocardial Infarction	CCU/MYO INFARC
2 Pulmonary Care	CCU/PULMONARY
3 Heart Transplant	CCU/TRANSPLANT
4 Intermed CCU	CCU/INTERMEDIATE
9 Other coronary care	CCU/OTHER

Ancillary Services

22X Special Charges	
0 General	SPECIAL CHARGES
1 Admission Charge	ADMIT CHARGE
2 Tech Support Charge	TECH SUPPT CHG
3 UR Service Charge	UR CHARGE
4 Late Discharge/Med Necess	LATE DISCH/MED NEC
9 Other Special Charges	OTHER SPEC CHG
23X Incremental Nursing Care	
0 General	NURSING INCREM
1 Nursery	NUR INCR/NURSERY
2 OB	NUR INCR/OB
3 ICU (inc transitional care)	NUR INCR/ICU
4 CCU (inc transitional care)	NUR INCR/CCU
5 Hospice	NUR INCR/HOSPICE
9 Other	NUR INCR/OTHER
24X All-Inclusive Ancillary	
0 General	ALL INCL ANCIL
1 Basic	ALL INCL BASIC
2 Comprehensive	ALL INCL COMP

(continues)

Figure 2–5 Continued

Notes

3 Specialty	ALL INCL SPECIAL
9 Other All-Inclusive Ancillary	ALL INCL ANCIL/OTHER
1 Generic Drugs	DRUGS/GENERIC
2 Non-generic Drugs	DRUGS/NONGENERIC
3 Take-Home Drugs	DRUGS/TAKEHOME
4 Drugs incident to Dx Serv	DRUGS/INCIDENT ODX
5 Drugs incident to Radiology	DRUGS/INCIDENT RAD
6 Experimental Drugs	DRUGS/EXPERIMT
7 Nonprescription Drugs	DRUGS/NONPSCRPT
8 IV Solutions	IV SOLUTIONS
9 Other Pharmacy	DRUGS/OTHER
26X IV Therapy	Usually requires HCPCS code(s)
0 General	IV THERAPY
1 Infusion Pump	IV THER/INFSN PUMP
2 IV Therapy/Pharmacy	IV THER/PHARM/SVC
3 IV Therapy/Drug/Supply/ Delivery	IV THER/DRUG/SUPPLY DELV
4 IV Therapy/Supplies	IV THER/SUPPLIES
9 Other IV Therapy	IV THERAPY/OTHER
27X Med/Surg Supplies/Devices	Only Non-Routine Billed With This RC
0 General	MED-SUR SUPPLIES
1 Non-Sterile Supply	NONSTER SUPPLY
2 Sterile Supply	STERILE SUPPLY
3 Take Home Supplies	TAKEHOME SUPPLY
4 Prostetic/Orthotic Devices	PROSTH/ORTH DEV
5 Pacemaker	PACE MAKER
6 Intraocular Lenses	INTRO OC LENS
7 Oxygen-Take Home	02/TAKEHOME
8 Other Implants	SUPPLY/IMPLANTS
9 Other Supplies/Devices	SUPPLY/OTHER
28X Oncology	
0 General	ONCOLOGY
9 Other Oncology	ONCOLOGY/OTHER
29X DME (Other Than Renal)	
0 General	MED EQUIP/DURAB
1 Rental	MED EQUIP/RENT
2 Purchase of new DME	MED EQUIP/NEW
3 Purchase of used DME	MED EQUIP/USED
4 Supplies/Drugs for DME Effectiveness (HHA)	MED EQUIP/SUPPLIES/DRUGS
9 Other Equipment	MED EQUIP/OTHER
30X Laboratory	
0 General	LABORATORY OR LAB
1 Chemistry	LAB/CHEMISTRY
2 Immunology	LAB/IMMUNOLOGY
3 Renal Patient (Home)	LAB/RENAL HOME

Figure 2–5 Continued

Notes

4 Nonroutine Dialysis	LAB/NR DIALYSIS
5 Hematology	LAB/HEMATOLOGY
9 Other Laboratory	LAB/OTHER
31X Laboratory Pathological	
0 General	PATHOLOGY LAB OR PATH LAB
1 Cytology	PATHOL/CYTOLOGY
2 Histology	PATHOL/HISTOLOGY
4 Biopsy	PATHOL/BIOPSY
9 Other	PATHOL/OTHER
32X Radiology-Diagnostic	
0 General	DX X-RAY
1 Angiocardiography	DX X-RAY/ANGIO
2 Arthrography	DX X-RAY/ARTH
3 Arteriography	DX X-RAY/ARTER
4 Chest X-Ray	DX X-RAY/CHEST
9 Other	DX X-RAY/OTHER
33X Radiology-Therapeutic	
0 General	RX X-RAY
1 Chemotherapy-Injected	CHEMOTHER/INJ
2 Chemotherapy-Oral	CHEMOTHER/ORAL
3 Radiation Therapy	RADIATION RX
5 Chemotherapy/IV	CHEMOTHERAP-IV
9 Other	RX X-RAY/OTHER
34X Nuclear Medicine	
0 General	NUCLEAR MEDICINE OR NUC MED
1 Diagnostic	NUC MED/DX
2 Therapeutic	NUC MED/RX
9 Other	NUC MED/OTHER
34X CT Scan	
0 General	CT SCAN
1 Head Scan	CT SCAN/HEAD
2 Body Scan	CT SCAN/BODY
9 Other CT Scans	CT SCAN/OTHER
36X Operating Room Services	
0 General	OR SERVICES
1 Minor Surgery	OR/MINOR
2 Organ Transplant/Not Kidney	OR/ORGAN TRANS
7 Kidney Transplant	OR/KIDNEY TSRANS
9 Other	OR/OTHER
37X Anesthesia	
0 General	ANESTHESIA
1 Anes Incident to RAD	ANESTHE/INCIDENT RAD
2 Anes Incident to Other Dx	ANESTHE/INCIDENT ODX
4 Acupuncture	ANESTHE/ACUPUNC
9 Other	ANESTHE/OTHER

(continues)

Figure 2–5 Continued

Notes

38X Blood	
0 General	BLOOD
1 Packed Red Cells	BLOOD/PKD RED
5 Leukocytes	BLOOD/LEUKOCYTES
6 Other Components	BLOOD/COMPONENTS
7 Other Derivatives	BLOOD/DERIVATIVES
9 Other Blood	BLOOD/OTHER
39X Blood Storage/Processing	
0 General	BLOOD/STOR-PROC
1 Blood Administration	BLOOD/ADMI
9 Other	BLOOD/OTHER STOR
40X Other Imaging	
0 General	IMAGE SERVICE
1 Dx Mammography	MAMMOGRAPHY
2 Ultrasound	ULTRASOUND
3 Screen Mammography	SCR MAMMOGRAPHY/GEN MAMMO
4 Positron Emission Tomography	PET SCAN
9 Other	OTHER IMAG SVS
41X Respiratory	
0 General	RESPIRATORY SVC
2 Inhalation Services	INHALATION SVC
3 Hyperbarbic Oxygen Therapy	HYPERBARIC 02
9 Other	OTHER RESPIR SVS
42X Physical Therapy	
0 General	PHYSICAL THERP
1 Visit Charge	PHYS THERAP/VISIT
2 Hourly Charge	PHYS THERP/HOUR
3 Group Rate	PHYS THERP/GROUP
4 Evaluation/Reevaluation	PHYS THERP/EVAL
9 Other	OTHER PHYS THERP
43X Occupational Therapy	
0 General	OCCUPATION THER
1 Visit Charge	OCCUP THERP/VISIT
2 Hourly Charge	OCCUP THERP/HOUR
3 Group Rate	OCCUP THERP/GROUP
4 Evaluation/Reevaluation	OCCUP THERP/EVAL
9 Other	OTHER OCCUP THER
44X Speech-Languaged Pathology	
0 General	SPEECH PATHOL
1 Visit Charge	SPEECH PATH/VISIT
2 Hourly Charge	SPEECH PATH/HOUR
3 Group Rate	SPEECH PATH/GROUP
4 Evaluation/Reevaluation	SPEECH PATH/EVAL
9 Other	OTHER SPEECH PAT

Figure 2–5 Continued

Notes

45X Emergency Room	450 Not to be Used with Any Other Code From Series
0 General	EMERG ROOM
1 EMTALA Med Screen Svcs	ER/EMTALA
0 General	PULMONARY FUNC
9 Other	OTHER PULMON FUNC
47X Audiology	
0 General	AUDIOLOGY
1 Diagnostic	AUDIOLOGY/DX
2 Treatment	AUDIOLOGY/RX
9 Other	OTHER AUDIOL
48X Cardiology	
0 General	CARDIOLOGY
1 Cardiac Cath Lab	CARDIAC CATH LAB
2 Stress Test	STRESS TEST
3 Echocardiology	ECHOCARDIOLOGY
9 Other	OTHER CARDIOL
49X Ambulatory Surgical Care	
0 General	AMBUL SURG
9 Other	OTHER AMBL SURG
50X Outpatient Services	
0 General	OUTPATIENT SVS
9 Other	OUTPATIENT/OTHER
51X Clinic	
0 General	CLINIC
1 Chronic Pain Center	CHRONIC PAIN CL
2 Dental Clinic	DENTAL CLINIC
3 Psychiatric Clinic	PSYCH CLINIC
4 Ob-Gyn Clinic	OB-GYN CLINIC
5 Pediatric Clinic	PEDS CLINIC
6 Urgent Care Clinic	URGENT CLINIC
7 Family Practice Clinic	FAMILY CLINIC
9 Other	OTHER CLINIC
52X Freestanding Clinic	
0 General	FREESTAND CLINIC
1 Rural Health-Clinic	RURAL/CLINIC
2 Rural Health-Home	RURAL/HOME
3 Family Practice Clinic	FR/STD FAMILY CLINIC
6 Urgent Care Clinic	FR/STD URGENT CLINIC
9 Other	OTHER FR/STD CLINIC
53X Osteopathic Services	
0 General	OSTEOPATH SVS
1 Osteopathic Therapy	OSTEOPATH RX
9 Other	OTHER OSTEOPATH
54X Ambulance	
0 General	AMBULANCE

(continues)

Figure 2–5 Continued

Notes

1 Supplies	AMBUL/SUPPLY	
2 Medical Transport	AMBUL/MED TRANS	
5 Air Ambulance	AIR AMBULANCE	
6 Neonatal Ambulance	AMBUL/NEO-NATAL	
7 Pharmacy	AMBUL/PHARMACY	
8 Telephone Transmission EKG	AMBUL/TELEPHONIC EKG	
9 Other	OTHER AMBULANCE	
55X Skilled Nursing		
0 General	SKILLED NURSING	
1 Visit Charge	SKILLED NURS/VISIT	
2 Hourly Charge	SKILLED NURS/HOUR	
9 Other	SKILLED NURS/OTHER	
56X Medical Social Services		
0 General	SOCIAL SVS	
1 Visit Charge	MED SOC SERV/VISIT	
2 Hourly Charge	MED SOC SERV/HOUR	
9 Other	MED SOC SERV/OTHER	
57X Home Health Aid		
0 General	AIDE/HOME HEALTH	
1 Visit Charge	AIDE/HOME HLTH/VISIT	
2 Hourly Charge	AIDE/HOME HLTH/HOUR	
9 Other	AIDE/HOME HLTH/OTHER	
58X Other Visits (Home Health)		
0 General	VISIT/HOME HEALTH	
1 Visit Charge	VISIT/HOME HLTH/VISIT	
2 Hourly Charge	VISIT/HOME HLTH/HOUR	
9 Other	VISIT/HOME HLTH/OTHER	
59X Units of Service (Home Health)		
0 General	UNIT/HOME HEALTH	
9 Other	UNIT/HOME HLTH/OTHER	
60X Oxygen (Home Health)		
0 General	02/HOME HEALTH	
1 Oxygen-Stat/Equip/Supp/or Contents	02/EQUIP/SUPPL/CONT	
2 Oxygen-Stat/Equip/Supp Under 1 LPM	02/STAT EQUIP/UNDER 1 LPM	
3 Oxygen-Stat/Equip/over 4 LPM	O2/STAT EQUIP/OVER 4 LPM	
4 Oxygen-Portable Add-On	02/STAT EQUIP/PORT ADD-ON	
61X Magnetic Resonance		
0 General	MRI	
1 Brain (inc Brain Stem)	MRI-BRAIN	
2 Spinal Cord (inc spine)	MRI-SPINE	
3 Reserved		
4 MRI-Other	MRI-OTHER	
5 MRA-Head/Neck	MRA-HEAD AND NECK	

Figure 2–5 Continued

Notes

6 MRA-Lower Extremities	MRA-LOWER EXTREMITIES
7 Reserved	
62X Med/Surg/Supp Extension of 27X	
1 Supplies incident Radiology	MED-SUR SUPP/INCIDNT RAD
2 Supplies incident Other Dx	MED-SUR SUPP INCIDNT ODX
3 Surgical Dressings	SURG DRESSING
4 FDA Investigation Devices	IDE
63X Pharmacy	
0 Reserved	
1 Single Source Drug	DRUG/SINGLE
2 Multiple Source Drug	DRUG/MULT
3 Restrictive Prescription	DRUG/RSTR
4 EPO < 10,000 units	DRUG/EPO/<10,000 UNITS
5 EPO >10,000 units	DRUG/EPO/>10,000 UNITS
6 Drugs Req Detailed Coding	DRUGS/DETAIL CODE
7 Self-Admin Drugs	DRUGS/SELFADMIN
64X Home IV Therapy Services	
0 General	IV THERAPY SVC
1 Nonroutine Nursing, Central Line	NON RT NURSING/CENTRAL
2 IV Site Care, Central Line	IV SISTE CARE/CENTRAL
3 IV Start/Change, Peripheral Line	IV STRT/CHNG/PERIPHAL
4 Nonroutine Nursing, Peripheral Line	NONRT NURSING/PERIPHRL
5 Training Patient/Caregiver, Central Line	TRNG/PT/CARGVR/CENTRAL
6 Training, Disabled Patient, Central Line	TRNG DSBLPT/CENTRAL
7 Training Patient/Caregiver, Peripheral Line	TRNG/PT/CARGVR/PERIPHRL
8 Training, Disabled Patient, Peripheral Line	TRNG/DSBLPAT/PERIPHRL
9 Other IV Therapy Services	OTHER IV THERAPY SVC
65X Hospice Services	
0 General	HOSPICE
1 Routine Home Care	HOSPICE/RTN HOME
2 Continuous Home Care	HOSPICE/CTNS HOME
3 Reserved	
4 Reserved	
5 Inpt Respite Care	HOSPICE/IP RESPITE
6 General Inpt Care (Nonrespite)	HOSPICE/IP NON RESPITE
7 Physician Services	HOSPICE/PHYSICIAN
9 Other Hospice	HOSPICE/OTHER
66X Respite Care (HHA Only)	
0 General	RESPITE CARE

Figure 2–5 Continued

(continues)

Notes

1 Hourly Chg/Skilled Nursing	RESPITE/SKILLED NURSE
2 Hourly Chg/HHA/Homemaker	RESPITE/HMEAID/HMEMKE
0 General	OP SPEC RES
1 Hospital-Based	OP SPEC RES/HOSP BASED
2 Contracted	OP SPEC RES/CONTRACTED
9 Other Special Residence	OP SPEC RES/OTHER
68X Not Assigned	
69X Not Assigned	
70X Cast Room	
0 General	CAST ROOM
9 Other Cast Room	OTHER CAST ROOM
71X Recovery Room	
0 General	RECOVERY ROOM
9 Other Recovery Room	OTHER RECOV RM
72X Labor Room/Delivery	
0 General	DELIVROOM/LAB
1 Labor	LABOR
2 Delivery	DELIVERY ROOM
3 Circumcision	CIRCUMCISION
4 Birthing Center	BIRTHING CENTER
9 Other Labor Room/Delivery	OTHER/DELIV-LABOR
73X EKG/ECG	
0 General	EKG/ECG
1 Holter Monitor	HOLTER MONT
2 Telemetry	TELEMETRY
9 Other EKG/ECG	OTHER EKG/ECG
74X EEG	
0 General	EEG
9 Other EEG	OTHER EEG
75X Gastrointestinal Services	
0 General	GASTRO-INTS SVS
9 Other Gastrointestinal	OTHER GASTRO-INTS
76X Treatment/Observation Rm	
0 General	TREATMENT/OBSERVATION RM
1 Treatment Room	TREATMENT ROOM
2 Observation Room	OBSERVATION RM
9 Other Treatment Room	OTHER TREATMENT RM
77X Preventative Care Services	
0 General	PREVENT CARE SVS
1 Vaccine Administration	VACCINE ADMIN
9 Other Prev Care Services	OTHER PREVENT
78X Telemedicine	
0 General	TELEMEDICINE
9 Other Telemedicine	TELEMEDICINE/OTHER

Figure 2–5 Continued

Notes

79X Lithotripsy	
0 General	LITHOTRIPSY
9 Other Lithotripsy	LITHOTRIPSY/OTHER
80X Inpatient Renal Dialysis Peritoneal Dialysis (CAPD)	
4 Inpt Continuous Ambulatory Cycling Peritoneal (CCPD)	DIALY/INPT/CCPT
9 Other Inpt Dialysis	DIALY/INPT/OTHER
81X Organ Acquisition	
0 General	ORGAN ACQUISIT
1 Living Donor	LIVING DONOR
2 Cavader Donor	CADAVER/DONOR
3 Unknown Donor	UNKNOWN/DONOR
4 Unsuccessful Organ Search Donor Bank Charge	UNSUCCESSFUL SEARCH
9 Other Organ Donor	OTHER/DONOR
82X Hemodialysis-Outpt/Home	
0 General	HEMO/OP OR HOME
1 Hemodialysis/Composite or Other Rate	HEMO/COMPOSITE
2 Home Supplies	HEMO/HOME/SUPPL
3 Home Equipment	HEMO/HOME/EQUIP
4 Maintenance/100%	HEMO/HOME/100%
5 Support Services	HEMO/HOME/SUPSERV
9 Other Outpt Hemodialysis	HEMO/HOME/OTHER
83X Peritoneal Dialysis- Outpatient/Home	
0 General	PERITONEAL/OP OR HOME
1 Peritoneal/Composite or Other Rate	PERTNL/COMPOSISTE
2 Home Supplies	PERTNL/HOME/SUPPL
3 Home Equipment	PERTNL/HOME/EQUIP
4 Maintenance/100%	PERTNL/HOME/100%
5 Support Services	PERTNL/HOME/SUPSERV
9 Other Peritoneal Dialysis	PERTNL/HOME/OTHER
84X Continuous Ambulatory Peritoneal Dialysis (CAPD) Outpatient/Home	
0 General	CAPD/OP OR HOME
1 CAPD/Composite or Other Rate	CAPD/COMPOSITE
2 Home Supplies	CAPD/HOME/SUPPL
3 Home Equipment	CAPD/HOME/EQUIP
4 Maintenance/100%	CAPD/HOME/100%
5 Support Services	CAPD/HOME/SUPSERV
9 Other CAPD Dialysis	CAPD/HOME/OTHER

Figure 2–5 Continued

(continues)

Notes

85X Continuous Cycling Peritoneal Dialysis (CCPD)	CCPD/OP OR HOME
1 CCPD/Composite or Other Rate	CCPD/COMPOSITE
2 Home Supplies	CCPD/HOME/SUPPL
3 Home Equipment	CCPD/HOME/EQUIP
4 Maintenance/100%	CCPD/HOME/100%
5 Support Services	CCPD/HOME/SUPSERV
9 Other CCPD Dialysis	CCPD/HOME/OTHER
86X Reserved Dialysis National Assignment	
87X Reserved Dialysis State Assignment	
88X Miscellaneous Dialysis	
0 General	DIALY/MISC
1 Ultrafiltration	DIALY/ULTRAFILT
2 Home Dialysis Aid Visit	HOME DIALYSIS AID VISIT
9 Misc Dialysis Other	DIALY/MISC/OTHER
89X Reserved Natl Assignment	
90X Psychiatric/Psychological Treatments	
0 General	PSTAY TREATMENT
1 Electroshock Treatment	ELECTRO SHOCK
2 Milieu Therapy	MILIEU THERAPY
3 Play Therapy	PLAY THERAPY
4 Activity Therapy	ACTIVITY THERAPY
9 Other	OTHER PSYCH RX
91X Psychiatric/Psychological Services	
0 General	PSYCH/SERVICES
1 Rehabilitation	PSYCH/REHAB
2 Partial Hosp-Less Intensive	PSYCH/PARTIAL HOSP
3 Partial Hosp-Intensive	PSYCH/PARTIAL INTENSIVE
4 Individual Therapy	PSYCH/INDIV RX
5 Group Therapy	PSYCH/GROUP RX
6 Family Therapy	PSYCH/FAMILY RX
7 Biofeedback	PSYCH/BIOFEED
8 Testing	PSYCH/TESTING
9 Other	PSYCH/OTHER
92X Other Dx Services	
0 General	OTHER DX SVS
1 Peripheral Vascular Lab	PERI VASCUL LAB
2 Electromyelogram	EMG
3 Pap Smear	PAP SMEAR
4 Allergy Test	ALLERGY TEST
5 Pregnancy Test	PREG TEST
9 Other Dx Service	ADDITIONAL DX SVS

Figure 2–5 Continued

Notes

93X Med Rehab Day Program	
2 Full Day	FULL DAY
94X Other Ther Services	
0 General	OTHE RX SVS
1 Recreational Therapy	RECREATION RX
2 Education/Training	EDUC/TRAINING
3 Cardiac Rehab	CARDIAC REHAB
4 Drug Rehab	DRUG REHAB
5 Alcohol Rehab	ALCOHOL REHAB
6 Complex Med Equip-Routine	RTN COMPLX MED EQUIP-ROUT
7 Complex Med Equip-Ancillary	COMPLX MED EQUIP-ANX
9 Other Ther Services	ADDITIONAL RX SVS
95X Other Ther Services Extension of 94X	
0 Reserved	
1 Athletic Training	ATHLETIC TRAINING
2 Kinesiotherapy	KINESIOTHERAPY
96X Professional Fees	
0 General	PRO FEE
1 Psychiatry	PRO FEE/PSYCH
2 Ophthalmology	PRO FEE/EYE
3 Anesthesiologist (MD)	PRO FEE/ANES MD
4 Anesthetist (CRNA)	PRO FEE/ANES CRNA
9 Other Prof Fees	OTHER PRO FEE
97X Prof Fees continued	
1 Laboratory	PRO FEE/LAB
2 Radiology-Dx	PRO FEE/RAD/DX
3 Radiology-Therapeutic	PRO FEE/RAD/RX
4 Radiology-Nuclear Med	PRO FEE/NUC MED
5 Operating Room	PRO FEE/OR
6 Respiratory Therapy	PRO FEE/RESPIR
7 Physical Therapy	PRO FEE/PHYSI
8 Occupational Therapy	PRO FEE/OCUPA
9 Speech Pathology	PRO FEE/SPEECH
98X Prof Fees continued	
1 Emergency Room	PRO FEE/ER
2 Outpatient Services	PRO FEE/OUTPT
3 Clinic	PRO FEE/CLINIC
4 Medical Social Services	PRO FEE/SOC SVC
5 EKG	PRO FEE/EKG
6 EEG	PRO FEE/EEG
7 Hospital Visit	PRO FEE/HOS VIS
8 Consultation	PRO FEE/CONSULT
9 Private Duty Nurse	PEE/PVT NURSE

(continues)

Figure 2–5 Continued

99X Patient Convenience Items	
0 General	PT CONVENIENCE
1 Cafeteria/Guest Tray	CAFETERIA
2 Private Linen Service	LINEN
3 Telephone/Telegraph	TELEPHONE
4 TV/Radio	TV/RADIO
5 Nonpt Room Rentals	NONPT ROOM RENT
6 Late Discharge Charge	LATE DISCHARGE
7 Admission Kits	ADMIT KITS
8 Beauty Shop/Barber	BARBER/BEAUTY
9 Other Pt Convenience Items	PT CONVENCE/OTHER
100X - 209X Reserved for Natl Assignment	
210X Alternative Therapy Svcs	
0 General	
1 Acupuncture	
2 Accupressure	
3 Massage	
4 Reflexology	
5 Biofeedback	
6 Hypnosis	
9 Other Alternative Ther Svcs	

Figure 2–5 Continued

PRACTICE EXERCISE 2–3

Let's also assign appropriate CDM descriptor codes.

CDM Code

1. Glucose, Blood   _____

2. ER Visit, Level 3   _____

3. Clinic Visit, Level 1   _____

4. IV Therapy   _____

5. Prothrombin Time   _____

6. Hematocrit   _____

7. Abdominal Ultrasound   _____

8. Sterile Supplies   _____

9. IM Demerol   _____

10. IV Lasix, 20 mg   _____

Notes

CODING AND HEALTH INFORMATION DEPARTMENT

Many of a facility's more involved procedures are captured through its coding or health information department. Services such as complex radiological procedures and surgeries are directed to this department, where trained personnel review the documentation and assign appropriate ICD-9-CM diagnostic and/or procedure codes, and CPT-4 codes when appropriate. Many of the services that are captured through the health information or coding department will be input directly into the billing system. The charge tickets or encounter forms mentioned above may be data-entered in the department where services are rendered, or in a specifically designated area.

BILLING DEPARTMENT

Once charge capturing has been accomplished, it is the responsibility of the billing department to ensure that all services are billed in accordance with third-party guidelines.

As with coding guidelines, many of the billing guidelines for the professional side are similar, if not identical, to facility guidelines. However, the basic concept for facility billing ensures that the facility has captured all resources they have expended in providing care to the patient.

All services will be billed on the UB-92 or Uniform Billing form, now known as the **CMS 1450**, commonly still referred to as HCFA 1450 or UB-92. An illustration of a CMS 1450 is shown in Figure 2–6. Chapter 3 of the Process Overview will deal specifically with the proper completion of this form for billing purposes.

It is also the responsibility of the billing office to ensure that payment is received, that it is appropriate, that it arrives on time and that appropriate patient billing occurs immediately following receipt of third-party carrier payments.

When payment is received, the carrier will forward an **Explanation of Benefits (EOB)**, which will detail the amount charged, the **allowance**—the amount agreed upon by the carrier and the provider as payment in full—and the reason(s) for any denial of payment or reduction in payment. An example is shown in Figure 2–7.

The EOB will be reviewed by billing office personnel, the payment posted, and the appropriate **contractual write-off**—the difference between the facility charge and the allowance—will be taken. Determination will be made as to whether appropriate reimbursement has been made, and if not, an **appeal**—a formal request for reconsideration—can be made.

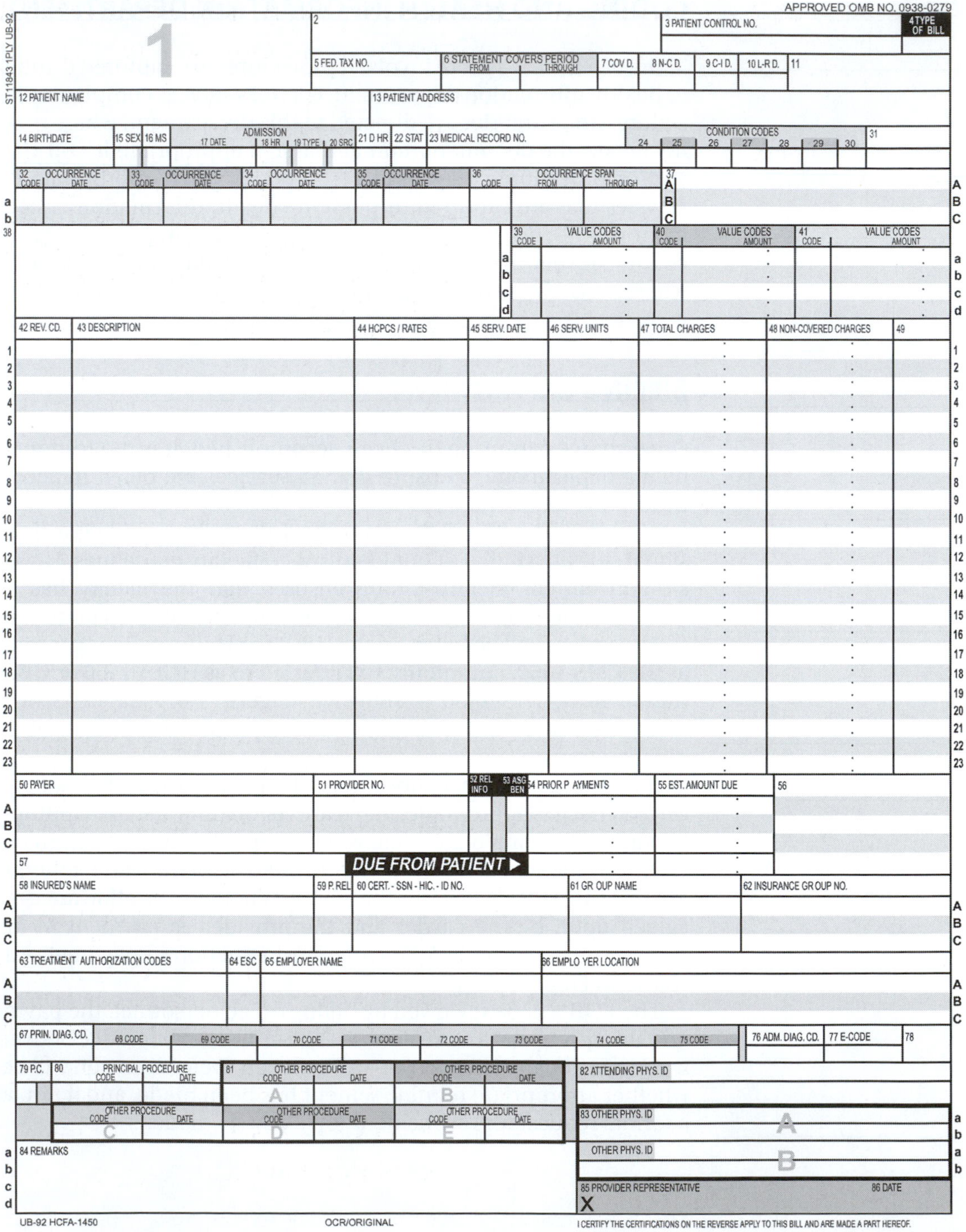
APPROVED OMB NO. 0938-0279
ST11843 1PLY UB-92
1
2
3 PATIENT CONTROL NO.
4 TYPE OF BILL
5 FED. TAX NO.
6 STATEMENT COVERS PERIOD FROM THROUGH
7 COV D.
8 N-C D.
9 C-I D.
10 L-R D.
11
12 PATIENT NAME
13 PATIENT ADDRESS
14 BIRTHDATE
15 SEX
16 MS
ADMISSION 17 DATE 18 HR 19 TYPE 20 SRC
21 D HR
22 STAT
23 MEDICAL RECORD NO.
CONDITION CODES 24 25 26 27 28 29 30
31
32 OCCURRENCE CODE DATE
33 OCCURRENCE CODE DATE
34 OCCURRENCE CODE DATE
35 OCCURRENCE CODE DATE
36 OCCURRENCE SPAN CODE FROM THROUGH
37 A B C
38
39 VALUE CODES CODE AMOUNT
40 VALUE CODES CODE AMOUNT
41 VALUE CODES CODE AMOUNT
42 REV. CD.
43 DESCRIPTION
44 HCPCS / RATES
45 SERV. DATE
46 SERV. UNITS
47 TOTAL CHARGES
48 NON-COVERED CHARGES
49
50 PAYER
51 PROVIDER NO.
52 REL INFO
53 ASG BEN
54 PRIOR PAYMENTS
55 EST. AMOUNT DUE
56
57
DUE FROM PATIENT ▶
58 INSURED'S NAME
59 P. REL
60 CERT. - SSN - HIC. - ID NO.
61 GROUP NAME
62 INSURANCE GROUP NO.
63 TREATMENT AUTHORIZATION CODES
64 ESC
65 EMPLOYER NAME
66 EMPLOYER LOCATION
67 PRIN. DIAG. CD.
68 CODE
69 CODE
70 CODE
71 CODE
72 CODE
73 CODE
74 CODE
75 CODE
76 ADM. DIAG. CD.
77 E-CODE
78
79 P.C.
80 PRINCIPAL PROCEDURE CODE DATE
81 OTHER PROCEDURE CODE DATE A
OTHER PROCEDURE CODE DATE B
OTHER PROCEDURE CODE DATE C
OTHER PROCEDURE CODE DATE D
OTHER PROCEDURE CODE DATE E
82 ATTENDING PHYS. ID
83 OTHER PHYS. ID A
OTHER PHYS. ID B
84 REMARKS
85 PROVIDER REPRESENTATIVE
X
86 DATE
UB-92 HCFA-1450
OCR/ORIGINAL
I CERTIFY THE CERTIFICATIONS ON THE REVERSE APPLY TO THIS BILL AND ARE MADE A PART HEREOF.

Figure 2–6 Blank CMS 1450 form.

CODING REGIONAL HOSPITAL

123 MAIN STREET
ANYWHERE, USA

MEDICARE EXPLANATION OF BENEFITS

PATIENT NAME: **MEDICARE #:**
STREET ADDRESS: **INFORMATION REGARDING MEDICARE CARRIER:**
CITY, STATE, ZIP: **NAME OF MEDICARE FISCAL INTERMEDIARY:**
                                           ADDRESS:
                                           CITY, STATE, ZIP:
                                           PHONE NUMBERS:
CLAIMS PROCESSED FROM: **TO:**

PART A—HOSPITAL INPATIENT BENEFITS

DATE OF SERVICE/ CLAIM NUMBER	BENFIT DAYS USED	NONCOVERED	DEDUCTIBLE COINSURANCE	PATIENT RESPONSIBLE	NOTES
01/01/xx-01/04/xx	3	0.00	$245.00	$245.00	I

EXPLANATION OF NOTES SECTION:

I   Patient Deductible Not Met

TOTAL AMOUNT PAID $ _____
TOTAL AMOUNT DUE FROM PATIENT $ _____
CONTRACTUAL WRITE-OFF AMOUNT $ _____

Figure 2–7   Example of a Medicare Explanation of Benefits for hospital services.

Notes

Billing office personnel are also responsible for follow-up on unpaid claims. A large percentage of third-party claims are never processed or paid without facility follow-up. **Accounts receivable (A/R)**—that is, unpaid accounts and uncollected balances—are attended to by the billing office, usually by A/R specialists trained in specific third-party guidelines and requirements for billing. Phone calls and letters are effective techniques for follow-up on unpaid claims that these personnel may utilize.

Business office personnel, or sometimes a separate department within the facility known as **Collections**, are responsible for billing and collection of patient balances.

PRACTICE EXERCISE 2–4

Take a look at the following EOBs and determine the amount paid, the amount due by the patient, and any contractual write-off that must be taken when the provider/facility is participating.

COLLECTION AND PAYMENT POLICIES

Each facility has specific policies and procedures that govern patient payment for services rendered. In some cases (e.g., when they represent co-payments or specific coinsurance amounts), these balances will be collected prior to services rendered, or payment arrangements will be made prior to services.

In many cases, contractual agreements with third-party carriers require the facility to refrain from billing the patient for their portion under after the third party has **adjudicated**, (i.e., advised the patient regarding processing of the claim).

Patients will be contacted by the collections department regarding payment or payment arrangements for the patient's portion of the facility bill. If the patient is unable to make appropriate arrangements, social services may become involved to determine if the patient qualifies for assistance of any type.

If it is determined that the patient does not qualify for any assistance and the balance is not paid within the period of time set by the facility's policies and procedures, the account may be sent to an outside **collection agency** or the facility's own internal collection department.

CODING REGIONAL HOSPITAL

**123 MAIN STREET
ANYWHERE, USA**

EXPLANATION OF BENEFITS #1

PATIENT NAME: John Smith   **MEDICARE #:** 325-82-xxxxA
STREET ADDRESS: 123 Beach Street
                    Orlando, FL 32xxx

CLAIMS PROCESSED: 01/03/xx–01/03/xx

PART A—HOSPITAL/FACILITY BENEFITS

DATE OF SERVICE/ CLAIM NUMBER	SERVICE	CHARGE	ALLOWANCE	DEDUCTIBLE COINSURANCE	PATIENT DUE	INSURANCE PAYMENT	NOTES
01/03/xx A034352	71020	$100.00	$100.00	$20.00	$20.00	$80.00	A
01/03/xx A034353	93005	$150.00	$100.00	$20.00	$20.00	$80.00	A
01/03/xx A034354	99281	$200.00	$150.00	$30.00	$30.00	$120.00	A
01/03/xx 1 of 1	74020	$150.00	$ 0.00	$0.00	$0.00	$ 0.00	B

EXPLANATION OF NOTES SECTION:

A   Patient Responsible for 20% of Allowance
    Your Facility Must Write Off Difference Between Charge and Allowance as Our Records Reflect You Are a Participating Provider
B   Service Not Medically Necessary
    Not Medicare ABN on File for This Service
    Patient Not Responsible

TOTAL AMOUNT PAID $ _____
TOTAL AMOUNT DUE FROM PATIENT $ _____
CONTRACTUAL WRITE-OFF AMOUNT $ _____

CODING REGIONAL HOSPITAL

123 MAIN STREET
ANYWHERE, USA

EXPLANATION OF BENEFITS #2

PATIENT NAME: Jane Berman

STREET ADDRESS: 4535 Orlando Street
Orlando, FL 32xxx

INSURANCE ID #: 335-12-xxxx

GROUP #: AS12T

CLAIMS PROCESSED: 02/03/xx–02/03/xx

PART A—HOSPITAL/FACILITY BENEFITS

DATE OF SERVICE/ CLAIM NUMBER	SERVICE	CHARGE	ALLOWANCE	DEDUCTIBLE COINSURANCE	PATIENT DUE	INSURANCE PAYMENT (80%)	NOTES
02/03/xx	71020	$100.00	$100.00	$20.00	$20.00	$80.00	
02/03/xx	93005	$150.00	$100.00	$20.00	$70.00	$80.00	A

EXPLANATION OF NOTES SECTION:

A   Our Records Reflect Your Facility is Non-Participating With Carrier
Patient Responsible for Amount Not Paid By Insurance

TOTAL AMOUNT PAID $ _____

TOTAL AMOUNT DUE FROM PATIENT $ _____

CONTRACTUAL WRITE-OFF AMOUNT $ _____

CODING REGIONAL HOSPITAL

123 MAIN STREET
ANYWHERE, USA

EXPLANATION OF BENEFITS #3

PATIENT NAME: Jerry Barber
STREET ADDRESS: 3539 Tampa Avenue
Orlando, FL 32xxx

INSURANCE ID #: 235-35-xxxx

CLAIMS PROCESSED: 04/25/xx–04/27/xx

PART A—HOSPITAL/FACILITY BENEFITS

DATE OF SERVICE/ CLAIM NUMBER	SERVICE	CHARGE	ALLOWANCE	DEDUCTIBLE COINSURANCE	PATIENT DUE	INSURANCE PAYMENT	NOTES
04/25/xx–04/27/xx #0358352A	R&B	$1,500.00	$1,100.00	$100.00	$320.00	$880.00	A,B
04/25/xx #0358352B	Med Supp	$1,000.00	$ 900.00	$ 0.00	$180.00	$720.00	A
04/25/xx #0358352C	IV Supp	$ 500.00	$ 400.00	$ 0.00	$80.00	$320.00	A

EXPLANATION OF NOTES SECTION:

A Patient Responsible for 20% of Allowance
Your Facility Must Write Off Difference Between Charge and Allowance as Our Records Reflect You Are a Participating Provider

B Deductible Not Met
Not Medicare ABN on File for This Service
Patient Not Responsible

TOTAL AMOUNT PAID $ _____
TOTAL AMOUNT DUE FROM PATIENT $ _____
CONTRACTUAL WRITE-OFF AMOUNT $ _____

CODING REGIONAL HOSPITAL

123 MAIN STREET
ANYWHERE, USA

EXPLANATION OF BENEFITS #4

PATIENT NAME: Jackie Green   **MEDICAID #:** 205-29-xxxx-xxx
STREET ADDRESS: 352 Briarwood
Orlando, FL 32xxx

CLAIMS PROCESSED: 09/04/xx–09/07/xx

PART A—HOSPITAL/FACILITY BENEFITS

DATE OF SERVICE/ CLAIM NUMBER	SERVICE	CHARGE	ALLOWANCE	DEDUCTIBLE COINSURANCE	PATIENT DUE	INSURANCE PAYMENT	NOTES
09/04/xx–09/07/xx Remit #83083A	R & B	$1,200.00	$ 0.00	$ 0.00	$1,200.00	$ 0.00	A
09/04/xx Remit #83083B	93005	$150.00	$ 0.00	$ 0.00	$ 150.00	$ 0.00	A
09/04/xx Remit #83083C	IV Supp	$200.00	$ 0.00	$ 0.00	$ 200.00	$ 0.00	A
09/04/xx–09/07/xx Remit #83083D	Sterile Supp	$150.00	$ 0.00	$0.00	$150.00	$ 0.00	A

EXPLANATION OF NOTES SECTION:

A No Medicaid Coverage For This Date(s) of Service
Patient Responsible

TOTAL AMOUNT PAID $ _____
TOTAL AMOUNT DUE FROM PATIENT $ _____
CONTRACTUAL WRITE-OFF AMOUNT $ _____

CODING REGIONAL HOSPITAL

123 MAIN STREET
ANYWHERE, USA

EXPLANATION OF BENEFITS #5

PATIENT NAME:	Jeremy Baker
STREET ADDRESS:	123 Virginia Avenue
	Orlando, FL 32xxx

SUN CITY HMO
ID #: 302-83-xxxx
GROUP #: ASN 4455

CLAIMS PROCESSED: 01/05/xx–01/05/xx

PART A—HOSPITAL/FACILITY BENEFITS

DATE OF SERVICE/ CLAIM NUMBER	SERVICE	CHARGE	ALLOWANCE	DEDUCTIBLE COINSURANCE	PATIENT DUE	INSURANCE PAYMENT	NOTES
0I/05/xx	99213	$200.00	$ 0.00	$ 0.00	$ 0.00	$ 0.00	A
0I/05/xx	93005	$150.00	$ 0.00	$ 0.00	$ 0.00	$ 0.00	A
01/05/xx	76705	$200.00	$ 0.00	$ 0.00	$ 0.00	$ 0.00	A
01/05/xx	71020	$150.00	$ 0.00	$ 0.00	$ 0.00	$ 0.00	A

EXPLANATION OF NOTES SECTION:

A   Services Not Pre-Authorized By Primary Care Physician
Patient Not Responsible

TOTAL AMOUNT PAID	$ _____
TOTAL AMOUNT DUE FROM PATIENT	$ _____
CONTRACTUAL WRITE-OFF AMOUNT	$ _____

CONCLUSION

The facility billing process involves numerous departments, individuals and forms. The successful completion of all of these processes results in effective and timely payment for services from third-party carriers and patients. After completing this chapter, the student should understand the many ways in which patients may be insured, as well as the process of capturing, authorizing and billing for services provided in the facility. After completing Practice Exercises 2–1 through 2–4, the student should understand the calculation of contractual allowances as well as patient and insurance payments, revenue codes and chargemaster codes. The student should also understand the components of the insurance Explanation of Benefits and how to use them to determine patient responsibility, which services are and are not covered, and the appropriate payment amount.

Chapter 3
UB-92 Overview

KEY TERMS

Birthday Rule
Center for Medicare and
   Medicaid Services (CMS)
Claims Scrubber
Clean Claim
Condition Codes

Dirty Claim
Electronic Media Claims (EMC)
Form Locators (FL)
Form Record
Lifetime Reserve Days
Occurrence Codes

Revenue Codes
UB-92
UPIN #
Working Aged

LEARNING OBJECTIVES

- Demonstrate an understanding of the UB-92/CMS-1450
- Discuss the requirements for Facility/Provider Information (FL 1-11)
- Identify Patient Information Data Fields (FL 12-23)
- Describe the proper use of Condition Codes (FL 24-31)
- Demonstrate the appropriate use of Occurrence Codes (FL 32-38)
- Discuss requirements for Value Codes/Amounts (FL 39-41)
- Identify Revenue Codes and associated information (FL 42-49)
- Demonstrate an understanding of Third Party Information (FL 50-66)
- Discuss requirements for Diagnosis/Procedure Code Information (FL 67-81)
- Describe the proper use of the Remarks Section (FL 84-86)

GENERAL OVERVIEW OF THE HOSPITAL BILLING FORM

The **UB-92** (Uniform Billing Form 1992), also known as the CMS-1450, is the universal claim form accepted by Medicare and Medical fiscal intermediaries as well as other insurance carriers for services provided by

Notes

a facility. All resources provided by the facility to provide a service are included on this form in a standardized format.

This form is typically NOT utilized for physician or professional charges; however, in some instances, the facility may contract the physician as a hospital employee and agree to bill those services utilizing the UB-92 and specific codes assigned to identify professional services.

The UB-92 represents a summary of all charges incurred by a patient during their inpatient or outpatient stay at a given facility. There are 86 data elements on the form, known as **form locators** or **FL,** that provide specific information necessary to process a claim. Each of these form locators has a specific format accepted by the insurance carriers. Because Medicare has some specific format requirements that differ from those of other insurance carriers, the information that follows indicates whether a specific field is required by Medicare and other carriers individually. The field formats vary; they can be alphabetic, numeric, alphanumeric or text-based.

Figure 3–1 shows an example of a completed UB-92 Form.

The following information specific to individual form locator fields on the UB-92 has been broken down into categories of information-gathering fields:

Provider information:	Form Locators 1-11
Patient demographic information:	Form Locators 12-23
Condition codes:	Form Locators 24-31
Occurrence codes and dates:	Form Locators 32-38
Value codes:	Form Locators 39-41
Revenue codes:	Form Locators 42-49
Third-party information:	Form Locators 50-66
Payer/insured/employer diagnosis/procedure codes:	Form Locators 67-81
Attending physician information:	Form Locators 82-83
Remarks:	Form Locators 84-86

There are seven additional form locators on the current UB-92/CMS-1450 form that are currently unlabeled and unutilized. These are reserved for state or national assignment when additional form locators and data are needed and should be left blank.

The UB-92 may be submitted in one of two formats: on paper or electronically. The latter process, termed an **electronic media claim (EMC),** allows one computer to transmit data to another electronically, similar to the transmission of e-mail. Overall, electronic claims are more efficient. They can be transmitted rather than mailed, eliminating the need for paper, printers, envelopes and postage; than are received by the carriers in a matter of hours rather than days, and they eliminate the problem of claims that are "lost" in processing or mailing. As a result of these efficiencies, electronic claims are typically processed and paid on a more timely basis than paper claims.

CODING REGIONAL HOSPITAL
123 MAIN STREET, ANYWHERE, USA

HOSPITAL ADMISSION FORM	ACCOUNT NUMBER		MEDICAL RECORD NUMBER 334357

PATIENT INFORMATION

PATIENT LAST NAME WHITE	FIRST NAME BLANCHE	MI J	DOB 02/18/1934	ADMIT DATE/TIME 04/26/20XX

STREET ADDRESS 4566 SYCAMORE DRIVE	CITY/STATE/ZIP ANYWHERE, ZA 10000	AREA CODE/PHONE NUMBER 111-344-84XX

SEX M ☐ F [X]	RACE	AGE	RELIGIOUS PREFERENCE	OCCUPATION	FT ☐ PT ☐

PATIENT'S EMPLOYER RETIRED	STREET ADDRESS	CITY/STATE/ZIP	AREA CODE/PHONE NUMBER

EMERGENCY CONTACT

#1 LAST NAME WHITE	FIRST NAME RICHARD	MI W	AREA CODE/PHONE NUMBER 111-344-84XX	RELATIONSHIP Husband
#2 LAST NAME	FIRST NAME	MI	AREA CODE/PHONE NUMBER	RELATIONSHIP

GUARANTOR

#1 LAST NAME WHITE	FIRST NAME BLANCHE	MI J	AREA CODE/PHONE NUMBER 111-344-84XX	RELATIONSHIP
#2 LAST NAME	FIRST NAME	MI	AREA CODE/PHONE NUMBER	RELATIONSHIP

ADMISSION INFORMATION

ADMISSION STATUS INPATIENT	PATIENT TYPE MED SURG	UNIT SURG	ROOM 356	ATTENDING MD ELIZABETH DIAMOND MD	UPIN # 1134711

ADMITTING DIAGNOSIS Abdominal Pain

INSURANCE INFORMATION

#1 PAYOR NAME MEDICARE/AETNA	STREET ADDRESS PO BOX 1440	CITY/STATE/ZIP ANYWHERE, ZA 10000	PHONE NUMBER 888-332-55XX

POLICY NUMBER 3824597XXA	GROUP NUMBER	GROUP NAME

SUBSCRIBER NAME Patient	DOB	AUTHORIZATION NUMBER	DEDUCTIBLE Inpatient $50

#2 PAYOR NAME BC BS OF ZA	STREET ADDRESS PO BOX 1492	CITY/STATE/ZIP ANYWHERE, ZA 10000	PHONE NUMBER 888-325-52XX

POLICY NUMBER 3824597XX	GROUP NUMBER INDIVIDUAL	GROUP NAME

SUBSCRIBER NAME SAME	DOB SAME	AUTHORIZATION NUMBER	DEDUCTIBLE Inpatient $100

PROVIDER NUMBER	PROCEDURES/SERVICES	
	Semi Private Visit	$550.00
	X-Ray, Abdomen	$175.00
Medicare Provider #005437	Abdomen US	$280.00
BCBS # 77374	IV Supplies (5)	$150.00
	IV Meds	$2,500.00
Admitted 04/26/xx Through ER	IV Solutions (5)	$100.00
	Lab Urol	$150.00
	Lab Chemistry	$1,500.00

CONTROL NUMBER

ATTENDING PHYSICIAN _____ DATE _____

PATIENT RECORD   ORIGINAL

Figure 3–1 Completed UB-92 form.

Notes

In addition, electronic claims can be sent through **claim scrubber** software, where errors can be detected and the claim returned to the sender almost immediately for correction and resubmission. Claims that are sent without errors or omissions and meet all predetermined specifications by the carrier are considered to be **clean claims.** Conversely, claims that are not clean are **dirty claims,** and will be returned to the sender for correction or denied.

There are few fields on electronic claims that differ significantly from those on paper claims; however, the date format must be completed differently and there are some specific guidelines that deal with the length of lists. The only other difference is the reference to each box on a paper claim as a form locator; in the electronic format, these are known as **form records.**

The discussion of the UB-92 or CMS-1450 has been divided into the same categories as the form itself. After discussion of the fields in a particular section, practice exercises will reinforce the information contained in that part of the form. At the conclusion of the chapter, all the information will be combined and practice in completing the entire UB-92/CMS-1450 will be offered.

FL 1-11:   FACILITY/PROVIDER INFORMATION

This section of the UB-92/CMS-1450 contains information specific to the facility or provider of services. In this particular section, punctuation is acceptable. The type of bill (FL4) provides information regarding the type of facility, type of care and the episode of care. Many of the fields on the form contain information that must coincide or agree with data in other fields. For instance, the total in FL6 (Statement Covers Period) must be equal to the sum of Covered Days (FL7) and Noncovered Days (FL8) in order for the claim to be clean. Medicare patients are allowed a total of 60 **lifetime reserve days,** a reserve of inpatient days that may be utilized by the Medicare beneficiary when covered hospital days and coinsurance days have been exceeded during a specific period of time.

Figure 3–2 shows FL 1-11 of the UB-92/CMS-1450 form and Table 3–1 provides completion instructions for this section of the form.

Figure 3–2 Form Locators 1-11.

TABLE 3–1   UB-92 Completion Details Provider Billing Information (FL 1-11).

FL#	Field Name	Specifics	# Digits	Digits (A)lpha (N)um	Medicare (R)eq (O)pt	Others (R)eq (O)pt
1	Line a - Name of Provider	Information on provider submitting bill		A/N	R	R
	Line b - Street Address, PO Box	Address where payment should be sent	A/N 5/9 zip	R A/N	R R	R
	Line c - City, St Abbreviation, Zip					
	Line d - Telephone and Fax # Country Code		10	N A	O	O
2	Unlabeled Field	Unlabeled Field				
3	Patient Control Number	Unique identification number assigned by provider to each patient	20	A/N	R	R
		Speeds up processing of checks, data entry				
4	Type of Bill	First digit - Type of Facility	1	N	R	R
		Second digit - Billing Classification	1	N	R	R
		Third digit - Frequency of Billing	1	N	R	R

Type of Bill
Except Clinics/Special Facilities

First Digit	Second Digit	Third Digit
0 - Not Applicable	0 - Not Applicable	0 - Nonpayment/zero claim
1 - Hospital	1 - Inpatient (Medicare Part A)	1 - Admit thru discharge claim
2 - Skilled Nursing	2 - Inpatient (Medicare Part B)	2 - Interim-First Claim
3 - Home Health Facility	3 - Outpatient	3 - Interim-Continuing Claim
4 - Religious nonmedical health care hospital (inpatient)	4 - Other (Medicare Part B)	4 - Interim-Last Claim
5 - Religious nonmedical health care posthospital (extended care)	5 - Intermediate Care Level I	5 - Late Charge(s) only claim
6 - Intermediate Care	6 - Intermediate Care Level II	6 - Adjustment of prior claim
7 - Clinic/hospital-based renal dialysis facility	7 - Subacute inpatient	7 - Replacement of prior claim
8 - Special facility/hospital ASC	8 - Swing bed	8 - Void/cancel a prior claim
9 - Reserved for national assignment	9 - Reserved for national assignment	9 - Final claim Home Health PPS episode

(continued)

TABLE 3–1   *continued*

FL#	Field Name	Specifics	# Digits	Digits (A)lpha (N)um	Medicare (R)eq (O)pt	Others (R)eq (O)pt

Clinics Only

First Digit	Second Digit	Third Digit
0 - Not Applicable	0 - Not Applicable	0 - Nonpayment/Zero Claim
1 - Hospital	1 - Rural Health Clinic (RHC)	1 - Admit Thru Discharge Claim
2 - Skilled Nursing	2 - Hospital-Based/ Independent Renal Dialysis Facility	2 - Interim-First Claim
3 - Home Health Facility	3 - Freestanding Provider-Based Federally Qualified Health Centers (FQHC)	3 - Interim-Continuing Claim
4 - Religious Nonmedical Health Care Hospital Inpatient	4 - Outpatient Rehabilitation Facility (CORF)	4 - Interim-Last Claim
5 - Religious Nonmedical Health Care Posthospital Extended Care	5 - Comprehensive Outpatient Rehabilitation Facility (CORF)	5 - Late Charge(s) Only Claim
6 - Intermediate Care	6 - Community Mental Health (CMHC)	6 - Adjustment Prior Claim
7 - Clinic/Hospital-Based Renal Dialysis Facility	7 - Reserved National Assignment	7 - Replacement Prior Claim
8 - Special Facility/Hospital ASC	8 - Reserved National Assignment	8 - Void/Cancel Prior Claim
9 - Reserved National Assignment	9 - Other	9 - Final Claim Home Health PPS Episode

Special Facilities Only

First Digit	Second Digit	Third Digit
0 - Not Applicable	0 - Not Applicable	0 - Nonpayment/Zero Claim
1 - Hospital	1 - Hospice (Nonhospital Based)	1 - Admit Thru Discharge Claim
2 - Skilled Nursing	2 - Hospice (Hospital-Based)	2 - Interim-First Claim
3 - Home Health Facility	3 - Ambulatory Surgery Center Services to Hospital Outpatients	3 - Interim-Continuing Claim
4 - Religious Nonmedical Health Care Hospital Inpatient	4 - Freestanding Birthing Center	4 - Interim-Last Claim
5 - Religious Nonmedical Health Care Posthospital Extended Care	5 - Critical Access Hospitals	5 - Late Charge(s) Only Claim
6 - Intermediate Care	6 - Residential Facility (Non-Medicare)	6 - Adjustment Prior Claim
7 - Clinic/Hospital-Based Renal Dialysis Facility	7 - Reserved For National Assignment	7 - Replacement Prior Claim
8 - Special Facility/ Hospital ASC	8 - Reserved National Assignment	8 - Void/Cancel Prior Claim
9 - Reserved National Assignment	9 - Other	9 - Final Claim Home Health PPS Episode

FL#	Field Name	Specifics	# Digits	Digits (A)lpha (N)um	Medicare (R)eq (O)pt	Others (R)eq (O)pt
5	Federal Tax ID Number	Federal TIN (Tax ID Number) OR EIN (Employer ID Number)	9	A/N	O	R
6	Statement Covers Period Same-Day Services Inpatient Interim/ No Discharge Final Bill	From/Thru Dates From/Thru Identical Thru calculated as part of FL 7-10 Thru Date of Discharge or Death No dashes/no slashes	8	N	R	R
7	Covered Days	Records total number inpatient days authorized by primary carrier within claim billing period Date of discharge/death not counted as covered date (unless patient elects to use Medicare lifetime reserve days) Hospitals: Maximum 150 days: 60 days hospitalization 60 lifetime reserve days 30 coinsurance days	3	N	R Inpt No Outpt	R Medi Carrier
8	Noncovered Days	Days not covered by primary carrier FL 7 + FL 8 = FL 6 days	4	N	R Inpt No Outpt	R Medi Carrier
9	Coinsurance Days	Inpatient hospital days occurring after 60th day and before 91st day in single benefit period of spell of illness Number cannot exceed 30 hospital days	2	N	R Inpt No Outpt	R Medi Carrier
10	Lifetime Reserve Days	Medicare patient used 60 covered hospital days and 30 coinsurance days may elect to use a lifetime reserve of up to 60 days inpatient hospital services	2	N	R Inpt No Outpt	R Medi Carrier
11	Unlabeled Field					

Notes

PRACTICE EXERCISE 3–1

Complete the information for FL 4 (Type of Bill).

	Digit 1	Digit 2	Digit 3

1. Outpatient Hospital, Admit Through Discharge   ____ ____ ____

2. Inpatient Hospital, Admit Through Discharge   ____ ____ ____

3. Outpatient Hospital, Physical Therapy,

    Second Month in Continuing Claim   ____ ____ ____

4. Inpatient Hospital, Admitted/Discharged
    Same Bill   ____ ____ ____

5. Outpatient Hospital, Late Charges Only   ____ ____ ____

6. Skilled Nursing Facility, Intermediate Care I,

    Admitted 2 Months Ago, Remaining in SNF   ____ ____ ____

7. Rural Health Clinic, One-Day Services   ____ ____ ____

8. Hospital ASC, One-Day Services   ____ ____ ____

9. Hospital-Based Outpatient Rehabilitation,
    30 Days (1 Mo.) Only   ____ ____ ____

10. Inpatient Hospital, Admitted 01-01-20xx,
    Continuing Inpatient, Billing for
    Month of 02-20xx   ____ ____ ____

Complete the information for FL 6, FL 7, FL 8 and FL 9 for the following scenarios:

1. Patient admitted 01/03/20xx, discharged 01/30/20xx.
    Insurance will cover entire admission period.
    FL 6 ____   FL 7 ____   FL 8 ____   FL 9____

2. Patient admitted 02/20/20xx, still inpatient billing for
    month of February only.
    Insurance will cover entire month of February.
    FL 6 ____   FL 7 ____   FL 8 ____   FL 9 ____

Notes

3. Patient receiving occupational therapy 01/31/20xx only. Service authorized for 01/31/20xx by insurance carrier.
   FL 6 _____   FL 7 _____   FL 8 _____   FL 9 _____

4. Patient receiving physical therapy from 01/04/20xx–01/08/20xx. Received 1 treatment daily. Insurance authorized 4 treatments only.
   FL 6 _____   FL 7 _____   FL 8 _____   FL 9 _____

5. Patient admitted on 03/01/20xx, discharged 03/17/20xx. First 10 days will be authorized in full; however, subsequent days will have a $100-per-day patient responsibility.
   FL 6 _____   FL 7 _____   FL 8 _____   FL 9 _____

FL 12-23:   PATIENT INFORMATION

The patient information contained in FL 12-23 is utilized for identifying the patient, and ensuring the benefits are being paid for the correct patient during the correct admission or encounter. Many carriers, including Medicare, require that the patient name listed in this section be exactly as listed on the insurance card. Nicknames and other changes to the patient name are not permitted. The address listed on the claim is utilized by Medicare and other carriers to send a duplicate Explanation of Benefits (EOB) to the patient containing information about how the claim was processed and paid. Age and sex information provided in this section are utilized by insurance carriers to determine conflicts in information, such as a gynecological procedure or admission performed on a male patient, or a newborn procedure performed on a 65-year-old.

Figure 3–3 shows FL 12-23 of the UB-92/CMS-1450 form and Table 3–2 provides completion instructions for this section of the form.

Figure 3–3 Form Locators 12-23.

TABLE 3–2   UB-92 COMPLETION DETAILS PATIENT INFORMATION (FL 12-23).

FL #	Field Name	Specifics	# Digits	Digits (A)lpha (N)um	Medicare (R)eq (O)pt	Others (R)eq (O)pt
12	Patient Name	No apostrophes, hyphens Titles are not used Medicare: must appear exactly as on Medicare card Last Name, First Name, MI		A	R	R
13	Patient Address	Street Name/PO Box City, State Abbreviation, ZIP (5–9 digits) First 3 ZIP digits must be valid	50	A/N	R	R
14	Patient Birth Date	If cannot obtain after reasonable efforts, should fill with zeros Do not leave blank	8	N	R	R
15	Patient Sex	M-Male F-Female U-Unknown	1	A	R	R
16	Patient Marital Status	S-Single M-Married P-Life partner (domestic partner) D-Divorced W-Widowed X-Legally separated U-Unknown	1	A	NO	NO

17	Admission/Start of Care Date	Admission Date
		** Required for inpatient,
		   home health, hospice,
		   outpatient rehab/facility
			8	N	R**	R**

18	Admission Hour	AM PM 0 12:00 mid-12:59 12 12:00-12:59 1 1:00-1:59 13 1:00-1:59 2 2:00-2:59 14 2:00-2:59 3 3:00-3:59 15 3:00-3:59 4 4:00-4:59 16 4:00-4:59 5 5:00-5:59 17 5:00-5:59 6 6:00-6:59 18 6:00-6:59 7 7:00-7:59 19 7:00-7:59 8 8:00-8:59 20 8:00-8:59	2	N	NO	R

FL #	Field Name	Specifics	# Digits	Digits (A)lpha (N)um	Medicare (R)eq (O)pt	Others (R)eq (O)pt
		9 9:00-9:59 21 9:00-9:59 10 10:00-10:59 22 10:00-10:59 11 11:00-11:59 23 11:00-11:59 99 Unknown				

19	Type of Admission	Code for establishing level of urgency for admission
		1 - Emergency
		  Severe, life-threatening, potentially disabling
		2 - Urgent
		  Patient should be admitted ASAP within 24–48 hours
		3 - Elective
		  Schedule in advance
		4 - Newborn
		  Used only when baby is born in the facility submitting the claim
		5 - Trauma Center
		  Must be properly licensed and so designated
		6-8 Reserved for national assignment
		9 - Information not available
			1	N	R Inpt No Outpt	R Inpt No Outpt

20 Inpt	Source of Admission	For all admissions except newborns: 1 - Physician referral 2 - Clinic referral 3 - HMO referral 4 - Transfer from hospital 5 - Transfer from SNF 6 - Transfer other health care facility 7 - Emergency room 8 - Court/law enforcement 9 - Information not available A - Transfer from critical access hosp B - Transfer from another home health agency (HHA) C - Readmission to same home health agency D-Z Reserved for national assignment Newborn admissions ONLY: 1 - Normal delivery	1	A/N	R	R

(continued)

TABLE 3–2 *continued*

FL #	Field Name	Specifics	# Digits	Digits (A)lpha (N)um	Medicare (R)eq (O)pt	Others (R)eq (O)pt
		2 - Premature delivery				
		3 - Sick baby				
		4 - Extramural birth				
		Born in nonsterile environment				
		5-8 Reserved for national assignment				
		9 - Do not use				
21	Discharge Hour	Use same table for discharge hour as for admission hour	2	N	NO	Pre-ferred
22	Patient Status	Patient's discharge status at the time of the "thru" date on the UB-92	2	N	R Part A	R Inpt
		01 - Discharged home/self-care				
		02 - Discharged/transferred short-term hosp for inpatient care				
		03 - Discharged/transferred SNF Not for swing bed, see 61				
		04 - Discharged/transferred ICF				
		05 - Discharged/transferred another type facility				
		06 - Discharged/transferred to home with home health care				
		07 - LMA (left against medical advice)				
		08 - Discharged/transferred to home IV care				
		09 - Admitted as inpt same facility				
		10-19 Discharged to be defined on state level				
		20 - Expired				
		21-29 Expired—defined at state level				
		30 - Active patient				
		31-39 Still a patient—defined state level				
		40 - Expired at home (hospice)				
		41 - Expired med facility (hospice)				
		42 - Expired place unknown (hospice)				
		43-49 Reserved national assignment				
		50 - Discharged to hospice-home				
		51 - Discharged to hospice-med fac				
		52-60 Reserved national assignment				
		61 - Discharged/transferrred within institution to swing bed				

FL #	Field Name	Specifics	# Digits	Digits (A)lpha (N)um	Medicare (R)eq (O)pt	Others (R)eq (O)pt
		62 - Discharged/transferred another rehab fac inc rehab distinct part units of hospital				
		63 - Discharged/transferred long-term care hospital				
		64-70 Reserved national assignment				
		71 - Discharged/transferred/ referred another institution for outpt svcs				
		72 - Discharged/transferred/referred to this institution for outpt svcs				
		73-99 Reserved national assignment				
23	Medical Record Number		17	A/N	R	REQ Tricare

Notes _____

(PRACTICE EXERCISE 3–2

Indicate appropriate format for the Admit/Discharge hours for FL 18 and FL 21.

1. Admit 8:15 AM _____   Discharge 1:15 PM _____

2. Admit 11:15 PM _____   Discharge 11:15 AM _____

3. Admit 7:00 AM _____   Discharge 9:00 PM _____

4. Admit 9:45 AM _____   Discharge 11:10 AM _____

5. Admit 10:15 AM _____   Discharge 7:11 PM _____

Identify the correct Type of Admission (FL 19), Source of Admission (FL 20) and Patient Status (FL 22) for each of the following scenarios:

1. Patient admitted through emergency room as emergency admission, later transferred to another facility.
   FL 19 (Type) _____   FL 20 (Source) _____   FL 22 (Status) _____

2. Patient admitted by attending physician (PCP) for elective surgical procedure, patient discharged home/self-care.
   FL 19 (Type) _____   FL 20 (Source) _____   FL 22 (Status) _____

3. Patient transferred from another hospital and expired.
   FL 19 (Type) _____   FL 20 (Source) _____   FL 22 (Status) _____

4. Patient admitted through outpatient clinic as urgent. Patient discharged home/self-care 2 days later.
   FL 19 (Type) _____   FL 20 (Source) _____   FL 22 (Status) _____

5. Patient admitted from SNF to facility, transferred to swing bed.
   FL 19 (Type) _____   FL 20 (Source) _____   FL 22 (Status) _____

FL 24-31:   CONDITION CODES

Condition codes are assigned to identify special circumstances, events or conditions that surround the services provided on the claim. They assist in determining eligibility for benefits by a specific carrier such as workers' compensation (condition code 02—Employment Related). These codes cover a variety of conditions, including those related to insurance issues, patient conditions, room conditions, special programs, approval and claim change conditions. When more than one condition code is appropriate, a total of seven codes may be utilized. They should be listed in ascending order—first numbers, then letters—and separated by commas.

Many condition codes require coordination with other form locator fields on the claim form. For example, the use of a room code such as Condition Code 38 (Semiprivate Room Not Available) requires the use of a corresponding revenue code in FL 42 (one of the Accommodation Revenue Codes).

Figure 3–4 shows FL 24-31 of the UB-92/CMS-1450 form and Table 3–3 provides instructions for completing this section of the form.

CONDITION CODES							31
24	25	26	27	28	29	30	

Figure 3–4 Form Locators 24-31.

TABLE 3–3   UB-92 COMPLETION DETAILS CONDITION CODES (FL 24-31).

FL #	Field Name	Specifics	# Digits	Digits (A)lpha (N)um	Medicare (R)eq (O)pt	Others (R)eq (O)pt
24-30	Condition Codes	Identifies special condition/unique circumstance. Assists carrier in determination of eligibility for coverage/payment. Up to seven (7) may be listed. List in ascending order, numbers then letters, separated by comma	2	AlphaNum	REQ If Applicable	REQ If Applicable

Condition Codes

Insurance Codes

01 - Military Service Related
02 - Employment Related
03 - Covered by Insurance Not on Claim
04 - Pt HMO Enrollee
05 - Lien Filed
06 - ESRD Pt First 19 Months Covered by Employer Plan
07 - Treatment Nonterminal Condition Hospice Patient
08 - Benficiary Would Not Provide Other Insur Info
09 - Patient/Spouse Employed
10 - Pt/Spouse Employed but No Employer Coverage
11 - Disabled Beneficiary No Employer Coverage
12-16 Payer Use Only

Patient Condition Codes

17 - Patient Homeless
18 - Maiden Name Retained
19 - Child Retain's Mother's Name
20 - Beneficiary Requested Billing
21 - Billing for Denial Notice
22 - Patient Multiple Drug Regimen
23 - Home Care Giver Available
24 - Home IV Patient Receiving HHA Services
25 - Patient Non-US Resident
26 - VA-Elig Patient Chooses Medicare-Certified Facility
27 - Pt Referred Sole Community Hosp Dx Laboratory Test(s)
28 - Pt/Spouse Employer 2nd to Care
29 - Disabled Beneficiary/Family Member Health Plan 2nd to Care
30 - Qualifying Clinical Trials
31 - Full-Time Day Student
32 - Student (Co-op/Work Study)
33 - Student (Full-Time Night)
34 - Student (Part-Time)
35 - Reserved National Assignment

Room Codes

36 - General Care Patient/Special Unit
37 - Ward Accomodation/Patient Request
38 - Semiprivate Room Not Available
39 - Private Room Medically Necessary
40 - Same-Day Transfer
41 - Partial Hospitalization
42 - Continuing Care Not Rel to Inpt Adm
43 - Continuing Care Not Provided within Prescribed Postdischarge Window
44-45 Reserved for National Assignment

TRICARE Codes

46 - Nonavailability Statement NOF
47 - Reserved for TRICARE
48 - Psych Residential Treatment Center
49-54 Reserved National Assignment
55 - SNF Bed Not Available
56 - Medical Appropriateness
57 - SNF Readmission
58 - Term Medicare+Choice Organization
59 - Reserved for National Assignment
60 - Day Outlier
61 - Cost Outlier
62-65 Payer Only Codes

(continued)

TABLE 3–3   *continued*

FL # Field Name	Specifics	# Digits	Digits (A)lpha (N)um	Medicare (R)eq (O)pt	Others (R)eq (O)pt

SPECIAL CODES

Other Special Codes

66 - Provider Does Not Wish Cost Outlier Payment
67 - Beneficiary Elects Not to Use Lifetime Reserve Days
68 - Beneficiary Elects to Use Lifetime Reserve Days
69 - Operating Indirect Medical Education Payment Only

Miscellaneous Codes

77 - Provider Accepts/ Obligated to Accept Payment Primary Payer as Payment in Full
78 - New Coverage Not Implemented by HMO
79 - CORDF Services Provided Off-Site
80-99 Reserved State Assignment

A6 - Medicare Pneumococcal Pneumonia Vaccine/Influenza
A7 - Induced Abortion-Danger to Life
A8 - Induced Abortion-Victim Rape/Incest
A9 - 2nd Opinion Surgery
B0 - Medicare Coordinated Care Demonstration Claim
B1 - Beneficiary Inelig Demonstration Prog
B2 - Critical Access Hosp Ambulance Attestation

Renal Dialysis Setting Codes

70 - Self-Administered Epoetin
71 - Full Care in Unit
72 - Self-Care in Unit
73 - Self-Care Training
74 - Home
75 - Home-100% Reimbursement
76 - Backup In-facility Dialysis

Special Programs

A0 - TRICARE External Partnership
A1 - EPSDT/CHAP
A2 - Physically Handicapped Children's Program
A3 - Special Federal Funding
A4 - Family Planning
A5 - Disability

B3-B9 Reserved National Assignment

QIO Approval Indicator Svcs

C0 - Reserved National Assignment
C1 - Approved as Billed
C2 - Auto Approval as Billed Based on Focused Review
C3 - Partial Approval
C4 - Admission/Service Denied
C5 - Postpayment Review
C6 - Admission Preauthorization

Claim Change Reasons

D0 - Changes to Service Dates
D1 - Changes to Charges
D2 - Changes in Revenue Codes/ HCPCS Codes
D3 - 2nd/Subsequent Interim PPS Bill
D4 - Change in Grouper Input
D5 - Cancel to Correct Claim # or Provider ID Number
D6 - Cancel Only to Repay

D7 - Change to Make Medicare 2nd
D8 - Change to Make Medicare Primary
D9 - Any Other Change
E0 - Change in Patient Status
E1-E9 Reserved National Assignment
G0 - Distinct Medical Visit
G1-G9 Reserved National Assignment
H0 - Delayed Filing, Statement of Intent Submitted
H1-H9 Reserved National Assignment

FL #	Field Name	Specifics	# Digits	Digits (A)lpha (N)um	Medicare (R)eq (O)pt	Others (R)eq (O)pt
	C7 - Extended Authorization C8-C9 Reserved National Assignment	Duplicate or OIG Overpayment		M0-M2 Payer Only Codes M3-M9 Reserved Payer Assignment N0-W9 Reserved National Assignment X0-Z9 Reserved State Assignment		
31	Unlabeled Field					

Notes

(PRACTICE EXERCISE 3–3

Assign the appropriate condition codes in the correct sequence for the following scenarios:

1. Homeless patient.   Condition Code(s) _____

2. Full-time day student. Admitted for induced abortion, danger to life.   Condition Code(s) _____

3. Child admitted who retains mother's maiden name.   Condition Code(s) _____

4. Claim submitted to change date of service.   Condition Code(s) _____

5. Admission preauthorized: private room medically necessary.   Condition Code(s) _____

6. Non-U.S. citizen, homeless, full-time night student.   Condition Code(s) _____

7. HMO patient, maiden name retained, semiprivate room not available.   Condition Code(s) _____

8. Medicare patient who received influenza vaccine during stay.   Condition Code(s) _____

9. Active military patient admitted without nonavailability statement.   Condition Code(s) _____

10. EPSDT services/admission.   Condition Code(s) _____

FL 32-38:   OCCURRENCE CODES/DATES

Form locator fields 32-38 will provide information to the insurance carrier known as **occurrence codes** regarding events connected to the claim that affect how it will be processed. In some instances, the event will be only one date (such as that of an automobile accident). In other instances, the occurrence or event spans multiple dates, in which case the occurrence span/dates field (FL 36) will be utilized instead. Examples would be hospitalization for several dates, or a benefit eligibility period that spans multiple days.

Responsible party information (FL 38) is utilized for determining financial responsibility for services incurred by the patient. This field may also be used in the event an insurance carrier is primary over Medicare.

Though FL 37 is "unlabeled," it is utilized to designate an internal control number. This number is assigned to all claims that have been processed previously by a carrier. In the event the facility or provider must resubmit a claim for changes, corrections or additions, this number must be indicated in FL 37 to prevent rejection as a duplicate claim.

Figure 3–5 shows FL 32-38 of the UB-92/CMS-1450 form and Table 3–4 provides instructions for completing this section of the form.

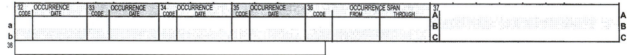

Figure 3–5 Form Locators 32-38.

TABLE 3–4   UB-92 COMPLETION DETAILS OCCURRENCE CODES/DATES (FL 32-38).

FL #	Field Name	Specifics	# Digits	Digits (A)lpha (N)um	Medicare (R)eq (O)pt	Others (R)eq (O)pt
32-35	Occurrence Codes/Dates	Significant event/occurrence that occurred in connection with service	2	A/N	R If Applicable	R If Applicable

Accident-Related Codes
01 - Auto Accident
02 - No-Fault/Auto/Other
03 - Accident/Tort Liability
04 - Accident/Employment
05 - Other Accident
06 - Crime Victim
07-08 Reserved National
    Assignment

Medical Condition Codes
09 - Start Infertility
    Treatment
10 - Last Menstrual Period
11 - Onset Symptoms/Illness
12 - Date Onset Chronically
    Dependent Individual
13-15 Reserved National
    Assignment

Insurance-Related Codes
16 - Date of Last Therapy
17 - Date Outpt Occupational Therapy
    Plan Established/Last Reviewed
18 - Date Retirement Pt/Beneficiary
19 - Date Retirement Spouse
20 - Guarantee of Payment Began
21 - UR Notice Received
22 - Date Active Care Ended
23 - Date Cancellation Hospice
    Elective Period
24 - Date Insurance Denied
25 - Date Benefits Terminated
    Primary Payer
26 - Date SNF Bed Available
27 - Date Hospice Cert or Recert
28 - Date Comprehensive Output
    Rehab Facility Plan Est/Reviewed
29 - Date Outpt Physical Therapy
    Plan Established/Last Reviewed
30 - Date Outpt Speech Path
    Plan Established/Last Reviewed
31 - Date Beneficiary Notified of
    Intent to Bill (Accommodations)
32 - Date Beneficiary Notified of
    Intent to Bill (Procedures/Trmts)
33 - 1st Day Medicare Coordination
    Period for ESRD Beneficiaries
    Covered by Employ Group Plan
34 - Date Election of Extended Care
35 - Date Treatment Started Phy Ther
36 - Date Inpt Hospital Discharge
    Covered Transplant Patient
37 - Date Inpt Hospital Discharge
    Noncovered Transplant Patient

Patient Service Codes
40 - Scheduled Date Admission
41 - Date 1st Test Preadmission
    Testing
42 - Date of Discharge
43 - Schedule Surgery Date
    Cancelled
44 - Date Occupational
    Therapy Started
45 - Date Speech Therapy Started
46 - Date Cardiac Rehab Started
47 - Date Cost Outer Status Began
48-49 Payer Codes
50-69 Reserved State Assignment
70-99 Reserved Occurrence
    Span Code
A0 - Reserved National assignment
A1 - Birth Date - Insured A
A2 - Effective Date-Insured A Policy
A3 - Benefits Exhausted
A4-A9 Reserved National
    Assignment
B0 - Reserved National Assignment
B1 - Birth Date - Insured B
B2 - Effective Date-Insured B Policy
B3 - Benefits Exhausted
B4-B9 Reserved National
    Assignment
C0 - Reserved National Assignment
C1 - Birth Date - Insured C
C2 - Effective Date - Insured C Policy
C3 - Benefits Exhausted
C4-C9 Reserved National
    Assignment

(continued)

TABLE 3–4   *continued*

FL #	Field Name	Specifics	# Digits	Digits (A)lpha (N)um	Medicare (R)eq (O)pt	Others (R)eq (O)pt
		38 - Date Treatment Start IV Home Therapy 39 - Date Discharged Continuous Course IV Therapy		D0-D9 Reserved National Assignment E0-G9 Follow same assignment for Insured E, F, G H0-I9 Reserved National Assignment J0-L9 Reserved State Assignment		
36	Occurrence Span Codes/Dates	Cannot be used in conjunction with Occurrence Codes If > 2 codes, may utilized occurrence code fields of additional listing(s)	2	A/N	REQR If Applicable	REQR If Applicable
	70 - Qualifying Stay Dates 71 - Prior Stay Date 72 - First/Last Visit 73 - Benefit Eligibility Period 74 - Noncovered Level of Care/Leave of Absence (LOA) 75 - SNF Level of Care	76 - Patient Liability 77 - Provider Liability Period Utilization Charged 78 - SNF Prior Stay Dates 79 - Payer Code 80-99 Reserved State Assignment		M0 - QIO/UR Approved Stay Dates M1 - Provider Liability-No Utilization M2 - Dates Inpatient Respite Care M3-W9 Reserved National Assignment X0-Z9 Reserved State Assignment		
37	Internal Control Number (ICN) Document Control Number (DCN)	Found on remittance voucher of original claim Must be reported for Medicare adjustment claims Subdivided into three (3) lines A - Primary Payer B - Secondary Payer C - Tertiary Payer			REQR Resubmissions	REQR
38	Responsible Party Name and Address	Guarantor on account May also be used when claim involves payer primary to Medicare		A/N	NO	NO

PRACTICE EXERCISE 3–4

Assign occurrence codes, dates (FL 32-35) and occurrence span codes, dates (FL 36) as applicable to the following:

1. Insurance carrier denied covered 01/01/20xx.

   Occurrence Code _____ Date _____

   Occurrence Code _____ Date _____

   Occurrence Span _____ From _____ Through _____

2. Auto accident 03/03/20xx.

   Occurrence Code _____ Date _____

   Occurrence Code_____ Date _____

   Occurrence Span _____ From _____ Through _____

3. Auto accident 04/01/20xx;
   benefits exhausted 04/10/20xx.

   Occurrence Code _____ Date _____

   Occurrence Code_____ Date _____

   Occurrence Span _____ From _____ Through _____

4. Patient liability from 01/16/20xx through 01/30/20xx.

   Occurrence Code _____ Date _____

   Occurrence Code_____ Date _____

   Occurrence Span _____ From _____ Through _____

5. SNF patient admitted, covered by Part A SNF benefits for 3
   hospital days, 01/01/20xx–01/03/20xx.

   Occurrence Code _____ Date _____

   Occurrence Code_____ Date _____

   Occurrence Span _____ From _____ Through _____

Determine the responsible party in each of the following instances:

1. Five-year-old child brought in by mother.

2. Five-year-old child brought in by mother, father carries insurance coverage.

3. Full-time college student covered by father's insurance.

4. Legal guardian for mentally handicapped adult, patient covered by Medicaid.

5. Female patient presents to emergency room indicating she has insurance coverage through her husband's employer.

FL 39-41:   VALUE CODES/AMOUNTS

Value codes are assigned to designate dollar amounts, units or the number of visits for a particular service. Anytime a value code is used, an amount must be entered. Because facilities may sometimes bill separately for Part A and Part B benefits, value codes 8-11 are used for Part A only, while A2, B2 and C2 are utilized for reporting Part B benefits that require the use of a value code and amount. As with many other form locator fields on the UB-92/CMS-1450, many of the value code/amount fields must correlate with other data fields on the claim.

Figure 3–6 shows FL 39-41 of the UB-92/CMS-1450 form and Table 3–5 provides instructions on completing this section of the form.

Figure 3–6 Form Locators 39-41.

TABLE 3–5   UB-92 COMPLETION DETAILS VALUE CODES AND AMOUNTS (FL 39-41).

FL #	Field Name	Specifics	# Digits	Digits (A)lpha (N)um	Medicare (R)eq (O)pt	Others (R)eq (O)pt
39-41	Value Code/Amount	Multiples should be reported in alphanumeric order	2/Code 8/Amts	A/N	R If Applicable	R If Applicable

Decimal points not keyed
Nondollars reported with 2 zeros
on end (EX: 45 = 45.00)

01 - Most Common Semiprivate Room Rate
02 - Hospital Has NO Semiprivate Room
03 - Reserved National Assignment
04 - Inpt Professional Component Charges Are Combined Billed
05 - Prof Component Inc in Charges/Billed Separately to Carrier
06 - Medicare Blood Deductible
07 - Reserved National Assignment
08 - Medicare Lifetime Reserve Amount in 1st Calendar Year
09 - Medicare Coinsurance Amount in 1st Calendar Year in Billing Period
10 - Medicare Lifetime Reserve Amount in 2nd Calendar Year in Billing Period
11 - Medicare Coinsurance Amt 2nd Calendar Year
12 - Working Aged Beneficiary/Spouse with Employer Health Plan
13 - ESRD Beneficiary in

Medicare Coordination Period with Employer Group Health
14 - No-Fault/Inc Auto/Other
15 - Workers' Compensation
16 - Public Health Service or Other Federal Agency
17–20 Reserved Payer Use
21 - Medicaid/Catastropic
22 - Medicaid/Surplus
23 - Medicaid/Recurring Monthly Income
24 - Medicaid Rate Code
25–29 Unassigned/Reserved for Medicaid National Assignment
30 - Preadmission Testing
31 - Patient Liability Amount
32-36 - Reserved National Assignment
37 - Pints of Blood Furnished
38 - Blood Deductible Pints
39 - Pints of Blood Replaced
40 - New Coverage Not Implemented by HMO (Inpt Only)
41 - Black Lung
42 - Veterans Affairs
43 - Disabled Beneficiary Under Age 65 with Group Health Plan

44 - Amount Provider Agreed to Accept Primary Insurer When Amount < Total Charges But > Primary Insured Payment
45 - Accident Hour as Follows:

AM		PM	
0	12:00-12:59	12	12:00-12:59
1	1:00-1:59	13	1:00-1:59
2	2:00-2:59	14	2:00-2:59
3	3:00-3:59	15	3:00-3:59
4	4:00-4:59	16	4:00-4:59
5	5:00-5:59	17	5:00-5:59
6	6:00-6:59	18	6:00-6:59
7	7:00-7:59	19	7:00-7:59
8	8:00-8:59	20	8:00-8:59
9	9:00-9:59	21	9:00-9:59
10	10:00-10:59	22	10:00-10:59
11	11:00-11:59	23	11:00-11:50
		99	Unknown

A1 - Deductible Payer A
B1 - Deductible Payer B
C1 - Deductible Payer C
A2 - Coinsurance Payer A
B2 - Coinsurance Payer B
C2 - Coinsurance Payer C
A3 - Estimated Responsibility Payer A
B3 - Estimated Responsibility Payer B

(continued)

Table 3–5   *continued*

FL #	Field Name	Specifics	# Digits	Digits (A)lpha (N)um	Medicare (R)eq (O)pt	Others (R)eq (O)pt

C3 - Estimated Responsibility Payer C
46 - Number of Grace Days
47 - Any Liability Insurance
48 - Hemoglobin Reading
49 - Hematocrit Reading
50 - Physical Therapy Visits
51 - Occupational Therapy Visits
52 - Speech Therapy Visits
53 - Cardiac Rehab Visits
54 - Newborn Birth Weight in Grams

55 - Reserved for National Assignment
Home Health Codes
56 - Skilled Nurse-Home Visit Hrs (HHA)
57 - Home Health Aid - Visit Hours
58 - Arterial Blood Bas
59 - Oxygen Saturation
60 - HHA Branch MSA
61 - Location Where Serv Furnished (HHA/Hospice)
62–65 Reserved for Payer Use

66 - Reserved National Assignment
67 - Peritoneal Dialysis
68 - EPO - Drug
69 - Reserved National Assignment
70–79 Reserved for Payer Use
80–99 Reserved State Assignment

Notes

PRACTICE EXERCISE 3–5

Indicate the appropriate value codes and amounts for the following:

1. Physical therapy, $50 per visit.   Code _____ Amount _____

2. Cardiac rehab visits, $100 per visit.   Code _____ Amount _____

3. Three units of blood furnished.   Code _____ Amount _____

   Three units of blood replaced.   Code _____ Amount _____

4. Four speech therapy visits.   Code _____ Amount _____

5. Most common semiprivate rate.   Code _____ Amount _____

Notes

Complete FL 1-41 for the following scenarios:

Scenario #1:

Patient Demographics

John Davis, Record #33546   DOB: 05/13/1957   SEX: M
430 Main Street   SSN: 334-56-3654
Miami, Fl 33435   MARITAL STATUS: SINGLE
Insurance Coverage: Aetna Insurance Company
                                 Deductible met, services authorized,
                                 accepts assignment through ABC
                                 Medical Supply.

Service Information

Main Street Hospital, 167 Metropolitan Way, Miami, FL 33435 Tax ID 59-55674
Admitted 03/11/20xx, 9:00 AM, discharged 03/18/20xx, 1:45 PM
Patient Number: 3355968SM
Admitted following automobile accident. Brought in by ambulance to
emergency room where he was admitted by Dr. Johnson.

Scenario #2:

Patient Demographics

Jane Houston, Record #56845   DOB: 04/23/1964   SEX: F
3344 Intrepid Lane   SSN: 503-40-6695
Miami, Fl 33435   MARITAL STATUS: SINGLE
Insurance Coverage: Medicare (Part A/B)
                                 Deductible met, accepts assignment.

Service Information

Main Street Hospital, 167 Metropolitan Way, Miami, FL 33435 Tax ID 59-55674
Admitted 02/01/20xx, 11:45 PM, discharged 02/18/20xx, 1:45 PM
Patient Number: 583649HO
Admitted with chest pain from Outpatient Clinic.

Figure form UB-92

FL 42-49: REVENUE CODES/INFORMATION

Notes

Specific services are listed on the UB-92/CMS-1450 in the revenue code fields (FL 42-49). **Revenue codes** are 4-digit codes, the first two digits of which designate the revenue code category. For example, Revenue Category 32X indicates services of a diagnostic nature performed in the Radiology Department. Within category 32X fall individually identified services such as:

320 Radiology, Diagnostic, General
321 Radiology, Diagnostic, Angiocardiography
322 Radiology, Diagnostic, Arthrography

An initial zero is usually programmed into the facility software to satisfy the 4-digit requirement for a revenue code. Originally, the revenue code assignment was only three digits; however, the need for additional codes necessitated the addition of a fourth digit. You will want to find out whether you need to add the initial zero manually or whether your system will make the necessary adjustments automatically.

When the last digit of a revenue code is 9, that indicates that other services within that category were performed that do not have a specific revenue code assignment. The use of a 0 for the last digit indicates the service was unspecified and a more specific assignment could not be made. As with ICD-9-CM coding, nonspecific codes should be avoided because many third-party carriers will not authorize payment for services that utilize them.

Figure 3–7 shows FL 42-49 of the UB-92/CMS-1450 form and Table 3–6 provides instructions for completing this section of the form.

42 REV. CD.	43 DESCRIPTION	44 HCPCS / RATES	45 SERV. DATE	46 SERV. UNITS	47 TOTAL CHARGES	48 NON-COVERED CHARGES	49	
1								1
2								2
3								3
4								4
5								5
6								6
7								7
8								8
9								9
10								10
11								11
12								12
13								13
14								14
15								15
16								16
17								17
18								18
19								19
20								20
21								21
22								22
23								23

Figure 3–7 Form Locators 42-49.

**TABLE 3–6   UB-92 COMPLETION
DETAILS REVENUE DESCRIPTIONS, CODES, CHARGES (FL 42-49).**

FL #	Field Name	Specifics	# Digits	Digits (A)lpha (N)um	Medicare (R)eq (O)pt	Others (R)eq (O)pt
42-43	Revenue Code/ Description	Revenue code identifies specific service being billed Last digit 0 = General code Last digit 9 = Other Detailed revenue codes (not ending in 0) required for following: 29X, 304, 33X, 367, 42X, 52X, 55-59X 624, 636, 80-85X 23 lines available Up to 9 pages (450 lines) acceptable on one claim List in ascending order by DOS except 001 Total Charges (last)	3	N	R	R

(continued)

TABLE 3–6 *continued*

FL #	Field Name	Specifics	# Digits	Digits (A)lpha (N)um	Medicare (R)eq (O)pt	Others (R)eq (O)pt
	Revenue Code	Standard Abbreviation				
	42 Revenue Code	43 Revenue Description				
	01X Reserved					
	02X Health Insurance PPS					
	0 Reserved					
	1 Reserved					
	2 SNF PPS System	SNF PPS (RUG)				
	3 Rehab Facility PPS	HH PPS				
	4 Inpatient Rehab Facility	IRF PPS				
	5-9 Reserved					
	03X-09X Reserved					
	Accommodation Codes					
	10X All-Inclusive Rate					
	0 All-Inclusive R & B Plus Ancillary	ALL INC R&B/ANC				
	1 All-inclusive R & B	ALL INCL R&B				
	11X R & B (Private/Med/Gen)					
	0 General	ROOM-BOARD/PVT				
	1 Med/Surg/Gyn	MED-SUR-GY/PVT				
	2 Obstetrics (OB)	OB/PVT				
	3 Pediatric	PEDS/PVT				
	4 Psychiatric	PSYCH/PVT				
	5 Hospice	HOSPICE/PVT				
	6 Detoxification	DETOX/PVT				
	7 Oncology	ONCOLOGY/PVT				
	8 Rehabilitation	REHAB/PVT				
	9 Other	OTHER/PVT				
	12X R & B (2 Bed/Med/Gen)					
	0 General	ROOM-BOARD/SEMI				
	1 Med/Surg/Gyn	MED-SUR-GY/2BED				
	2 Obstetrics (OB)	OB/2BED				
	3 Pediatric	PEDS/2BED				
	4 Psychiatric	PSYCH/2BED				
	5 Hospice	HOSPICE/2BED				
	6 Detoxification	DETOX/2BED				
	7 Oncology	ONCOLOGY/2BED				
	8 Rehabilitation	REHAB/2BED				
	9 Other	OTHER/2BED				
	13X R & B (3-4 Beds)					
	0 General	ROOM-BOARD/3&4 BED				
	1 Med/Surg/Gyn	MED-SUR-GY/3&4 BED				

FL #	Field Name	Specifics	# Digits	Digits (A)lpha (N)um	Medicare (R)eq (O)pt	Others (R)eq (O)pt
	2 Obstetrics (OB)	OB/3&4BED				
	3 Pediatric	PEDS/3&4BED				
	4 Psychiatric	PSYCH/3&4BED				
	5 Hospice	HOSPICE/3&4BED				
	6 Detoxification	DETOX/3&4BED				
	7 Oncology	ONCOLOGY/3&4BED				
	8 Rehabilitation	REHAB/3&4 BED				
	9 Other	OTHER/3&4BED				
14X	Private (Deluxe)					
	0 General	ROOM-BOARD/PVT/DLX				
	1 Med/Surg/Gyn	MED-SUR-GY/DLX				
	2 Obstetrics (OB)	OB/DLX				
	3 Pediatric	PEDS/DLX				
	4 Psychiatric	PSYCH/DLX				
	5 Hospice	HOSPICE/DLX				
	6 Detoxification	DETOX/DLX				
	7 Oncology	ONCOLOGY/DLX				
	8 Rehabilitation	REHAB/DLX				
	9 Other	OTHER/DLX				
15X	R & B (Ward/Med/Gen)					
	0 General	ROOM-BOARD/WARD				
	1 Med/Surg/Gyn	MED-SUR-GY/WARD				
	2 Obstetrics (OB)	OB/WARD				
	3 Pediatric	PEDS/WARD				
	4 Psychiatric	PSYCH/WARD				
	5 Hospice	HOSPICE/WARD				
	6 Detoxification	DETOX/WARD				
	7 Oncology	ONCOLOGY/WARD				
	8 Rehabilitation	REHAB/WARD				
	9 Other	OTHER/WARD				
16X	Other R & B					
	0 General	R&B				
	4 Sterile Environment	R&B/STERILE				
	7 Self-Care	R&B/SELF				
	9 Other	R&B/OTHER				
17X	Nursing					
	0 General	NURSERY				
	1 Newborn Level I Routine Newborn Care	NURSERY/LEVEL I				
	2 Newborn Level II Low Birthweight Neonates	NURSERY/LEVEL II				

(continued)

TABLE 3–6 *continued*

FL #	Field Name	Specifics	# Digits	Digits (A)lpha (N)um	Medicare (R)eq (O)pt	Others (R)eq (O)pt
	3 Newborn Level III Sick Neonates/Not NICU	NURSERY/LEVEL III				
	4 Newborn Level IV Sick Neonates/NICU	NURSERY/LEVEL IV				
18X	Leave of Absence (LOA)					
	0 General	LOA OR LEAVE OF ABSENCE				
	1 Reserved					
	2 Pt Convenience-Billable	LOA/PT CONV CHGS BILLABLE				
	3 Therapeutic Leave	LOA/THERAP				
	4 ICF Mentally Retarded	LOA/ICF/MR				
	5 Nursing Home (Hosp)	LOA/NURS HOME				
	9 Other LOA	LOA/OTHER				
19X	Subacute Care					
	0 General	SUBACUTE				
	1 Subacute Level I Minimal Nursing Care	SUBACUTE/LEVEL I				
	2 Subacute Level II Moderate Nursing Care	SUBACUTE/LEVEL II				
	3 Subacute Level III Mod/Extensive Nursing	SUBACUTE/LEVEL III				
	4 Subacute Level IV Extensive Nurs/Tech	SUBACUTE/LEVEL IV				
20X	Intensive Care					
	0 General	INTENSIVE CARE OR ICU				
	1 Surgical	ICU/SURGICAL				
	2 Medical	ICU/MEDICAL				
	3 Pediatric	ICU/PEDS				
	4 Psychiatric	ICU/PSTAY				
	6 Intermediate ICU	ICU/INTERMEDIATE				
	7 Burn Care	ICU/BURN CARE				
	8 Trauma	ICU/TRAUMA				
	9 Other ICU	ICU/OTHER				
21X	Coronary Care					
	0 General	CORONARY CARE OR CCU				
	1 Myocardial Infarction	CCU/MYO INFARC				
	2 Pulmonary Care	CCU/PULMONARY				
	3 Heart Transplant	CCU/TRANSPLANT				
	4 Intermed CCU	CCU/INTERMEDIATE				
	9 Other Coronary Care	CCU/OTHER				

FL #	Field Name	Specifics	# Digits	Digits (A)lpha (N)um	Medicare (R)eq (O)pt	Others (R)eq (O)pt
	Ancillary Services					
	22X Special Charges					
	0 General	SPECIAL CHARGES				
	1 Admission Charge	ADMIT CHARGE				
	2 Tech Support Charge	TECH SUPPT CHG				
	3 UR Service Charge	UR CHARGE				
	4 Late Discharge/Med Necess	LATE DISCH/MED NEC				
	9 Other Special Charges	OTHER SPEC CHG				
	23X Incremental Nursing Care					
	0 General	NURSING INCREM				
	1 Nursery	NUR INCR/NURSERY				
	2 OB	NUR INCR/OB				
	3 ICU (inc transitional care)	NUR INCR/ICU				
	4 CCU (inc transitional care)	NUR INCR/CCU				
	5 Hospice	NUR INCR/HOSPICE				
	9 Other	NUR INCR/OTHER				
	24X All-Inclusive Ancillary					
	0 General	ALL INCL ANCIL				
	1 Basic	ALL INCL BASIC				
	2 Comprehensive	ALL INCL COMP				
	3 Specialty	ALL INCL SPECIAL				
	9 Other All-Inclusive Ancillary	ALL INCL ANCIL/OTHER				
	25X Pharmacy					
	0 General	PHARMACY				
	1 Generic Drugs	DRUGS/GENERIC				
	2 Nongeneric Drugs	DRUGS/NONGENERIC				
	3 Take-Home Drugs	DRUGS/TAKEHOME				
	4 Drugs Incident to Dx Serv	DRUGS/INCIDENT ODX				
	5 Drugs Incident to Radiology	DRUGS/INCIDENT RAD				
	6 Experimental Drugs	DRUGS/EXPERIMT				
	7 Nonprescription Drugs	DRUGS/NONPSCRPT				
	8 IV Solutions	IV SOLUTIONS				
	9 Other Pharmacy	DRUGS/OTHER				
	26X IV Therapy	Usually requires HCPCS code(s)				
	0 General	IV THERAPY				
	1 Infusion Pump	IV THER/INFSN PUMP				
	2 IV Therapy/Pharmacy	IV THER/PHARM/SVC				
	3 IV Therapy/Drug/Supply/ Delivery	IV THER/DRUG/SUPPLY DELV				
	4 IV Therapy/Supplies	IV THER/SUPPLIES				
	9 Other IV Therapy	IV THERAPY/OTHER				

(continued)

TABLE 3–6   *continued*

FL #	Field Name	Specifics	# Digits	Digits (A)lpha (N)um	Medicare (R)eq (O)pt	Others (R)eq (O)pt
	27X Med/Surg Supplies/Devices	Only Nonroutine Billed with This RC				
	0 General	MED-SUR SUPPLIES				
	1 Nonsterile Supply	NONSTER SUPPLY				
	2 Sterile Supply	STERILE SUPPLY				
	3 Take-Home Supplies	TAKEHOME SUPPLY				
	4 Prosthetic/Orthotic Devices	PROSTH/ORTH DEV				
	5 Pacemaker	PACE MAKER				
	6 Intraocular Lenses	INTRO OC LENS				
	7 Oxygen-Take Home	02/TAKEHOME				
	8 Other Implants	SUPPLY/IMPLANTS				
	9 Other Supplies/Devices	SUPPLY/OTHER				
	28X Oncology					
	0 General	ONCOLOGY				
	9 Other Oncology	ONCOLOGY/OTHER				
	29X DME (Other Than Renal)					
	0 General	MED EQUIP/DURAB				
	1 Rental	MED EQUIP/RENT				
	2 Purchase of new DME	MED EQUIP/NEW				
	3 Purchase of used DME	MED EQUIP/USED				
	4 Supplies/Drugs for DME Effectiveness (HHA)	MED EQUIP/SUPPLIES/ DRUGS				
	9 Other Equipment	MED EQUIP/OTHER				
	30X Laboratory					
	0 General	LABORATORY OR LAB				
	1 Chemistry	LAB/CHEMISTRY				
	2 Immunology	LAB/IMMUNOLOGY				
	3 Renal Patient (Home)	LAB/RENAL HOME				
	4 Nonroutine Dialysis	LAB/NR DIALYSIS				
	5 Hematology	LAB/HEMATOLOGY				
	6 Bacteriology/Microbiology	LAB/BACT-MICRO				
	7 Urology	LAB/UROLOGY				
	9 Other Laboratory	LAB/OTHER				
	31X Laboratory Pathological					
	0 General	PATHOLOGY LAB OR PATH LAB				
	1 Cytology	PATHOL/CYTOLOGY				
	2 Histology	PATHOL/HISTOLOGY				
	4 Biopsy	PATHOL/BIOPSY				
	9 Other	PATHOL/OTHER				

FL #	Field Name	Specifics	# Digits	Digits (A)lpha (N)um	Medicare (R)eq (O)pt	Others (R)eq (O)pt
32X	Radiology-Diagnostic					
	0 General	DX X-RAY				
	1 Angiocardiography	DX X-RAY/ANGIO				
	2 Arthrography	DX X-RAY/ARTH				
	3 Arteriography	DX X-RAY/ARTER				
	4 Chest X-Ray	DX X-RAY/CHEST				
	9 Other	DX X-RAY/OTHER				
33X	Radiology-Therapeutic					
	0 General	RX X-RAY				
	1 Chemotherapy-Injected	CHEMOTHER/INJ				
	2 Chemotherapy-Oral	CHEMOTHER/ORAL				
	3 Radiation Therapy	RADIATION RX				
	5 Chemotherapy/IV	CHEMOTHERAP-IV				
	9 Other	RX X-RAY/OTHER				
34X	Nuclear Medicine					
	0 General	NUCLEAR MEDICINE OR NUC MED				
	1 Diagnostic	NUC MED/DX				
	2 Therapeutic	NUC MED/RX				
	9 Other	NUC MED/OTHER				
35X	CT Scan					
	0 General	CT SCAN				
	1 Head Scan	CT SCAN/HEAD				
	2 Body Scan	CT SCAN/BODY				
	9 Other CT Scans	CT SCAN/OTHER				
36X	Operating Room Services					
	0 General	OR SERVICES				
	1 Minor Surgery	OR/MINOR				
	2 Organ Transplant/Not Kidney	OR/ORGAN TRANS				
	7 Kidney Transplant	OR/KIDNEY TRANS				
	9 Other	OR/OTHER				
37X	Anesthesia					
	0 General	ANESTHESIA				
	1 Anes Incident to RAD	ANESTHE/INCIDENT RAD				
	2 Anes Incident to Other Dx	ANESTHE/INCIDENT ODX				
	4 Acupuncture	ANESTHE/ACUPUNC				
	9 Other	ANESTHE/OTHER				
38X	Blood					
	0 General	BLOOD				
	1 Packed Red Cells	BLOOD/PKD RED				
	2 Whole Blood	BLOOD/WHOLE				

(continued)

TABLE 3–6   *continued*

FL #	Field Name	Specifics	# Digits	Digits (A)lpha (N)um	Medicare (R)eq (O)pt	Others (R)eq (O)pt
	3 Plasma	BLOOD/PLASMA				
	4 Platelets	BLOOD/PLATELETS				
	5 Leukocytes	BLOOD/LEUKOCYTES				
	6 Other Components	BLOOD/COMPONENTS				
	7 Other Derivatives	BLOOD/DERIVATIVES				
	9 Other Blood	BLOOD/OTHER				
39X	Blood Storage/Processing					
	0 General	BLOOD/STOR-PROC				
	1 Blood Administration	BLOOD/ADMI				
	9 Other	BLOOD/OTHER STOR				
40X	Other Imaging					
	0 General	IMAGE SERVICE				
	1 Dx Mammography	MAMMOGRAPHY				
	2 Ultrasound	ULTRASOUND				
	3 Screen Mammography	SCR MAMMOGRAPHY/ GEN MAMMO				
	4 Positron Emission Tomography	PET SCAN				
	9 Other	OTHER IMAG SVS				
41X	Respiratory					
	0 General	RESPIRATORY SVC				
	2 Inhalation Services	INHALATION SVC				
	3 Hyperbaric Oxygen Therapy	HYPERBARIC 02				
	9 Other	OTHER RESPIR SVS				
42X	Physical Therapy					
	0 General	PHYSICAL THERP				
	1 Visit Charge	PHYS THERAP/VISIT				
	2 Hourly Charge	PHYS THERP/HOUR				
	3 Group Rate	PHYS THERP/GROUP				
	4 Evaluation/Reevaluation	PHYS THERP/EVAL				
	9 Other	OTHER PHYS THERP				
43X	Occupational Therapy					
	0 General	OCCUPATION THER				
	1 Visit Charge	OCCUP THERP/VISIT				
	2 Hourly Charge	OCCUP THERP/HOUR				
	3 Group Rate	OCCUP THERP/GROUP				
	4 Evaluation/Reevaluation	OCCUP THERP/EVAL				
	9 Other	OTHER OCCUP THER				

FL #	Field Name	Specifics	# Digits	Digits (A)lpha (N)um	Medicare (R)eq (O)pt	Others (R)eq (O)pt
44X	Speech-Languaged Pathology					
	0 General	SPEECH PATHOL				
	1 Visit Charge	SPEECH PATH/VISIT				
	2 Hourly Charge	SPEECH PATH/HOUR				
	3 Group Rate	SPEECH PATH/GROUP				
	4 Evaluation/Reevaluation	SPEECH PATH/EVAL				
	9 Other	OTHER SPEECH PAT				
45X	Emergency Room	450 Not to Be Used with Any Other Code from Series				
	0 General	EMERG ROOM				
	1 EMTALA Med Screen Svcs	ER/EMTALA				
	2 ER beyond EMTALA Screen	ER/BEYOND EMTALA				
	6 Urgent Care	URGENT CARE				
	9 Other	OTHER EMER ROOM				
46X	Pulmonary Function					
	0 General	PULMONARY FUNC				
	9 Other	OTHER PULMON FUNC				
47X	Audiology					
	0 General	AUDIOLOGY				
	1 Diagnostic	AUDIOLOGY/DX				
	2 Treatment	AUDIOLOGY/RX				
	9 Other	OTHER AUDIOL				
48X	Cardiology					
	0 General	CARDIOLOGY				
	1 Cardiac Cath Lab	CARDIAC CATH LAB				
	2 Stress Test	STRESS TEST				
	3 Echocardiology	ECHOCARDIOLOGY				
	9 Other	OTHER CARDIOL				
49X	Ambulatory Surgical Care					
	0 General	AMBUL SURG				
	9 Other	OTHER AMBL SURG				
50X	Outpatient Services					
	0 General	OUTPATIENT SVS				
	9 Other	OUTPATIENT/OTHER				
51X	Clinic					
	0 General	CLINIC				
	1 Chronic Pain Center	CHRONIC PAIN CL				
	2 Dental Clinic	DENTAL CLINIC				

(continued)

TABLE 3–6   *continued*

FL #	Field Name	Specifics	# Digits	Digits (A)lpha (N)um	Medicare (R)eq (O)pt	Others (R)eq (O)pt
	3 Psychiatric Clinic	PSYCH CLINIC				
	4 Ob-Gyn Clinic	OB-GYN CLINIC				
	5 Pediatric Clinic	PEDS CLINIC				
	6 Urgent Care Clinic	URGENT CLINIC				
	7 Family Practice Clinic	FAMILY CLINIC				
	9 Other	OTHER CLINIC				
52X	Freestanding Clinic					
	0 General	FREESTAND CLINIC				
	1 Rural Health-Clinic	RURAL/CLINIC				
	2 Rural Health-Home	RURAL/HOME				
	3 Family Practice Clinic	FR/STD FAMILY CLINIC				
	6 Urgent Care Clinic	FR/STD URGENT CLINIC				
	9 Other	OTHER FR/STD CLINIC				
53X	Osteopathic Services					
	0 General	OSTEOPATH SVS				
	1 Osteopathic Therapy	OSTEOPATH RX				
	9 Other	OTHER OSTEOPATH				
54X	Ambulance					
	0 General	AMBULANCE				
	1 Supplies	AMBUL/SUPPLY				
	2 Medical Transport	AMBUL/MED TRANS				
	3 Heart Mobile	AMBUL/HEARTMOBL				
	4 Oxygen	AMBUL/OXY				
	5 Air Ambulance	AIR AMBULANCE				
	6 Neonatal Ambulance	AMBUL/NEO-NATAL				
	7 Pharmacy	AMBUL/PHARMACY				
	8 Telephone Transmission EKG	AMBUL/TELEPHONIC EKG				
	9 Other	OTHER AMBULANCE				
55X	Skilled Nursing					
	0 General	SKILLED NURSING				
	1 Visit Charge	SKILLED NURS/VISIT				
	2 Hourly Charge	SKILLED NURS/HOUR				
	9 Other	SKILLED NURS/OTHER				
56X	Medical Social Services					
	0 General	SOCIAL SVS				
	1 Visit Charge	MED SOC SERV/VISIT				
	2 Hourly Charge	MED SOC SERV/HOUR				
	9 Other	MED SOC SERV/OTHER				

FL #	Field Name	Specifics	# Digits	Digits (A)lpha (N)um	Medicare (R)eq (O)pt	Others (R)eq (O)pt
57X	Home Health Aid					
	0 General	AIDE/HOME HEALTH				
	1 Visit Charge	AIDE/HOME HLTH/VISIT				
	2 Hourly Charge	AIDE/HOME HLTH/HOUR				
	9 Other	AIDE/HOME HLTH/OTHER				
58X	Other Visits (Home Health)					
	0 General	VISIT/HOME HEALTH				
	1 Visit Charge	VISIT/HOME HLTH/VISIT				
	2 Hourly Charge	VISIT/HOME HLTH/HOUR				
	9 Other	VISIT/HOME HLTH/OTHER				
59X	Units of Service (Home Health)					
	0 General	UNIT/HOME HEALTH				
	9 Other	UNIT/HOME HLTH/OTHER				
60X	Oxygen (Home Health)					
	0 General	02/HOME HEALTH				
	1 Oxygen-Stat/Equip/Supp/or Contents	02/EQUIP/SUPPL/CONT				
	2 Oxygen-Stat/Equip/Supp Under 1 LPM	02/STAT EQUIP/ UNDER 1 LPM				
	3 Oxygen-Stat/Equip/Over 4 LPM	O2/STAT EQUIP/ OVER 4 LPM				
	4 Oxygen-Portable Add-On	02/STAT EQUIP/ PORT ADD-ON				
61X	Magnetic Resonance					
	0 General	MRI				
	1 Brain (inc brain stem)	MRI-BRAIN				
	2 Spinal Cord (inc spine)	MRI-SPINE				
	3 Reserved					
	4 MRI-Other	MRI-OTHER				
	5 MRA-Head/Neck	MRA-HEAD AND NECK				
	6 MRA-Lower Extremities	MRA-LOWER EXTREMITIES				
	7 Reserved					
	8 MRA-Other	MRA-OTHER				
	9 Other	MRI-OTHER				
62X	Med/Surg/Supp Extension of 27X					
	1 Supplies Incident Radiology	MED-SUR SUPP/INCIDNT RAD				
	2 Supplies Incident Other Dx	MED-SUR SUPP INCIDNT ODX				
	3 Surgical Dressings	SURG DRESSING				
	4 FDA Investigation Devices	IDE				

(continued)

TABLE 3-6 *continued*

FL #	Field Name	Specifics	# Digits	Digits (A)lpha (N)um	Medicare (R)eq (O)pt	Others (R)eq (O)pt
	63X Pharmacy					
	0 Reserved					
	1 Single Source Drug	DRUG/SINGLE				
	2 Multiple Source Drug	DRUG/MULT				
	3 Restrictive Prescription	DRUG/RSTR				
	4 EPO > 10,000 units	DRUG/EPO/ > 10,000 UNITS				
	5 EPO < 10,000 units	DRUG/EPO/ < 10,000 UNITS				
	6 Drugs Req Detailed Coding	DRUGS/DETAIL CODE				
	7 Self-Admin Drugs	DRUGS/SELFADMIN				
	64X Home IV Therapy Services					
	0 General	IV THERAPY SVC				
	1 Nonroutine Nursing, Central Line	NON RT NURSING/CENTRAL				
	2 IV Site Care, Central Line	IV SISTE CARE/CENTRAL				
	3 IV Start/Change, Peripheral Line	IV STRT/CHNG/PERIPHRL				
	4 Nonroutine Nursing, Peripheral Line	NONRT NURSING/PERIPHRL				
	5 Training Patient/Caregiver, Central Line	TRNG/PT/CARGVR/CENTRAL				
	6 Training, Disabled Patient, Central Line	TRNG DSBLPT/CENTRAL				
	7 Training Patient/Caregiver, Peripheral Line	TRNG/PT/CARGVR/PERIPHRL				
	8 Training, Disabled Patient, Peripheral Line	TRNG/DSBLPAT/PERIPHRL				
	9 Other IV Therapy Services	OTHER IV THERAPY SVC				
	65X Hospice Services					
	0 General	HOSPICE				
	1 Routine Home Care	HOSPICE/RTN HOME				
	2 Continuous Home Care	HOSPICE/CTNS HOME				
	3 Reserved					
	4 Reserved					
	5 Inpt Respite Care	HOSPICE/IP RESPITE				
	6 General Inpt Care (nonrespite)	HOSPICE/IP NON RESPITE				
	7 Physician Services	HOSPICE/PHYSICIAN				
	9 Other Hospice	HOSPICE/OTHER				

FL #	Field Name	Specifics	# Digits	Digits (A)lpha (N)um	Medicare (R)eq (O)pt	Others (R)eq (O)pt
	66X Respite Care (HHA Only)					
	0 General	RESPITE CARE				
	1 Hourly Chg/Skilled Nursing	RESPITE/SKILLED NURSE				
	2 Hourly Chg/HHA/ Homemaker	RESPITE/HMEAID/ HMEMKE				
	9 Other Respite Care	RESPITE/CARE				
	67X Oupt Special Residence					
	0 General	OP SPEC RES				
	1 Hospital-Based	OP SPEC RES/HOSP BASED				
	2 Contracted	OP SPEC RES/CONTRACTED				
	9 Other Special Residence	OP SPEC RES/OTHER				
	68X Not Assigned					
	69X Not Assigned					
	70X Cast Room					
	0 General	CAST ROOM				
	9 Other Cast Room	OTHER CAST ROOM				
	71X Recovery Room					
	0 General	RECOVERY ROOM				
	9 Other Recovery Room	OTHER RECOV RM				
	72X Labor Room/Delivery					
	0 General	DELIVROOM/LAB				
	1 Labor	LABOR				
	2 Delivery	DELIVERY ROOM				
	3 Circumcision	CIRCUMCISION				
	4 Birthing Center	BIRTHING CENTER				
	9 Other Labor Room/Delivery	OTHER/DELIV-LABOR				
	73X EKG/ECG					
	0 General	EKG/ECG				
	1 Holter Monitor	HOLTER MONT				
	2 Telemetry	TELEMETRY				
	9 Other EKG/ECG	OTHER EKG/ECG				
	74X EEG					
	0 General	EEG				
	9 Other EEG	OTHER EEG				
	75X Gastrointestinal Services					
	0 General	GASTRO-INTS SVS				
	9 Other Gastrointestinal	OTHER GASTRO-INTS				
	76X Treatment/Observation Rm					
	0 General	TREATMENT/ OBSERVATION RM				
	1 Treatment Room	TREATMENT ROOM				

(continued)

TABLE 3–6 *continued*

FL #	Field Name	Specifics	# Digits	Digits (A)lpha (N)um	Medicare (R)eq (O)pt	Others (R)eq (O)pt
	2 Observation Room	OBSERVATION RM				
	9 Other Treatment Room	OTHER TREATMENT RM				
77X	Preventative Care Services					
	0 General	PREVENT CARE SVS				
	1 Vaccine Administration	VACCINE ADMIN				
	9 Other Prev Care Services	OTHER PREVENT				
78X	Telemedicine					
	0 General	TELEMEDICINE				
	9 Other Telemedicine	TELEMEDICINE/OTHER				
79X	Lithotripsy					
	0 General	LITHOTRIPSY				
	9 Other Lithotripsy	LITHOTRIPSY/OTHER				
80X	Inpatient Renal Dialysis					
	0 General	RENAL DIALYSIS				
	1 Inpt Hemodialysis	DIALY/INPT				
	2 Inpt Peritoneal (Non-CAPD)	DIALY/INPT/PER				
	3 Inpt Continuous Ambulatory Peritoneal Dialysis (CAPD)	DIALY/INPT/CAPD				
	4 Inpt Continuous Ambulatory Cycling Peritoneal (CCPD)	DIALY/INPT/CCPT				
	9 Other Inpt Dialysis	DIALY/INPT/OTHER				
81X	Organ Acquisition					
	0 General	ORGAN ACQUISIT				
	1 Living Donor	LIVING DONOR				
	2 Cadaver Donor	CADAVER/DONOR				
	3 Unknown Donor	UNKNOWN/DONOR				
	4 Unsuccessful Organ Search Donor Bank Charge	UNSUCCESSFUL SEARCH				
	9 Other Organ Donor	OTHER/DONOR				
82X	Hemodialysis-Outpt/Home					
	0 General	HEMO/OP OR HOME				
	1 Hemodialysis/Composite or Other Rate	HEMO/COMPOSITE				
	2 Home Supplies	HEMO/HOME/SUPPL				
	3 Home Equipment	HEMO/HOME/EQUIP				
	4 Maintenance/100%	HEMO/HOME/100%				
	5 Support Services	HEMO/HOME/SUPSERV				
	9 Other Outpt Hemodialysis	HEMO/HOME/OTHER				

FL #	Field Name	Specifics	# Digits	Digits (A)lpha (N)um	Medicare (R)eq (O)pt	Others (R)eq (O)pt
83X	Peritoneal Dialysis-Outpatient/Home					
	0 General	PERITONEAL/OP OR HOME				
	1 Peritoneal/Composite or Other Rate	PERTNL/COMPOSISTE				
	2 Home Supplies	PERTNL/HOME/SUPPL				
	3 Home Equipment	PERTNL/HOME/EQUIP				
	4 Maintenance/100%	PERTNL/HOME/100%				
	5 Support Services	PERTNL/HOME/SUPSERV				
	9 Other Peritoneal Dialysis	PERTNL/HOME/OTHER				
84X	Continuous Ambulatory Peritoneal Dialysis (CAPD) Outpatient/Home					
	0 General	CAPD/OP OR HOME				
	1 CAPD/Composite or Other Rate	CAPD/COMPOSITE				
	2 Home Supplies	CAPD/HOME/SUPPL				
	3 Home Equipment	CAPD/HOME/EQUIP				
	4 Maintenance/100%	CAPD/HOME/100%				
	5 Support Services	CAPD/HOME/SUPSERV				
	9 Other CAPD Dialysis	CAPD/HOME/OTHER				
85X	Continuous Cycling Peritoneal Dialysis (CCPD) Outpatient/Home					
	0 General	CCPD/OP OR HOME				
	1 CCPD/Composite or Other Rate	CCPD/COMPOSITE				
	2 Home Supplies	CCPD/HOME/SUPPL				
	3 Home Equipment	CCPD/HOME/EQUIP				
	4 Maintenance/100%	CCPD/HOME/100%				
	5 Support Services	CCPD/HOME/SUPSERV				
	9 Other CCPD Dialysis	CCPD/HOME/OTHER				
86X	Reserved Dialysis National Assignment					
87X	Reserved Dialysis State Assignment					
88X	Miscellaneous Dialysis					
	0 General	DIALY/MISC				
	1 Ultrafiltration	DIALY/ULTRAFILT				
	2 Home Dialysis Aid Visit	HOME DIALYSIS AID VISIT				
	9 Misc Dialysis Other	DIALY/MISC/OTHER				

(continued)

TABLE 3–6   *continued*

FL #	Field Name	Specifics	# Digits	Digits (A)lpha (N)um	Medicare (R)eq (O)pt	Others (R)eq (O)pt
	89X Reserved National Assignment					
	90X Psychiatric/Psychological Treatments					
	0 General	PSTAY TREATMENT				
	1 Electroshock Treatment	ELECTRO SHOCK				
	2 Milieu Therapy	MILIEU THERAPY				
	3 Play Therapy	PLAY THERAPY				
	4 Activity Therapy	ACTIVITY THERAPY				
	9 Other	OTHER PSYCH RX				
	91X Psychiatric/Psychological Services					
	0 General	PSYCH/SERVICES				
	1 Rehabilitation	PSYCH/REHAB				
	2 Partial Hosp-Less Intensive	PSYCH/PARTIAL HOSP				
	3 Partial Hosp-Intensive	PSYCH/PARTIAL INTENSIVE				
	4 Individual Therapy	PSYCH/INDIV RX				
	5 Group Therapy	PSYCH/GROUP RX				
	6 Family Therapy	PSYCH/FAMILY RX				
	7 Biofeedback	PSYCH/BIOFEED				
	8 Testing	PSYCH/TESTING				
	9 Other	PSYCH/OTHER				
	92X Other Dx Services					
	0 General	OTHER DX SVS				
	1 Peripheral Vascular Lab	PERI VASCUL LAB				
	2 Electromyelogram	EMG				
	3 Pap Smear	PAP SMEAR				
	4 Allergy Test	ALLERGY TEST				
	5 Pregnancy Test	PREG TEST				
	9 Other Dx Service	ADDITIONAL DX SVS				
	93X Med Rehab Day Program					
	1 Half Day	HALF DAY				
	2 Full Day	FULL DAY				
	94X Other Ther Services					
	0 General	OTHE RX SVS				
	1 Recreational Therapy	RECREATION RX				
	2 Education/Training	EDUC/TRAINING				
	3 Cardiac Rehab	CARDIAC REHAB				
	4 Drug Rehab	DRUG REHAB				
	5 Alcohol Rehab	ALCOHOL REHAB				

FL #	Field Name	Specifics	# Digits	Digits (A)lpha (N)um	Medicare (R)eq (O)pt	Others (R)eq (O)pt
	6 Complex Med Equip-Routine	RTN COMPLX MED EQUIP-ROUT				
	7 Complex Med Equip-Ancillary	COMPLX MED EQUIP-ANX				
	9 Other Ther Services	ADDITIONAL RX SVS				
95X	Other Ther Services Extension of 94X					
	0 Reserved					
	1 Athletic Training	ATHLETIC TRAINING				
	2 Kinesiotherapy	KINESIOTHERAPY				
96X	Professional Fees					
	0 General	PRO FEE				
	1 Psychiatry	PRO FEE/PSYCH				
	2 Ophthalmology	PRO FEE/EYE				
	3 Anesthesiologist (MD)	PRO FEE/ANES MD				
	4 Anesthetist (CRNA)	PRO FEE/ANES CRNA				
	9 Other Prof Fees	OTHER PRO FEE				
97X	Prof Fees continued					
	1 Laboratory	PRO FEE/LAB				
	2 Radiology-Dx	PRO FEE/RAD/DX				
	3 Radiology-Therapeutic	PRO FEE/RAD/RX				
	4 Radiology-Nuclear Med	PRO FEE/NUC MED				
	5 Operating Room	PRO FEE/OR				
	6 Respiratory Therapy	PRO FEE/RESPIR				
	7 Physical Therapy	PRO FEE/PHYSI				
	8 Occupational Therapy	PRO FEE/OCUPA				
	9 Speech Pathology	PRO FEE/SPEECH				
98X	Prof Fees continued					
	1 Emergency Room	PRO FEE/ER				
	2 Outpatient Services	PRO FEE/OUTPT				
	3 Clinic	PRO FEE/CLINIC				
	4 Medical Social Services	PRO FEE/SOC SVC				
	5 EKG	PRO FEE/EKG				
	6 EEG	PRO FEE/EEG				
	7 Hospital Visit	PRO FEE/HOS VIS				
	8 Consultation	PRO FEE/CONSULT				
	9 Private Duty Nurse	PEE/PVT NURSE				
99X	Patient Convenience Items					
	0 General	PT CONVENIENCE				
	1 Cafeteria/Guest Tray	CAFETERIA				
	2 Private Linen Service	LINEN				

(continued)

TABLE 3–6 *continued*

FL #	Field Name	Specifics	# Digits	Digits (A)lpha (N)um	Medicare (R)eq (O)pt	Others (R)eq (O)pt
	3 Telephone/Telegraph	TELEPHONE				
	4 TV/Radio	TV/RADIO				
	5 Nonpt Room Rentals	NONPT ROOM RENT				
	6 Late Discharge Charge	LATE DISCHARGE				
	7 Admission Kits	ADMIT KITS				
	8 Beauty Shop/Barber	BARBER/BEAUTY				
	9 Other Pt Convenience Items	PT CONVENCE/OTHER				
	100X-209X Reserved for National Assignment					
	210X Alternative Therapy Svcs					
	0 General					
	1 Acupuncture					
	2 Accupressure					
	3 Massage					
	4 Reflexology					
	5 Biofeedback					
	6 Hypnosis					
	9 Other Alternative Ther Svcs					
44	HCPCS/Rates/HIPPS	Accommodation Code or HCPCS Code	2/Codes	A/N	R	R
	Rate Codes	Outpatient Claims Accommodation Code Inpatient Claims Supplies/ESRD Services/ Drugs NO HCPCS Code Req Outpt Claim Multiple Codes List in Revenue Code Sequence Rates - Dollar value whole numbers decimal point/cents	8/Amts			
45	Service Date	Line item dates of service required where HCPCS code required Dates must fall within dates in FL6	8	N	R Outpt	R Outpt

FL #	Field Name	Specifics		# Digits	Digits (A)lpha (N)um	Medicare (R)eq (O)pt	Others (R)eq (O)pt
46	Service Units	Required for following revenue code groups:		7	N per line	R Out- pt	R Out- pt
		10X-15X	636				
		20X-21X	274				
		38X	30X-31X				
		51X, 52X	410/420/ 430/440				
		80X	480/910/943				
		29X	60X				
		450/452/459	32X/333/34X 35X/40X/61X				
47	Total Charges	Units X Line Item Service Grand Total Listed as Last Line Item Revenue Code 01 Includes Covered/ Noncovered Chgs EXCEPT Medicare (only covered)		9	N	R	R
48	Noncovered Charges	Utilized when noncovered days are indicated in FL 8			N	R If Appli- cable	R If Appli- cable
49	Unlabeled Field						

Notes

PRACTICE EXERCISE 3–6

Identify the appropriate revenue codes and descriptions for the following. When multiple codes are necessary, assign them in the appropriate sequence:

                                                 Code(s)   Description(s)

1. Room and board—oncology, semiprivate, 2 beds.   ____   _____

2. Room and board—medical, semiprivate, 2 beds.   ____   _____

3. Intensive care—surgical.   ____   _____

4. Routine newborn care.   _____   _____

5. Nonsterile supply.   _____   _____

6. DME equipment rental.   _____   _____

7. CT head.   _____   _____

8. Lab—hematology.   _____   _____

9. Chest X-ray.   _____   _____

10. Diagnosis mammogram.   _____   _____

11. Room and board—medical, private.

    IV Infusion Supplies.

    IV Drugs.

	Code	Description
	_____	_____
	_____	_____
	_____	_____
	_____	_____
	_____	_____

12. Room and board—medical, semiprivate.

    Chest X-ray.

    Lab—chemistry.

	Code	Description
	_____	_____
	_____	_____
	_____	_____
	_____	_____
	_____	_____

Notes

13. Room and board—mICU, private.

Chest X-ray.

Lab—chemistry.

EKG.

EEG.

Spirometry.

Code	Description
____	____
____	____
____	____
____	____
____	____

14. Room and board—medical, private.

IV Pharmacy Drugs.

IV Supplies.

Chest X-ray.

CT Scan Abdomen.

Code	Description
____	____
____	____
____	____
____	____
____	____

15. Room and board—medical, private.

Peripheral Vascular Study.

MRI Brain.

EKG.

Code	Description
____	_____
____	_____
____	_____
____	_____
____	_____

Complete FL 42-49 for each of the following scenarios:

1. 4 days semiprivate, 2 bed days, $880 per day.
EKG done on 04/01/20xx, 93010, $200.
Clinical lab tests, total $2,892.46.

42 REV. CD.	43 DESCRIPTION	44 HCPCS / RATES	45 SERV. DATE	46 SERV. UNITS	47 TOTAL CHARGES	48 NON-COVERED CHARGES	49
1							1
2							2
3							3
4							4
5							5
6							6
7							7
8							8
9							9
10							10
11							11
12							12
13							13
14							14
15							15
16							16
17							17
18							18
19							19
20							20
21							21
22							22
23							23

Notes

Chest X-rays, 2, done 04/01 and 04/02, 71020-TC, total $240.

Medical supplies, total $737.20.

Pharmacy, total $3,788.94.

2. Seven days, semiprivate, 2 bed days, $880 per day, 08/17-08/23/20xx.

Minor surgery room charge, 08/17/20xx, $890.

Surgical supplies, 08/17/20xx, $870.

Medical supplies, total $3,450.

Pharmacy supplies, $8,453.

Clinical lab tests, total $1,783.50.

Pathology lab tests, total $837.

42 REV. CD.	43 DESCRIPTION	44 HCPCS / RATES	45 SERV. DATE	46 SERV. UNITS	47 TOTAL CHARGES	48 NON-COVERED CHARGES	49
1							1
2							2
3							3
4							4
5							5
6							6
7							7
8							8
9							9
10							10
11							11
12							12
13							13
14							14
15							15
16							16
17							17
18							18
19							19
20							20
21							21
22							22
23							23

3. Five days, inpatient rehab facility, $500 per day, 01/02/20xx–01/06/20xx.

Physical therapy, 01/02/20xx–01/05/20xx, $80 per day.

Medical supplies, total $350.

Pharmacy supplies, $253.

42 REV. CD.	43 DESCRIPTION	44 HCPCS / RATES	45 SERV. DATE	46 SERV. UNITS	47 TOTAL CHARGES	48 NON-COVERED CHARGES	49	
1								1
2								2
3								3
4								4
5								5
6								6
7								7
8								8
9								9
10								10
11								11
12								12
13								13
14								14
15								15
16								16
17								17
18								18
19								19
20								20
21								21
22								22
23								23

Notes

4. Three days, coronary care, myocardial infarction, $1,500 per day. 05/01/20xx–05/03/20xx.

   Operating room charge, 05/01/20xx, $3,500.

   Surgical supplies, 05/01/20xx, $4,870.

   Medical supplies, total $5,400.

   Pharmacy supplies, $9,700.

   Clinical lab tests, total $3,555.50.

   Pathology lab tests, total $837.

   EKG, 3, code 93010, $200 each, 05/01/20xx, 05/02/20xx, 05/03/20xx.

   Chest X-ray, 71020, $120, 05/01/20xx.

42 REV. CD.	43 DESCRIPTION	44 HCPCS / RATES	45 SERV. DATE	46 SERV. UNITS	47 TOTAL CHARGES	48 NON-COVERED CHARGES	49
1							1
2							2
3							3
4							4
5							5
6							6
7							7
8							8
9							9
10							10
11							11
12							12
13							13
14							14
15							15
16							16
17							17
18							18
19							19
20							20
21							21
22							22
23							23

Notes

5. Two days, semiprivate, 2 bed days, $880 per day, 04/04/20xx–04/06/20xx.
Medical supplies, total $1,750.
Pharmacy supplies, $783.
Clinical lab tests, total $883.50.
Pathology lab tests, total $237.

42 REV. CD.	43 DESCRIPTION	44 HCPCS / RATES	45 SERV. DATE	46 SERV. UNITS	47 TOTAL CHARGES	48 NON-COVERED CHARGES	49
1							1
2							2
3							3
4							4
5							5
6							6
7							7
8							8
9							9
10							10
11							11
12							12
13							13
14							14
15							15
16							16
17							17
18							18
19							19
20							20
21							21
22							22
23							23

FL 50-66:   THIRD-PARTY INFORMATION (PAYER, INSURED, EMPLOYER)

The payer field in FL 50 indicates responsibility for payment processing of the claim. Sequencing carriers correctly is essential to proper payment and processing. For instance, while Medicare is primary in a number of instances, there are also cases where Medicare is secondary—such as the **Working Aged**, those Medicare-eligible patients who also possess group health insurance coverage through an employer. In such instances, the group health insurance will be listed in FL 50, Line A as primary, and Medicare will be listed FL 50, Line B as secondary.

Many times children will have insurance through both parents, in which case the **birthday rule** applies. The rule specifies that if coverage for a child is through both parents, the carrier of the parent whose birthday is closer to the child's birthday (first by month, then by day if necessary) will be primary. This means that children in the same household covered by both parents' insurances may have different primary and secondary carriers.

The Assignment of Benefits Certification Indicator (FL 53) determines where payment will be sent. In the event an assignment of benefits was not obtained by the facility or provider, "N" will be marked in FL 53 and payment for services on the claim will be sent to the patient.

The Insured's Name indicated in FL 58 should indicate the name of the individual who has the coverage listed in FL 50 (Payer). Lines A, B and C should correspond to the name of the insured name or the policyholder for each of the insurances listed in 50 A, B and C. The Patient's Relationship to Insured (FL 59) should correspond as well, as should the rest of the fields in this section (FL 60-66).

Figure 3–8 shows FL 50-66 of the UB-92/CMS-1450 form and Table 3–7 provides instructions for completing this section of the form.

Figure 3–8 Form Locators 50-66.

TABLE 3–7   UB-92 COMPLETION DETAILS PAYER/INSURED/EMPLOYER INFO (FL 50-66).

FL #	Field Name	Specifics	# Digits	Digits (A)lpha (N)um	Medicare (R)eq (O)pt	Others (R)eq (O)pt
50	Payer Identification	A Primary Payer B Secondary Payer C Tertiary Payer Electronic must include Payer ID# Paper must include Carrier Code# and Name (Available from FI)	25	A/N	R	R
51	Provider Number	Assigned by Payer listed in 50		A/N	R	R most
52	Release of Information Certification Indicator	Y - Yes (On File) N - No (Not on File) R - Restricted (Limited Authority)	1	A	R	R most
53	Assignment of Benefits Certification Indicator	Y - Yes/Benefits Assigned Payment to Provider N - No/Benefits Not Assigned Payment to Insured	1	A	R	R
54	Prior Payments-Payers and Pt	All services other than Medicare Inpt 7 positions - dollars 2 positions - cents 1 position - character space for credit if applicable	10	N Outpt	R	R
55	Estimated Amount Due	Estimated Due from Payer - Any Payments 10 positions in each line (A-D) 7 positions - dollars 2 positions - cents 1 position - character space for credit if applicable	10	N	NO	
56-57	Unlabeled Fields					
58	Insured's Name	Patient or Policyholder 25 characters Line A-D Must be exactly as on insurance card Use comma to separate names No titles	25	A/N	R	R
59	Patient's Relationship to Insured		2	N	R Care 2nd	R
		01 - Patient Insured 02 - Spouse 03 - Natural Child 04 - Natural Child/Insured Not Responsible				

(continued)

FL #	Field Name	Specifics	# Digits	Digits (A)lpha (N)um	Medicare (R)eq (O)pt	Others (R)eq (O)pt
		05 - Stepchild				
		06 - Foster Child				
		07 - Ward of Court				
		08 - Employee				
		09 - Unknown				
		10 - Handicapped Dependent				
		11 - Organ Donor				
		12 - Cadaver Donor				
		13 - Grandchild				
		14 - Niece/Nephew				
		15 - Insured Plaintiff				
		16 - Sponsored Dependent				
		17 - Minor Dependent of a Minor Dependent				
		18 - Parent				
		19 - Grandparent				
		20 - Life Partner				
		21-99 Reserved National Assignment				
60	Certificate/Social Security #/ Health Insurance Claim #	No spaces/hyphens/characters	19	A/N	R	R
61	Insured Group Name		14	A/N	R	R If Applicable
62	Insured Group Number		17	A/N	NO	NO
63	Treatment Authorization Codes		18	A/N	R	NO
64	Employment Status Code of the Insured			N	R MSP	NO
		1 - Employed Full-Time				
		2 - Employed Part-Time				
		3 - Not Employed				
		4 - Self-Employed				
		5 - Retired				
		6 - Active Military Duty				
		7-8 Reserved National Assignment				
65	Employer Name of the Insured		24	A/N	R	R
66	Employer Location of the Insured	Can be specific city, employer location 35 AlphaNum per Line (A-C)	35	A/N	R	

PRACTICE EXERCISE 3–7

Determine the (P)rimary Carrier, (S)econdary Carrier and (T)ertiary Carrier in these instances:

1. Patient has Medicare/Medicaid coverage. _____

2. Patient has Aetna Insurance and the encounter is related to a Workers' Compensation injury through Risk Management Insurance, employer ABC Medical Supply. _____

3. Child covered by Medicaid as well as mother's insurance: Aetna through employer. _____

4. Patient has Medicare/Medicaid coverage; services provided not covered by Medicare, but covered by Medicaid. _____

5. Seventy-three-year-old patient, employed, has Aetna through employer, as well as Medicare coverage. _____

6. Child, DOB 05/18/xxxx, covered by mother's and father's insurance as follows:
    Mother: Aetna, DOB 05/01/19xx.
    Father: CIGNA, DOB 10/03/19xx. _____

7. Patient has coverage through employer as well as through spouse's employer. _____

8. Patient has auto insurance as well as health insurance coverage. Encounter is for X-rays related to auto accident. _____

9. Child lives with father and has insurance coverage through mother. _____

10. Child lives with father and has insurance coverage through both mother and father. _____

FL 67-81: DIAGNOSIS/PROCEDURE CODES

Diagnosis and procedure codes listed in these form locator fields 67-81 are ICD-9-CM diagnostic codes (FL 67-77) and ICD-9-CM procedural codes (FL 80-81) only. CPT-4/HCPCS codes should be utilized in Form Locator 44 (HCPCS/Rates) only when appropriate. These fields contain patient clinical information necessary in processing charges for payment. These diagnostic and procedure codes assist in the determination of medical necessity for services rendered. We will discuss the appropriate coding and assignment of diagnosis/procedure codes later on, when we cover hospital coding systems.

The Principal Procedure Code and Date (FL 80) is used to identify the most significant procedure performed and, usually, the procedure that most closely relates to the principal diagnosis.

Because different coding systems are utilized by third-party carriers, FL 79 (Procedure Coding Method Used) is utilized to identify the methods used on the current claim form.

Figure 3–9 shows FL 67-82 of the UB-92/CMS-1450 form and Table 3–8 provides instructions for completing this section of the form.

Figure 3–9 Form Locators 67-81.

TABLE 3–8   UB-92 COMPLETION DETAILS DIAGNOSIS/PROCEDURE CODES (FL 67-81).

FL #	Field Name	Specifics	# Digits	Digits (A)lpha (N)um	Medicare (R)eq (O)pt	Others (R)eq (O)pt
67	Principal Diagnosis Code	Condition established after study chiefly responsible for resulting in hospital admission or hospital services Cannot be E Code	6	A/N	R	R
68-75	Other Diagnosis Codes	Patient condition(s) that co-exist at the time of admission/service or develop during the hospital stay or encounter	6	A/N	R If Applicable	R If Applicable

FL #	Field Name	Specifics	# Digits	Digits (A)lpha (N)um	Medicare (R)eq (O)pt	Others (R)eq (O)pt
76	Admitting Diagnosis/Patient's Reason for Visit	ICDD-9-CM that best describes the patient's diagnosis or reason for visit in the patient's words	6	A/N	R	R
77	External Cause of Injury	External cause for injury, poisoning, adverse effect	6	A/N Reg	State Reg	State
78	Unlabeled Field					
79	Procedure Coding Method Used	1-3 Reserved State Assignment 4 CPT-4 5 HCPCS 6-8 Reserved National Assignment 9 ICD-9-CM		A/N	NO	R
80	Principal Procedure Code/Date	Inpatient principal procedure	7/Proc 8/Date	A/N Inpt Surgery	R	R
81	Other Procedure Code/Date	Additional inpatient procedures or outpt procedures when applicable	7/Proc 8/Date	A/N	R If Applic- able	R If Applic- able

FL 82-83:   ATTENDING PHYSICIAN INFORMATION

Fields 82-83 are utilized for listing the physicians or providers that are primarily responsible for the patient during the encounter or admission. Typically the attending physician is the provider who admits the patient and establishes their treatment plan. FL 83 is utilized to identify the provider of the principal procedure listed.

Medicare and many other carriers require the listing of a **UPIN** (Unique Physician Identification Number) in field 82. This number is assigned by the **Center for Medicare and Medicaid Services (CMS)** as a unique identifier for every physician in the nation. When patients are seen by interns, residents and in the emergency departments, the UPIN would be assigned as follows:

SLF000   **Emergency Room Self-Referrals**

INT000   **Interns**

RES000   **Residents**

PHS000   **Public Health Service Physicians**

Notes
_____
_____
_____
_____
_____
_____
_____
_____
_____
_____

VAD000   Department of Veterans Affairs Physicians

RET000   Retired Physicians

OTH000   Other

BIA   Bureau of Indian Affairs

If the physician indicated in FL 82 is the same as for FL 83, the number should be repeated rather than left blank.

Figure 3–10 shows FL 82-83 of the UB-92/CMS-1450 form and Table 3–9 provides instructions for completing this section of the form.

Figure 3–10 Form Locators 82-83.

TABLE 3–9   UB-92 COMPLETION DETAILS ATTENDING PHYSICIAN INFORMATION (FL 82-83).

FL #	Field Name	Specifics	# Digits	Digits (A)lpha (N)um	Medicare (R)eq (O)pt	Others (R)eq (O)pt
82	Attending Physician ID	Physician primarily responsible for patient's medical care/ treatment FORMAT: UPIN__LastName_First Name_MI	25	A/N	R	R
83	Other Physician ID	Name of other than attending Physician performing principal procedure First line optional exc Medicare Lower line required if procedure inpatient/outpatient claims	25/upper 32/lower	A/N		

Notes

FL 84-86:   REMARK SECTION

The Remarks field (FL 84) is utilized as a "miscellaneous" field for overflow or information that does not fit in other field locator areas. On Medicare claims, this field is often utilized to report noncovered days that are not explainable by Occurrence Codes such as FL 20, 21 and 22. This field is also used when an unlisted CPT-4 code must be utilized on an outpatient claim; the description of the corresponding service should be listed in FL 84. This field is also used for overflow in the event the occurrence code and dates, occurrence span codes and dates, and value codes and amounts fields are insufficient for reporting purposes. Formatting would be as follows:

FL Number: Code Number, Dates or Values

24:                     17

The signature of the provider representative signifies that the physician's certification is on file at the facility. Some carriers will accept a facsimile signature, including Medicare, which will accept a signature stamp. Check with individual carriers before permitting the use of anything other than a signature in this field.

Figure 3–11 shows FL 84-86 of the UB-92/CMS-1450 form and Table 3–10 provides instructions for completing this section of the form.

Figure 3–11 Form Locators 84-86.

TABLE 3–10   UB-92 COMPLETION DETAILS REMARKS (FL 84-86).

FL #	Field Name	Specifics	# Digits	Digits (A)lpha (N)um	Medicare (R)eq (O)pt	Others (R)eq (O)pt
84	Remarks	Explain reason for reporting noncovered days OR Overflow information FL 32-35, FL 36, FL 24-30 and FL 39-41 Format Ex: FL XX: Code, Date, Value	48	A/N	R If Applicable	R
85	Provider Representative Signature	Signature certifies provider conforms with certifications on UB-92	22	A/N	R	R
86	Date Bill Submitted	Date UB-92 Signed/Sent to Payer	10	N	No	R

Notes

_____

_____

_____

_____

_____

_____

_____

_____

_____

_____

_____

CHAPTER SUMMARY EXERCISES

Additional exercises in the completion of the UB-92 are included in the CD-ROM located in the back of the text. Case scenarios and complete UB-92 forms are included in these exercises.

Review the case scenarios, assigning the appropriate ICD-9-CM diagnostic and procedural codes and CPT-4 and HCPCS codes, then complete the UB-92 form for these services. Make certain the UB-92 form is completed according to guidelines for inpatient or outpatient facility service, as applicable. Any additional information needed to complete these forms can be found in the Inpatient and Outpatient Coding/Billing sections of this textbook.

These case scenarios may be completed now or at the conclusion of the Inpatient and Outpatient Coding/Billing sections, where a more thorough review of completing inpatient and outpatient UB-92 forms is provided.

CONCLUSION

After finishing this chapter, you should be able to complete a basic UB-92/CMS 1450 form and understand the requirements for completion of each of the form locators on it. Individual requirements for fields, such as revenue codes, condition codes, and occurrence codes, should be understood, as well as the importance of completing the UB-92 without errors or omissions for appropriate and timely payment for services rendered.

Section II

Inpatient Coding/ Billing

Chapter 4
Inpatient Coding

KEY TERMS

Admitting Diagnosis
Complications and
   Comorbidities (CCs)

Diagnosis Related Group (DRG)
Encoding Software
Query Process

LEARNING OBJECTIVES

- Apply the use of appropriate inpatient coding tools
- Explain the basic ICD-9-CM inpatient diagnostic coding guidelines
- Describe the difference between principal, secondary, and admitting diagnosis
- Demonstrate the appropriate use of complications and comorbidity codes
- Explain the use of the query process in obtaining appropriate documentation for inpatient coding assignment
- Describe additional diagnostic coding considerations for inpatient use
- Discuss the guidelines for assigning ICD-9-CM procedure code

ICD-9-CM DIAGNOSTIC CODING TOOLS

Facility inpatient coding is based on the premise that the facility should be reimbursed for the resources it expends in evaluating and treating the patient. While the physician codes and bills for professional services performed, the facility is coding and billing for resources such as room, board, operating room, technical services, and supplies and materials.

The inpatient coding process depends solely on the assignment of ICD-9-CM diagnostic and procedural codes for billing and appropriate reimbursement. The correct assignment of an appropriate principal diagnosis—i.e., the condition determined after diagnostic and therapeutic

_____

_____

_____

_____

_____

_____

studies to be chiefly responsible for the hospital admission—will determine whether appropriate payment is made. Due to the complexity of the hospital inpatient process, a number of diagnoses and diagnostic statements are made during the course of the hospitalization. All chart documentation must be reviewed and a preliminary listing of principal diagnoses established. This requires review of a massive amount of data. Often a clinical background or a solid knowledge of anatomy, physiology and pharmacology is helpful.

Tools such as those illustrated in Tables 4–1 and 4–2 and Figure 4–1 are helpful when evaluating the inpatient hospital record. In addition, many facilities, especially larger ones, utilize **encoding software** that not only allows the coder to enter the diagnosis and procedures, but also assists in assigning the correct ICD-9-CM diagnostic and procedural codes and applying coding principles correctly to obtain the optimal principal diagnosis for DRG assignment.

TABLE 4–1   Laboratory Values.

	Male	Female
Hematology/Coagulation Studies		
Red Blood Cells (RBCs)	4.5–6.2	4.2–5.4
Hematocrit (HCT)	40–54	37–47
Hemoglobin (Hgb)	13.5–18	12–16
MCV (mean corpuscular volume)	80–94	84–99
MCH (mean corpuscular Hgb)	26–34	26–34
MCHC (mean corpuscular Hgb concentrate)	32–36	32–36
White Blood Cells (WBCs)	5,000–10,000	5,000–10,000
Differential WBCs		
Neutrophils	48–77 (3,000–7,500/mm)	48–77 (3,000–7,500/mm)
Bands	3–8 (150–700/mm)	3–8 (150–700/mm)
Eosinophils	1–4 (50–400/mm)	1–4 (50–400/mm)
Basophils	0–1 (25–100/mm)	0–1 (25–100/mm)
Monocytes	1–9 (100–500/mm)	1–9 (100–500/mm)
Lymphtocutes	25–40 (1,500–4,500/mm)	25–40 (1,500–4,500/mm)
T Lymphocytes	60–80% lymphocytes	60–80% lymphocytes
B Lymphocytes	10–20% of lymphocytes	10–20% of lymphocytes
Platelets	150,000–450,000/mm	150,000–450,000/mm
Bleeding Time	3–9 minutes	3–9 minutes
Prothrombin Time (PT)	9.6–11.8 seconds	9.5–11.3 seconds
Partial Thromboplastin Time (PTT)	25–38 seconds	25–38 seconds
Whole Blood Clotting Time	5–15 minutes	5–15 minutes
Thrombin Time	10–15 seconds	10–15 seconds

	Male	*Female*
Cardiac Enzymes		
CK-MB	0.7 U/L >0.05 fraction of Total CK Taken at 4–6 hours and 18–24 hours	0.7 U/L >0.05 fraction of Total CK Taken at 4–6 hours and 18–24 hours
LDH1	29–37% 0.15–0.40 Fraction of Total Taken at 48 hours and 4–6 days	29–37% 0.15–0.40 Fraction of Total Taken at 48 hours and 4–6 days
LDH2	42–48 % 0.20–0.45 Fraction of Total Taken at 48 hours and 4–6 days	42–48 % 0.20–0.45 Fraction of Total Taken at 48 hours and 4–6 days
SGOT, AST	7–27 U/L Taken at 8–12 hours and repeat at 48 hours	7–27 U/L Taken at 8–12 hours and repeat at 48 hours
Electrolytes		
Calcium	4.5–5.5 mEq/L Increased Ranges: Respiratory Acidosis Bacteremia Kidney Disorders Hepatic Disease	4.5–5.5 mEq/L Decreased Ranges: GI Malabsorption Alkalosis Burns Cachexia Celiac Disease Chronic Renal Disease Diarrhea
Potassium	3.5–5.3 mEq/L Increased Ranges: Acidosis Adrenocorticol Insufficiency Anemia Asthma Burns Dialysis Dysrhythmia Hypoventilations	3.5–5.3 mEq/L Decreased Ranges: Vomiting Diarrhea Kidney Disorder Intestinal Fistula Alcoholism Alkalosis Bradycardia Colon Cancer Chest Pain Chronic Cirrhosis Congestive Heart Failure Chron's Disease

(continued)

TABLE 4–1 *continued*

	Male	*Female*
Sodium	135–145 mEq/L Increased Ranges: Congestive Heart Failure Diabetes Insipidus Diaphoresis Diarrhea Hypertension Ostomies Toxemia Vomiting	135–145 mEq/L Decreased Ranges: GI Malabsorption Diarrhea Ascites in Cardiac Failure Bowel Obstruction Burns Chest Pain Cirrhosis Diabetes Mellitus Emphysema
Chloride	97–107 mEq/L Increased Ranges: Alcoholism Respiratory Acidosis Anemia Congestive Heart Failure Dehydration Fever Head Trauma	97–107 mEq/L Decreased Ranges: Metabolic Acidosis Burns Central Nervous System Disorders Edema Emphysema GI Loss
Magnesium	1.5–2.5 mEq/L Increased Ranges: Renal Disease Renal Failure Diabetic Ketoacidosis Hyperparathyroidism	1.5/2.5 mEq/L Decreased Ranges: Use of Drugs Chronic Alcoholism
Phosphate	2.5–4.5 mEq/L Increased Ranges: Renal Failure Hypoparathyroidism Trauma Heat Stroke	2.5–4.5 mEq/L Decreased Ranges: Alkalosis Diabetes Mellitus Chronic Alcoholism Malnutrition Diarrhea

Arterial Blood Gas Values

Value	Normal Range	Respiratory Acidosis	Respiratory Alkalosis
Ph	7.35–7.45	<7.35	>7.45
PCO2	35–45 mmHg	>45 mmHg	<35 mmHg
HCO3	22–28 mEq/L	<22 mEq/L Metabolic	>28 mEq/L Metabolic

TABLE 4–2   Common Documentation Abbreviations.

ABG	*Arterial Blood Gas*
Ac	before meals
ADL	activities of daily living
Ad Lib	as desired
AP	anterior and posterior
ASHD	arteriosclerotic heart disease
AV	arteriovenous, atrioventricular
Bid	twice a day
Bpm	beats per minute
$\bar{C}$	with
CAD	coronary artery disease
cc	cubic centimeter, chief complaint
cm	Centimeter
CSF	cerebrospinal fluid
C & S	culture and sensitivity
FUO	fever of unknown original
G or gm	Gram
Gt, Gtt	Drops
H	Hour
HS	at bedtime
IM	Intramuscular
IV	Intravenous
KUB	kidneys, ureters, bladder
KVO	keep vein open
L	Liter
lb	Pound
LLQ	left lower quadrant
LUQ	left upper quadrant
M	Meter
mg	Milligram
mcg	Microgram
ml	Milliliter
mm	Millimeter
NPO	nothing by mouth
OD	right eye
OS	left eye
OTC	over the counter
OU	both eyes
oz	Ounce
pc	after meals
PERRLA	pupils equal, round, reactive to light and accommodation
po	by mouth
prn	as needed

(continued)

TABLE 4–2 *continued*

ABG	Arterial Blood Gas
PTCA	percutaneous transluminal coronary angioplasty
q	every
q am	every morning
qid	four times a day
qod	every other day
R/O	rule out
ROM	range of motion
RLQ	right lower quadrant
RUQ	right upper quadrant
rx	prescription
$\bar{s}$	without
sq	subcutaneous
SOB	shortness of breath
stat	immediately
supp	suppository
T & C	type and crossmatch
tid	three times a day
tsp	teaspoon
UA	urinalysis
URI	upper respiratory infection
UTI	urinary tract infection

INPATIENT ICD-9-CM DIAGNOSTIC CODING

While the assignment of actual ICD-9-CM codes is the same for both inpatient and outpatient facility records, the selection of those codes varies dramatically. Selecting the principal diagnosis is foremost in the inpatient coding process. This principal diagnosis guides the assignment of a DRG code for reimbursement purposes, and therefore is integral to proper payment.

Here are some general guidelines in the correct selection of a principal diagnosis:

1. The principal diagnosis is not the admitting diagnosis, but rather the diagnosis found after workup and/or surgery.
2. When two or more diagnoses meet the definition for principal diagnosis equally, and ICD-9-CM diagnosis guidelines do not direct otherwise, the coder may assign in any order. However, when treatment is directed towards one condition (such as surgery), that condition would be assigned as the principal diagnosis.

INPATIENT HOSPITAL CODING DOCUMENTATION REVIEW

Patient Name: Admit Date:
                                       Discharge Date: Status:

DIAGNOSTIC INFORMATION: PREVIOUS DIAGNOSES:
Diagnostic Statements:

_____   _____
_____   _____
_____   _____
_____   _____
_____
_____
_____
_____
_____   ANCILLARY TESTS/RESULTS
                                       Pathology:
Principal Diagnosis:
_____   _____
                                       _____
Secondary Diagnoses: _____
_____
_____
_____   Radiology:
_____
_____   _____
_____   _____
                                       _____
Admitting Diagnosis: Ancillary (Other):
_____
                                       _____
PROCEDURE INFORMATION   _____
_____   _____
_____   _____
_____
_____   Patient Age:
Principal Procedure: CCs: Yes_____ No _____
_____
                                       DRG ASSIGNMENT:
Secondary Procedure(s):
_____   _____
_____
_____
_____

Figure 4–1 Sample of Worksheet to Capture Inpatient Coding Information.

_____

_____

_____

_____

_____

_____

_____

_____

_____

_____

_____

_____

_____

_____

_____

_____

_____

_____

3. When contrasting conditions are listed as either/or, both diagnoses are coded as though confirmed, with the rules regarding principal diagnosis governing which, if either, will be assigned as principal diagnosis.

4. When symptoms as well as comparative/contrasting diagnoses are listed, the symptom would be assigned first, unless it is an integral part of one or more of the diagnoses. Again, keep in mind that ICD-9-CM diagnostic coding rules are always primary in the consideration of coding assignment.

5. When the original treatment plan is not carried out during the admission yet still remains the primary reason for the admission, it would still be considered the principal diagnosis.

Try applying the above coding guidelines to determine the principal diagnoses in the following exercises.

PRACTICE EXERCISE 4–1

Determine the principal diagnosis and assign ICD-9-CM code(s) for all appropriate diagnoses:

1. Patient admitted for acute bronchitis.
   During admission found to be result of COPD.
   Cough.
   Fever.

   Principal Diagnosis: _____ Code: _____

   Secondary Diagnosis: _____ Code: _____

   Secondary Diagnosis: _____ Code: _____

   Secondary Diagnosis: _____ Code: _____

2. Patient admitted for shortness of breath.
   Chest x-ray, arterial blood gas indicate congestive heart failure.
   Patient also has diabetes mellitus, hypertension, chronic renal failure.

   Principal Diagnosis: _____ Code: _____

   Secondary Diagnosis: _____ Code: _____

Secondary Diagnosis: _____ Code: _____

Secondary Diagnosis: _____ Code: _____

3. Lump, right breast.
Excision of breast mass.
Surgical pathology indicating malignant neoplasm, breast,
left outer quadrant.
Acute anemia due to blood loss.

Principal Diagnosis: _____ Code: _____

Secondary Diagnosis: _____ Code: _____

Secondary Diagnosis: _____ Code: _____

Secondary Diagnosis: _____ Code: _____

4. Patient who is 2 months pregnant, wishes therapeutic abortion.
Due to her advanced maternal age, she will be admitted for
therapeutic abortion.

Principal Diagnosis: _____ Code: _____

Secondary Diagnosis: _____ Code: _____

Secondary Diagnosis: _____ Code: _____

Secondary Diagnosis: _____ Code: _____

5. Patient admitted for possible intracranial injury as the result of falling
from ladder during the course of painting house. During the course of
the hospitalization, the patient was also treated for open wounds to the
arm and leg as well as contusions to the cheek.

Principal Diagnosis: _____ Code: _____

Secondary Diagnosis: _____ Code: _____

Secondary Diagnosis: _____ Code: _____

Secondary Diagnosis: _____ Code: _____

6. Patient admitted to hospital as a result of a staph infection. Patient has been seen in physician's office for urinary retention, and staph infection resulted from catheter. Patient had catheter removed in the emergency room and was started on antibiotics, switched to oral antibiotics and released.

    Principal Diagnosis: _____ Code: _____

    Secondary Diagnosis: _____ Code: _____

    Secondary Diagnosis: _____ Code: _____

    Secondary Diagnosis: _____ Code: _____

7. Patient admitted for open reduction, internal fixation of a closed fracture of the left distal radius as a result of a fall while roller-skating.

    Principal Diagnosis: _____ Code: _____

    Secondary Diagnosis: _____ Code: _____

    Secondary Diagnosis: _____ Code: _____

    Secondary Diagnosis: _____ Code: _____

8. Patient admitted with epigastric pain, believed to be due from Barrett's esophagus. Performed upper GI endoscopy, where an esophageal stricture was diagnosed and dilated during the GI endoscopy.

    Principal Diagnosis: _____ Code: _____

    Secondary Diagnosis: _____ Code: _____

    Secondary Diagnosis: _____ Code: _____

    Secondary Diagnosis: _____ Code: _____

9. Twenty-four-year-old female admitted with fatigue, loss of appetite and cough for approximately one month. Culture showed E coli pneumonia. Patient experienced extreme shortness of breath, required nebulizer treatments. Chest x-ray confirmed E coli pneumonia and

Notes

the patient was treated further with nebulizer treatments and IV antiobiotics for 4 days and then released.

Principal Diagnosis: _____ Code: _____

Secondary Diagnosis: _____ Code: _____

Secondary Diagnosis: _____ Code: _____

Secondary Diagnosis: _____ Code: _____

10. Patient admitted with acute low back pain, elevated WBC, with suspected appendicitis. Patient taken to surgery on hospital day 2, where an appendectomy was performed. The appendix had ruptured and generalized peritonitis was diagnosed. Patient was started on IV antibiotics for 4 days postoperatively and released.

Principal Diagnosis: _____ Code: _____

Secondary Diagnosis: _____ Code: _____

Secondary Diagnosis: _____ Code: _____

Secondary Diagnosis: _____ Code: _____

ADDITIONAL ICD-9-CM DIAGNOSTIC CODING GUIDELINES

In addition to the rules for determining principal diagnosis, there are a number of other general diagnostic coding guidelines that must be considered when assigning codes for inpatient charts.

1. Previous conditions stated in the diagnostic statement should only be coded when they have an impact on the current care or treatment. Conditions that are no longer present, such as "history of" or "status post," should only be assigned as such when they influence the current care or treatment; otherwise, it is not necessary to report these conditions.

2. Diagnosis with no documentation to report or substantiation should not be coded. If the coder feels the condition was present during the

Notes

admission and played an integral role in the treatment and care, the physician should be queried.

3. Chronic conditions that are not involved in the treatment or do not influence the care during the current episode, yet still require evaluation and monitoring, should be coded; however, they do not meet the criteria of a principal diagnosis.

4. Conditions that are considered a sign or symptom of a disease process need not be coded.

5. Conditions that are documented only as a sign or symptom and are an integral component of the treatment or care during the episode of care should be assigned the appropriate ICD-9-CM diagnositic codes.

6. Abnormal conditions or findings should be assigned codes only when the physician has been unable to determine a specific diagnosis, but indicates that the abnormal condition had an impact on the care and treatment during the admission. Care should be taken to not assign codes for such abnormal findings as laboratory or radiological findings based solely on the lab or radiological value, since these do not always indicate a significant finding.

In light of these additional guidelines, check your answers in Practice Exercise 4–1 to make certain that the principal diagnoses and secondary diagnoses you selected are still appropriate.

Admitting Diagnosis

The **admitting diagnosis** is reported on the billing form (UB-92) for inpatient hospital; however, it is not necessarily the principal diagnosis. The admitting diagnosis usually involves:

- A sign or symptom that prompted the patient's arrival for the encounter or episode of care.
- A working diagnosis based on findings such as lab and x-ray.
- An injury or accident.
- Encounter for other than illness or injury, such as normal pregnancy, need for inoculation, or postoperative exam.

Typically, an admitting diagnosis:

- Should reflect the diagnosis provided by the admitting physician at the time of admission.
- Should not be changed to coincide with the principal diagnosis, or vice versa.

PRACTICE EXERCISE 4–2

Take a look at the following scenarios and determine the admitting diagnosis and principal diagnosis for each:

1. Patient admitted with lower abdominal pain, diagnosed during admission as acute pancreatitis.

    Admitting Diagnosis: _____

    Principal Diagnosis: _____

2. Patient admitted with lower abdominal and epigastric pain, nausea, vomiting and diarrhea. Discharge diagnosis was possible gastroenteritis.

    Admitting Diagnosis: _____

    Principal Diagnosis: _____

3. Patient admitted for lower back pain, possible urinary tract infection. Diagnosed during hospitalization with pyelonephritis.

    Admitting Diagnosis: _____

    Principal Diagnosis: _____

4. Patient admitted for malaise, fatigue, increased WBC, for possible upper respiratory infection, due to cough and production of yellow phlegm. Patient diagnosed with pneumonia, culture did not identify organism.

    Admitting Diagnosis: _____

    Principal Diagnosis: _____

5. Patient admitted with chest pain, shortness of breath and possible abnormal cardiac enzymes, with myocardial infarction ruled out. EKG, chest x-ray, and repeat cardiac enzymes returned normal and the patient was discharged 2 days after admission.

    Admitting Diagnosis: _____

    Principal Diagnosis: _____

6. Patient admitted for vaginal hysterectomy due to abnormal uterine bleeding. Hysterectomy was performed, which revealed a massive fibroid in the cervix uteri that was removed as well as the hysterectomy performed abdominally.

   Admitting Diagnosis: _____

   Principal Diagnosis: _____

7. Patient admitted for repair full thickness skin graft to repair area of old burn received approximately 6 months ago as the result of a kitchen fire.

   Admitting Diagnosis: _____

   Principal Diagnosis: _____

8. Patient admitted for shortness of breath, past history of COPD. Patient treated with steroids, nebulizer treatments; CXR performed that showed acute exacerbation of COPD as well as newly diagnosed CHF.

   Admitting Diagnosis: _____

   Principal Diagnosis: _____

9. Patient admitted for possible internal abdominal injuries as the result of an altercation with her husband. Abdominal ultrasound showed the possibility of a contused kidney; however, abdominal pain resolved over the period of 24–48 hours, a follow-up ultrasound was negative and the patient was released home.

   Admitting Diagnosis: _____

   Principal Diagnosis: _____

10. Patient admitted as the result of a gunshot wound to the chest received during a bank robbery. The patient is a bank security guard who attempted to apprehend the burglar and was shot at point-blank range in the upper chest area. Patient was taken to surgery, bullet removed, and the patient was started on IV antibiotics prophylactically.

    Admitting Diagnosis: _____

    Principal Diagnosis: _____

Notes

Specific ICD-9-CM Inpatient Diagnostic Coding Rules

- Code diagnoses stated as possible, probable, likely, or suspected at the time of discharge as if the condition exists. This is due to the fact that the inpatient facility services were the same whether the condition really exists or not.
- Rule-out diagnoses are coded as if the condition exists when stated at the time of discharge. However, "ruled out" indicates that that condition is no longer a possibility and should not be coded.
- Acute conditions should always be sequenced first, as they are considered the chief reason for the admission or episode of care.
- Signs and symptoms should NOT be utilized as principal diagnoses when related diagnoses are established. When no related condition is identified and the symptom is the reason for the encounter, a sign/symptom would be appropriate as the principal diagnosis.
- Aftercare visit codes (V codes) are used when the initial treatment for an injury or disease has been completed, and the patient returns for follow-up or aftercare management.
- Fracture care codes should only be utilized for encounter for initial treatment; then aftercare codes (V codes) should be utilized.
- When a patient is admitted for the purpose of surveillance subsequent to original treatment, a V code for follow-up will be assigned.
- When the encounter or episode of care is primarily for a condition suspected but not found, a V code will be assigned as the principal diagnosis. These codes typically would be only a principal diagnosis, due to the fact that if a condition is found, it would be assigned as principal and the V code would be omitted.

Certain V codes may only be assigned as principal or additional/subsequent codes only. The following represent specific V codes and their specific usage:

Acceptable Only as Principal Diagnosis

- V20   Health Supervision of Infant/Child
- V22.0   Supervision of Normal First Pregnancy
- V22.1   Supervision of Other Normal Pregnancy
- V24   Postpartum Care and Exam
- V29   Observe/Evaluation of Newborn Suspected Conditions Not Found

  (Codes V30–V39 may be coded before V29 on the newborn record only.)
- V30–V39   Liveborn infant based on type of birth
- V58.0   Encounter for Radiotherapy
- V58.1   Encounter for Chemotherapy

Notes

Acceptable Only as Subsequent Diagnosis Code(s)

- V09.x   Infection by Drug-Resistant Microorganisms
- V14.x   Personal History Allergy to Medicinal Agents
- V15.x   Other Personal History Presenting Hazards to Health (Exception: V15.7 Personal History of Contraception)
- V21.x   Constitutional States in Development
- V22.2   Pregnant State, Incidental
- V26.5   Sterilization Status
- V27.x   Outcome of Delivery
- V42.x   Organ/Tissue Replaced by Transplant
- V43.x   Organ/Tissue Replaced by Other Means
- V44.x   Artificial Opening Status
- V45.x   Other Postsurgical States (Exception: V45.7 Acquired Absence of Organ)
- V46.x   Other Dependence of Machines
- V49.6x   Upper Limb Amputation Status
- V49.7x   Lower Limb Amputation Status
- V49.82   Dental Sealant Status
- V60.x   Housing, Household and/or Economic Circumstances
- V62.x   Other Psychosocial Circumstances
- V64.x   Persons Encountering Health Services for Specified Procedure Not Carried Out
- V66.7   Palliative Care

Other V codes may be utilized as principal or subsequent codes as appropriate by coding guidelines.

Complications and Comorbidity Diagnoses

Specific diagnoses are recognized as **complications and comorbidities** (known as "**CCs**") as part of the DRG assignment process. We will discuss the assignment of DRGs or **diagnosis related groups (DRGs)** as part of the inpatient billing process; however, these diagnoses have a significant impact on reimbursement, and the correct assignment of a DRG, a code assigned based on the diagnostic evaluation performed during the patient's inpatient stay. When one of the diagnoses listed in Table 4–3 is listed as a secondary diagnosis, it would be considered a complication or comorbidity that could affect the assignment of the DRG and reimbursement.

As these complications and comorbidities affect reimbursement, it is imperative to review documentation thoroughly and identify clinical findings

Notes

TABLE 4–3   Common Complications and Comorbidities.

Complications and Comorbidities

Alcoholism
Anemia, due to blood loss, acute/chronic
Angina Pectoris
Atrial Fibrillation/Flutter
Atelectasis
Cachexia
Cardiogenic Shock
Cardiomyopathy
Cellulitis
Congestive Heart Failure (CHF)
Chronic Obstructive Pulmonary Disease (COPD)
Decubitus Ulcer
Dehydration
Diabetes Mellitus, Insulin Dependent (IDDM)
Furuncles
Hematuria
Hematemesis
Hypertensive Heart Disease with CHF
Hyponatremia
Malnutrition
Melena
Pelural Effusion
Pneumothorax
Renal Failure, Acute/Chronic
Respiratory Failure
Urinary Retention
Urinary Tract Infection

and/or diagnosis of these conditions. If the diagnostic statement is not documented by the physician, a query may need to be made requesting additional clarification.

The Query Process

The **query process** has met with much conflict with third-party carriers. When querying or questioning the physician, the coder must be certain that questions are not directed in a manner that influences the answers given by the physician. The coder may not lead the physician or ask for a specific diagnosis during the process. Some carriers discourage this process, and when the query process is utilized, there are specific requirements regarding the documentation obtained and how it should be incorporated into the medical record.

In certain principal diagnoses, certain complications and comorbidities would not be considered complications, since these conditions are closely related or an integral part of the principal diagnosis. The following guidelines are utilized for making the determination whether these conditions should be coded as secondary diagnoses:

- Chronic or acute manifestations of the same condition should NOT be coded.
- Nonspecific diagnosis codes for a condition should NOT be considered complications and comorbidities for each other.
- Conditions that cannot coexist, such as unilateral and bilateral or benign and malignant, should not be considered as CCs for each other.
- The same condition in anatomical proximity should not be considered as a CC.
- Closely related conditions should not be considered as CCs to each other.

SPECIAL INPATIENT ICD-9-CM CODING CONSIDERATIONS

In addition to the general ICD-9-CM diagnostic coding guidelines, there are other guidelines specific to certain coding scenarios. These are listed in order of the ICD-9-CM diagnostic category.

Infectious and Parasitic Diseases

Infections are classified by body site and organism. Organisms may be bacteria, parasites, fungi and/or viruses. The location of the infection often suggests the common pathogen causing the infection, as illustrated in Table 4–4.

Bacteremia vs. Septicemia

Bacteremia is defined as the presence of bacteria that have entered the bloodstream after injury or mild infection. Septicemia is a systemic infection that can lead to death if not treated aggressively. Documentation that might be present in the medical record that would substantiate septicemia would be treatment with IV antibiotics and the use of medications to raise blood pressure. Septicemia is classified by the underlying organism, with bacterial septicemia coded as category 038, further divided based on the identified bacteria. Code 038.9 is utilized when the specific organism is not identified or not documented.

Notes

TABLE 4–4   Common Infection Pathogens.

Infection Origin	Common Cause
Arteriovenous Shunt	S. aureus, S. epidermidis
Biliary Tract	E. coli, Klebsiella, Enterococci
Burn Wounds Early	Streptococci, S. aureus
Burn Wounds Later	Gram-negative bacilli
Cellulitis, Wound	S. aureus, Streptococci
Osteomyelitis	S. aureus, gram-negative, high-risk patients
Pelvic Abscess	Anaerobic streptococci, E. coli, Enterococci
Peritonitis	E. coli, Klebsiella, Enterococci
Intra-Abdominal Abscess	E. coli, Klebsiella, Enterococci
Urinary Tract Infection	E. coli, Klebsiella, Pseudomonas, Enterococci

Gram-Negative vs. Gram-Positive

Gram-negative and gram-positive bacteria are referred to as groups of bacteria. When the specific organism is not identified, these general categories would be assigned. However, when the specific organism has been identified, a more specific code for that organism would be assigned.

Some common examples of gram-negative and gram-positive organisms are listed in Table 4–5.

HIV Infection Coding

An exception to the inpatient coding rule regarding the assignment of codes for conditions stated as suspected, possible, or probable is the case of HIV infection. This condition may be coded only if the physician documentation supports the statement of HIV-positive or HIV-related illness.

When a patient requests testing to determine HIV status, Code V73.89, Screening for Other Specified Viral Disease, would be appropriate. If the patient tests positive for the HIV virus yet shows no signs or symptoms of the disease, Code V08, Asymptomatic Human Immunodeficiency Infection Status, would be assigned.

If a patient is admitted for HIV treatment, Code 042, Human Immunodeficiency Virus, is assigned as the principal diagnosis. If a patient is admitted inpatient for conditions unrelated to HIV, Code 042 would be assigned as a secondary/subsequent diagnosis.

Viral Infections

Viral infections are categorized based on the following:

- Body site.
- Severity (acute or chronic).

Notes

TABLE 4–5   Common Gram-Negative/Gram-Positive Organisms.

Gram-Positive	Gram-Negative
Actinomyces	Aeromonas
Bacillus	Branhamella
Clostridium	Campylobacter
Corynebacterium	Citrobacter
Lactobacillis	Enterobacteriaceae
Listeria	Klebsiella
Peptococcus	Proteus
Peptostreptococcus	Serratia
Staphylococcus	Shigella
Streptococcus	Salmonella Proteus

- Organism or parasite.
- Causation.
- Any associated signs or symptoms.

Neoplasms

As stated previously in the general coding guidelines, neoplasms are coded as to the nature of the neoplasm (malignant, benign, undetermined, unspecified) and primary, secondary, or in situ. The appropriate order of these diagnoses is based on the chief reason for the episode of care. Keep in mind that secondary malignant diagnostic codes may be utilized as principal diagnoses if they are the chief reason for admission following tests and treatment.

In addition, V codes such as Encounter for Chemotherapy may be assigned as the chief reason for the encounter when appropriate, followed by the neoplasms being treated, in order of significance.

When a sign or symptom or other disease is the main reason for admission following tests and treatment, it should be assigned as the principal diagnosis, rather than the underlying neoplasm(s).

When cancer is identified as "metastatic from," the site indicated is considered primary. "Metastatic to" indicates the secondary site: where the cancer has spread to.

Morphology Neoplasm Codes

Morphology codes identify the histological type of neoplasm. These codes are not utilized for coding purposes, but for tumor registry within the hospital. The morphology code typically is located next to the appropriate ICD-9-CM neoplasm code.

Notes
_____
_____
_____
_____
_____
_____
_____
_____
_____
_____
_____
_____
_____
_____
_____
_____
_____
_____
_____
_____

TABLE 4–6   Fifth Digit ICD-9-CM Morphology Codes.

Fifth Digit	Meaning
0	Benign
1	Uncertain whether benign/malignant
	Borderline malignancy
2	Carcinoma in situ
	Noninvasive
	Noninfiltrating
3	Malignant, primary
6	Malignant, secondary site
9	Malignant, uncertain whether primary or secondary

The last digit of the morphology code identifies the behavior of the neoplasm, as outlined in Table 4–6.

Endocrine, Nutritional, Metabolic Diseases and Immunity Disorders

Laboratory findings of blood sugar analysis typically confirm the diagnosis of diabetes. The following findings are indicative of the diagnosis of diabetes mellitus. Of course, the physician must state this diagnosis in order for diabetes to be coded.

Glucose Tolerance Test (1 hour)   160 mg/100 ml
Glucose Tolerance Test (2 hour)   120 mg/100 ml

Because diabetes is treated either by diet or by oral and injectable medication, the codes for diabetes are assigned based on "noninsulin" dependent (NIDDM) and "insulin" dependent (IDDM).

Remember that the coding of diabetes always requires five digits. The fifth digit indicates the type of diabetes as well as the current state (controlled or uncontrolled).

When assigning diabetic diagnostic codes during a hospitalization, it should not be assumed that the patient is insulin dependent simply because they are receiving insulin while hospitalized. Many patients need insulin only during illness or exacerbations of diabetic problems and are, in fact, not insulin dependent.

The diabetic code is coded as primary (if chiefly responsible for episode of care) followed by the specific manifestation when one is present. This rule is based on the fact that the original condition (diabetes) must be present for the

Notes

manifestation to exist. Code 250 is subdivided based on the presence or absence or manifestations of diabetes such as:

250.1x	Ketoacidosis
250.2x	Hyperosmolarity
250.3x	Other Coma
250.4x	Renal Manifestations
250.5x	Ophthalmic Manifestations
250.6x	Neurological Manifestations
250.7x	Peripheral Circulatory Disorders
250.8x	Other Specified Manifestations
250.9x	Unspecified Manifestations

Diseases of Blood and Blood-Forming Organs

Because acute blood-loss anemia can occur as the result of an acute event such as trauma, whereas chronic blood-loss anemia may not be precipitated by an acute event, different ICD-9-CM diagnostic codes are utilized for these conditions.

When the condition is not specified as acute or chronic, Code 280.0 should be assigned. If documentation of trauma with heavy bleeding, or a significant, acute drop in hemoglobin and/or hematocrit, is noted in the medical record, the coder may wish to forward a query to the physician to clarify whether the condition is acute or chronic.

Mental Disorders

Mental-disorder diagnostic codes are often misused by the physician and the coder. Make certain that the chief reason for the encounter or admission following workup is indeed of a psychiatric nature. In addition to the typical psychiatric diagnosis, keep in mind that altered mental status as well as alcohol and drug abuse and dependence are also considered psychiatric diagnoses.

When assigning 780.0x for altered mental status, the condition should not be associated with any other conditions such as delirium or coma.

Also note that alcohol and drug abuse may only be assigned codes when the physician documents this information in the medical record. If the patient presents in an acute state of alcohol intoxication with the additional diagnosis of alcohol abuse, Code 303.0x should be assigned. If the patient presents with the diagnosis of alcohol, but is not diagnosed with acute alcohol intoxication, 303.9x would be appropriate. There is also a diagnosis code for history of alcoholism, V11.3, should a patient present who no longer has the diagnosis of alcohol abuse. The patient may be coded with the alcohol abuse code with a fifth digit indicating remission if the patient has not made a complete

Notes

and full recovery. These same rules apply to the use of the drug and substance abuse codes as well.

In the event the patient actually presents for problems related to the alcohol or drug problem, and those problems are the chief reason for the encounter or admission, they should be sequenced first.

Central Nervous System

When infectious diseases are present in the nervous system, the ICD-9-CM guidelines should be followed closely to determine which condition should be coded as primary.

When hemiplegia occurs as a result of a CVA but is transient, it need not be coded. When the hemiplegia does not clear by the time of discharge for that CVA event, a code from category 342 should be assigned.

If the patient is readmitted with hemiplegia from a previous CVA and/or previous admission, the hemiplegia code should be assigned, along with a late effect code.

Disorders of the Eye and Ocular Adnexa

The most common error made in assigning ICD-9-CM codes for the eye involve the diagnostic coding of cataracts. If the type of cataract has not been specified, it cannot be assumed that the cataract is senile or mature due to the patient's age. A code of 366.9 would be appropriate in these instances.

Diseases of the Ear

Care should be taken in assigning ICD-9-CM diagnostic codes for otitis media. As was the case with diagnosing cases for eye conditions, assumptions cannot be made regarding the nature of the ear inflammation, such as chronic, supportative, or serous. Follow the documentation clearly in order to code the otitis media correctly. Some of the most common otitis media codes are as follows:

- 381.00 Nonsuppurative, unspecified
- 381.01 Acute serous
- 381.10 Chronic serous, simple/unspecified
- 381.3 Other/unspecified chronic nonsuppurative
- 381.4 Nonsuppurative
- 382.00 Acute suppurative w/o ruptured eardrum
- 382.01 Acute suppurative w/ruptured eardrum

Notes

- 382.3 Chronic suppurative, unspecified
- 382.4 Suppurative, unspecified
- 382.9 Unspecified/unspecified acute/chronic

Diseases of the Circulatory System

We previously discussed in Process Overview, Coding, that no causal relationship could be assumed between hypertension and other conditions, other than chronic renal failure. In the event two diagnoses, one of which is hypertension, could be related, the coder must review the documentation carefully and make no assumptions. If the coder feels there may be a causal relationship, they may query the physician for clarification.

Initial myocardial infarctions are coded to the fifth digit to the location of the MI, if known. Code 410.9, acute myocardial infarction, unspecified site, is utilized in such instances. In the event the patient is being seen as the result of an MI experienced in the previous eight weeks, the old MI, Code 412, would be utilized, unless the chief reason for the encounter is a new MI.

Note that angina is coded when it is the chief reason for the encounter; however, when it is the precursor to ischemic heart disease, that condition would take precedence over the angina. For instance, a patient presents with angina, and prior to discharge is diagnosed with preinfarction angina or intermediate coronary syndrome. In such instances, the intermediate coronary syndrome code would be assigned.

The cardiac arrest code can only be assigned when a patient arrives at the hospital in cardiac arrest and cannot be resuscitated and is pronounced dead before a reason can be determined for the cause of death.

Diseases of the Respiratory System

One of the most common diagnostic conditions of the respiratory system is pneumonia. The coder should make every effort to identify the organism that resulted in pneumonia. However, if that information is not present or available, Code 486 would be appropriate.

Patients with asthma will often be seen in the emergency room or admitted to the hospital due to symptoms related to their asthma. In order to qualify as "status asthmaticus," one or more of the following conditions must be met:

- Prolonged, severe, intractable wheezing despite treatment.
- Prolonged, severe respiratory distress.
- Respiratory failure.
- Absence of breath sounds.
- Lethargic, confused state due to prolonged asthmatic attack.

Notes

The fifth digit of the ICD-9-CM diagnostic code for asthma identifies the specific type of asthma:

Fifth Digit	Type of Asthma
.0	Extrinsic (caused by outside/environmental factors)
.1	Intrinsic (caused by immune response)
.2	Chronic
.9	Unspecified

Patients with COPD (chronic obstructive pulmonary disease) are typically admitted to the hospital as the result of an acute exacerbation. When acute bronchitis with COPD is present, Code 491.21 should be coded for both conditions.

Respiratory failure may result from either acute or chronic illness, and the use of this diagnosis as a principal diagnosis is typically dependent on the underlying disease. If the failure is the chief reason for the encounter, it would be appropriately assigned as the principal diagnosis; however, if it arises following admission and as a result of another diagnosis, that diagnosis would be considered primary.

Specific coding rules are in place for the proper sequencing of the respiratory failure codes:

- If the patient is admitted with respiratory failure that is due to or associated with another acute nonrespiratory condition, the acute condition would be coded first.

- If the patient is admitted with respiratory failure that is due to or associated with an acute exacerbation of a chronic nonrespiratory condition, that acute condition would be coded first.

- When a patient is admitted with respiratory failure due to or associated with a chronic nonrespiratory condition, the respiratory condition is coded first.

Diseases of the Digestive System

Combination codes are utilized when ulcers are present with obstruction or complications. Hernias are also assigned codes that indicate the location of the hernia, as well as whether the hernia is unilateral or bilateral, with obstruction and/or gangrene.

Gastroenteritis is coded based on its cause, as follows:

- 003.0   Due to salmonella
- 005.9   Food poisoning
- 008.8   Viral
- 009.0   Infectious
- 556.9   Ulcerative colitis
- 558.3   Allergic
- 558.9   Other/unspecified noninfectious

Diseases of the Genitourinary System

Renal failure indicates the loss of renal function, which can be either acute or chronic. Documentation that may indicate renal failure is present would include:

- Elevated serum creatinine or BUN.
- Clinical findings such as anemia, hyperphosphatemia, hyperkalemia, or acidemia.
- Signs and symptoms such as nausea, vomiting, edema, dyspnea, lethargy, or coma.

Chronic renal failure typically develops as a result of other diseases. End-stage renal disease is a progression of chronic renal failure and is defined as the point at which chronic maintenance dialysis or kidney transplantation is required in order to sustain life. Chronic renal failure and end-stage renal disease are both coded to the 585 category.

When hematuria is a symptom of a specific genitourinary disease, it need not be coded; however, if that condition is not documented or diagnosed at the conclusion of that encounter or admission, the hematuria may be assigned a code.

Complications of Pregnancy, Childbirth and Puerperium

We have discussed pregnancy coding in our overview of the coding process. However, remember that conditions that are diagnosed or treated during the pregnancy state are assumed to be complications of pregnancy unless stated otherwise by the physician.

In the event a condition is treated during the pregnancy that is unrelated to it, a V22.2, incidental pregnancy code, would be assigned.

Abortion is defined as the extraction or spontaneous expulsion of all or part of the products of conception weighing less than 500 grams. Abortion may occur spontaneously or by induction, and therefore code categories are classified as follows:

- 634   Spontaneous
- 635   Legally induced
- 636   Illegally induced
- 637   Unspecified
- 638   Failed attempt
- 639   Complications following abortion, ectopic, molar pregnancies

Diseases of the Skin and Subcutaneous Tissue

Skin infections or inflammations affect a large population and result in a number of encounters and admissions. Because many of these conditions are the

Notes

result of drugs or biologicals, keep in mind the coding guidelines for utilizing the Table of Drugs and Chemicals reviewed in our Coding Overview earlier.

Diseases of the Musculoskeletal System and Connective Tissue

Keep in mind that fractures can be assigned codes from the following categories:

- Closed fracture stated as closed, or not otherwise stated
- Comminuted
- Depressed
- Greenstick
- Simple
- Spiral
- Open fracture stated as open, or report indicates bone protruding through skin
- Infected
- Compound
- Pathological fracture resulting from bone weakened by disease

Also keep in mind that the diagnostic code assigned does not necessarily have to correlate with the procedure or procedures performed. For example: A closed-fracture diagnosis could require an open repair, and therefore the codes would appear not to agree.

Congenital Anomalies and Conditions Arising from Perinatal Period

Keep in mind that congenital anomalies can be coded whether they present themselves at birth or do not manifest until a later date, but still can be attributed as being present at birth.

Injuries and Poisonings

Keep in mind that multiple injuries treated during the same encounter or admission are coded based on severity. When coding for poisoning, the use of the Table of Drugs and Chemicals that was reviewed in the Process Overview chapters is appropriate.

Burns should be coded with the following guidelines:

- Always code to the highest degree.
- Code nonhealing burns as acute burns.

- Assign code series 948 when site of burn is not listed.
- Use 958.3 for infected burns.
- Use late-effect codes for sequelae to original burns.

ICD-9-CM PROCEDURAL CODING

The coding of inpatient encounters requires assignment of ICD-9-CM codes for procedures performed as well.

Inpatient coding guidelines specify that the principal procedure should be the definitive treatment, not exploratory, diagnostic procedures. Multiple ICD-9-CM procedural codes may be assigned; however, it is imperative that the principal procedure be listed first.

Additional procedural codes may be listed for the following:

- Other definitive procedures
- Diagnostic procedures
- Therapeutic procedures

Only procedures that are defined as "significant" should be assigned ICD-9-CM procedural codes. "Significant" is defined as:

- Surgical procedures
- Procedures associated with an anesthetic risk
- Procedures associated with procedural risk
- Procedures requiring specialized training

Once the determination has been made that a procedural code should be assigned, selection of the code should be made based on the type of procedure performed. As with ICD-9-CM diagnostic coding, the code should be located first in the alphabetical listing utilizing the main headings of:

- Anastomosis
- Closure
- Excision
- Implant
- Insertion
- Procedure
- Repair
- Suture
- Biopsy
- Division
- Graft
- Incision
- Operation
- Removal
- Replacement

The ICD-9-CM procedure code requires a minimum of three digits for proper code assignment. The third digit specifies the type of procedure

Notes

performed within the body system. In some instances, a fourth digit is necessary to further specify the procedure performed.

ICD-9-CM Procedure Code Index

The selection of the code should then be cross-referenced (as with diagnostic coding) with the numerical index. Codes are categorized by body system, and a general index is listed in Table 4–7.

A more detailed listing of the procedures contained in the Volume 3, Procedure Codes, for ICD-9-CM was listed in the Coding Overview.

As with CPT-4 coding, only the definitive procedure should be assigned ICD-9-CM procedural codes. For instance, it is not necessary to code the approach, such as an incision and closure, for a surgical procedure.

It is appropriate to assign an ICD-9-CM procedural code when a significant evaluation and management service occurs that requires the use of facility resources. If significant facility resources are not expended, the evaluation and management ICD-9-CM procedural code would not be necessary.

Specific Coding Guidelines for ICD-9-CM Procedural Coding

There are a number of guidelines specific to an anatomical site, type of procedure or body area or organ system. Though these are extensive, the most commonly miscoded or overlooked procedures follow.

TABLE 4–7   ICD-9-CM Procedure Index.

Body System/Organ	Category Range
Nervous System	01–05
Endocrine System	05–07
Eye	08–16
Ear	18-20
Nose, Mouth, Pharynx	21–29
Respiratory System	30–34
Cardiovascular System	35–39
Hemic/Lymphatic System	40–41
Digestive System	42–54
Urinary System	55–59
Male Genital Organs	60–64
Female Genital Organs	65–71
Obstetrics	72–75
Musculoskeletal System	76–84
Integumentary System	85–86
Miscellaneous	87–99

Notes

Incomplete Procedure

When a procedure needs to be terminated prior to completion, an ICD-9-CM procedural code should be assigned for the extent completed. For example:

1. If an exploration was not performed, the incision would be assigned a code.
2. If a body cavity or body area was entered but no surgical intervention was accomplished, code the exploratory procedure.
3. If no incision is made, no ICD-9-CM procedural code would be assigned.

Nervous System

Until endoscopic codes are assigned for excision, destruction of lesions, or brain tissues, open codes (i.e., 01.59) should be utilized.

When chemotherapy agents are implanted following the excision of a brain lesion, two ICD-9-CM procedural codes are necessary: 01.59 (Excision, Destruction Lesion, Brain Tissue) and 99.25 (Injection or Infusion Cancer Chemotherapy Agent).

In instances where a morphine infusion pump is implanted (typically for intractable back pain), multiple codes may be necessary for the several different procedures that may be performed as part of this service. Code 03.99 would be assigned for insertion of the catheter into the subarachnoid space, while pump implantation would be assigned 86.09. When morphine is subsequently infused, the addition of Code 03.91 would also be appropriate.

Endocrine System

When two or more parathyroid glands are excised during the course of a thyroidectomy, additional codes need not be assigned.

Eye

When cataract extraction is performed followed by an intraocular lenses implantion, two ICD-9-CM procedure codes will be necessary: 13.41 for the extracapsular cataract extraction, as well as 13.71 when the intraocular lens is implantable during the same encounter.

Ear

There are a number of ICD-9-CM procedure codes for the implantation and repair of cochlear implants. Code 20.96 should be assigned for implantation of the cochlear implant when documentation does not specify whether the implant is single or multiple channel. In the event of a replacement cochlear implant, should the implant not be complete (i.e., coils or electrodes only), Code 20.99 (Other Procedures, Middle or Inner Ear) would be appropriately assigned.

Notes

Nose, Mouth Pharynx

When UPPP (uvulopalatopharyngoplasty) is performed, typically two ICD-9-CM procedure codes would be appropriate: Code 29.4 for plastic repair/operation of the pharynx, as well as 27.69 for repair of the palate.

Respiratory System

Endoscopic lung biopsy codes are assigned based on where the procedure is performed: 33.27 when it is performed into the lung alveoli, or 33.24 when within the lumen of the trachea or bronchus. If lung biopsies are performed in both locations, both Code 33.27 and 33.24 would be assigned.

> 33.27   Biopsy Taken Endoscopically Bronchus into Lung Alveoli
> 33.24   Endoscopic Biopsy within Lumen of Trachea and Bronchus

Cardiovascular/Heart Assist System

When the removal of a heart assist device such as a pacemaker or defibrillator is necessary, the code assignment is based upon whether operative or nonoperative removal is required. Code 97.44 would be assigned for nonoperative removal, while Code 37.64 would be appropriate when operative removal is necessary.

For the assignment of central lines and venous access devices, codes are distinguished based on a percutaneous catheter brought out through the skin: Code 38.93, known as a central line, or Code 86.07 for a totally implantable catheter, also known as a venous access device. Key documentation words would include the placement of the catheter within a "pocket" created in the chest for the totally implantable catheter, versus the securing of an intravenous line "hub" or "lumen" on the outside of the skin for Code 38.93.

Hemic and Lymphatic System

Care should be taken in the review of documentation to determine whether radical excision of lymphatics has been accomplished. Radical excision would be defined as involving the muscle and deep fascia.

Digestive System

When adhesions prevent the surgeon from accessing the organ or area to be addressed, both the surgery and the lysis procedure should be coded. However, when adhesions do not increase the difficulty of performing the operative procedure, the lysis should not be coded.

Urinary System

The placement of ureteral stents requires the assignment of ICD-9-CM procedural code 59.8. Note that ICD-9-CM distinguishes between ureteral stents and urethral stents; asssign codes accordingly.

Male Genital Organs

One of the more difficult ICD-9-CM procedural codes to locate in the male genital system is for the balloon dilation of the prostate. Code 60.99 would be appropriate when this procedure is performed.

Female Genital Organs

In the female genital section of ICD-9-CM procedure codes, Code 67.32 should be assigned for the performance of a LEEP, or cone biopsy of the cervix. Code 69.09, not 69.01, should be utilized for the dilation and curettage of a blighted ovum.

Obstetrics

When suturing or incision is required during the course of a delivery, Code 73.6 includes the episiotomy or episiorrhaphy that may be required. This coincides with the CPT-4 guidelines for a vaginal delivery as well.

Musculoskeletal System

A somewhat new procedure is the percutaenous repair of a vertebra, known as a percutaenous vertebroplasty. When this procedure is performed, it is appropriate to assign ICD-9-CM procedure code 78.49. Revision of hip replacements includes the removal of the previous prosthesis. Again, this is consistent with CPT-4 procedure coding guidelines as well.

Integumentary System

When bilateral breast implants are removed for nonmedical reasons, such as patient request, Code 89.54 should be listed twice to indicate the procedure has been performed on both the right and left breasts.

As with CPT-4 coding, ICD-9-CM procedural coding distinguishes between the biopsy or sample of tissue of a breast lesion (Code 85.12) and the excision of the entire breast lesion (85.21).

Notes
_____

_____

_____

_____

_____

_____

_____

_____

_____

_____

_____

_____

_____

_____

_____

_____

_____

Miscellaneous

Unlike CPT-4 format, the injection of therapeutic substances into a joint or ligament, known as arthrocentesis, is not included in the musculoskeletal section, but is located in the miscellaneous section of ICD-9-CM procedure codes, utilizing Code 81.92.

ICD-9-CM procedure code 99.29 is utilized when a therapeutic or prophylactic substance is injected or infused.

PRACTICE EXERCISE 4–3

Assign Volume 3 ICD-9-CM procedure codes for the following:

ICD-9-CM Procedure Code

1. Exploratory laparotomy.   _____

2. Repair fractured femur.   _____

3. Cholecystectomy.   _____

4. CABG (Coronary Artery Bypass Graft).   _____

5. Mastectomy.   _____

6. Upper GI endoscopy (EGD).   _____

7. Radical abdominal hysterectomy.   _____

8. PTCA.   _____

9. Craniotomy.   _____

10. Trabeculectomy.   _____

11. Corneal transplant.   _____

12. Stapedectomy.   _____

13. Tympanoplasty.   _____

Notes
_____

_____

_____

_____

_____

_____

_____

_____

_____

_____

_____

_____

_____

_____

_____

_____

_____

_____

_____

14. Revision of tympanoplasty.   _____

15. CABG, 3 arteries.   _____

16. Ligation of coronary artery.   _____

17. Ultrasonic shattering of urinary stones.   _____

18. Dilation of urethra.   _____

19. Sphincterotomy of bladder.   _____

20. STSG breast.   _____

21. Mastectomy.   _____

22. Fitting of prosthetic lower leg.   _____

23. Measles vaccination.   _____

24. Insulin injection.   _____

25. Transfusion packed cells.   _____

The process of inpatient coding involves all the processes we have discussed, including determining admitting and principal diagnoses, secondary diagnosis (when appropriate), and ICD-9-CM procedural codes.

PRACTICE EXERCISE 4–4

Review each of the following inpatient scenarios and try assigning all the codes appropriately.

1. Patient presents for admission with low-grade fever, lethargy, altered mental status, with complaints of cough, shortness of breath and dyspnea for the past 24–48 hours. CXR indicates lower lobe pneumonia, organism unknown. Patient inpatient for approximately 4 days, during which time he receives IV antibiotics; however, accumulated lung fluid requires a thoracentesis with drainage tube insertion. Tube is left in

Notes

place for approximately 2 days, at which time the tube is removed, the patient is placed on oral antibiotics and discharged.

Admitting Diagnosis: _____ Code: _____

Principal Diagnosis: _____ Code: _____

Secondary Diagnosis: _____ Code: _____

Secondary Diagnosis: _____ Code: _____

Secondary Diagnosis: _____ Code: _____

Principal Procedure: _____ Code: _____

Secondary Procedure: _____ Code: _____

Secondary Procedure: _____ Code: _____

2. Patient presents with long-standing history of IDDM and is admitted with blood sugars uncontrolled. Patient was switched from oral diabetic medication to sliding-scale insulin regimen. She improved over the next 3 days and was discharged for follow-up with a home health nurse.

Admitting Diagnosis: _____ Code: _____

Principal Diagnosis: _____ Code: _____

Secondary Diagnosis: _____ Code: _____

Secondary Diagnosis: _____ Code: _____

Secondary Diagnosis: _____ Code: _____

Principal Procedure: _____ Code: _____

Secondary Procedure: _____ Code: _____

3. Eight-six-year-old patient admitted with severe decubitus ulcer of the foot and toes. The patient was taken to the operating room X2 during his hospitalization where the physician debrided the ulcer, including

Notes
_____

_____

_____

_____

_____

_____

_____

_____

_____

_____

_____

_____

_____

_____

_____

_____

_____

_____

_____

_____

_____

amputation of the distal phalanx of the left fifth toe. IV antibiotic treatment was instituted at admission, and continued through the fifth day of admission, at which time the patient was switched to oral antibiotics, and seemed to tolerate that well with no change in the appearance of the wounds. Discharged on the sixth day.

Admitting Diagnosis: _____ Code: _____

Principal Diagnosis: _____ Code: _____

Secondary Diagnosis: _____ Code: _____

Secondary Diagnosis: _____ Code: _____

Secondary Diagnosis: _____ Code: _____

Principal Procedure: _____ Code: _____

Secondary Procedure: _____ Code: _____

4. Patient presented to the emergency room with relatives with increasing confusion and inability to remember dates and events, according to family members. The patient has also become incontinent and smells strongly of urine. We will admit and workup for any urological problems; however, we believe the patient is suffering from senile dementia, in which case we will discharge to a nursing facility for continual care. Urinalysis was negative.

Admitting Diagnosis: _____ Code: _____

Principal Diagnosis: _____ Code: _____

Secondary Diagnosis: _____ Code: _____

Secondary Diagnosis: _____ Code: _____

Secondary Diagnosis: _____ Code: _____

Principal Procedure: _____ Code: _____

Secondary Procedure: _____ Code: _____

Notes

5. Patient brought to the floor in respiratory failure, ventilator already placed in the emergency room. Long-standing patient with history of CHF. CXR now shows CHF with pleural effusion and acute pulmonary edema. EKG was also performed. Patient was treated with IV Lasix and weaned from the ventilation. He was then placed in the Medical Unit for additional 2 days and released.

Admitting Diagnosis: _____   Code: _____

Principal Diagnosis: _____   Code: _____

Secondary Diagnosis: _____   Code: _____

Secondary Diagnosis: _____   Code: _____

Secondary Diagnosis: _____   Code: _____

Principal Procedure: _____   Code: _____

Secondary Procedure: _____   Code: _____

Actual chart review is obviously more complicated and involved due to the volume and complexity of the medical data.

Additional inpatient charts are included in the student CD-ROM for further practice assigning codes.

PRACTICE EXERCISE 4–5

Read each case scenario and assign codes appropriately, including ICD-9-CM diagnostic codes as well as procedural codes when necessary.

1. Patient is a 78-year-old female with a known history of metastatic carcinoma of the left breast. The patient has been experiencing extreme pain, accompanied by shortness of breath, especially in the right upper quadrant. The patient also has a history of diabetes, COPD and s/p mastectomy for her breast cancer approximately 4 years ago. The patient has been treated in the past with chemotherapy as well as radiation therapy; her primary site has never been identified.

The patient was treated with IV pain meds and sliding-scale insulin and her pain subsided over the next several days. She was switched to oral pain meds which she tolerated well, and was discharged on day 5.

Medications at discharge were: Aldactone, 25 mg daily, Tamoxifen, 10 mg, Lanoxin 0.125 mg daily, Tolinase 250 mg tablet, Reglan, 10 mg, Lasix 20 mg bid, and Vicodin tablets, 1 every 4–6 hours as needed for pain.

Discharge Diagnosis:

Uncontrolled pain secondary to metastatic breast carcinoma. Dehydration, NIDDM, uncontrolled at the time of admission.

Admitting Diagnosis: _____ Code: _____

Principal Diagnosis: _____ Code: _____

Secondary Diagnosis: _____ Code: _____

Secondary Diagnosis: _____ Code: _____

Secondary Diagnosis: _____ Code: _____

Principal Procedure: _____ Code: _____

Secondary Procedure: _____ Code: _____

Secondary Procedure: _____ Code: _____

Secondary Procedure: _____ Code: _____

2. Forty-five-year-old female admitted for long history of abdominal pain, primarily in the left lower quadrant. The pain has been present for some time now, and does not seem related to food, position, or stress. Patient has been worked up by her primary care physician with an EGD and colonoscopy, both of which were negative. Duodenitis was an incidental finding on the EGD, for which she was prescribed Prevacid.

She is admitted for further workup due to unrelenting abdominal pain. She received an ultrasound of the abdomen as well as a CT. A mass was found in in the kidney that appears to also involve the pancreas.

Patient went to the operating room for a nephrectomy. The metastatic pancreatic site was not explored, but will be treated with chemotherapy at this time. The involvement in the pancreas did not

Notes

appear to be significant, and whatever the outcome, it was felt that the chemotherapy would be as beneficial as any surgical intervention we would have to offer her.

The patient tolerated the procedure well and was sent to the intensive care unit where she began experiencing difficulties, including the need for blood transfusions. Following several additional days of intensive care, the patient's condition improved and the patient was then transferred to the oncology floor.

Her first dose of chemotherapy was administered as an inpatient, and she will be treated aggressively for the metastatic pancreatic cancer.

Prognosis is guarded, and the patient and her husband are so informed.

Admitting Diagnosis: _____ Code: _____

Principal Diagnosis: _____ Code: _____

Secondary Diagnosis: _____ Code: _____

Secondary Diagnosis: _____ Code: _____

Secondary Diagnosis: _____ Code: _____

Principal Procedure: _____ Code: _____

Secondary Procedure: _____ Code: _____

Secondary Procedure: _____ Code: _____

Secondary Procedure: _____ Code: _____

3. This 24-year-old female presented to the emergency room following an altercation with her boyfriend yesterday evening. She received a direct blow to the left eye and face, and has already been to the police station, filed a complaint and had photographs taken. She also complained of left lower quadrant abdominal pain.

She has swelling and a hematoma below her left eye with a swollen, tender inferior orbital rim. She has tenderness and pain along the inferior orbital rim, with some diploplia with extraocular movement. Her nose is tender along the bridge. Neck has some contusions and abrasions, although minor. She shows exquisite tenderness to palpation of her abdomen, with guarding. CT of the abdomen was negative, so we will watch her abdomen during her hospitalization.

X-rays of the inferior orbital rim show a blowout fracture of the right orbit. Nasal x-rays were negative.

The patient was taken to the operating room, where the orbital fracture was reduced and placement of an implant in the right orbital floor area was done. She recovered postoperatively during the next 2–3 days, her abdominal pain resolved, contusions resolved, and she appeared stable for discharge. She was instructed to return in 3–5 days for suture removal.

Admitting Diagnosis: _____ Code: _____

Principal Diagnosis: _____ Code: _____

Secondary Diagnosis: _____ Code: _____

Secondary Diagnosis: _____ Code: _____

Secondary Diagnosis: _____ Code: _____

Principal Procedure: _____ Code: _____

Secondary Procedure: _____ Code: _____

Secondary Procedure: _____ Code: _____

Secondary Procedure: _____ Code: _____

4. The patient is an 82-year-old female who is s/p right colectomy for cancer. She had a post-op wound infection and has one persistent area of chronic sinus drainage without evidence of overt infection or foreign body. This area has not resolved after approximately 3 months of wound care. She presents for admission for excision of the entire sinus tract. Patient also has a history of hypertension, arthritis and a history of chronic alcoholism.

The patient was brought to the OR and placed in the supine position. We excised the area of surrounding fistulous tract without entering the tract itself. The deepest part was just above the fascia. There was no fascial defect to repair. The area was irrigated with saline, we closed the subcutaneous tissue with Vicyrl and the skin was closed with staples.

She will remain in the hospital for 24–48 hours to make certain this resolves her problem. She will receive her chemotherapy for her colon carcinoma while an inpatient and continue as an outpatient after discharge.

Notes
_____

_____

_____

_____

_____

_____

_____

_____

_____

_____

_____

_____

_____

_____

_____

_____

_____

_____

_____

_____

_____

Admitting Diagnosis: _____ Code: _____

Principal Diagnosis: _____ Code: _____

Secondary Diagnosis: _____ Code: _____

Secondary Diagnosis: _____ Code: _____

Secondary Diagnosis: _____ Code: _____

Principal Procedure: _____ Code: _____

Secondary Procedure: _____ Code: _____

Secondary Procedure: _____ Code: _____

Secondary Procedure: _____ Code: _____

5. This is a 58-year-old known diabetic female who recently underwent debridement of a decubitus ulcer of the plantar aspect of the foot X4. Despite conservative therapy as well as wound care, the ulcer has enlarged and the second toe on the left foot appears to be gangrenous. She also has arrythmia problems, and had a pacemaker implanted approximately 6 years ago. She also has a past history of hypertension and CHF for which she takes Lasix 40 mg per day.

   She indicates in her history that she has also suffered an MI; however, we could find no documentation to substantiate this occurred. Perhaps she is referring to her episodes of arrythmia that necessitated the pacemaker.

   Exam reveals second toe with erythema into the foot; however, toe itself appears to not be viable at this time.

   We will proceed with an amputation of the second toe of the left foot and begin IV antibiotic treatment.

   Diagnosis: Necrotic 2nd toe, left foot

   We will schedule surgical procedure for tomorrow and begin IV antibiotic therapy preoperatively.

   Patient was taken to the operating room, where the digit was prepped and draped in the usual sterile fashion. The 2nd phalanx on the left foot was sharply excised and the bone rasped smooth with a file. The wound was irrigated copiously, dressed and the patient was returned from the operating room in satisfactory condition. We will aggressively treat the wound, as she has experienced difficulties in the past; will order bedrest, elevation, soaks and IV Garamycin.

Notes _____

_____

_____

_____

_____

_____

_____

_____

_____

_____

_____

_____

_____

_____

_____

_____

_____

_____

_____

_____

_____

On the 5-day postoperative, her wound was clean and dry, and her glucose levels were within normal range. She will be switched to oral antibiotics for the next 24 hours in preparation for discharge.

Admitting Diagnosis: _____ Code: _____

Principal Diagnosis: _____ Code: _____

Secondary Diagnosis: _____ Code: _____

Secondary Diagnosis: _____ Code: _____

Secondary Diagnosis: _____ Code: _____

Principal Procedure: _____ Code: _____

Secondary Procedure:_____ Code: _____

Secondary Procedure:_____ Code: _____

Secondary Procedure:_____ Code: _____

CONCLUSION

The assignment of ICD-9-CM diagnostic codes and procedural codes is only one aspect of hospital coding and billing. Proper application of the selected codes is also instrumental in ensuring appropriate reimbursement on a timely basis. We will take what has been introduced in this chapter and add the reimbursement perspective in the next chapter.

Upon completing this chapter, the student should be capable of identifying and assigning the appropriate inpatient diagnostic codes, including differentiating between the principal diagnosis, supporting diagnoses and admitting diagnoses. The student should also be able to identify complications and comorbidities that add to the complexity of the inpatient admission, and will result in assignment of a DRG to include complications and/or comorbidities. The student must also demonstrate the ability to assign the appropriate Volume 3 ICD-9-CM procedural codes to significant procedures.

Chapter 5
Inpatient Billing

KEY TERMS

Diagnosis Related Group (DRG)
Fee-for-Service (FFS)
Major Diagnostic
  Category (MDC)

Per Diem
Prospective Payment
  System (PPS)

LEARNING OBJECTIVES

- Describe the basic methodologies for reimbursement of inpatient services
- Demonstrate and understand the basic concepts of the Prospective Payment System (PPS)
- Describe the different Diagnosis Related Groups (DRGs)
- Discuss additional considerations for DRG assignments
- Demonstrate the proper completion of the UB-92 for inpatient services

METHODOLOGIES FOR INPATIENT SERVICES

There are three basic reimbursement methodologies for inpatient hospital service. While the most common and most recognized would be the Prospective Payment System, there are still a number of third-party carriers that utilize other methodologies for reimbursement.

Fee for Service (FFS) is perhaps the oldest methodology for inpatient facility reimbursement. It uses the actual expenses incurred by the facility for providing the medically necessary services to the patient. All services that are deemed medically necessary for the treatment and diagnosis of the patient's condition are considered for reimbursement.

Under the **Per Diem** methodology, a fixed rate per day is paid for all services performed or provided by the hospital facility. Individual charges are

Notes

not considered for reimbursement, but the per diem (per day) reimbursement is based on a daily rate for the type of admission of level of service provided to the patient. This same methodology is utilized by rehabilitation centers and other facilities for negotiating reimbursement by third-party carriers.

These two methodologies have largely given way to the **Prospective Payment System (PPS),** first introduced by Medicare under Title VI of the Social Security Amendments of 1983. The design and development of this methodology began as far back as the 1960s, with its first application in New Jersey in the 1970s. Under PPS, payment rates to hospitals are established prospectively (thus *prospective payment system*)—i.e., before services are rendered—and are based on a reimbursement rate in which patients are categorized according to diagnosis and treatment that entails similar lengths of stay.

Concept of Prospective Payment System

The categories of diagnosis and treatment into which patients are grouped under PPS methodology are called **Diagnosis Related Groups (DRGs).** Payments for each DRG are based on a "relative weight" assigned to each case, and the individual hospital rate. The relative weight represents the average resources necessary to provide services to a specific diagnosis, while the individual hospital rate is determined by a nationally standard amount that takes into consideration the type and designation of hospital and a wage index for the area in which it is located.

Outliers are considered for additional reimbursement. Typically these cases involve patients who require significantly more medically necessary services than others assigned the same principal diagnosis, and reflect the same DRG.

The assignment of the DRG is not performed by the facility; instead, it is assigned by the carrier at the time the claim is processed, much like the outpatient billing methodology of Ambulatory Payment Classifications (APCs). However, the facility has the ability to determine not just the DRG that should be assigned, but also the expected reimbursement, based on such factors as:

- Principal and secondary diagnoses
- Principal and secondary procedures
- Patient age
- Patient discharge status
- Presence of documented complications and/or comorbidities

The facility may also determine their case mix for patients by adding the relative weight for all patients discharged within a specific period and dividing the number by the number of patients discharged within that period. This case mix can be calculated for all patients, for Medicare patients only, or for any other defined patient population.

Notes

Other factors that contribute to the facility's case mix are:

- Severity of illness
- Prognosis
- Treatment difficulty
- Need for intervention
- Resource intensity

A facility's case-mix index for Medicare patients is determined each year based on the cases received by Medicare from that facility during the past fiscal year. This information is available online for each hospital by provider number. Thus, a hospital can calculate their potential reimbursement with the case-mix index for the year and the relative weight assigned to each DRG.

ALERT: Case-mix index information is available on the Medicare website at www.cms.gov.

Diagnosis Related Groups

The main categorization of diagnosis related groups is based on patients who are clinically similar and use similar hospital resources. Therefore, the primary breakdown of principal diagnoses is referred to as **Major Diagnostic Categories (MDCs).** These MDCs are then further broken down with more specificity, taking into consideration the other factors listed above.

The Major Diagnostic Categories are listed in Table 5–1:

TABLE 5–1   Major Diagnostic Categories (MDCs).

MDC	Descriptor/Category
1	Nervous System
2	Eye
3	Ear, Nose, Mouth, Throat
4	Respiratory
5	Circulatory
6	Digestive
7	Hepatobiliary/Pancreas
8	Musculoskeletal/Connective Tissue
9	Skin, Subcutaneous Tissue, Breast

(continued)

TABLE 5–1 _continued_

MDC	Descriptor/Category
10	Endocrine, Nutritional, Metabolic
11	Kidney and Urinary Tract
12	Male Reproductive
13	Female Reproductive
14	Pregnancy, Childbirth and Puerperium
15	Newborns, Neonates, Conditions Originating in Perinatal Period
16	Blood and Blood-Forming Organs, Immunology
17	Myeloproliferative Diseases, Poorly Differentiated Neoplasms
18	Infectious, Parasitic
19	Mental
20	Alcohol/Drug Use, Alcohol/Drug-Induced Organic Mental Disorders
21	Injury, Poisoning, Toxic Effects of Drugs
22	Burns
23	Factors Influencing Health Status and Other Contacts with Health Services
24	Multiple Significant Trauma
25	Human Immunodeficiency Virus (HIV) Infections

Most of the MDCs are based on an organ systems rather than etiology. However, there are also six pre-MDC designations:

- Heart transplant
- Tracheostomy (nonface, mouth, neck)
- Liver transplant
- Bone marrow transplant
- Lung transplant
- Tracheostomy (face, mouth, neck)

Following the establishment of major diagnostic groups, these groups were then further divided based on surgical and nonsurgical patients. Patients having procedures performed in the operating room consume a significant amount of additional resources, and therefore consistently incur significantly additional services and charges.

Additionally, some DRG classifications are based on patient age, patient discharge status and presence or absence of complications and/or comorbidities.

EXAMPLE OF NONSURGICAL DRG

Patient with syncope for which no surgery intervention was performed would be assigned as follows:

MDC 05   Circulatory System Diseases/Disorders

Medical/Not Surgical

DRG 141   If complications/comorbidities

DRG 142   No complications/comorbidities

(COMPLICATIONS AND COMORBIDITIES WERE DISCUSSED IN CHAPTER 1, *INPATIENT HOSPITAL CODING*.)

EXAMPLE OF SURGICAL DRG

An example of a DRG assignment based on age and complications/comorbidities:

One-year-old male admitted for inguinal hernia repair

MDC 06   Digestive System Diseases/Disorders

Surgical/Not Medical (Inguinal Hernia Repair in Operating Room)

DRG 161   Inguinal/Femoral Hernia Repair Age > 17 with CC

DRG 162   Inguinal/Femoral Hernia Repair Age > 17 without CC

DRG 163   Inguinal/Femoral Hernia Repair 0–17 Years

A listing of DRGs categorized by MDC and Surgical/Nonsurgical is contained in Table 5–2.

TABLE 5–2   Diagnosis Related Groups by MDC and Surgical/Nonsurgical Categories.

Surgical Medical	With CC	W/O CC	Descriptor
MDC 01 - Nervous System			
Surg	1		Craniotomy Except for Trauma, Age >17
Surg	2		Craniotomy for Trauma, Age >17
Surg	3		Craniotomy, Age 0–17

(continued)

Notes

_____

_____

_____

_____

_____

_____

_____

_____

_____

_____

_____

_____

_____

_____

_____

_____

_____

_____

_____

_____

TABLE 5–2   *continued*

Surgical Medical	With CC	W/O CC	Descriptor
Surg	4		Spinal Procedures
Surg	5		Extracranial Vascular Procedures
Surg	6		Carpal Tunnel Release
Surg	7	8	Peripheral, Cranial Nerve, Other Nervous System Procedures
Med	9		Spinal Disorders and Injuries
Med	10	11	Nervous System Neoplasms
Med	12		Degenerative Nervous System Disorders
Med	13		Multiple Sclerosis and Cerebellar Ataxia
Med	14		Specific Cerebrovascular Disorders, Except TIA
Med	15		Transient Ischemic Attack and Precerebral Occlusions
Med	16	17	Nonspecific Cerebrovascular Disorders
Med	18	19	Cranial and Peripheral Nerve Disorders
Med	20		Nervous System Infection Except Viral Meningitis
Med	21		Viral Meningitis
Med	22		Hypertensive Encephalopathy
Med	23		Nontraumatic Stupor and Coma
Med	24	25	Seizure and Headache, Age > 17
Med	26		Seizure and Headache, Age 0–17
Med	27		Traumatic Stupor and Coma > 1 Hr
Med	28	29	Traumatic Stupor and Coma < 1 Hr, Age >17
Med	30		Traumatic Stupor and Coma < 1 Hr, Age 0–17
Med	31	32	Concussion, Age >17
Med	33		Concussion, Age 0–17
Med	34	35	Other Disorders of Nervous System
MDC 02 - Eye			
Surg	36		Retinal Procedures

Notes

Surgical Medical	With CC	W/O CC	Descriptor
Surg	37		Orbital Procedures
Surg	38		Primary Iris Procedures
Surg	39		Lens Procedures with or without Vitrectomy
Surg	40		Extraocular Procedures Except Orbit, Age >17
Surg	41		Extraocular Procedures Except Orbit, Age 0–17
Surg	42		Intraocular Procedures Except Retina, Iris and Lens
Med	43		Hyphema
Med	44		Acute Major Eye Infections
Med	45		Neurological Eye Disorders
Med	46	47	Other Disorders of Eye, Age >17
Med	48		Other Disorders of Eye, Age 0–17

MDC 03 - Ears, Nose, Mouth, Throat

Surg	49		Major Head and Neck Procedure
Surg	50		Sialoadenectomy
Surg	51		Salivary Gland Procedures Except Sialoadenectomy
Surg	52		Cleft Lip and Palate Repair
Surg	53		Sinus and Mastoid Procedure, Age >17
Surg	54		Sinus and Mastoid Procedures, Age 0–17
Surg	55		Miscellaneous Ear, Nose, Mouth and Throat Procedures
Surg	56		Rhinoplasty
Surg	57		Tonsillectomy and Adenoidectomy (Both Performed), Age >17
Surg	58		Tonsillectomy and Adenoidectomy (Both Performed), Age 0–17
Surg	59		Tonsillectomy or Adenoidectomy Only, Age >17
Surg	60		Tonsillectomy or Adenoidectomy Only, Age 0–17

(continued)

TABLE 5–2   *continued*

Surgical Medical	With CC	W/O CC	Descriptor
Surg	61		Myringotomy with Tube Insertion, Age >17
Surg	62		Myringotomy with Tube Insertion, Age 0–17
Surg	63		Other Ear, Nose, Throat, Mouth OR Procedures
Surg	168	169	Mouth Procedures
Med	64		Ear, Nose, Mouth and Throat Malignancy
Med	65		Disequilibrium
Med	66		Epistaxis
Med	67		Epiglottitis
Med	68	69	Otitis Media and Upper Respiratory Infection, Age >17
Med	70		Otitis Media and Upper Respiratory Infection, Age 0–17
Med	71		Laryngotracheitis
Med	72		Nasal Trauma and Deformity
Med	73		Other Ear, Nose, Mouth and Throat Diagnoses, Age >17
Med	74		Other Ear, Nose, Mouth and Throat Diagnoses, Age 0–17
Med	185		Dental and Oral Disease Except Extractions/Restorations, Age >17
Med	186		Dental and Oral Disease Except Extractions/Restorations, Age 0–17
Med	187		Dental Extractions and Restorations
MDC 04 - Respiratory			
Surg	75		Major Chest Procedures
Surg	76	77	Other Respiratory System OR Procedures
Med	78		Pulmonary Embolism
Med	79	80	Respiratory Infections and Inflammations, Age >17

Notes

Surgical Medical	With CC	W/O CC	Descriptor
Med	81		Respiratory Infections and Inflammations, Age 0–17
Med	82		Respiratory Neoplasms
Med	83	84	Major Chest Trauma
Med	85	86	Pleural Effusion
Med	87		Pulmonary Edema and Respiratory Failure
Med	88		Chronic Obstructive Pulmonary Disease
Med	89	90	Simple Pneumonia and Pleurisy, Age >17
Med	91		Simple Pneumonia and Pleurisy, Age 0–17
Med	92	93	Interstitial Lung Disease
Med	94	95	Pneumothorax
Med	96	97	Bronchitis and Asthma, Age >17
Med	98		Bronchitis and Asthma, Age 0–17
Med	99	100	Respiratory Signs and Symptoms
Med	101	102	Other Respiratory System Diagnoses
Med	475		Respiratory System Diagnosis with Ventilator Support

MDC 05 - Circulatory System

Surgical Medical	With CC	W/O CC	Descriptor
Surg	104		Cardiac Valve and Other Major Cardiothoracic Procedure with Cardiac Catheterization
Surg	105		Cardiac Valve and Other Major Cardiothoracic Procedure without Cardiac Catheterization
Surg	106		Coronary Bypass with PTCA
Surg	107		Coronary Bypass with Cardiac Catheterization
Surg	108		Other Cardiothoracic Procedures
Surg	109		Coronary Bypass without PTCA or Cardiac Catheterization
Surg	110	111	Major Cardiovascular Procedures
Surg	112		Percutaneous Cardiovascular Procedures

(continued)

Notes

_____

_____

_____

_____

_____

_____

_____

_____

_____

_____

_____

_____

_____

_____

_____

_____

_____

_____

_____

_____

_____

TABLE 5–2   *continued*

Surgical Medical	With CC	W/O CC	Descriptor
Surg	113		Amputation for Circulatory System Disorders Except Upper Limb and Toe
Surg	114		Upper Limb and Toe Amputation for Circulatory System Disorder
Surg	115		Permanent Cardiac Pacemaker Implantation with Acute Myocardial Infarction, Heart Failure or Shock or AICD Lead of Generator Procedure
Surg	116		Other Permanent Cardiac Pacemaker Implantation or PTCA with Coronary Artery Stent Implantation
Surg	117		Cardiac Pacemaker Revision Except Device Replacement
Surg	118		Cardiac Pacemaker Device Replacement
Surg	119		Vein Ligation and Stripping
Surg	120		Other Circulatory System OR Procedures
Surg	478	479	Other Vascular Procedures
Med	121		Circulatory Disorders with Acute Myocardial Infarction and Major Complications, Discharged Alive
Med	122		Circulatory Disorders without Acute Myocardial Infarction without Major Complications, Discharged Alive
Med	123		Circulatory Disorders with Acute Myocardial Infarction, Expired
Med	124		Circulatory Disorders Except Acute Myocardial Infarction, with Cardiac Catheterization and Complex Diagnostics
Med	125		Circulatory Disorders Except Acute Myocardial Infarction
			Cardiac Catheterization without Complex Diagnostics
Med	126		Acute and Subacute Endocarditis

Notes

Surgical Medical	With CC	W/O CC	Descriptor
Med	127		Heart Failure and Shock
Med	128		Deep Vein Thrombophlebitis
Med	129		Cardiac Arrest, Unexplained
Med	130	131	Peripheral Vascular Disorders
Med	132	133	Atherosclerosis
Med	134		Hypertension
Med	135	136	Cardiac Congenital and Valvular Disorders, Age >17
Med	137		Cardiac Congenital and Valvular Disorders, Age 0–17
Med	138	139	Cardiac Arrhythmia and Conduction Disorders
Med	140		Angina Pectoris
Med	141	142	Syncope and Collapse
Med	143		Chest Pain
Med	144	145	Other Circulatory System Diagnoses
Med	475		Respiratory System Diagnosis with Ventilator Support
Pre-Surg	103		Pre-Surg MDC - Heart Transplant

MDC 06 - Digestive Disease/GI System

Surgical Medical	With CC	W/O CC	Descriptor
Surg	146	147	Rectal Resection
Surg	148	149	Major Small and Large Bowel Procedures
Surg	150	151	Peritoneal Adhesiolysis
Surg	152	153	Minor Small and Large Bowel Procedures
Surg	154	155	Stomach, Esophageal and Duodenal Procedures, Age >17
Surg	156		Stomach, Esophageal and Duodenal Procedures, Age 0–17
Surg	157	158	Anal and Stomal Procedures
Surg	159	160	Hernia Procedures Except Inguinal and Femoral, Age >17

(continued)

Notes
_____
_____
_____
_____
_____
_____
_____
_____
_____
_____
_____
_____
_____
_____
_____
_____
_____
_____
_____
_____

TABLE 5–2 *continued*

Surgical / Medical	With CC	W/O CC	Descriptor
Surg	161		Hernia Procedures Inguinal and Femoral Only, Age >17
Surg	162		Hernia Procedures Inguinal and Femoral Only, Age 0–17
Surg	163		Hernia Procedures, Age 0–17
Surg	164	165	Appendectomy with Complicated Principal Diagnosis
Surg	166	167	Appendectomy without Complicated Principal Diagnosis
Surg	170	171	Other Digestive System OR Procedures
Med	172	173	Digestive Malignancy
Med	174	175	GI Hemorrhage
Med	176		Complicated Peptic Ulcer
Med	177	178	Uncomplicated Peptic Ulcer
Med	179		Inflammatory Bowel Disease
Med	180	181	GI Obstruction
Med	182	183	Esophagitis, Gastroenteritis and Miscellaneous Digestive Disorders, Age >17
Med	184		Esophagitis, Gastroenteritis and Miscellaneous Digestive Disorders, Age 0–17
Med	188	189	Other Digestive System Diagnoses, Age >17
Med	190		Other Digestive System Diagnoses, Age 0–17

MDC 07 - Hepatobiliary System

Surg	191	192	Pancreas, Liver and Shunt Procedures
Surg	193	194	Biliary Tract Procedures Except Only Cholecysto with or without CDE
Surg	195	196	Cholecystectomy with CDE
Surg	197	198	Cholecystectomy Except by Laparoscope without CDE
Surg	199		Hepatobiliary Diagnostic Procedure for Malignancy

Notes

Surgical Medical	With CC	W/O CC	Descriptor
Surg	200		Hepatobiliary Diagnostic Procedure for Non-Malignancy
Surg	201		Other Hepatobiliary or Pancreas OR Procedures
Surg	493	494	Laparoscopic Cholecystectomy without CDE
Med	202		Cirrhosis and Alcoholic Hepatitis
Med	203		Malignancy of Hepatobiliary System or Pancreas
Med	204		Disorders of Pancreas Except Malignancy
Med	205	206	Disorders of Liver Except Malignancy, Cirrhosis, Alcoholic Hepatitis
Med	207	208	Disorders of Biliary Tract

DRG 08 - Musculoskeletal

Surgical Medical	With CC	W/O CC	Descriptor
Surg	209		Major Joint and Limb Reattachment Procedures, Lower Extremity
Surg	210	211	Hip and Femur Procedures Except Major Joint, Age >17
Surg	212		Hip and Femur Procedures Except Major Joint, Age 0–17
Surg	213		Amputation Musculoskeletal System and Connective Tissue Disorders
Surg	216		Biopsies of Musculoskeletal System and Connective Tissue
Surg	217		Wound Debridement and Skin Graft Except Hand for Musculoskeletal and Connective Tissue Disease
Surg	218	219	Lower Extremity and Humerus Procedures Except Hip, Foot, Femur, Age >17
Surg	220		Lower Extremity and Humerus Procedures Except Hip, Foot, Femur, Age 0–17
Surg	223	224	Major Shoulder, Elbow, Other Upper Extremities
Surg	225		Foot Procedures
Surg	226	227	Soft Tissue Procedures

(continued)

TABLE 5–2   *continued*

Surgical Medical	With CC	W/O CC	Descriptor
Surg	228	229	Major Thumb, Joint Procedures, Hand, or Wrist
Surg	230		Local Excision, Removal Internal Fixation Devices, Hip and Femur
Surg	231		Local Excision, Removal Internal Fixation Devices, Except Hip and Femur
Surg	232		Arthroscopy
Surg	233	234	Other Musculoskeletal, Connective Tissue OR Procedures
Surg	471		Bilateral, Multiple Major Joint Procedures, Lower Extremity
Surg	491		Major Joint and Limb Reattachment Procedures, Upper Extremity
Surg	496		Combined Anterior/Posterior Spinal Fusion
Surg	497	498	Spinal Fusion
Surg	499	500	Back, Neck Procedures Except Spinal Fusion
Surg	501	502	Knee Procedures with Principal Diagnosis Infection
Surg	503		Knee Procedures without Principal Diagnosis of Infection
Med	235		Fractures of Femur
Med	236		Fractures of Hip and Pelvis
Med	237		Sprains, Strains, Dislocations of Hip, Pelvis, Thigh
Med	238		Osteomyelitis
Med	239		Pathological Fractures and Musculoskeletal/Connective Tissue Malignancy
Med	240	241	Connective Tissue Disorders
Med	242		Septic Arthritis
Med	243		Medical Back Problems
Med	244	245	Bone Disease, Specific Arthropathies
Med	246		Nonspecific Arthropathies

Notes

Surgical Medical	With CC	W/O CC	Descriptor
Med	247		Signs, Symptoms Musculoskeletal System/Connective Tissue
Med	248		Tendonitis, Myositis, Bursitis
Med	249		Aftercare, Musculoskeletal System/Connective Tissue
Med	250	251	Fracture, Sprain, Strain, Dislocations Forearm, Hand, Foot, Age >17
Med	252		Fracture, Sprain, Strain, Dislocations Forearm, Hand, Foot, Age 0–17
Med	253	254	Fracture, Sprain, Strain, Dislocations Upper Arm, Lower Leg, Age >17
Med	255		Fracture, Sprain, Strain, Dislocations Upper Arm, Lower Leg, Age 0–17
Med	256		Other Musculoskeletal System/Connective Tissue Diagnoses
DRG 09 - Skin and Breast			
Surg	257	258	Total Mastectomy for Malignancy
Surg	259	260	Subtotal Mastectomy for Malignancy
Surg	261		Breast Procedure for Nonmalignancy Except Biopsy/Local Excision
Surg	262		Breast Biopsy and Local Excision for Nonmalignancy
Surg	263	264	Skin Graft/Debridement for Skin Ulcer/Cellulitis
Surg	265	266	Skin Graft/Debridement Except Skin Ulcer/Cellulitis
Surg	267		Perianal and Pilonidal Procedures
Surg	268		Skin, Subcutaneous Tissue, Breast Plastic Procedures
Surg	269	270	Other Skin, Subcutaneous Tissue, Breast Procedures
Med	272	273	Major Skin Disorder

(continued)

Notes

_____

_____

_____

_____

_____

_____

_____

_____

_____

_____

_____

_____

_____

_____

_____

_____

_____

_____

_____

_____

TABLE 5–2   *continued*

Surgical Medical	With CC	W/O CC	Descriptor
Med	274	275	Malignant Breast Disorders
Med	276	276	Nonmalignant Breast Disorders
Med	277	278	Cellulitis, Age >17
Med	279	279	Cellulitis, Age 0–17
Med	280	281	Trauma Skin, Subcutaneous Tissue, Breast, Age >17
Med	282	282	Trauma Skin, Subcutaneous Tissue, Breast, Age 0–17
Med	283	284	Minor Skin Disorders
DRG 10 - Endocrine Disorders			
Surg	285		Amputation Lower Limb, Endocrine, Nutritional, Metabolic Disorder
Surg	286		Adrenal and Pituitary Procedures
Surg	287		Skin Grafts, Wound Debridement for Endocrine, Nutritional Metabolic Disorders
Surg	288		OR Procedures for Obesity
Surg	289		Parathyroid Procedures
Surg	290		Thyroid Procedures
Surg	291		Thyroglossal Procedures
Surg	292	293	Other Endocrine, Nutritional, Metabolic OR Procedures
Med	294		Diabetes, Age >35
Med	295		Diabetes, Age 0–35
Med	296	297	Nutritional, Miscellaneous Metabolic Disorders, Age >17
Med	298		Nutritional, Miscellaneous Metabolic Disorders, Age 0–17
Med	299		Inborn Errors for Metabolism
Med	300	301	Endocrine Disorders
DRG 11 - Urinary System			

Notes

Surgical Medical	With CC	W/O CC	Descriptor
Surg	302		Kidney Transplant
Surg	303		Kidney, Ureter and Major Bladder Procedures for Neoplasm
Surg	304	305	Kidney, Ureter and Major Bladder Procedures for Non-Neoplasm
Surg	306	307	Prostatectomy
Surg	308	309	Minor Bladder Procedures
Surg	310	311	Transurethral Procedures
Surg	312	313	Urethral Procedures, Age >17
Surg	314		Urethral Procedures, Age 0–17
Surg	315		Other Kidney and Urinary Tract OR Procedures
Med	316		Renal Failure
Med	317		Admit for Renal Dialysis
Med	318	319	Kidney and Urinary Tract Neoplasms
Med	320	321	Kidney and Urinary Tract Infection, Age >17
Med	322	322	Kidney and Urinary Tract Infection, Age 0–17
Med	323		Urinary Stones with CC and/or ESW Lithotripsy
Med		324	Urinary Stones
Med	325	326	Kidney and Urinary Tract Signs/Symptoms, Age >17
Med	327	327	Kidney and Urinary Tract Signs/Symptoms, Age 0–17
Med	328	329	Urethral Stricture, Age >17
Med	330	330	Urethral Stricture, Age 0–17
Med	331	332	Other Kidney and Urinary Tract Diagnoses, Age >17
Med	333	333	Other Kidney and Urinary Tract Diagnoses, Age 0–17

DRG 12 - Male Reproductive System

| Surg | 334 | 335 | Major Male Pelvic Procedures |

(continued)

TABLE 5–2   _continued_

Surgical Medical	With CC	W/O CC	Descriptor
Surg	336	337	Transurethral Prostatectomy
Surg	338	338	Testes Procedures for Malignancy
Surg	339	339	Testes Procedures for Nonmalignancy, Age >17
Surg	340	340	Testes Procedures for Nonmalignancy, Age 0–17
Surg	341	341	Penis Procedures
Surg	342	342	Circumcision, Age >17
Surg	343	343	Circumcision, Age 0–17
Surg	344	344	Other Male Reproductive System OR Procedures for Malignancy
Surg	345	345	Other Male Reproductive System OR Procedures for Nonmalignancy
Med	346	347	Malignancy, Male Reproductive System
Med	348	349	Benign Prostatic Hypertrophy
Med	350	350	Inflammation of Male Reproductive System
Med	351	351	Sterilization, Male
Med	352	352	Other Male Reproductive System Diagnoses

DRG 13 - Female Reproductive System

Surg	353		Pelvic Evisceration, Radical Hysterectomy and Radical Vulvectomy
Surg	354	355	Uterine, Adnexa Procedure for Nonovarian/Adnexal Malignancy
Surg	356		Female Reproductive System Reconstructive Procedures
Surg	357	358	Uterine and Adnexa Procedure for Ovarian/Adnexal Malignancy
Surg	360		Vagina, Cervix, Vulva Procedures
Surg	361		Laparoscopy and Incisional Tubal Interruption
Surg	362		Endoscopic Tubal Interruption
Surg	363		D & C, Conization and Radio-Implant for Malignancy

Notes

Surgical Medical	With CC	W/O CC	Descriptor
Surg	364		D & C, Conization Except for Malignancy
Surg	365		Other Female Reproductive System OR Procedures
Med	366	367	Malignancy, Female Reproductive System
Med	368		Infections, Female Reproductive System
Med	369		Menstrual and Other Female Reproductive System Disorders

DRG 14 - Pregnancy and Childbirth

Surgical Medical	With CC	W/O CC	Descriptor
Surg	370	371	Cesarean Section
Surg	372		Vaginal Delivery with Complicating Diagnoses
Surg	373		Vaginal Delivery without Complicating Diagnoses
Surg	374		Vaginal Delivery with Sterilization and/or D & C
Surg	375		Vaginal Delivery with OR Procedures Except Sterilization and/or D & C
Surg	376		Postpartum and Postabortion Diagnoses without OR Procedure
Surg	377		Postpartum and Postabortion Diagnoses with OR Procedure
Med	378		Ectopic Pregnancy
Med	379		Threatened Abortion
Med	380		Abortion without D & C
Med	381		Abortion with D & C, Aspiration Curettage, or Hysterotomy
Med	382		False Labor
Med	383		Other Antepartum Diagnoses with Medical Complications
Med	384		Other Antepartum Diagnoses without Medical Complications

DRG 15 - Newborns and Neonates

Surgical Medical	With CC	W/O CC	Descriptor
Med	385		Neonates, Died or Transferred to Another Acute Care Facility

(continued)

TABLE 5–2 _continued_

Surgical Medical	With CC	W/O CC	Descriptor
Med	386		Extreme Immaturity or Respiratory Distress Syndrome, Neonate
Med	387		Prematurity with Major Problems
Med	388		Prematurity without Major Problems
Med	389		Full Term Neonate with Major Problems
Med	390		Neonate with Other Significant Problems
Med	391		Normal Newborn
DRG 16 - Blood Disorders			
Surg	392		Splenectomy, Age >17
Surg	393		Splenectomy, Age 0–17
Surg	394		Other OR Procedures of the Blood and Blood-Forming Organs
Med	395		Red Blood Cells Disorders, Age >17
Med	396		Red Blood Cells Disorders, Age 0–17
Med	397		Coagulation Disorders
Med	398	399	Reticuloendothelial and Immunity Disorders
DRG 17 - Myeloproliferative Neoplasm			
Surg	400		Lymphoma and Leukemia with Major OR Procedure
Surg	401	402	Lymphoma and Nonacute Leukemia with Other OR Procedures
Surg	406	407	Myeloproliferative Disorders or Poorly Differentiated Neoplasm with Major OR Procedure
Surg	408		Myeloproliferative Disorders or Poorly Differentiated Neoplasm with Other OR Procedure
Surg	473		Acute Leukemia without Major OR Procedure, Age >17
Med	403	404	Lymphoma and Nonacute Leukemia

Notes

Surgical Medical	With CC	W/O CC	Descriptor
Med	405		Acute Leukemia without Major OR Procedure, Age 0–17
Med	409		Radiotherapy
Med	410		Chemotherapy without Acute Leukemia as Secondary Diagnosis
Med	411		History of Malignancy without Endoscopy
Med	412		History of Malignancy with Endoscopy
Med	413	414	Other Myeloproliferative Disorders or Poorly Differentiated Neoplasm Diagnosis
Med	492		Chemotherapy with Acute Leukemia as Secondary Diagnosis

DRG 18 - Infectious and Parasitic Disease

Surgical Medical	With CC	W/O CC	Descriptor
Surg	415		OR Procedure for Infectious and Parasitic Diseases
Med	416		Septicemia, Age >17
Med	417		Septicemia, Age 0–17
Med	418		Postoperative and Post-Traumatic Infections
Med	419	420	Fever of Unknown Origin, Age >17
Med	421		Viral Illness, Age >17
Med	422		Viral Illness and Fever of Unknown Origin, Age 0–17
Med	423		Other Infectious and Parasitic Diseases Diagnoses

DRG 19 - Psychiatric

Surgical Medical	With CC	W/O CC	Descriptor
Surg	424		OR Procedure with Principal Diagnoses of Mental Illness
Med	425		Acute Adjustment Reaction and Psychological Dysfunction
Med	426		Depressive Neuroses
Med	427		Neuroses Except Depressive
Med	428		Disorders of Personality and Impulse Control
Med	429		Organic Disturbances and Mental Retardation
Med	430		Psychoses

(continued)

TABLE 5–2 _continued_

Surgical Medical	With CC	W/O CC	Descriptor
Med	431		Childhood Mental Disorders
Med	432		Other Mental Disorder Diagnoses
DRG 20 - Alcohol and/or Drug Disorders			
Med	433		Alcohol/Drug Abuse or Dependence, Left AMA
Med	434	435	Alcohol/Drug Abuse or Dependence or Other Symptom Treatment
Med	436		Alcohol/Drug Dependence with Rehabilitation Therapy
Med	437		Alcohol/Drug Dependence, Combined Rehabilitation and Detox Therapy
DRG 21 - Injury and Poisoning			
Surg	439		Skin Grafts for Injuries
Surg	440		Wound Debridements for Injuries
Surg	441		Hand Procedures for Injuries
Surg	442	443	Other OR Procedures for Injuries
Med	444	445	Traumatic Injury, Age >17
Med	446		Traumatic Injury, Age 0–17
Med	447		Allergic Reactions, Age >17
Med	448		Allergic Reactions, Age 0–17
Med	449	450	Poisoning and Toxic Effects of Drugs, Age >17
Med	451		Poisoning and Toxic Effects of Drugs, Age 0–17
Med	452	453	Complications of Treatment
Med	454	455	Other Injury, Poisoning and Toxic Effect Diagnosis
DRG 22 - Burns			
Surg	504		Extensive 3rd-Degree Burns with Skin Graft
Surg	505		Extensive 3rd-Degree Burns without Skin Graft
Surg	506	507	Full Thickness Burn with Skin Graft or Inhal Injury or Significant Trauma

Notes

Surgical Medical	With CC	W/O CC	Descriptor
Surg	508	509	Full Thickness Burn without Skin Graft or Inhal Injury or Significant Trauma
Surg	510	511	Nonextensive Burns with or without CC or Significant Trauma

DRG 23 - V Codes

Surg	461		OR Procedures with Diagnoses of Other Contact with Health Services
Med	462		Rehabilitation
Med	463	464	Signs and Symptoms
Med	465		Aftercare with History of Malignancy as Secondary Diagnosis
Med	466		Aftercare without History of Malignancy as Secondary Diagnosis
Med	467		Other Factors Influencing Health Status

DRG 24 - Multiple Significant Trauma

Surg	484		Craniotomy for Multiple Significant Trauma
Surg	485		Limb Reattachment, Hip and Femur Procedures, Multiple Significant Trauma
Surg	486		Other OR Procedures for Multiple Significant Trauma
Med	487		Other Multiple Significant Trauma

DRG 25 - HIV Infections

Surg	488		HIV with Extensive OR Procedures
Med	489		HIV with Major Related Conditions
Med	490		HIV with or without Other Related Conditions

NON-MDC DRGs

	468		Extensive OR Procedure Unrelated to Principal Diagnosis
	469		Principal Diagnosis Invalid as Discharge Diagnosis
	476		Prostatic OR Procedure Unrelated to Principal Diagnosis

(continued)

TABLE 5–2 *continued*

Surgical Medical	With CC	W/O CC	Descriptor
PreSurg	480		Liver Transplant
PreSurg	481		Bone Marrow Transplant
PreSurg	482		Tracheostomy for Face, Mouth, Neck Diagnoses
PreSurg	483		Tracheostomy Except Face, Mouth, Neck Diagnoses
PreSurg	495		Lung Transplant

Special DRG Assignments

In addition to the above criteria of principal diagnosis, surgical/medical categorization, patient age, discharge status and presence or absence of complications or comorbidities, the DRG Definitions Manual published by CMS (Center for Medicare Services) formerly known as HCFA (Healthcare Financial Administration) outlines specific guidelines for specific DRGs. These additional categories and their definitions are listed below:

- Prinicipal Diagnosis

  A specific set of principal diagnoses is utilized in the DRG definition.

  Only admissions with a principal diagnosis included in the list for that DRG may be assigned that DRG designation.

- Operating Room Procedures

  This DRG designation is intended for use only when the principal diagnosis involves a specified surgical procedure performed in the operating room.

- Nonoperating Room Procedures

  DRGs from this category are assigned when procedures do not involve the use of the OR are performed. An performed An excellent example would be cardiac catheterization, which normally does not require the use of the OR.

- With or without Operating Room Procedures

  These DRGs may be utilized regardless of whether the procedures performed are done in the operating room. For instance, the removal of calculi may be performed in the OR laparoscopically (OR) or by the use of lithotripsy (non-OR).

- Any Operating Room Procedure

  This designation is assigned to DRGs when any OR procedures performed for the principal diagnosis assigned to the DRG are performed.

Notes

- Operating Room Procedures and Comorbidity

  Specific OR procedures are assigned to the specific DRG as well as the presence of complications and/or comorbidities.

- Any Combination of Two or More Operating Room Procedures

  In order for DRGs from this category to be assigned, two or more procedures from the listing under the DRG must be documented on the patient record.

- Any of the Following Procedure Combinations

  The combination of procedures listed in the specified DRG must all be listed on the patient's record in order for the specified DRG to be assigned.

- Principal or Secondary Diagnosis

  The most common category of DRG assignments, this designation is assigned when a principal or secondary diagnosis listed is included in the patient record.

- Secondary Diagnosis

  Specific secondary diagnoses are assigned to the patient's encounter in conjunction with specific principal diagnoses in order for these DRG designations to be utilized.

- Only Secondary Diagnosis

  In these instances, only a specific set of secondary diagnoses may be assigned to that designated DRG.

PRACTICE EXERCISE 5–1

Let's combine the knowledge from Chapter 4, *Inpatient Coding*, with the information above regarding DRG assignment. Take the same charts to in which you assigned ICD-9-CM diagnostic and procedure codes in Chapter 5, Practice Exercise 4–5, and designate the proper DRG for each chart. If you have already coded these charts, simply bring your diagnostic codes forward for this exercise, or utilize the charts in this chapter to code and assign DRGs to practice the whole process.

1. Patient is a 78-year-old female with a known history of metastatic carcinoma of the left breast. The patient has been experiencing extreme pain, accompanied by shortness of breath, especially in the right upper quadrant. The patient also has a history of diabetes, COPD and s/p mastectomy for her breast cancer approximately 4 years ago. The patient has been treated in the past with chemotherapy as well as radiation therapy; her primary site has never been identified.

The patient was treated with IV pain meds, sliding scale insulin and her pain subsided over the next several days. She was switched to oral pain meds which she tolerated well, and was discharged on day 5.

Medications at discharge were: Aldactone, 25 mg daily; Tamoxifen, 10 mg; Lanoxin, 0.125 mg daily; Tolinase, 250 mg tablet; Reglan; 10 mg; Lasix, 20 mg bid; and Vicodin tablets, 1 every 4–6 hours as needed for pain.

Discharge Diagnosis:

Uncontrolled pain secondary to metastatic breast carcinoma. Dehydration, NIDDM, uncontrolled at the time of admission.

Admitting Diagnosis: _____ Code: _____

Principal Diagnosis: _____ Code: _____

Secondary Diagnosis: _____ Code: _____

Secondary Diagnosis: _____ Code: _____

Secondary Diagnosis: _____ Code: _____

Principal Procedure: _____ Code: _____

Secondary Procedure: _____ Code: _____

Secondary Procedure: _____ Code: _____

Secondary Procedure: _____ Code: _____

DRG ASSIGNMENT: _____

2. Forty-five-year-old female admitted for long history of abdominal pain, primarily in the left lower quadrant. The pain has been present for some time now, and does not seem related to food, position, or stress. Patient has been worked up by her primary care physician with an EGD and colonoscopy, both of which were negative. Duodenitis was an incidental finding on the EGD for which she was prescribed Prevacid.

She is admitted for further workup due to unrelenting abdominal pain. She received an ultrasound of the abdomen as well as a CT. A mass was found in in the kidney that appears to also involve the pancreas.

Patient went to the operating room for a nephrectomy. The metastatic pancreatic site was not explored, but will be treated with chemotherapy

Notes

at this time. The involvement in the pancreas did not appear to be significant, and whatever the outcome, it was felt that the chemotherapy would be as beneficial as any surgical intervention we would have to offer her.

The patient tolerated the procedure well and was sent to the intensive care unit where she began experiencing difficulties, including the need for blood transfusions. Following several additional days of intensive care, the patient's condition improved and the patient was then transferred to the oncology floor.

Her first dose of chemotherapy was administered as an inpatient, and she will be treated aggressively for the metastatic pancreatic cancer.

Prognosis is guarded, and the patient and her husband are so informed.

Admitting Diagnosis: _____ Code: _____

Principal Diagnosis: _____ Code: _____

Secondary Diagnosis: _____ Code: _____

Secondary Diagnosis: _____ Code: _____

Secondary Diagnosis: _____ Code: _____

Principal Procedure: _____ Code: _____

Secondary Procedure: _____ Code: _____

Secondary Procedure: _____ Code: _____

Secondary Procedure: _____ Code: _____

DRG ASSIGNMENT: _____

3. This 24-year-old female presented to the emergency room following an altercation with her boyfriend yesterday evening. She received a direct blow to the left eye and face, and has already been to the police station, filed a complaint and had photographs taken. She also complained of left lower quadrant abdominal pain.

She has swelling and a hematoma below her left eye with a swollen, tender inferior orbital rim. She has tenderness and pain along the inferior orbitalrim, with some diploplia with extraocular movement. Her nose is tender along the bridge. Neck has some contusions and abrasions, although minor. She shows exquisite tenderness to palpation of her abdomen, with guarding. CT of the abdomen was negative, so we will watch her abdomen during her hospitalization.

X-rays of the inferior orbital rim show a blowout fracture of the right orbit. Nasal x-rays were negative.

The patient was taken to the operating room, where the orbital fracture was reduced and placement of an implant in the right orbital floor area was done. She recovered postoperatively during the next 2–3 days, her abdominal pain resolved, contusions resolved and she appeared stable for discharge. She was instructed to return in 3–5 days for suture removal.

Admitting Diagnosis: _____ Code: _____

Principal Diagnosis: _____ Code: _____

Secondary Diagnosis: _____ Code: _____

Secondary Diagnosis: _____ Code: _____

Secondary Diagnosis: _____ Code: _____

Principal Procedure: _____ Code: _____

Secondary Procedure: _____ Code: _____

Secondary Procedure: _____ Code: _____

Secondary Procedure: _____ Code: _____

DRG ASSIGNMENT: _____

4. The patient is an 82-year-old female who is s/p right colectomy for cancer. She had a post-op wound infection and has one persistent area of chronic sinus drainage without evidence of overt infection or foreign body. This area has not resolved after approximately 3 months of wound care. She presents for admission for excision of the entire sinus tract. Patient also has a history of hypertension, arthritis and a history of chronic alcoholism.

The patient was brought to the OR and placed in the supine position. We excised the area of surrounding fistulous tract without entering the tract itself. The deepest part was just above the fascia. There was no fascial defect to repair. The area was irrigated with saline, and closed the subcutaneous tissue with Vicryl and the skin was closed with staples.

Notes

She will remain in the hospital for 24–48 hours to make certain this resolves her problem. She will receive her chemotherapy for her colon carcinoma while an inpatient and continue as an outpatient after discharge.

Admitting Diagnosis: _____ Code: _____

Principal Diagnosis: _____ Code: _____

Secondary Diagnosis: _____ Code: _____

Secondary Diagnosis: _____ Code: _____

Secondary Diagnosis: _____ Code: _____

Principal Procedure: _____ Code: _____

Secondary Procedure: _____ Code: _____

Secondary Procedure: _____ Code: _____

Secondary Procedure: _____ Code: _____

DRG ASSIGNMENT: _____

5. This is a 58-year-old known diabetic female who recently underwent debridement of a decubitus ulcer of the plantar aspect of the foot X4. Despite conservative therapy as well as wound care, the ulcer has enlarged and the second toe on the left foot appears to be gangrenous. She also has arrythmia problems, and had a pacemaker implanted approximately 6 years ago. She also has a past history of hypertension and CHF for which she takes Lasix 40 mg per day.

She indicates in her history that she has also suffered an MI; however, we could find no documentation to substantiate this occurred. Perhaps she is referring to her episodes of arrythmia that necessitated the pacemaker.

Exam reveals second toe with erythema into the foot; however, toe itself appears to not be viable at this time.

We will proceed with an amputation of the second toe of the left foot and begin IV antibiotic treatment.

Diagnosis: Necrotic 2nd toe, left foot

We will schedule surgical procedure for tomorrow and begin IV antibiotic therapy preoperatively.

Patient was taken to the operating room, where the digit was prepped and draped in the usual sterile fashion. The 2nd phalanx on the left foot was sharply excised and the bone rasped smooth with a file. The wound was irrigated copiously, dressed and the patient was returned from the operating room in satisfactory condition. We will aggressively treat the wound, as she has experienced difficulties in the past; will order bedrest, elevation, soaks and IV Garamycin.

On the 5th day postoperative, her wound was clean and dry, and her glucose levels were within normal range. She will be switched to oral antibiotics for the next 24 hours in preparation for discharge.

Admitting Diagnosis: _____ Code: _____

Principal Diagnosis: _____ Code: _____

Secondary Diagnosis: _____ Code: _____

Secondary Diagnosis: _____ Code: _____

Secondary Diagnosis: _____ Code: _____

Principal Procedure: _____ Code: _____

Secondary Procedure: _____ Code: _____

Secondary Procedure: _____ Code: _____

Secondary Procedure: _____ Code: _____

DRG ASSIGNMENT: _____

Due to the fact that, as mentioned earlier, hospital rates differ based on the hospital's designation and location, the calculation for reimbursement would vary from facility to facility.

While the principal and secondary diagnosis assignments directly affect the third-party DRG designation and reimbursement, there are many other elements in the inpatient billing process that drive proper reimbursement.

Many facilities utilize a reference text known as a DRG Optimizer to assist in the assignment of the most appropriate diagnostic code for the principal diagnosis. As mentioned in Chapter 4, *Inpatient Coding*, this may be utilized in lieu of encoding software, or in combination with the software. Since facilities typically bill for several thousands of dollars in reimbursement, proper DRG assignment is integral to maximizing reimbursement appropriate to the resources expended by the facility.

Notes

Table 5–3 (located at the end of this chapter) indicates the specific fields necessary in the proper completion of the UB-92. We have previously reviewed a general overall completion of this form in Section II—Process Overview. However, Table 5–3 is specific to the completion of the UB-92 from the inpatient perspective.

CONCLUSION

After completing this chapter, student should be capable of properly completing the UB-92/CMS 1450 for inpatient facility services as well as determining the appropriate DRG assignment that will determine reimbursement. This includes comprehending additional considerations for changes in DRG assignments such as complications and comorbidities.

Now that we have completed a review of the inpatient coding and billing process, complete the CMS 1450/UB-92 claim exercises located on the CD-ROM that accompanies this text. Keep in mind that the assignment of DRGs is not completed within the text of the UB-92; however, the facility should know the appropriate DRG assignment in order to determine the reimbursement expected. You may still wish to assign DRGs to each case study to identify the level of reimbursement that may be expected. Always keep in mind that the order of the diagnostic codes—e.g., principal diagnosis followed by complications and/or comorbidities—makes the determination for the DRG assignment. Choose your principal diagnosis carefully. Many facilities will look at each diagnosis and its relative weight, determine whether other diagnoses could be considered as principal and, after careful consideration, make their final assignment.

TABLE 5–3   INPATIENT UB-92 COMPLETION DETAILS.

FL	Field Name	Specifics	# Digits	Digits (A)lpha (N)um	Medicare (R)eq (O)pt	Others (R)eq (O)pt
PROVIDER BILLING INFORMATION (FL 1-11)						
1	Line a - Name of Provider	Information on Provider Submitting Bill		AlphaNum	REQ	REQ
	Line b - Street Address, PO Box	Address Where Payment Should Be Sent		AlphaNum	REQ	REQ
	Line c - City, St Abbreviation, Zip		5/9 zip	AlphaNum	REQ	REQ
	Line d - Telephone and Fax # Country Code		10	Num Alpha	OPT	OPT

(continued)

TABLE 5–3   *continued*

FL	Field Name	Specifics	# Digits	Digits (A)lpha (N)um	Medicare (R)eq (O)pt	Others (R)eq (O)pt
2	Unlabeled Field	Unlabeled Field				
3	Patient Control Number	Unique identification number assigned by provider to each patient. Speeds up processing of checks, data entry	20	AlphaNum	REQ	REQ
4	Type of Bill	First digit - Type of Facility	1	Num	REQ	REQ
		Second digit - Billing Classification	1	Num	REQ	REQ
		Third digit - Frequency of Billing	1	Num	REQ	REQ
	Type of Bill	Except Clinics/Special Facilities				

First Digit

0 - Not Applicable
1 - Hospital
2 - Skilled Nursing
3 - Home Health Facility
4 - Relig nonmedical health care hospital inpatient
5 - Relig nonmedical health care post-hospital extended care
6 - Intermediate Care
7 - Clinic/hospital-based renal dialysis facility
8 - Special facility/hospital ASC
9 - Reserved for national assignment

Second Digit

0 - Not Applicable
1 - Inpatient (Medicare Part A)
2 - Inpatient (Medicare Part B)
4 - Other (Medicare Part B)
5 - Intermediate Care Level I
6 - Intermediate Care Level II
7 - Subacute inpatient
8 - Swing bed
9 - Reserved for national assignment

Third Digit

0 - Nonpayment/zero claim
1 - Admit thru discharge claim
2 - Interim-First Claim
3 - Interim-Continuing Claim
4 - Interim-Last Claim
5 - Late Charge(s) only claim
6 - Adjustment prior claim
7 - Replacement prior claim
8 - Void/cancel prior claim
9 - Final claim Home Health PPS episode

Clinics Only

First Digit

0 - Not Applicable
1 - Hospital
2 - Skilled Nursing

Second Digit

0 - Not Applicable
2 - Hospital-Based/Independent Renal Dialysis

Third Digit

0 - Nonpayment/zero claim
1 - Admit thru discharge claim
2 - Interim-First Claim

FL	Field Name	Specifics	# Digits	Digits (A)lpha (N)um	Medicare (R)eq (O)pt	Others (R)eq (O)pt
	3 - Home Health Facility				3 - Interim-Continuing Claim	
	4 - Relig nonmedical health care hospital inpatient				4 - Interim-Last Claim	
	5 - Relig nonmedical health care post-hospital extended care	5 - Comprehensive outpatient			5 - Late Charge(s) only claim	
	6 - Intermediate Care	6 - Community mental health (CMHC)			6 - Adjustment prior claim	
	7 - Clinic/hospital-based renal dialysis facility	7 - Reserved for national assignment			7 - Replacement prior claim	
		8 - Reserved for national assignment			8 - Void/cancel prior claim	
	9 - Reserved for national assignment	9 - Other			9 - Final claim Home Health PPS episode	

Special Facilities Only

First Digit	Second Digit	Third Digit
0 - Not Applicable	0 - Not Applicable	0 - Nonpayment/zero claim
1 - Hospital		1 - Admit thru discharge claim
2 - Skilled Nursing	2 - Hospital (Hospital-Based)	2 - Interim-First Claim
3 - Home Health Facility		3 - Interim-Continuing Claim
4 - Relig nonmedical health care hospital inpatient	4 - Freestanding birthing center	4 - Interim-Last Claim
5 - Relig nonmedical health care post-hospital extended care	5 - Critical access hospitals	5 - Late Charge(s) only claim
6 - Intermediate Care	6 - Residential facility (Non-Medicare)	6 - Adjustment prior claim
7 - Clinic/hospital-based renal dialysis facility	7 - Reserved for national assignment	7 - Replacement prior claim
8 - Special facility/hospital ASC	8 - Reserved for national assignment	8 - Void/cancel prior claim
9 - Reserved for national assignment	9 - Other	9 - Final claim Home Health PPS episode

FL	Field Name	Specifics	# Digits	Digits (A)lpha (N)um	Medicare (R)eq (O)pt	Others (R)eq (O)pt
5	Federal Tax ID Number	Federal TIN (Tax ID Number) OR EIN (Employer ID Number)	9	AlphaNum	OPT	REQ
6	Statement Covers Period Same-Day Services Inpatient Interim/No Discharge Final Bill	From/Thru Dates From/Thru Identical Thru calculated as part of FL 7-10 Thru Date of Discharge or Death No dashes/no slashes	8	Num	REQ	REQ

(continued)

TABLE 5–3 *continued*

FL	Field Name	Specifics	# Digits	Digits (A)lpha (N)um	Medicare (R)eq (O)pt	Others (R)eq (O)pt
7	Covered Days	Records total number inpatient days authorized by primary carrier within claim billing period Date of discharge/death not counted as covered date (Unless patient elects to use Medicare lifetime reserve days) Hospitals: Maximum 150 days: 60 days hospitalization 60 lifetime reserve days 30 coinsurance days	3	Num	REQ	REQ Medi as carrier
8	Noncovered Days	Days not covered by primary carrier FL 7 + FL 8 = FL 6 days	4	Num	REQ	REQ Medi as carrier
9	Coinsurance Days	Inpatient hospital days occurring after 60th day and before 91st day in single benefit period of spell of illness # cannot exceed 30 hospital days	2	Num	REQ	REQ Medi as carrier
10	Lifetime Reserve Days	Medicare patient used 60 covered hospital days and 30 coinsurance days may elect to use a lifetime reserve of up to 60 days inpatient hospital services	2	Num	REQ	REQ Medi as carrier
11	Unlabeled Field					

Patient Information (FL 12-23)

| 12 | Patient Name | No apostrophes, hyphens Titles not used Medicare: must appear exactly as on Medicare card Last Name, First Name, MI | | Alpha | REQ | REQ |

FL	Field Name	Specifics		# Digits	Digits (A)lpha (N)um	Medicare (R)eq (O)pt	Others (R)eq (O)pt
13	Patient Address	Street Name/PO Box City, State Abbreviation, Zip 5-9 digits 1st 3 zip digits must be valid		50	AlphaNum	REQ	REQ
14	Patient Birth Date	If cannot obtain after reasonable efforts, should fill with zeros Do not leave blank		8	Num	REQ	REQ
15	Patient Sex	M-Male F-Female U-Unknown		1	Alpha	REQ	REQ
16	Patient Marital Status	S-Single M-Married P-Life partner (domestic partner) D-Divorced W-Widowed X-Legally separated U-Unknown		1	Alpha	NO	NO
17	Admission/ Start of Care Date	Admission Date ** Required for inpatient, home health, hospice, outpatient rehab/ facility		8	Num	REQ**	REQ**
18	Admission Hour	AM	PM	2	Num	NO	REQ
	0	12:00 mid-12:59	12 12:00-12:59				
	1	1:00-1:59	13 1:00-1:59				
	2	2:00-2:59	14 2:00-2:59				
	3	3:00-3:59	15 3:00-3:59				
	4	4:00-4:59	16 4:00-4:59				
	5	5:00-5:59	17 5:00-5:59				
	6	6:00-6:59	18 6:00-6:59				
	7	7:00-7:59	19 7:00-7:59				
	8	8:00-8:59	20 8:00-8:59				
	9	9:00-9:59	21 9:00-9:59				
	10	10:00-10:59	22 10:00-10:59				
	11	11:00-11:59	23 11:00-11:59 99 Unknown				

(continued)

TABLE 5–3 *continued*

FL	Field Name	Specifics	# Digits	Digits (A)lpha (N)um	Medicare (R)eq (O)pt	Others (R)eq (O)pt
Patient Information (FL 12-23)						

19	Type of Admission	Code for establishing level of urgency for admission
		1 - Emergency
		   Severe, life-threatening, potentially disabling
		2 - Urgent
		   Patient should be admitted ASAP
		   Within 24–48 hours
		3 - Elective
		   Schedule in advance
		4 - Newborn
		   Used only when baby is born in the facility submitting the claim
		5 - Trauma Center
		   Must be properly licensed and so designated
		6-8 Reserved for national assignment
		9 - Information Not Available
			1	Num	REQ	REQ

20	Source of Admission	For All Admissions Except Newborns: 1 - Physician Referral 2 - Clinic Referral 3 - HMO Referral 4 - Transfer from Hospital 5 - Transfer from SNF 6 - Transfer other health care facility 7 - Emergency Room 8 - Court/law enforcement 9 - Information not available A - Transfer from critical access hosp	1	AlphaNum	REQ	REQ

FL	Field Name	Specifics	# Digits	Digits (A)lpha (N)um	Medicare (R)eq (O)pt	Others (R)eq (O)pt
		B - Transfer from another home health agency (HHA)				
		C - Readmission to same home health agency				
		D-Z Reserved for national assignment				
		Newborn Admissions ONLY:				
		1 - Normal Delivery				
		2 - Premature Delivery				
		3 - Sick baby				
		4 - Extramural birth Born in nonsterile environment				
		5-8 Reserved for national assignment				
		9 - Do not use				
21	Discharge Hour	Use Same Table for Discharge Hour as for Admission Hour	2	Num	NO	PREF
22	Patient Status	Patient's discharge status at the time of the "thru" date on the UB-92	2	Num	REQ Part A	REQ
		01 - Discharged Home/Self-Care				
		02 - Discharged/Transferred Short-Term Hosp for Inpatient Care				
		03 - Discharged/Transferred SNF Not for swing bed, see 61				
		04 - Discharged/Transferred ICF				
		05 - Discharged/Transferred another type facility				
		06 - Discharged/transferred to home with Home Health Care				
		07 - LMA (left against medical advice)				
		08 - Discharged/transferred to home IV care				
		09 - Admitted as inpt same facility				
		10-19 Discharged to be defined on state level				

(continued)

TABLE 5–3   *continued*

FL	Field Name	Specifics	# Digits	Digits (A)lpha (N)um	Medicare (R)eq (O)pt	Others (R)eq (O)pt
		20 - Expired				
		21-29 Expired - defined at state level				
		30 - Active patient				
		31-39 Still a patient-defined state level				
		40 - Expired at home (hospice)				
		41 - Expired med facility (hospice)				
		42 - Expired place unknown (hospice)				
		43-49 Reserved national assignment				
		50 - Discharged to hospice-home				
		51 - Discharged to hospice-med fac				
		52-60 Reserved national assignment				
		61 - Discharged/transferred within institution to swing bed				
		62 - Discharged/transferred another rehab fac inc rehab distinct part units of hospital				
		63 - Discharged/transferred long-term care hospital				
		64-70 Reserved national assignment				
		71 - Discharged/transferred/referred another institution for outpt svcs				
		72 - Discharged/transferred/referred to this institution for outpt svcs				
		73-99 Reserved national assignment				
23	Medical Record Number		17	AlphaNum	REQ	REQ TRICARE

FL	Field Name	Specifics	# Digits	Digits (A)lpha (N)um	Medicare (R)eq (O)pt	Others (R)eq (O)pt
CONDITION CODES (FL 24-31)						
24-30	Condition Codes	Identifies special condition/unique circumstance. Assist carrier in determination of eligibility for coverage/payment. Up to seven (7) may be listed. List in ascending order, numbers then letters, separated by comma	2	AlphaNum	REQ If Applicable	REQ If Applicable

Insurance Codes

01 - Military Service Related
02 - Employment Related
03 - Covered by Insurance Not on Claim
04 - Pt HMO Enrollee
05 - Lien Filed
06 - ESRD Pt First 19 Months Covered by Employer Plan
07 - Treatment Nonterminal Condition Hospice Patient
08 - Beneficiary Would Not Provider Other Insur Info
09 - Patient/Spouse Employed
10 - Pt/Spouse Employed but No Employer Coverage
11- Disabled Beneficiary No Employer Coverage
12-16 Payer Use Only
17 - Patient Homeless
18 - Maiden Name Retained
19 - Child Retain's Mother's Name
20 - Beneficiary Requested Billing
21 - Billing for Denial Notice
22 - Patient Multiple Drug Regimen
23 - Home Caregiver Available
24 - Home IV Patient Receiving HHA Services

Patient Condition Codes

25 - Patient Non-US Resident
26 - VA-Elig Patient Chooses Medicare-Certified Facility
27 - Pt Referred Sole Community Hosp Dx Laboratory Test(s)
28 - Pt/Spouse Employer 2nd to Care
29 - Disabled Beneficiary/Family Member Health Plan 2nd to Care
30 - Qualifying Clinical Trials
31 - Full-Time Day Student
32 - Student (Coop/Work Study)
33 - Student (Full-Time Night)
34 - Student (Part-Time)
35 - Reserved for National Assignment
36 - General Care Patient/Special Unit
37 - Ward Accommodation/ Patient Request
38 - Semiprivate Room Not Available
39 - Private Room Medically Necessary
40 - Same-Day Transfer

Room Codes

41 - Partial Hospitalization
42 - Continuing Care Not Rel to Inpt Adm
43 - Continuing Care Not Provided within Prescribed Postdischarge Window
44-45 Reserved for National Assignment

TRICARE Codes

46 - Nonavailability Statement NOF
47 - Reserved for TRICARE
48 - Psych Residential Treatment Center
49-54 Reserved for National Assignment
55 - SNF Bed Not Available
56 - Medical Appropriateness
57 - SNF Readmission
58 - Term Medicare + Choice Organization
59 - Reserved for National assignment
60 - Day Outlier
61 - Cost Outlier
62-65 Payer Only Codes

(continued)

TABLE 5–3   *continued*

FL	Field Name	Specifics	# Digits	Digits (A)lpha (N)um	Medicare (R)eq (O)pt	Others (R)eq (O)pt

SPECIAL CODES

Other Special Codes

66 - Provider Does Not Wish Cost Outlier Payment

67 - Beneficiary Elects Not to Use Lifetime Reserve Days

68 - Beneficiary Elects to Use Lifetime Reserve Days

69 - Operating Indirect Medical Education Payment Only

Renal Dialysis Setting Codes

70 - Self-Administered Epoetin

71 - Full Care in Unit

72 - Self-Care in Unit

73 - Self-Care Training

74 - Home

75 - Home-100% Reimbursement

76 - Backup In-facility Dialysis

QIO Approval Indicator Svcs

C0 - Reserved National assignment

C1 - Approved as Billed

C2 - Auto Approval As Billed Based on Focused Review

C3 - Partial Approval

C4 - Admission/Service Denied

C5 - Postpayment Review

C6 - Admission Preauthorization

C7 - Extended Authorization

C8-C9 Reserved for National Assignment

Miscellaneous Codes

77 - Provider Accepts/Obligated to Accept Payment Primary Payer as Payment in Full

78 - New Coverage Not Implemented by HMO

79 - CORD Services Provided Off-Site

80-99 Reserved State Assignment

Special Programs

A0 - TRICARE External Partnership

A1 - EPSDT/CHAP

A2 - Physically Handicapped Children's Program

A3 - Special Federal Funding

A4 - Family Planning

A5 - Disability

Claim Change Reasons

D0 - Changes to Service Dates

D1 - Changes to Charges

D2 - Changes in Revenue Codes/ HCPCS Codes

D3 - 2nd/Subsequent Interim PPS Bill

D4 - Change in Grouper Input

D5 - Cancel to Correct Claim # or Provider ID Number

D6 - Cancel Only to Repay Duplicate Or OIG Overpayment

D7 - Change to Make Medicare 2nd

D8 - Change to Make Medicare Primary

D9 - Any Other Change

E0 - Change in Patient Status

A6 - Medicare Pneumococcal Pneumonia Vaccine/ Influenza

A7 - Induced Abortion-Danger to Life

A8 - Induced Abortion-Victim Rape/Incest

A9 - 2nd Opinion Surgery

B0 - Medicare Coordinated Care Demonstration Claim

B1 - Beneficiary Inelig Demonstration Prog

B2 - Critical Access Hosp Ambulance Attestation

B3-B9 Reserved for National Assignment

E1-E9 Reserved for National Assignment

G0 - Distinct Medical Visit

G1-G9 Reserved for National Assignment

H0 - Delayed Filing, Statement of Intent Submitted

H1-H9 Reserved for National Assignment

M0-M2 Payer Only Codes

M3-M9 Reserved for Payer Assignment

N0-W9 Reserved for National Assignment

X0-Z9 Reserved for State Assignment

31   Unlabeled Field

FL	Field Name	Specifics	# Digits	Digits (A)lpha (N)um	Medicare (R)eq (O)pt	Others (R)eq (O)pt

OCCURRENCE CODES/DATES (FL 32-38)

FL	Field Name	Specifics	# Digits	Digits (A)lpha (N)um	Medicare (R)eq (O)pt	Others (R)eq (O)pt
32-35	Occurrence Codes/ Dates	Significant event/occurrence that occurred in connection with service	2	AlphaNum	REQ if applic	REQ if applic

Accident-Related Codes

01 - Auto Accident
02 - No-Fault/Auto/Other
03 - Accident/Tort Liability
04 - Accident/Employment
05 - Other Accident
06 - Crime Victim
07-08 Reserved for National Assignment

Medical Condition Codes

09 - Start Infertility Treatment
10 - Last Menstrual Period
11 - Onset Symptoms/Illness
12 - Date Onset Chronically Dependent Individual
13-15 Reserved for National Assignment

Insurance-Related Codes

16 - Date of Last Therapy
17 - Date Outpt Occupational Therapy Plan Established/ Last Reviewed
18 - Date Retirement Pt/ Beneficiary
19 - Date Retirement Spouse
20 - Guarantee of Payment Began
21 - UR Notice Received
22 - Date Active Care Ended
23 - Date Cancellation Hospice Elective Period
24 - Date Insurance Denied
25 - Date Benefits Terminated Primary Payer
26 - Date SNF Bed Available
27 - Date Hospice Cert or Recert
28 - Date Comprehensive Outpt Rehab Facility Plan Est/ Reviewed
29 - Date Outpt Physical Therapy Plan Established/Last Reviewed
30 - Date Outpt Speech Path Plan Established/Last Reviewed
31 - Date Beneficiary Notified of Intent to Bill (Accommodations)
32 - Date Beneficiary Notified of Intent to Bill (Procedures/Trmts)
33 - 1st Day Medicare Coordination Period for ESRD Beneficiaries Covered by Employ Group Plan

Patient Service Codes

40 - Scheduled Date Admission
41 - Date 1st Test Preadmission Testing
42 - Date of Discharge
43 - Schedule Surgery Date Cancelled
44 - Date Occupational Therapy Started
45 - Date Speech Therapy Started
46 - Date Cardiac Rehab Started
47 - Date Cost Outlier Status Began
48-49 Payer Codes
50-69 Reserved for State Assignment
70-99 Reserved Occurrence Span Codes
A0 - Reserved for National Assignment
A1 - Birth Date - Insured A
A2 - Effective Date-Insured A Policy
A3 - Benefits Exhausted
A4-A9 Reserved for National Assignment
B0 - Reserved for National Assignment
B1 - Birth Date - Insured B
B2 - Effective Date-Insured B Policy
B3 - Benefits Exhausted
B4-B9 Reserved for National Assignment

(continued)

TABLE 5-3 *continued*

FL	Field Name	Specifics	# Digits	Digits (A)lpha (N)um	Medicare (R)eq (O)pt	Others (R)eq (O)pt
		34 - Date Election of Extended Care		C0 - Reserved for National Assignment		
		35 - Date Treatment Started Phy Ther		C1 - Birth Date - Insured C		
		36 - Date Inpt Hospital Discharge Covered Transplant Patient		C2 - Effective Date - Insured C Policy		
		37 - Date Inpt Hospital Discharge Noncovered Transplant Patient		C3 - Benefits Exhausted C4-C9 Reserved for National Assignment		
		38 - Date Treatment Start IV Home Therapy		D0-D9 Reserved for National Assignment		
		39 - Date Discharged Continuous Course IV Therapy		E0-G9 Follow same assignment for Insured E, F, G		
				H0-I9 Reserved for National Assignment		
				J0-L9 Reserved for State Assignment		
36	Occurrence Span Codes/Dates	Cannot be used in conjunction with Occurrence Codes If > 2 codes, may utilized occurrence code fields of additional listing(s)	2	AlphaNum	REQ if applic	REQ if applic
	70 - Qualifying Stay Dates	76 - Patient Liability		M0 - QIO/UR Approved Stay Dates		
	71 - Prior Stay Date	77 - Provider Liability Period Utilization Charged		M1 - Provider Liability-No Utilization		
	72 - First/Last Visit	78 - SNF Prior Stay Dates		M2 - Dates Inpatient Respite Care		
	73 - Benefit Eligibility I Period	79 - Payer Code		M3-W9 Reserved for National Assignment		
	74 - Noncovered Leve of Care/Leave of Absence LOA	80-99 Reserved for State Assignment		X0-Z9 Reserved for State Assignment		
	75 - SNF Level of Care					
37	Internal Control Number (ICN) Document Control Number (DCN)	Found on remittance voucher of original claim Must be reported for Medicare adjustment claims Subdivided into three (3) lines A - Primary Payer B - Secondary Payer C - Tertiary Payer			REQ Resubmissions	REQ

FL	Field Name	Specifics	# Digits	Digits (A)lpha (N)um	Medicare (R)eq (O)pt	Others (R)eq (O)pt
38	Responsible Party Name and Address	Guarantor on account May also be used when claim involves payer primary to Medicare		AlphaNum	NO	NO

VALUE CODES AND AMOUNTS (FL 39-41)

FL	Field Name	Specifics	# Digits	Digits (A)lpha (N)um	Medicare (R)eq (O)pt	Others (R)eq (O)pt
39-41	Value Code/Amount	Multiples should be reported in alphanumeric order Decimal points not keyed Nondollars reported with 2 zeros on end (e.g., 45 = 45.00)	2/Code 8/Amts	AlphaNum	REQ If Applic	REQ If Applic

01 - Most Common Semiprivate Room Rate
02 - Hospital Has NO Semi-private Room
03 - Reserved for National Assignment
04 - Inpt Professional Component Charges Are Combined Billed
05 - Prof Component Inc in Charges/Billed Separately
06 - Medicare Blood Deductible
07 - Reserved for National Assignment
08 - Medicare Lifetime Reserve Amount in 1st Calendar Year
09 - Medicare Coinsurance Amount in 1st Calendar Year in Billing Period
10 - Medicare Lifetime Reserve Amount in 2nd Calendar Year in Billing Period
11- Medicare Coinsurance Amt 2nd Calendar Year
12 - Working Aged Beneficiary/ Spouse with Employer Health Plan

21 - Medicaid/Catastrophic
22 - Medicaid/Surplus
23 - Medicaid/Recurring Monthly Income
24 - Medicaid Rate Code
25-29 Unassigned/Reserved for Medicaid National Assignment
30 - Preadmission Testing to Carrier
31 - Patient Liability Amount
32-36 Reserved for National Assignment
37 - Pints of Blood Furnished
38 - Blood Deductible Pints
39 - Pints of Blood Replaced
40 - New Coverage Not Implemented by HMO (Inpt Only)
41 - Black Lung
42 - Veterans Affairs
43 - Disabled Beneficiary Under Age 65 with Group Health Plan
44 - Amount Provider Agreed to Accept Primary Insurer When Amount < Total Charges But > Primary Insured Payment

46 - Number of Grace Days
47 - Any Liability Insurance
48 - Hemoglobin Reading
49 - Hematocrit Reading
50 - Physical Therapy Visits
51 - Occupational Therapy Visits
52 - Speech Therapy Visits
53 - Cardiac Rehab Visits
54 - Newborn Birth Weight in Grams
55 - Reserved for National Assignment

Home Health Codes
56 - Skilled Nurse-Home Visit Hours (HHA)
57 - Home Health Aid - Visit Hours
58 - Arterial Blood Bas
59 - Oxygen Saturation
60 - HHA Branch MSA
61 - Location Where Service Furnished (HHA/Hospice)
62-65 for Payer Use
66 - Reserved for National Assignment
67 - Peritoneal Dialysis
68 - EPO - Drug

(continued)

TABLE 5–3   *continued*

FL	Field Name	Specifics		# Digits	Digits (A)lpha (N)um	Medicare (R)eq (O)pt	Others (R)eq (O)pt
	13 - ESRD Beneficiary in Medicare Coordination Period with Employer Group Health 14 - No-Fault/Inc Auto/Other 15 - Workers' Compensation 16 - Public Health Service or Other Federal Agency 17-20 Reserved for Payer Use	45 - Accident Hour as follows: AM 0 12:00-12:59 1 1:00-1:59 2 2:00-2:59 3 3:00-3:59 4 4:00-4:59 5 5:00-5:59 6 6:00-6:59 7 7:00-7:59 8 8:00-8:59 9 9:00-9:59 10 10:00-10:59 11 11:00-11:59	PM 12 12:00-12:59 13 1:00-1:59 14 2:00-2:59 15 3:00-3:59 16 4:00-4:59 17 5:00-5:59 18 6:00-6:59 19 7:00-7:59 20 8:00-8:59 21 9:00-9:59 22 10:00-10:59 23 11:00-11:50 99 Unknown			69 - Reserved National Assignment 70-79 Reserved for Payer Use 80-99 Reserved for State Assignment	
		A1 - Deductible Payer A B1 - Deductible Payer B C1 - Deductible Payer C A2 - Coinsurance Payer A B2 - Coinsurance Payer B C2 - Coinsurance Payer C A3 - Estimated Responsibility Payer A B3 - Estimated Responsibility Payer B C3 - Estimated Responsibility Payer C					

REVENUE DESCRIPTIONS, CODES, CHARGES (FL 42-49)

| 42-43 | Revenue Code/ Description | Revenue code identifies specific service being billed
Last digit 0 = general code
Last digit 9 = Other
Detailed revenue codes (not ending in 0) required for following:
29X, 304, 33X, 367, 42X, 52X, 55-59X
624, 636, 80-85X
23 lines available | 3 | Num | REQ | REQ |

FL	Field Name	Specifics	# Digits	Digits (A)lpha (N)um	Medicare (R)eq (O)pt	Others (R)eq (O)pt
		Up to 9 pages (450 lines) acceptable on one claim List in ascending order by DOS except 001 Total Charges (last)				
	Revenue Code (Subcategory)	Standard Abbreviation				

42 Revenue Code   **43 Revenue Description**

01X Reserved

02X Health Insurance PPS

0 Reserved

1 Reserved

2 SNF PPS System   SNF PPS (RUG)

3 Rehab Facility PPS   HH PPS

4 Inpatient Rehab   IRF PPS
   Facility

5-9 Reserved

03X - 09X Reserved

Accommodation Codes

10X All-Inclusive Rate

    0 All-Inclusive   ALL INC R&B/ANC
      R & B Plus Ancillary

    1 All-Inclusive R & B   ALL INCL R&B

11X R & B (Private/Med/Gen)

    0 General   ROOM-BOARD/PVT

    1 Med/Surg/Gyn   MED-SUR-GY/PVT

    2 Obstetrics (OB)   OB/PVT

    3 Pediatric   PEDS/PVT

    4 Psychiatric   PSYCH/PVT

    5 Hospice   HOSPICE/PVT

    6 Detoxification   DETOX/PVT

    7 Oncology   ONCOLOGY/PVT

    8 Rehabilitation   REHAB/PVT

    9 Other   OTHER/PVT

12X R & B (2 Bed/Med/Gen)

    0 General   ROOM-BOARD/SEMI

    1 Med/Surg/Gyn   MED-SUR-GY/2BED

    2 Obstetrics (OB)   OB/2BED

    3 Pediatric   PEDS/2BED

    4 Psychiatric   PSYCH/2BED

(continued)

TABLE 5–3   *continued*

FL	Field Name	Specifics	# Digits	Digits (A)lpha (N)um	Medicare (R)eq (O)pt	Others (R)eq (O)pt
	5 Hospice	HOSPICE/2BED				
	6 Detoxification	DETOX/2BED				
	7 Oncology	ONCOLOGY/2BED				
	8 Rehabilitation	REHAB/2BED				
	9 Other	OTHER/2BED				
13X R & B (3-4 Beds)						
	0 General	ROOM-BOARD/3&4 BED				
	1 Med/Surg/Gyn	MED-SUR-GY/3&4 BED				
	2 Obstetrics (OB)	OB/3 & 4BED				
	3 Pediatric	PEDS/3 & 4BED				
	4 Psychiatric	PSYCH/3 & 4BED				
	5 Hospice	HOSPICE/3 & 4BED				
	6 Detoxification	DETOX/3 & 4BED				
	7 Oncology	ONCOLOGY/3&4BED				
	8 Rehabilitation	REHAB/3&4 BED				
	9 Other	OTHER/3&4BED				
14X Private (Deluxe)						
	0 General	ROOM-BOARD/PVT/DLX				
	1 Med/Surg/Gyn	MED-SUR-GY/DLX				
	2 Obstetrics (OB)	OB/DLX				
	3 Pediatric	PEDS/DLX				
	4 Psychiatric	PSYCH/DLX				
	5 Hospice	HOSPICE/DLX				
	6 Detoxification	DETOX/DLX				
	7 Oncology	ONCOLOGY/DLX				
	8 Rehabilitation	REHAB/DLX				
	9 Other	OTHER/DLX				
15X R & B (Ward/Med/Gen)						
	0 General	ROOM-BOARD/WARD				
	1 Med/Surg/Gyn	MED-SUR-GY/WARD				
	2 Obstetrics (OB)	OB/WARD				
	3 Pediatric	PEDS/WARD				
	4 Psychiatric	PSYCH/WARD				
	5 Hospice	HOSPICE/WARD				
	6 Detoxification	DETOX/WARD				
	7 Oncology	ONCOLOGY/WARD				
	8 Rehabilitation	REHAB/WARD				
	9 Other	OTHER/WARD				

FL	Field Name	Specifics	# Digits	Digits (A)lpha (N)um	Medicare (R)eq (O)pt	Others (R)eq (O)pt
16X Other R & B						
	0 General	R&B				
	4 Sterile Environment	R&B/STERILE				
	7 Self-Care	R&B/SELF				
	9 Other	R&B/OTHER				
17X Nursing						
	0 General	NURSERY				
	1 Newborn Level I Routine Newborn Care	NURSERY/LEVEL I				
	2 Newborn Level II Low Birthweight Neonates	NURSERY/LEVEL II				
	3 Newborn Level III Sick Neonates/Not NICU	NURSERY/LEVEL III				
	4 Newborn Level IV Sick Neonates/NICU	NURSERY/LEVEL IV				
18X Leave of Absence (LOA)						
	0 General	LOA OR LEAVE OF ABSENCE				
	1 Reserved					
	2 Pt Convenience-Billable	LOA/PT CONV CHGS BILLABLE				
	3 Therapeutic Leave	LOA/THERAP				
	4 ICF Mentally Retarded	LOA/ICF/MR				
	5 Nursing Home (Hosp)	LOA/NURS HOME				
	9 Other LOA	LOA/OTHER				
19X Subacute Care						
	0 General	SUBACUTE				
	1 Subacute Level I Minimal Nursing Care	SUBACUTE/LEVEL I				
	2 Subacute Level II Moderate Nursing Care	SUBACUTE/LEVEL II				
	3 Subacute Level III Mod/Extensive Nursing	SUBACUTE/LEVEL III				
	4 Subacute Level IV Extensive Nurs/Tech	SUBACUTE/LEVEL IV				
20X Intensive Care						
	0 General	INTENSIVE CARE OR ICU				
	1 Surgical	ICU/SURGICAL				
	2 Medical	ICU/MEDICAL				
	3 Pediatric	ICU/PEDS				
	4 Psychiatric	ICU/PSTAY				
	6 Intermed ICU	ICU/INTERMEDIATE				

(continued)

TABLE 5–3 *continued*

FL	Field Name	Specifics	# Digits	Digits (A)lpha (N)um	Medicare (R)eq (O)pt	Others (R)eq (O)pt
	7 Burn Care	ICU/BURN CARE				
	8 Trauma	ICU/TRAUMA				
	9 Other ICU	ICU/OTHER				
	21X Coronary Care					
	0 General	CORONARY CARE OR CCU				
	1 Myocardial Infarction	CCU/MYO INFARC				
	2 Pulmonary Care	CCU/PULMONARY				
	3 Heart Transplant	CCU/TRANSPLANT				
	4 Intermediate CCU	CCU/INTERMEDIATE				
	9 Other Coronary Care	CCU/OTHER				
	Ancillary Services					
	22X Special Charges					
	0 General	SPECIAL CHARGES				
	1 Admission Charge	ADMIT CHARGE				
	2 Tech Support Charge	TECH SUPPT CHG				
	3 UR Service Charge	UR CHARGE				
	4 Late Discharge/Med Necess	LATE DISCH/MED NEC				
	9 Other Special Charges	OTHER SPEC CHG				
	23X Incremental Nursing Care					
	0 General	NURSING INCREM				
	1 Nursery	NUR INCR/NURSERY				
	2 OB	NUR INCR/OB				
	3 ICU (inc transitional care)	NUR INCR/ICU				
	4 CCU (inc transitional care)	NUR INCR/CCU				
	5 Hospice	NUR INCR/HOSPICE				
	9 Other	NUR INCR/OTHER				
	24X All-Inclusive Ancillary					
	0 General	ALL INCL ANCIL				
	1 Basic	ALL INCL BASIC				
	2 Comprehensive	ALL INCL COMP				
	3 Specialty	ALL INCL SPECIAL				
	9 Other All-Inclusive Ancillary	ALL INCL ANCIL/OTHER				
	25X Pharmacy					
	0 General	PHARMACY				
	1 Generic Drugs	DRUGS/GENERIC				
	2 Nongeneric Drugs	DRUGS/NONGENERIC				
	3 Take-Home Drugs	DRUGS/TAKEHOME				
	4 Drugs Incident to Dx Serv	DRUGS/INCIDENT ODX				

FL	Field Name	Specifics	# Digits	Digits (A)lpha (N)um	Medicare (R)eq (O)pt	Others (R)eq (O)pt
	5 Drugs Incident to Radiology	DRUGS/INCIDENT RAD				
	6 Experimental Drugs	DRUGS/EXPERIMT				
	7 Nonprescription Drugs	DRUGS/NONPSCRPT				
	8 IV Solutions	IV SOLUTIONS				
	9 Other Pharmacy	DRUGS/OTHER				

26X IV Therapy — **Usually Requires HCPCS Code(s)**
- 0 General — IV THERAPY
- 1 Infusion Pump — IV THER/INFSN PUMP
- 2 IV Therapy/Pharmacy — IV THER/PHARM/SVC
- 3 IV Therapy/Drug/Supply/Delivery — IV THER/DRUG/SUPPLY DELV
- 4 IV Therapy/Supplies — IV THER/SUPPLIES
- 9 Other IV Therapy — IV THERAPY/OTHER

27X Med/Surg Supplies/Devices — **Only Nonroutine Billed with This RC**
- 0 General — MED-SUR SUPPLIES
- 1 Nonsterile Supply — NONSTER SUPPLY
- 2 Sterile Supply — STERILE SUPPLY
- 3 Take-Home Supplies — TAKEHOME SUPPLY
- 4 Prostetic/Orthotic Devices — PROSTH/ORTH DEV
- 5 Pacemaker — PACEMAKER
- 6 Intraocular Lenses — INTRO OC LENS
- 7 Oxygen-Take Home — 02/TAKEHOME
- 8 Other Implants — SUPPLY/IMPLANTS
- 9 Other Supplies/Devices — SUPPLY/OTHER

28X Oncology
- 0 General — ONCOLOGY
- 9 Other Oncology — ONCOLOGY/OTHER

29X DME (Other Than Renal)
- 0 General — MED EQUIP/DURAB
- 1 Rental — MED EQUIP/RENT
- 2 Purchase of New DME — MED EQUIP/NEW
- 3 Purchase of Used DME — MED EQUIP/USED
- 4 Supplies/Drugs for DME Effectiveness (HHA) — MED EQUIP/SUPPLIES/DRUGS
- 9 Other Equipment — MED EQUIP/OTHER

30X Laboratory
- 0 General — LABORATORY OR LAB
- 1 Chemistry — LAB/CHEMISTRY
- 2 Immunology — LAB/IMMUNOLOGY

(continued)

TABLE 5–3   *continued*

FL	Field Name	Specifics	# Digits	Digits (A)lpha (N)um	Medicare (R)eq (O)pt	Others (R)eq (O)pt
	3 Renal Patient (Home)	LAB/RENAL HOME				
	4 Nonroutine Dialysis	LAB/NR DIALYSIS				
	5 Hematology	LAB/HEMATOLOGY				
	6 Bacteriology/Microbiology	LAB/BACT-MICRO				
	7 Urology	LAB/UROLOGY				
	9 Other Laboratory	LAB/OTHER				
31X	**Laboratory Pathological**					
	0 General	PATHOLOGY LAB OR PATH LAB				
	1 Cytology	PATHOL/CYTOLOGY				
	2 Histology	PATHOL/HISTOLOGY				
	4 Biopsy	PATHOL/BIOPSY				
	9 Other	PATHOL/OTHER				
32X	**Radiology-Diagnostic**					
	0 General	DX X-RAY				
	1 Angiocardiography	DX X-RAY/ANGIO				
	2 Arthrography	DX X-RAY/ARTH				
	3 Arteriography	DX X-RAY/ARTER				
	4 Chest X-Ray	DX X-RAY/CHEST				
	9 Other	DX X-RAY/OTHER				
33X	**Radiology-Therapeutic**					
	0 General	RX X-RAY				
	1 Chemotherapy-Injected	CHEMOTHER/INJ				
	2 Chemotherapy-Oral	CHEMOTHER/ORAL				
	3 Radiation Therapy	RADIATION RX				
	5 Chemotherapy/IV	CHEMOTHERAP-IV				
	9 Other	RX X-RAY/OTHER				
34X	**Nuclear Medicine**					
	0 General	NUCLEAR MEDICINE OR NUC MED				
	1 Diagnostic	NUC MED/DX				
	2 Therapeutic	NUC MED/RX				
	9 Other	NUC MED/OTHER				
34X	**CT Scan**					
	0 General	CT SCAN				
	1 Head Scan	CT SCAN/HEAD				
	2 Body Scan	CT SCAN/BODY				
	9 Other CT Scans	CT SCAN/OTHER				
36X	**Operating Room Services**					
	0 General	OR SERVICES				
	1 Minor Surgery	OR/MINOR				

FL	Field Name	Specifics	# Digits	Digits (A)lpha (N)um	Medicare (R)eq (O)pt	Others (R)eq (O)pt
	2 Organ Transplant/ Not Kidney	OR/ORGAN TRANS				
	7 Kidney Transplant	OR/KIDNEY TRANS				
	9 Other	OR/OTHER				
37X Anesthesia						
	0 General	ANESTHESIA				
	1 Anes Incident to RAD	ANESTHE/INCIDENT RAD				
	2 Anes Incident to Other Dx	ANESTHE/INCIDENT ODX				
	4 Acupuncture	ANESTHE/ACUPUNC				
	9 Other	ANESTHE/OTHER				
38X Blood						
	0 General	BLOOD				
	1 Packed Red Cells	BLOOD/PKD RED				
	2 Whole Blood	BLOOD/WHOLE				
	3 Plasma	BLOOD/PLASMA				
	4 Platelets	BLOOD/PLATELETS				
	5 Leukocytes	BLOOD/LEUKOCYTES				
	6 Other Components	BLOOD/COMPONENTS				
	7 Other Derivatives	BLOOD/DERIVATIVES				
	9 Other Blood	BLOOD/OTHER				
39X Blood Storage/Processing						
	0 General	BLOOD/STOR-PROC				
	1 Blood Administration	BLOOD/ADMI				
	9 Other	BLOOD/OTHER STOR				
40X Other Imaging						
	0 General	IMAGE SERVICE				
	1 Dx Mammography	MAMMOGRAPHY				
	2 Ultrasound	ULTRASOUND				
	3 Screen Mammography	SCR MAMMOGRAPHY/GEN MAMMO				
	4 Positron Emission Tomography	PET SCAN OTHER IMAG SVS				
	9 Other					
41X Respiratory						
	0 General	RESPIRATORY SVC				
	2 Inhalation Services	INHALATION SVC				
	3 Hyperbaric Oxygen Therapy	HYPERBARIC 02 OTHER RESPIR SVS				
	9 Other					

(continued)

TABLE 5–3 *continued*

FL	Field Name	Specifics	# Digits	Digits (A)lpha (N)um	Medicare (R)eq (O)pt	Others (R)eq (O)pt
42X Physical Therapy						
	0 General	PHYSICAL THERP				
	1 Visit Charge	PHYS THERAP/VISIT				
	2 Hourly Charge	PHYS THERP/HOUR				
	3 Group Rate	PHYS THERP/GROUP				
	4 Evaluation/Reevaluation	PHYS THERP/EVAL				
	9 Other	OTHER PHYS THERP				
43X Occupational Therapy						
	0 General	OCCUPATION THER				
	1 Visit Charge	OCCUP THERP/VISIT				
	2 Hourly Charge	OCCUP THERP/HOUR				
	3 Group Rate	OCCUP THERP/GROUP				
	4 Evaluation/Reevaluation	OCCUP THERP/EVAL				
	9 Other	OTHER OCCUP THER				
44X Speech-Language Pathology						
	0 General	SPEECH PATHOL				
	1 Visit Charge	SPEECH PATH/VISIT				
	2 Hourly Charge	SPEECH PATH/HOUR				
	3 Group Rate	SPEECH PATH/GROUP				
	4 Evaluation/Reevaluation	SPEECH PATH/EVAL				
	9 Other	OTHER SPEECH PAT				
45X Emergency Room		450 Not to Be Used with Any Other Code from Series				
	0 General	EMERG ROOM				
	1 EMTALA Med Screen Svcs	ER/EMTALA				
	2 ER beyond EMTALA Screen	ER/BEYOND EMTALA				
	6 Urgent Care	URGENT CARE				
	9 Other	OTHER EMER ROOM				
46X Pulmonary Function						
	0 General	PULMONARY FUNC				
	9 Other	OTHER PULMON FUNC				
47X Audiology						
	0 General	AUDIOLOGY				
	1 Diagnostic	AUDIOLOGY/DX				
	2 Treatment	AUDIOLOGY/RX				
	9 Other	OTHER AUDIOL				

FL	Field Name	Specifics	# Digits	Digits (A)lpha (N)um	Medicare (R)eq (O)pt	Others (R)eq (O)pt
48X Cardiology						
	0 General	CARDIOLOGY				
	1 Cardiac Cath Lab	CARDIAC CATH LAB				
	2 Stress Test	STRESS TEST				
	3 Echocardiology	ECHOCARDIOLOGY				
	9 Other	OTHER CARDIOL				
49X Ambulatory Surgical Care						
	0 General	AMBUL SURG				
	9 Other	OTHER AMBL SURG				
50X Outpatient Services						
	0 General	OUTPATIENT SVS				
	9 Other	OUTPATIENT/OTHER				
51X Clinic						
	0 General	CLINIC				
	1 Chronic Pain Center	CHRONIC PAIN CL				
	2 Dental Clinic	DENTAL CLINIC				
	3 Psychiatric Clinic	PSYCH CLINIC				
	4 Ob-Gyn Clinic	OB-GYN CLINIC				
	5 Pediatric Clinic	PEDS CLINIC				
	6 Urgent Care Clinic	URGENT CLINIC				
	7 Family Practice Clinic	FAMILY CLINIC				
	9 Other	OTHER CLINIC				
52X Free-Standing Clinic						
	0 General	FREESTAND CLINIC				
	1 Rural Health-Clinic	RURAL/CLINIC				
	2 Rural Health-Home	RURAL/HOME				
	3 Family Practice Clinic	FR/STD FAMILY CLINIC				
	6 Urgent Care Clinic	FR/STD URGENT CLINIC				
	9 Other	OTHER FR/STD CLINIC				
53X Osteopathic Services						
	0 General	OSTEOPATH SVS				
	1 Osteopathic Therapy	OSTEOPATH RX				
	9 Other	OTHER OSTEOPATH				
54X Ambulance						
	0 General	AMBULANCE				
	1 Supplies	AMBUL/SUPPLY				
	2 Medical Transport	AMBUL/MED TRANS				
	3 Heart Mobile	AMBUL/HEARTMOBL				
	4 Oxygen	AMBUL/OXY				

(continued)

TABLE 5–3   *continued*

FL	Field Name	Specifics	# Digits	Digits (A)lpha (N)um	Medicare (R)eq (O)pt	Others (R)eq (O)pt
	5 Air Ambulance	AIR AMBULANCE				
	6 Neonatal Ambulance	AMBUL/NEO-NATAL				
	7 Pharmacy	AMBUL/PHARMACY				
	8 Telephone Transmission EKG	AMBUL/TELEPHONIC EKG				
	9 Other	OTHER AMBULANCE				
55X	**Skilled Nursing**					
	0 General	SKILLED NURSING				
	1 Visit Charge	SKILLED NURS/VISIT				
	2 Hourly Charge	SKILLED NURS/HOUR				
	9 Other	SKILLED NURS/OTHER				
56X	**Medical Social Services**					
	0 General	SOCIAL SVS				
	1 Visit Charge	MED SOC SERV/VISIT				
	2 Hourly Charge	MED SOC SERV/HOUR				
	9 Other	MED SOC SERV/OTHER				
57X	**Home Health Aid**					
	0 General	AIDE/HOME HEALTH				
	1 Visit Charge	AIDE/HOME HLTH/VISIT				
	2 Hourly Charge	AIDE/HOME HLTH/HOUR				
	9 Other	AIDE/HOME HLTH/OTHER				
58X	**Other Visits (Home Health)**					
	0 General	VISIT/HOME HEALTH				
	1 Visit Charge	VISIT/HOME HLTH/VISIT				
	2 Hourly Charge	VISIT/HOME HLTH/HOUR				
	9 Other	VISIT/HOME HLTH/OTHER				
59X	**Units of Service (Home Health)**					
	0 General	UNIT/HOME HEALTH				
	9 Other	UNIT/HOME HLTH/OTHER				
60X	**Oxygen (Home Health)**					
	0 General	02/HOME HEALTH				
	1 Oxygen-Stat/Equip/ Supp/or Contents	02/EQUIP/SUPPL/CONT				
	2 Oxygen-Stat/Equip/Supp Under 1 LPM	02/STAT EQUIP/UNDER 1 LPM				
	3 Oxygen-Stat/Equip/Over 4 LPM	O2/STAT EQUIP/OVER 4 LPM				
	4 Oxygen-Portable Add-On	02/STAT EQUIP/PORT ADD-ON				

FL	Field Name	Specifics	# Digits	Digits (A)lpha (N)um	Medicare (R)eq (O)pt	Others (R)eq (O)pt
	61X Magnetic Resonance					
	0 General	MRI				
	1 Brain (inc Brain Stem)	MRI-BRAIN				
	2 Spinal Cord (inc spine)	MRI-SPINE				
	3 Reserved					
	4 MRI-Other	MRI-OTHER				
	5 MRA-Head/Neck	MRA-HEAD AND NECK				
	6 MRA-Lower Extremities	MRA-LOWER EXTREMITIES				
	7 Reserved					
	8 MRA-Other	MRA-OTHER				
	9 Other	MRI-OTHER				
	62X Med/Surg/Supp **Extension of 27X**					
	1 Supplies Incident Radiology	MED-SUR SUPP/INCIDNT RAD				
	2 Supplies Incident Other Dx	MED-SUR SUPP INCIDNT ODX				
	3 Surgical Dressings	SURG DRESSING				
	4 FDA Investigation Devices	IDE				
	63X Pharmacy					
	0 Reserved					
	1 Single Source Drug	DRUG/SINGLE				
	2 Multiple Source Drug	DRUG/MULT				
	3 Restrictive Prescription	DRUG/RSTR				
	4 EPO < 10,000 units	DRUG/EPO/ < 10,000 UNITS				
	5 EPO > 10,000 units	DRUG/EPO/ > 10,000 UNITS				
	6 Drugs Req Detailed Coding	DRUGS/DETAIL CODE				
	7 Self-Admin Drugs	DRUGS/SELFADMIN				
	64X Home IV Therapy Services					
	0 General	IV THERAPY SVC				
	1 Nonroutine Nursing, Central Line	NON RT NURSING/CENTRAL				
	2 IV Site Care, Central Line	IV SITE CARE/CENTRAL				
	3 IV Start/Change, Peripheral Line	IV STRT/CHNG/PERIPHRL				
	4 Nonroutine Nursing, Peripheral Line	NONRT NURSING/PERIPHRL				
	5 Training Patient/Caregiver, Central Line	TRNG/PT/CARGVR/CENTRAL				

(continued)

TABLE 5–3   *continued*

FL	Field Name	Specifics	# Digits	Digits (A)lpha (N)um	Medicare (R)eq (O)pt	Others (R)eq (O)pt
	6 Training, Disabled Patient, Central Line	TRNG DSBLPT/CENTRAL				
	7 Training Patient/Caregiver, Peripheral Line	TRNG/PT/CARGVR/PERIPHRL				
	8 Training, Disabled Patient, Peripheral Line	TRNG/DSBLPAT/PERIPHRL				
	9 Other IV Therapy Services	OTHER IV THERAPY SVC				
	65X Hospice Services					
	0 General	HOSPICE				
	1 Routine Home Care	HOSPICE/RTN HOME				
	2 Continuous Home Care	HOSPICE/CTNS HOME				
	3 Reserved					
	4 Reserved					
	5 Inpt Respite Care	HOSPICE/IP RESPITE				
	6 General Inpt Care (Nonrespite)	HOSPICE/IP NONRESPITE				
	7 Physician Services	HOSPICE/PHYSICIAN				
	9 Other Hospice	HOSPICE/OTHER				
	66X Respite Care (HHA Only)					
	0 General	RESPITE CARE				
	1 Hourly Chg/Skilled Nursing	RESPITE/SKILLED NURSE				
	2 Hourly Chg/HHA/ Homemaker	RESPITE/HMEAID/HMEMKE				
	9 Other Respite Care	RESPITE/CARE				
	67X Oupt Special Residence					
	0 General	OP SPEC RES				
	1 Hospital-Based	OP SPEC RES/HOSP BASED				
	2 Contracted	OP SPEC RES/CONTRACTED				
	9 Other Special Residence	OP SPEC RES/OTHER				
	68X Not Assigned					
	69X Not Assigned					
	70X Cast Room					
	0 General	CAST ROOM				
	9 Other Cast Room	OTHER CAST ROOM				
	71X Recovery Room					
	0 General	RECOVERY ROOM				
	9 Other Recovery Room	OTHER RECOV ROOM				

FL	Field Name	Specifics	# Digits	Digits (A)lpha (N)um	Medicare (R)eq (O)pt	Others (R)eq (O)pt
72X Labor Room/Delivery						
	0 General	DELIVROOM/LAB				
	1 Labor	LABOR				
	2 Delivery	DELIVERY ROOM				
	3 Circumcision	CIRCUMCISION				
	4 Birthing Center	BIRTHING CENTER				
	9 Other Labor Room/ Delivery	OTHER/DELIV-LABOR				
73X EKG/ECG						
	0 General	EKG/ECG				
	1 Holter Monitor	HOLTER MONT				
	2 Telemetry	TELEMETRY				
	9 Other EKG/ECG	OTHER EKG/ECG				
74X EEG						
	0 General	EEG				
	9 Other EEG	OTHER EEG				
75X Gastro-Intestinal Services						
	0 General	GASTRO-INTS SVS				
	9 Other Gastrointestinal	OTHER GASTRO-INTS				
76X Treatment/Observation Rm						
	0 General	TREATMENT/OBSERVATION RM				
	1 Treatment Room	TREATMENT ROOM				
	2 Observation Room	OBSERVATION RM				
	9 Other Treatment Room	OTHER TREATMENT RM				
77X Preventative Care Services						
	0 General	PREVENT CARE SVS				
	1 Vaccine Administration	VACCINE ADMIN				
	9 Other Prev Care Services	OTHER PREVENT				
78X Telemedicine						
	0 General	TELEMEDICINE				
	9 Other Telemedicine	TELEMEDICINE/OTHER				
79X Lithotripsy						
	0 General	LITHOTRIPSY				
	9 Other Lithotripsy	LITHOTRIPSY/OTHER				
80X Inpatient Renal Dialysis						
	0 General	RENAL DIALYSIS				
	1 Inpt Hemodialysis	DIALY/INPT				
	2 Inpt Peritoneal (Non-CAPD)	DIALY/INPT/PER				

(continued)

TABLE 5–3 *continued*

FL	Field Name	Specifics	# Digits	Digits (A)lpha (N)um	Medicare (R)eq (O)pt	Others (R)eq (O)pt
	3 Inpt Continuous Ambulatory Peritoneal Dialysis (CAPD)	DIALY/INPT/CAPD				
	4 Inpt Continuous Ambulatory Cycling Peritoneal (CCPD)	DIALY/INPT/CCPT				
	9 Other Inpt Dialysis	DIALY/INPT/OTHER				
81X	**Organ Acquisition**					
	0 General	ORGAN ACQUISIT				
	1 Living Donor	LIVING DONOR				
	2 Cadaver Donor	CADAVER/DONOR				
	3 Unknown Donor	UNKNOWN/DONOR				
	4 Unsuccessful Organ Search Donor Bank Charge	UNSUCCESSFUL SEARCH				
	9 Other Organ Donor	OTHER/DONOR				
82X	**Hemodialysis-Outpt/Home**					
	0 General	HEMO/OP OR HOME				
	1 Hemodialysis/Composite or Other Rate	HEMO/COMPOSITE				
	2 Home Supplies	HEMO/HOME/SUPPL				
	3 Home Equipment	HEMO/HOME/EQUIP				
	4 Maintenance/100%	HEMO/HOME/100%				
	5 Support Services	HEMO/HOME/SUPSERV				
	9 Other Outpt Hemodialysis	HEMO/HOME/OTHER				
83X	**Peritoneal Dialysis-Outpatient/Home**					
	0 General	PERITONEAL/OP OR HOME				
	1 Peritoneal/Composite or Other Rate	PERTNL/COMPOSISTE				
	2 Home Supplies	PERTNL/HOME/SUPPL				
	3 Home Equipment	PERTNL/HOME/EQUIP				
	4 Maintenance/100%	PERTNL/HOME/100%				
	5 Support Services	PERTNL/HOME/SUPSERV				
	9 Other Peritoneal Dialysis	PERTNL/HOME/OTHER				

FL	Field Name	Specifics	# Digits	Digits (A)lpha (N)um	Medicare (R)eq (O)pt	Others (R)eq (O)pt
	84X Continuous Ambulatory Peritoneal Dialysis (CAPD) Outpatient/Home					
	0 General	CAPD/OP OR HOME				
	1 CAPD/Composite or Other Rate	CAPD/COMPOSITE				
	2 Home Supplies	CAPD/HOME/SUPPL				
	3 Home Equipment	CAPD/HOME/EQUIP				
	4 Maintenance/100%	CAPD/HOME/100%				
	5 Support Services	CAPD/HOME/SUPSERV				
	9 Other CAPD Dialysis	CAPD/HOME/OTHER				
	85X Continuous Cycling Peritoneal Dialysis (CCPD) Outpatient/Home					
	0 General	CCPD/OP OR HOME				
	1 CCPD/Composite or Other Rate	CCPD/COMPOSITE				
	2 Home Supplies	CCPD/HOME/SUPPL				
	3 Home Equipment	CCPD/HOME/EQUIP				
	4 Maintenance/100%	CCPD/HOME/100%				
	5 Support Services	CCPD/HOME/SUPSERV				
	9 Other CCPD Dialysis	CCPD/HOME/OTHER				
	86X Reserved Dialysis National Assignment					
	87X Reserved Dialysis State Assignment					
	88X Miscellaneous Dialysis					
	0 General	DIALY/MISC				
	1 Ultrafiltration	DIALY/ULTRAFILT				
	2 Home Dialysis Aid Visit	HOME DIALYSIS AID VISIT				
	9 Misc Dialysis Other	DIALY/MISC/OTHER				
	89X Reserved Natl Assignment					
	90X Psychiatric/Psychological Treatments					
	0 General	PSTAY TREATMENT				
	1 Electroshock Treatment	ELECTROSHOCK				
	2 Milieu Therapy	MILIEU THERAPY				
	3 Play Therapy	PLAY THERAPY				

(continued)

TABLE 5–3 *continued*

FL	Field Name	Specifics	# Digits	Digits (A)lpha (N)um	Medicare (R)eq (O)pt	Others (R)eq (O)pt
	4 Activity Therapy	ACTIVITY THERAPY				
	9 Other	OTHER PSYCH RX				
	91X Psychiatric/Psychological Services					
	0 General	PSYCH/SERVICES				
	1 Rehabilitation	PSYCH/REHAB				
	2 Partial Hosp-Less Intensive	PSYCH/PARTIAL HOSP				
	3 Partial Hosp-Intensive	PSYCH/PARTIAL INTENSIVE				
	4 Individual Therapy	PSYCH/INDIV RX				
	5 Group Therapy	PSYCH/GROUP RX				
	6 Family Therapy	PSYCH/FAMILY RX				
	7 Biofeedback	PSYCH/BIOFEED				
	8 Testing	PSYCH/TESTING				
	9 Other	PSYCH/OTHER				
	92X Other Dx Services					
	0 General	OTHER DX SVS				
	1 Peripheral Vascular Lab	PERI VASCUL LAB				
	2 Electromyelogram	EMG				
	3 Pap Smear	PAP SMEAR				
	4 Allergy Test	ALLERGY TEST				
	5 Pregnancy Test	PREG TEST				
	9 Other Dx Service	ADDITIONAL DX SVS				
	93X Med Rehab Day Program					
	1 Half Day	HALF DAY				
	2 Full Day	FULL DAY				
	94X Other Ther Services					
	0 General	OTHE RX SVS				
	1 Recreational Therapy	RECREATION RX				
	2 Education/Training	EDUC/TRAINING				
	3 Cardiac Rehab	CARDIAC REHAB				
	4 Drug Rehab	DRUG REHAB				
	5 Alcohol Rehab	ALCOHOL REHAB				
	6 Complex Med Equip-Routine	RTN COMPLX MED EQUIP-ROUT				
	7 Complex Med Equip-Ancillary	COMPLX MED EQUIP-ANX				
	9 Other Ther Services	ADDITIONAL RX SVS				

FL	Field Name	Specifics	# Digits	Digits (A)lpha (N)um	Medicare (R)eq (O)pt	Others (R)eq (O)pt

95X Other Ther Services
Extension of 94X
0 Reserved
1 Athletic Training   ATHLETIC TRAINING
2 Kinesiotherapy   KINESIOTHERAPY

96X Professional Fees
0 General   PRO FEE
1 Psychiatry   PRO FEE/PSYCH
2 Ophthalmology   PRO FEE/EYE
3 Anesthesiologist (MD)   PRO FEE/ANES MD
4 Anesthetist (CRNA)   PRO FEE/ANES CRNA
9 Other Prof Fees   OTHER PRO FEE

97X Prof Fees continued
1 Laboratory   PRO FEE/LAB
2 Radiology-Dx   PRO FEE/RAD/DX
3 Radiology-Therapeutic   PRO FEE/RAD/RX
4 Radiology-Nuclear Med   PRO FEE/NUC MED
5 Operating Room   PRO FEE/OR
6 Respiratory Therapy   PRO FEE/RESPIR
7 Physical Therapy   PRO FEE/PHYSI
8 Occupational Therapy   PRO FEE/OCUPA
9 Speech Pathology   PRO FEE/SPEECH

98X Prof Fees continued
1 Emergency Room   PRO FEE/ER
2 Outpatient Services   PRO FEE/OUTPT
3 Clinic   PRO FEE/CLINIC
4 Medical Social Services   PRO FEE/SOC SVC
5 EKG   PRO FEE/EKG
6 EEG   PRO FEE/EEG
7 Hospital Visit   PRO FEE/HOS VIS
8 Consultation   PRO FEE/CONSULT
9 Private Duty Nurse   PEE/PVT NURSE

99X Patient Convenience Items
0 General   PT CONVENIENCE
1 Cafeteria/Guest Tray   CAFETERIA
2 Private Linen Service   LINEN
3 Telephone/Telegraph   TELEPHONE
4 TV/Radio   TV/RADIO
5 Nonpt Room Rentals   NONPT ROOM RENT

(continued)

TABLE 5–3   *continued*

FL	Field Name	Specifics	# Digits	Digits (A)lpha (N)um	Medicare (R)eq (O)pt	Others (R)eq (O)pt
	6 Late Discharge Charge 7 Admission Kits 8 Beauty Shop/ Barber 9 Other Pt Convenience Items	LATE DISCHARGE ADMIT KITS BARBER/BEAUTY PT CONVENCE/OTHER				
	100X - 209X Reserved for Natl Assignment					
	210X-Alternative Therapy Svcs 0 General 1 Acupuncture 2 Accupressure 3 Massage 4 Reflexology 5 Biofeedback 6 Hypnosis 9 Other Alternative Ther Svcs					
44	HCPCS/Rates/HIPPS Rate Codes	Accommodation Code or HCPCS Code Outpatient Claims Accommodation Code Inpatient Claims Supplies/ESRD Services/ Drugs NO HCPCS Code Req Outpt Claim Multiple Codes List in Revenue Code Sequence Rates - Dollar value whole numbers decimal point/cents	2/Codes 8/Amts	AlphaNum	REQ	REQ
45	Service Date	Line item dates of service required where HCPCS code required Dates must fall within dates in FL 6	8	Num	See Note	See Note
46	Service Units	Required for following revenue code groups: 10X-15X 636 20X-21X 274	7 per line	Num	See Note	See Note

FL	Field Name	Specifics	# Digits	Digits (A)lpha (N)um	Medicare (R)eq (O)pt	Others (R)eq (O)pt
		38X 30X-31X 51X, 52X 410/420/430/440 80X 480/910/943 29X 60X 450/452/459 32X/333/34X 35X/40X/61X				
47	Total Charges	Units X Line Item Service Grand Total Listed as last line item Revenue Code 01 Includes Covered/Noncovered Chgs EXCEPT Medicare (only covered)	9	Num	REQ	REQ
48	Noncovered Charges	Utilized when noncovered days are indicated in FL 8		Num	REQ if applic	REQ if applic
49	Unlabeled Field					

PAYER/INSURED/EMPLOYER INFO (FL 50-66)

FL	Field Name	Specifics	# Digits	Digits (A)lpha (N)um	Medicare (R)eq (O)pt	Others (R)eq (O)pt
50	Payer Identification	A Primary Payer B Secondary Payer C Tertiary Payer Electronic must include Payer ID# Paper must include Carrier Code# and Name (Available from FI)	25	AlphaNum	REQ	REQ
51	Provider Number	Assigned by Payer listed in 50		AlphaNum	REQ	REQ most
52	Release of Information Certification Indicator	Y - Yes (On File) N - No (Not on File) R - Restricted (Limited Authority)	1	Alpha	REQ	REQ most
53	Assignment of Benefits Certification Indicator	Y - Yes/Benefits Assigned Payment to Provider N - No/Benefits Not Assigned Payment to Insured	1	Alpha	REQ	REQ
54	Prior Payments-Payers and Pt	All services other than Medicare inpt 7 positions - dollars 2 positions - cents 1 position - character space for credit if applicable	10	Num	REQ	REQ

(continued)

TABLE 5–3   *continued*

FL	Field Name	Specifics	# Digits	Digits (A)lpha (N)um	Medicare (R)eq (O)pt	Others (R)eq (O)pt
55	Estimated Amount Due	Estimated Due from Payer - Any Payments 10 positions in each line (A-D) 7 positions - dollars 2 positions - cents 1 position - character space for credit if applicable	10	Num	NO	
56-57	Unlabeled Fields					
58	Insured's Name	Patient or Policyholder 25 characters Line A-D Must be exactly as on insurance card Use comma to separate names No titles	25	AlphaNum	REQ	REQ
59	Patient's Relationship to Insured		2	Num	REQ Care 2nd	REQ

01 - Patient Insured
02 - Spouse
03 - Natural Child
04 - Natural Child/Insured Not
       Responsible
05 - Stepchild
06 - Foster Child
07 - Ward of Court
08 - Employee
09 - Unknown
10 - Handicapped Dependent
11 - Organ Donor
12 - Cadaver Donor
13 - Grandchild
14 - Niece/Nephew
15 - Insured Plaintiff
16 - Sponsored Dependent
17 - Minor Dependent of a Minor
       Dependent
18 - Parent
19 - Grandparent
20 - Life Partner
21-99 Reserved for National Assignment

FL	Field Name	Specifics	# Digits	Digits (A)lpha (N)um	Medicare (R)eq (O)pt	Others (R)eq (O)pt
60	Certificate/Social Security #/ Health Insurance Claim #	No spaces/hyphens/characters	19	AlphaNum	REQ	REQ
61	Insured Group Name		14	AlphaNum	REQ	REQ if applic
62	Insured Group Number		17	AlphaNum	NO	NO
63	Treatment Authorization Codes		18	AlphaNum	REQ	NO
64	Employment Status Code of the Insured			Num	REQ MSP	NO
		1 - Employed Full-Time 2 - Employed Part-Time 3 - Not Employed 4 - Self-Employed 5 - Retired 6 - Active Military Duty 7-8 Reserved for National Assignment				
65	Employer Name of the Insured		24	AlphaNum	REQ	REQ
66	Employer Location of the Insured	Can be specific city, employer location 35 AlphaNum per Line (A-C)	35	AlphaNum	REQ	

DIAGNOSIS/PROCEDURE CODES (FL 67-81)

FL	Field Name	Specifics	# Digits	Digits (A)lpha (N)um	Medicare (R)eq (O)pt	Others (R)eq (O)pt
67	Principal Diagnosis Code	Condition established after study chiefly responsible for resulting in hospital admission or hospital services cannot be E Code	6	AlphaNum	REQ	REQ
68-75	Other Diagnosis Codes	Patient condition(s) that co-exist at the time of admission/service or develop during the hospital stay or encounter	6	AlphaNum	REQ if applic	REQ if applic

(continued)

TABLE 5–3   *continued*

FL	Field Name	Specifics	# Digits	Digits (A)lpha (N)um	Medicare (R)eq (O)pt	Others (R)eq (O)pt
76	Admitting Diagnosis/ Patient's Reason for Visit	ICD-9-CM that best describes the patient's diagnosis or reason for visit in the patient's words	6	AlphaNum	REQ	REQ
77	External Cause of Injury	External cause for injury, poisoning, adverse effect	6	AlphaNum	State Reg	State Reg
78	Unlabeled Field					
79	Procedure Coding Method Used	1-3 Reserved for State Assignment 4 CPT-4 5 HCPCS 6-8 Reserved for National Assignment 9 ICD-9-CM		AlphaNum	NO	REQ
80	Principal Procedure Code/Date	Inpatient principal procedure	7/Proc 8/Date	AlphaNum	REQ Inpt Surgery	
81	Other Procedure Code/Date	Additional inpatient procedures or outpt procedures when applicable	7/Proc 8/Date	AlphaNum	REQ if applic	

ATTENDING PHYSICIAN INFORMATION (FL 82-83)

FL	Field Name	Specifics	# Digits	Digits (A)lpha (N)um	Medicare (R)eq (O)pt	Others (R)eq (O)pt
82	Attending Physician ID	Physician primarily responsible for patient's medical care/treatment FORMAT: UPIN__LastName_First Name_MI	25	AlphaNum	REQ	REQ
83	Other Physician ID	Name of other than Attending Physician performing principal procedure First line optional exc Medicare Lower line required if procedure inpatient claims	25/ upper 32/ lower	AlphaNum		

FL	Field Name	Specifics	# Digits	Digits (A)lpha (N)um	Medicare (R)eq (O)pt	Others (R)eq (O)pt
REMARKS (FL 84-86)						
84	Remarks	Explain reason for reporting noncovered days OR overflow information FL 32-35, FL 36, FL 24-30 and FL 39-41 Format Ex: FL XX: Code, Date, Value	48	AlphaNum	REQ if applic	REQ
85	Provider Representative Signature	Signature certifies provider conforms with certifications on UB-92	22	AlphaNum	REQ	REQ
86	Date Bill Submitted	Date UB-92 Signed/ Sent to Payer	10	Num	NO	REQ

Section III

Outpatient Coding/Billing

Current Procedural Terminology (CPT) © 2005 American Medical Association. All Rights Reserved.

Chapter 6

Outpatient Coding

Acuity Levels
Add-on Procedures
Ambulatory Payment
   Classifications (APCs)
Each/Each Additional/Per

Global Service
Outpatient Prospective
   Payment System (OPPS)
Separate Procedures
Unlisted Procedure

LEARNING OBJECTIVES

- Identify key documentation elements for assigning outpatient codes
- Describe basic ICD-9-CM diagnostic codes for outpatient coding
- Describe additional ICD-9-CM diagnostic coding considerations
- Demonstrate the concepts of assigning ICD-9-CM procedure codes from the outpatient coding perspective
- Describe the appropriate use of HCPCS codes for outpatient coding purposes
- Apply key concepts for assigning CPT-4 code for outpatient purposes
- Apply the appropriate coding concepts for proper use of CPT-4 modifier codes
- Describe the various methods utilized for determining Evaluation and Management codes under outpatient coding
- Discuss the general and specific guidelines for assigning outpatient codes for surgery services
- Apply the organization of the radiology section of CPT-4
- Apply the coding concepts for radiological services for outpatient services
- Describe the organization of the pathology section of CPT-4
- Apply the concepts for pathology services for coding outpatient services
- Identify the various aspects of the medicine section of CPT-4
- Apply the concepts for assigning codes in the medicine section of CPT-4 for outpatient services

249

Current Procedural Terminology (CPT) © 2005 American Medical Association. All Rights Reserved.

Notes

INTRODUCTION

Hospital outpatient coding presents perhaps as some of the most complex coding challenges, as it encompasses ICD-9-CM diagnostic coding, CPT-4 and HCPCS Level II coding as well as ICD-9-CM Volume 3 Procedural Coding. It requires the outpatient facility coder to master all coding nomenclatures and apply coding principles specific to facility and professional coders alike. Recently, some third-party carriers (i.e., insurance companies) have dropped the requirement for assigning ICD-9-CM procedural codes. The facility coder will need to be familiar with third-party contracts for the facility to code correctly, as the information systems department may program the computer software to convert the codes appropriately by carrier.

DOCUMENTATION REVIEW FOR KEY ELEMENTS

Documentation is crucial to the reimbursement process for outpatient and inpatient facility services as well as for professional services. "If not documented, the service or procedure did not occur" is frequently quoted by professionals when services are disallowed and rejected by third-party carriers because documentation does not support that the service was provided as coded and billed.

Documentation requirements will vary based on the need for information, whether it be diagnostic information or service information; however, the basic guidelines apply to the documentation for coding and billing services:

- If it is not documented, the service did not occur.
- Make certain all services and/or procedures assigned codes are substantiated by medical necessity (i.e., diagnoses).
- Make certain codes (both diagnostic and procedural) are assigned based on documentation of the text body dictated, not the titles or summarizations such as those contained in operative report titles, discharge summaries and so on.
- Always code from the operative report text, rather than straight from the title of the procedure. The surgeon may have indicated only the primary procedure performed or may be unfamiliar with additional procedures that may be assigned codes.

GENERAL ICD-9-CM DIAGNOSTIC CODING GUIDELINES

General guidelines for outpatient ICD-9-CM diagnostic coding follow. The most significant difference between the inpatient and outpatient ICD-9-CM diagnostic guidelines is the ability of the inpatient coder to utilize

Current Procedural Terminology (CPT) © 2005 American Medical Association. All Rights Reserved.

Notes

diagnostic statements such as "rule out, possible, probable." Outpatient hospital guidelines typically mimic the professional or physician coder in basic guidelines.

- List primary diagnosis, condition, problem, or reason for medical service, procedure, or encounter.
- Always utilize the highest level of specificity for codes assigned.
- Never utilize statements such as "rule out, possible, probably, suspect."
- When no definitive diagnosis is documented during the encounter, code signs or symptoms as opposed to "rule-out" statements.
- Distinguish between acute and chronic conditions.
- Determine external causes, and code when appropriate.
- Assign chronic condition codes or secondary diagnoses only when treatment or consideration is given for these conditions.
- Do not code conditions that are no longer present (use "history-of" codes).
- Always utilize the alphabetic and numeric indexes for coding assignments.
- Code secondary and additional codes for conditions that are managed or impact the medical management during that encounter.
- Assign "significant procedures" only when required by certain third-party payors. Significant procedures are defined as:
  - Carrying a procedural risk
  - Carrying an anesthestic risk
  - Requiring specialized training
  - Surgical in nature
- Secondary procedures are assigned in the following order:
  - Definitive procedures
  - Therapeutic procedures
  - Diagnostic procedures
  - Other procedures
- Codes that describe signs or symptoms are acceptable when diagnosis has not been established or confirmed by the provider at the conclusion of the outpatient contact or encounter.
- When the encounter is for circumstances other than a disease or injury, a code may be assigned from the Supplementary Classification of Factors Influencing Health Status and Contact with Health Services (V01.0–V83.02).
- For preoperative evaluations, utilize a code from category V72.8 as well as a code to indicate the condition that is the reason for surgery.
- For ambulatory surgery, utilize the diagnosis that indicates the reason the surgery was performed. If preoperative and postoperative diagnoses are provided, utilize the postoperative diagnosis.

Current Procedural Terminology (CPT) © 2005 American Medical Association. All Rights Reserved.

ICD-9-CM Code Index

The ICD-9-CM procedure code index is divided into chapters based on body areas and organ systems. A brief outline of the index follows:

	Code Range
• Infectious and Parasitic Diseases	001–139
• Neoplasms	140–239
• Endocrine, Nutritional, Metabolic, Immunity Disorders	240–279
• Blood/Blood-Forming Diseases	280–289
• Mental Disorders	290–319
• Nervous System	320–349
• Eye and Adnexa Disorders	360–379
• Ear and Mastoid Disorders	380–389
• Circulatory Disorders	390–459
• Respiratory Disorders	450–519
• Digestive System Disorders	520–579
• Genitourinary Disorders	580–629
• Complications of Pregnancy, Childbirth, Puerperium	630–677
• Skin and Subcutaneous Tissues Disorders	680–709
• Musculoskeletal/Connective Tissue Disorders	710–739
• Congenital Anomalies	740–759
• Perinatal Period Disorders	760–779
• Symptoms, Signs, Ill-Defined Disorders	780–799
• Injury and Poisoning	800–999

Specific Outpatient ICD-9-CM Coding Considerations

While we have discussed general ICD-9-CM coding situations in our overview of coding, there are some ICD-9-CM coding situations that are more common in the outpatient setting than in inpatient scenarios.

HIV/AIDS Infection

The code must make certain to distinguish between the actual acquired immunodeficiency syndrome versus exposure to the disease and/or testing positive for the presence of the AIDS virus.

Current Procedural Terminology (CPT) © 2005 American Medical Association. All Rights Reserved.

Notes

Code 042 should be assigned for the following:

- AIDS
- Acquired immunodeficiency syndrome
- AIDS-related conditions

In contrast, Code V01.7 should be assigned for the following:

- Exposure to AIDS
- Exposure to AIDS without diagnosis of AIDS
- Positive AIDS test without active HIV

Diabetes/Complications and Manifestations

Diabetes is a common diagnostic code for outpatient encounters as well as out-patient ancillary services. The rules for coding diabetes on an outpatient basis are consistent with the inpatient coding guidelines we have already discussed.

Mental Disorders

When the patient encounter is for substance-related psychosis, code psychosis first, followed by the alcohol/drug dependence or abuse code.

Postoperative Complication

As a large majority of postoperative complications will be addressed in the outpatient setting, it is appropriately mentioned in this section. The diagnosis of postoperative complication should not be assigned unless specified and documented by the physician.

Pneumonia

Often in the outpatient setting, additional diagnostic information is not available regarding the organism resulting in the diagnosis of pneumonia. When the organism is not specified, Code 486, Pneumonia, organism unspecified, should be utilized. Lobar pneumonia may not be utilized unless specifically indicated by the provider or physician.

Hypertension

Hypertension will also be a common outpatient diagnostic code. This condition should be assigned an ICD-9-CM diagnostic code from the hypertension table previously discussed if that condition is part of the evaluative process during the encounter. Chronic system diseases are only assigned codes when treatment or consideration is given to these conditions during the encounter.

Current Procedural Terminology (CPT) © 2005 American Medical Association. All Rights Reserved.

Notes

Contraceptive Management

When the primary reason for the encounter is contraceptive management, a V code for the appropriate method of contraceptive management should be utilized. When the encounter is specifically for sterilization, assign a code from the V25.2 series. Again, these services are typically performed on an outpatient basis.

Late Effect Codes

Late effects are defined as conditions that remain after the acute phase of an illness or injury. The late effect must be documented as associated with the previous condition, and the chief reason for the encounter would be coded first—typically, the late effect, followed by the original illness or injury that precipitated it.

Neoplasm Codes

Neoplasms are some of the diagnoses most often incorrectly assigned. While the rules for assigning neoplasm codes do not differ, keep in mind that the outpatient rule which specifies conditions stated as "rule out, suspect, possible" probably are not codable in the outpatient coding field.

Visits and encounters primarily for chemotherapy or radiation therapy would be assigned a primary V code for the therapy, with secondary code(s) for the neoplasm site(s).

PRACTICE EXERCISE 6–1

Assign ICD-9-CM diagnostic codes to the following scenarios:

	ICD-9-CM Diagnostic Code(s)
1. Breast mass, suspect breast carcinoma.	_____
2. Chemotherapy visit for metastatic pancreatic ca.	_____
3. Metastatic brain ca from the cervix.	_____
4. Old myocardial infarction.	_____
5. Coma due to overdose of phenobarbital.	_____
6. Gestational diabetes.	_____

Current Procedural Terminology (CPT) © 2005 American Medical Association. All Rights Reserved.

7. Pneumonia, probably streptococcal. _____

8. NIDDM. _____

9. Elevated blood pressure. _____

10. Encounter for oral contraceptive. _____

ICD-9-CM PROCEDURE CODING

Unlike physician/professional coding, outpatient hospital coding requires the use of both ICD-9-CM diagnostic coding and procedural coding from Volume III of the ICD-9-CM code book (except in those instances stated earlier). The typical physician coder usually utilizes an ICD-9-CM coding book that contains only Volumes I and II (alphabetic and numeric) diagnostic codes only. Therefore, the outpatient facility code will need to utilize an ICD-9-CM diagnostic code book with all three volumes.

A number of the guidelines that apply to ICD-9-CM diagnostic coding for hospital outpatient also apply to ICD-9-CM procedural coding. In addition to the general ICD-9-CM guidelines listed above, the following guidelines are specific to ICD-9-CM procedural code selection:

- If the procedure code description does not specify "bilateral," the service should be coded twice if performed on both the right and left sides of the body.
- When procedures are started but not completed, code to the extent completed only.
- Biopsy codes are utilized only when a portion of the lesion is removed, while excision codes should be utilized if the entire lesion is removed.
- When procedures are converted from laparoscopic to open, only the open procedure is assigned an ICD-9-CM procedural code.
- When endoscopic procedures are performed, only the most significant procedure in the body region is coded.

PRACTICE EXERCISE 6–2

Assign ICD-9-CM procedural codes to the following:

ICD-9-CM Procedure Code

1. Tonsillectomy with adenoidectomy. _____

2. Tympanostomy. _____

Current Procedural Terminology (CPT) © 2005 American Medical Association. All Rights Reserved.

Notes

3. Extracapsular cataract extraction with IOL. _____

4. D & C for incomplete abortion. _____

5. Blood transfusion. _____

6. Laceration repair. _____

7. IV infusion. _____

8. Diagnostic arthroscopy of knee. _____

9. Bronchoscopy with biopsy. _____

10. EGD with FB removal. _____

GENERAL PROCEDURE CODING GUIDELINES (CPT-4/HCPCS)

With the implementation of the **Outpatient Prospective Payment System (OPPS)** and **Ambulatory Payment Classifications (APCs),** outpatient hospital services required services be assigned HCPCS codes, a three-level coding system that includes CPT-4 codes.

HCPCS (Healthcare Common Procedure Coding System) codes encompass three levels of procedure codes utilized for identifying procedures and services provided. Level I HCPCS codes, which are known as CPT-4 codes, are five-digit numeric codes developed and maintained by the American Medical Association. When they were originally developed, their primary purpose was to identify professional and physician services for coding and billing purposes. However, with the implementation of OPPS, these codes are now utilized for hospital outpatient services as well. Table 6–1 shows those outpatient facility services that require HCPCS codes:

TABLE 6–1   Outpatient Revenue Codes Requiring HCPCS/CPT Codes.

Revenue Code	Service/Description
260	IV Therapy
261	Infusion Pump
274	Prosthetics and Orthotics

Current Procedural Terminology (CPT) © 2005 American Medical Association. All Rights Reserved.

Notes

Revenue Code	Service/Description
31x	Laboratory (Pathology)
32x	Diagnostic Radiology
33x	Therapeutic Radiology
333	Radiation Therapy
34x	Nuclear Medicine
35x	CT Scan
36x	OR (Operating Room)
38x	Blood
40x	Other Not Specified Imaging Services
401	Diagnostic Mammograms
402	Screening Mammograms
41x	Respiratory Services
513	Hyperbaric Therapy
42x	Physical Therapy
43x	Occupational Therapy
44x	Speech/Language Therapy
45x	Emergency Room
46x	Pulmonary Function

(continued)

Current Procedural Terminology (CPT) © 2005 American Medical Association. All Rights Reserved.

TABLE 6–1 *Continued*

Revenue Code	Service/Description
47x	Audiology
471	Diagnostic Audiology
48x	Cardiovascular Therapeutic
480	Cardiology
481	Cardiac Catheterization
482	Stress Test
483	Echocardiology
49x	Ambulatory Surgery Center
51x	Clinic
61x	Magnetic Resonance Technology
623	Surgical Dressings
636	Drugs Requiring Additional Coding
70x	Cast Room
71x	Recovery Room
73x	EKG/ECG
731	Holter Monitor
732	Telemetry
74x	EKG/ECG

Current Procedural Terminology (CPT) © 2005 American Medical Association. All Rights Reserved.

Notes

Revenue Code	Service/Description
75x	Gastroenterology Service
76x	Treatment/Observation Room
77x	Preventive Care Services
79x	Lithotripsy
900	Psychiatric/Psychological Treatment
901	Electroshock
904	Activity Therapy
91x	Psychiatric/Psychological Services
92x	Other Diagnostic Services
921	Peripheral Vascular Lab
922	Electromyography (EMG)
923	Allergy Testing
94x	Other Therapeutic Services
940	Therapeutic Phlebotomy
943	Cardiac Rehabilitation
949	Allergy Therapy

CPT-4 General Coding Guidelines

CPT-4, the common acronym for Current Procedural Terminology, 4th edition—is utilized by the outpatient and professional/physician coder for the assignment of codes for services or procedures performed. In Section III, "Inpatient Hospital," the inpatient coder utilized ICD-9-CM diagnostic and procedural codes for the assignment of services.

While the outpatient coder will continue to utilize these codes, they will utilize CPT-4 codes primarily to describe services. These CPT-4 codes will drive

Current Procedural Terminology (CPT) © 2005 American Medical Association. All Rights Reserved.

Notes

the outpatient reimbursement process, the assignment of APCs (Ambulatory Payment Classifications), and thus, reimbursement.

As the inpatient coder does not utilize CPT-4 coding, a brief review of the layout and conceptual usage of CPT-4 would be appropriate.

As we discussed in our general coding overview in Section I, the CPT-4 book is comprised of six sections: Evaluation and Management, Anesthesia, Surgery, Radiology, Pathology and Medicine.

To review how each section is organized, it may be appropriate at this time to return to Section I, Chapter 1.

! **ALERT:** HCPCS codes are updated quarterly. Certain updates are made to the chargemaster on a quarterly basis.

Some general guidelines apply to the use of CPT-4 codes by the outpatient facility coder. These rules differ from those applying to the professional/provider coder due to the nature of facility coding.

- The concept of "global" periods does not apply; therefore, the preoperative and postoperative periods do not apply to facility coding.
- All services and supplies should be assigned codes, as the facility must capture all services and supplies for reporting purposes.
- Unlike professional/provider coding, it is NOT necessary to sequence procedures based on significance. Payment-status indicators will indicate whether reductions should be made in payment for subsequent services.

Modifier Codes

Upon selection of the appropriate CPT-4 codes, attention should then be turned to the application or usage of any necessary modifier codes. Modifier codes were introduced to handle situations that require additional consideration for payment in unusual circumstances. These codes consist of two extra digits added to the five-digit CPT-4 codes. Some instances of the unusual circumstances that would call for modifier codes are: services greater than or less than normally provided; individualized portions of surgical services provided, and services provided during a surgical encounter that usually would be included in the reimbursement for that code. Usage of these modifier codes in the outpatient setting differs from their professional/physician coder use.

Table 6–2 is a listing of the appropriate usage of modifier codes for the outpatient/hospital facility.

When the use of more than one modifier is necessary, the modifier code that is most significant to appropriate reimbursement should be listed first.

Keep in mind there are significant differences in the proper assignment of usage of both CPT-4 codes and modifier codes, as they are utilized by both the outpatient facility coder and the physician coder.

Current Procedural Terminology (CPT) © 2005 American Medical Association. All Rights Reserved.

Notes

TABLE 6–2   Modifier Codes for Outpatient Facility.

HCPCS Level I

25	Significantly Separately Identifiable Evaluation and Management
27	Multiple Outpatient Visits Same Date
50	Bilateral Procedures
52	Reduced Services
58	Staged/Related Service
59	Distinct Services
73	Discontinued Outpatient Hospital Procedure Prior to Administration of Anesthesia
74	Discontinued Outpatient Hospital Procedure After Administration of Anesthesia
76	Repeat Procedure Same Physician
77	Repeat Procedure Different Physician
78	Return to Operating Room for Related Procedure during Post-op Period
79	Unrelated Procedure/Service Same Physician during Post-op Period

HCPCS Level II

LT	Left side of body
RT	Right side of body
E1	Upper left eyelid
E2	Lower left eyelid
E3	Upper right eyelid
E4	Lower right eyelid
FA	1st digit, left hand
F1	2nd digit, left hand
F2	3rd digit, left hand
F3	4th digit, left hand
F4	5th digit, left hand
F5	1st digit, right hand

(continued)

Current Procedural Terminology (CPT) © 2005 American Medical Association. All Rights Reserved.

TABLE 6–2 *Continued*

HCPCS Level II

F6	2nd digit, right hand
F7	3rd digit, right hand
F8	4th digit, right hand
F9	5th digit, right hand
TA	1st digit, left foot
T1	2nd digit, left foot
T2	3rd digit, left foot
T3	4th digit, left foot
T4	5th digit, left foot
T5	1st digit, right foot
T6	2nd digit, right foot
T7	3rd digit, right foot
T8	4th digit, right foot
T9	5th digit, right foot
LC	Left circumflex artery
LD	Left descending artery
RC	Right coronary artery
QM	Ambulatory under arrangement by provider
QN	Ambulance furnished by provider

Probably the most significant overall difference in the interpretation of CPT-4 language in the outpatient setting is the absence of any words pertaining to the physician. For instance, if the descriptor indicates "provided by the physician" or "supervised by the physician," these phrases are to be omitted for purposes of outpatient facility coding.

One must also keep in mind that the services being assigned codes are facility services, or resources utilized by the facility in providing the services coded). For instance, when the facility codes CPT-4 Code 12001 for a laceration repair, the facility is requesting reimbursement for all facility resources utilized to perform that service. This would include such items as medications, supplies, nursing

Current Procedural Terminology (CPT) © 2005 American Medical Association. All Rights Reserved.

Notes

services and any other items typically necessary to perform the laceration repair. The APC reimbursement under APC 0024 encompasses reimbursement for all these services. Services that are not integral to the performance of the diagnostic colonoscopy would still be codable and/or reimbursable, such as an x-ray or a laboratory procedure. Accommodation is also made for services such as drugs and supplies that are highly expensive, (e.g., special medical devices that are medically necessary). This will be discussed more extensively in the outpatient billing portion of this section.

PRACTICE EXERCISE 6–3

Take each of the following coding scenarios and determine whether a modifier code would be appropriate, as well as which modifier would be most appropriate:

1. Patient arrives in the emergency room at 10:30 AM on 01/01/20xx and returns at 3:30 PM.   Yes_____ No_____ Modifier_____

2. Patient receives two chest x-rays on the same date of service.   Yes_____ No_____ Modifier_____

3. Office visit and chest x-ray.   Yes_____ No_____ Modifier_____

4. Colonoscopy with FB removal and polyp removal by snare.   Yes_____ No_____ Modifier_____

5. EGD (upper GI endoscopy) and colonoscopy on same date.   Yes_____ No_____ Modifier_____

6. Laparoscopic tubal ligation.   Yes_____ No_____ Modifier_____

7. Cystourethroscopy.   Yes_____ No_____ Modifier_____

8. IUD implantation.   Yes_____ No_____ Modifier_____

9. Diagnostic bronchoscopy with FB removal.   Yes_____ No_____ Modifier_____

10. Cataract extraction with IOL insertion.   Yes_____ No_____ Modifier_____

CPT-4 SPECIFIC SECTION GUIDELINES

Within each subsection or chapter of the CPT-4 code book, there are guidelines specific to that section. General guidelines for each section precede the

Current Procedural Terminology (CPT) © 2005 American Medical Association. All Rights Reserved.

code range for each of these sections, and the pages are usually color coded to indicate guidelines rather than code listing. Many of these guidelines apply ONLY to codes from that section, or to specific codes within that section.

Outpatient Evaluation and Management CPT-4 Coding Considerations

With the inception of APCs in mid-2000, CMS (Center for Medicare Services), formerly known as HCFA (Health Care Finance Administration), mandated that each facility would be accountable for developing and implementing its own methodology and ensuring compliance with it.

Some facilities chose to utilize the same methodology utilized by physician coders by assigning levels of complexities based on history, examination and medical decision-making components. Others utilized methods such as developing acuity sheets with **acuity levels,** assigning a point system for each service performed, or some combination of these methods for assigning levels of service. The key component to any of these methods is consistency. Obviously, each facility will not arrive at the same level of service for an identical service; however, the facility is expected to track levels of service and maintain that the distribution of services represents the level of complexity of services performed.

For example: If a small facility performs low-acuity services, one would expect that facility to assign acuity levels accordingly. Therefore, that facility's distribution of levels of service might appear as follows:

EXAMPLE OF SMALL-FACILITY ACUITY LEVELS OF DISTRIBUTION

Level 1 (Minimal)	20%
Level 2 (Low)	30%
Level 3 (Moderate)	30%
Level 4 (Mod/High)	20%
Level 5 (High)	10%

In contrast, a larger facility providing high-level services, such as a trauma center, would expect a higher-level distribution such as:

EXAMPLE OF LARGE-FACILITY ACUITY LEVELS OF DISTRIBUTION

Level 1 (Minimal)	10%
Level 2 (Low)	10%
Level 3 (Moderate)	20%
Level 4 (Mod/High)	30%
Level 5 (High)	30%

Current Procedural Terminology (CPT) © 2005 American Medical Association. All Rights Reserved.

Notes

TABLE 6–3   **Example of Facility E & M Acuity Levels.**

99281	99282	99283	99284	99285
Uncomplicated Insect Bite	Venipuncture Urine	Foley Catheter Heplock	Thoracentesis Ultrasound	Central Line Chest Tube
Prescription Refill	X-Rays	EKG	IVs	Transfer OR
Recheck, No Treatment	Ace Wrap	Dermabond	ABGs	TPA
DOA, No Treatment	Bandages	I & D	Lumbar Puncture	Full Code
Suture Removal	Straight Catheter	Pelvic Exam	IVPs	Trauma Level
Admit Observation	STD Cultures	Slit Lamp	Epistaxis Cautery	Auto Accident w/ Intraabdominal Complaints
	Fetal Heart Tones	Irrigation	Charcoal Treatment	
		Enema	Paracentesis	
		Breath Treatment	Echo	Conscious Sedation
			Endoscopy	

Acuity Levels Based on Resources, Not E & M Levels

Whatever methodology the facility elects to utilize for assigning levels of service, it should successfully reflect the complexity distribution of the facility.

Table 6–3 is an example of levels of service based on Evaluation and Management acuity level.

Other evaluation and management coding concerns include:

- Regardless of whether the facility chooses to utilize the CPT-4 Evaluation and Management methodology or some other method of assigning E & M codes, CMS has indicated that it does not expect to see a correlation between the level of service codes reported by the facility and those reported by the physician.

- Multiple visits provided in the outpatient setting on the same day are reimbursable provided they are separate and distinct, and that any subsequent services have the modifier 27 amended.

Current Procedural Terminology (CPT) © 2005 American Medical Association. All Rights Reserved.

Notes

- The use of modifier 25 is appropriate when an evaluation and management service is performed that is "separately identifiable" from an additional procedure or service by the facility. Again, modifier 25 is not utilized in the same manner as with physician coding.

- Critical care is reimbursed only for CPT-4 Code 99291 (Critical Care, First Hour). Again remember that the portion of the description that states "physician" should be omitted or ignored for facility purposes. In addition, CMS has indicated that the portion of this code that indicates all services provided by the physician is not applicable on the facility side, as the facility has expended additional resources to provide those services. Therefore, code assignment of x-rays, electrocardiograms, and other diagnostic and therapeutic services would be permitted under the outpatient facility coding methodology. However, the portion of that descriptor that indicates the patient should be "critically ill and unstable" would still be applicable.

- Observation care is reimbursable only under specific circumstances:

  - Specific diagnosis

    Chest Pain

    Congestive Hear Failure

    Asthma

  - Reported with HCPCS Code G0378 for minimum of 8 hours

  - E & M level must be coded/billed for same day or day before observation care

  - Must span minimum of 8 hours and listed as "units" on UB-92/CMS 1450

  - Must be under care of physician during time of observation

  - Medical record documentation must indicate that specific review criteria was utilized to determine the patient would benefit from observation

  - No payment status indicator "T" procedure were performed subsequent to the admission for observation care

In addition, outpatient hospitals may also code for patients directly admitted for observation services with code CG379.

In addition to the above observation care services, infusion therapy provided in combination with these services is also codable utilizing C8950.

Current Procedural Terminology (CPT) © 2005 American Medical Association. All Rights Reserved.

Notes

> ‼ ***ALERT*** Each facility has implemented its own mechanism for levels of service (E & M). While facilities are not compared to another based on levels of service, consistency within the same facility and the proper use, implementation and interpretation by facility staff of the methodology chosen may be reviewed.

PRACTICE EXERCISE 6–4

Utilizing the acuity levels in Table 6–3, assign outpatient E & M levels for each of the following scenarios:

1. Patient arrives in emergency room, where the following occurs:
   - Exam by ER physician
   - Chest x-ray
   - EKG

   Patient given Darvocet and instructed to return in needed.

   Diagnosis: Noncardiac chest pain.

   E & M Acuity Level: _____

2. Patient arrives in ER, where patient is examined by ER physician. Patient instructed in care of contusions received in auto accident.

   Diagnosis: Arm contusions, automobile accident

   E & M Acuity Level: _____

3. Patient arrives in ER and is examined by ER physician. CBC, urinalysis for dysuria, chest x-ray were performed that indicated pneumonia. IV penicillin was given and patient was ordered to return the next day.

   Diagnosis: Pneumonia, rule out urinary tract infection

   E & M Acuity Level: _____

4. Patient arrived in ER with lacerated finger. Examination was performed by ER physician. Wound cleansed, sutured. Patient to return in 7–10 days for suture removal.

   Diagnosis: Finger laceration, cut with electric can opener

   E & M Acuity Level: _____

Current Procedural Terminology (CPT) © 2005 American Medical Association. All Rights Reserved.

Notes

_____

_____

_____

_____

_____

_____

_____

_____

_____

_____

_____

_____

_____

_____

_____

_____

_____

_____

_____

_____

_____

5. Patient arrives in ER for recheck of laceration and suture removal. Exam was performed by ER physician, sutures removed by ER nurse, dressing of wound by ER nurse. Discharge instructions to return PRN.

   Diagnosis: Finger laceration, suture removal

   E & M Acuity Level: _____

Anesthesia Coding Guidelines

As the administration of anesthesia is included in the reimbursement for the surgical procedure performed, codes need not be assigned. When the anesthesiologist performs services outside of the anesthesia section of the CPT-4 book, such as epidural injections, pain management, or evaluation or management services, these would be coded according to the guidelines for that particular section.

Outpatient CPT-4 Surgery Coding Guidelines

Due to the comprehensive nature of the surgery section, it is subdivided by anatomical system as follows:

- Integumentary
- Musculoskeletal
- Respiratory
- Cardiovascular
- Digestive
- Urinary
- Male
- Female
- Nervous
- Eye
- Ear

General Surgery Definitions

Because the Surgery section is subdivided into the types of procedures performed, some vocabulary may be appropriate to correctly assign codes from this section. A few of these terms are outlined in Table 6–4.

Current Procedural Terminology (CPT) © 2005 American Medical Association. All Rights Reserved.

Notes

TABLE 6–4 Surgery Terminology.

Procedure	Definition
Split-Thickness Skin Graft (STSG)	Encompasses the dermis/epidermis
Full-Thickness Skin Graft (FTSG)	Full thickness of all 3 layers of skin
Allograft	Grafts from similar species
Autograft	Graft from patient's (self) body
Xenograft	Graft from different species
Muscle Flap	Transfer of layer of muscle
Island Pedicle Flap	Single artery/vein running length of FTSG
Arthrocentesis	Puncture/injection joint
Incision	Cut into or incise
Excision	Cutting or removing
Introduction/Removal	Scope, irrigate, inject, insert, remove, or replace

General Surgical Guidelines

Before beginning specific guidelines for areas within the Surgery section of CPT-4, some basic guidelines for coding surgery services should be reviewed.

The designation **"separate procedure"** is given to surgical codes (those in the 10000–69999 range) when the procedure is performed alone, for a specific reason at the time of that surgical session, as an integral part of another procedure, or incidental to another procedure.

EXAMPLE

A diagnostic knee arthroscopy (29870/separate procedure) is performed at the same time as an arthroscopic medial meniscectomy (29881). In this instance, 29870 would be considered incidental to the meniscectomy, as that procedure was the primary procedure performed and the diagnostic arthroscopy served as the approach technique for accomplishing the primary procedure.

Correct Coding assignment would be 29881 only.

Add-on procedures are those performed during the same session as another procedure or surgical code. They are never performed alone, and therefore should never be assigned as code without the addition of the primary procedure.

EXAMPLE

Three breast lesions are excised that were previously identified by radiological marker.

Current Procedural Terminology (CPT) © 2005 American Medical Association. All Rights Reserved.

Code 19125 would be assigned for the first lesion, followed by add-on Code 19126 for "each additional lesion."

Correct Code Assignment:

Code 19125

Code 19126, 2 units

Codes designated with the term **"each"** or **"each additional"** or **"per"** are to be coded as units when coding for these services. In the event multiple services NOT containing one of these terms that indicate the possibility of multiple units of service, those services would be listed as individual line items, and, in the event that identical CPT-4 code is utilized, the modifier 76 or 77 would be utilized.

See example above for "in addition to" guidelines.

Example of nonmultiple term language:
Electrocardiogram performed three (3) times during encounter. Code 93005 would be listed as follows.

93005

93005–76

93005–76

From the physician/professional perspective, codes in the Surgery section are considered **"global,"** meaning the reimbursement for the surgical services is inclusive of all preoperative, postoperative and surgical services performed by the surgeon and/or provider. However, this guideline is disregarded for outpatient facility coding.

For each subsection in the CPT-4 code book, there is a designated **"unlisted"** code that should be utilized ONLY when a procedure or surgery is performed for which there is no specific CPT-4 code. As these codes can be utilized for a multitude of coding scenarios, it would be appropriate to file these claims manually with documentation attached and an explanation of what specific services are being assigned these codes.

The use of modifier codes in the surgery section of CPT-4 is essential in defining the specific procedures performed, and obtaining correct reimbursement for them. Modifier codes were listed in the overview of CPT-4 outpatient facility coding earlier in this textbook; however, a detailed discussion of the appropriate usage of each of these modifiers would be appropriate. Note also that not all modifiers are appropriate for usage in the surgical section of CPT-4; therefore, modifier codes such as 25 and 27 are missing from this explanation.

Make certain when assigning modifier codes, especially anatomical modifiers (those that refer to a specific location on the body or side of the body such as LT, RT, E1, F2), that the CPT descriptors refer only to those body areas.

EXAMPLE

Code 12001 indicates "simple repair of superficial wounds of the scalp, neck, axillae, external genitalia, trunk and/or extremities (including hands/feet), 2.5 cm or less."

Current Procedural Terminology (CPT) © 2005 American Medical Association. All Rights Reserved.

Notes

As this code descriptor encompasses multiple anatomical sites, the use of any anatomical modifier would not be appropriate as it would not provide additional clarification of the area involved.

CPT-4 Surgical Modifier Codes

50 Bilateral Procedures

Should only be utilized for performing identical (same CPT-4 code) procedures on each side of the body. Modifier 50 should be appended to the CPT-4 code as one line item only, unless otherwise specified by third-party carrier. There are some carriers that prefer these services be coded as two line items: one line item with the first CPT-4 code, the second line item with the identical CPT-4 code plus the addition of modifier 50. Be aware of third-party carrier requirements regarding the use of this modifier.

52 Reduced Services

In this instance, the services performed based on the operative report do not encompass the full services as designated by the CPT-4 descriptor.

EXAMPLE

A colonoscopy was performed, but due to poor bowel prep, the cecum could not be visualized. The scope was removed.

Code 45378 specifically indicates that the scope must visualize the cecum. Therefore, in this instance, the CPT-4 descriptor was not completely met. The addition of modifier 52 would be appropriate in this instance.

58 Staged/Related Procedure

This modifier should be assigned when a second procedure is performed during a subsequent day that was either planned at the time of the original procedure (staged) or required and/or more extensive than the original (related).

Modifier 58 is assigned only to the subsequent procedure performed.

EXAMPLE

A closed reduction of a distal radial fracture was performed one day; however, upon radiological exam of the fracture site, it was determined that further reduction with internal fixation would be needed. Modifier 58 would be appended to the Open Reduction, Internal Fixation, Distal Radius procedure performed on a subsequent day.

59 Distinct Procedure

Modifier codes should be appended to procedure codes that are normally considered included or incidental or performed on different

Current Procedural Terminology (CPT) © 2005 American Medical Association. All Rights Reserved.

Notes

_____

_____

_____

_____

_____

_____

_____

_____

_____

_____

_____

_____

_____

_____

_____

_____

_____

_____

_____

_____

_____

_____

_____

body sites or anatomical parts, and therefore are "distinct" and codable and billable. Again, the modifier code is assigned only to the subsequent code.

EXAMPLE

A colonoscopy was performed, and the patient requested a lesion be removed from her back at the same time, same surgical session.

Code 45378 would be assigned for the colonoscopy, while an appropriate CPT-4 code would be assigned for the lesion, based on nature, size and location, with a modifier 59 appended to the lesion to indicate it was excised from a separate, distinct location.

73 Discontinued OP/ASC Procedure Prior to Administration of Anesthesia

This modifier is utilized when a procedure is terminated after patient preparation but before the administration of anesthesia. While physicians and providers cannot bill for services not provided, the outpatient facility has already expended services in preparation for the patient's surgery as well as utilizing operating room time, supplies and other technical services. As a result, carriers believe it appropriate to reimburse the facility for the portion of services provided. Typically the reimbursement would be 50 percent of the usual reimbursement for the CPT-4 code assigned.

In addition, some carriers require the use of a diagnostic code from the V64 series to indicate the reason the procedure was terminated.

74 Discontinued OP/ASC Procedure After Anesthesia

This modifier would be added when the procedure has been started, such as incision made, scope inserted, at which time the procedure is discontinued. As the majority of the outpatient facility services have already been expended at this point, reimbursement would typically be made at 100 percent of the reimbursement for the surgical service. Use of a diagnostic code from the V64 series as outlined above may also be deemed necessary by some third-party carriers.

76 Repeat Procedure Same Physician

When the same procedure must be performed on the same day, modifier 76 should be appended to all subsequent repetitions of the same procedure.

EXAMPLE

Patient had two chest x-rays (71020) performed on the same date:

71020   First chest x-ray
71020–76   Subsequent chest x-ray

77 Repeat Procedure Different Physician

Utilized the same as with modifier 76, except a different physician is utilized to perform the subsequent service or services.

Current Procedural Terminology (CPT) © 2005 American Medical Association. All Rights Reserved.

Notes

EXAMPLE

Patient had three chest x-rays (71020) performed on the same date; however, the subsequent chest x-rays were performed by another radiologist.

71020	First chest x-ray
71020–77	Subsequent chest x-ray
71020–77	Additional subsequent chest x-ray

78 Return to the Operating Room for Related Procedure during Postoperative Period

While several of these modifier codes speak of "during the postoperative period," they were originally utilized only by physicians, who are reimbursed for the total global period for that procedure, from preoperative to surgical to postoperative. In the outpatient facility setting, however, this meaning has been interpreted as operating room procedures that are related to OR procedures performed on the same day.

79 Unrelated Procedure during Postoperative Period

This modifier would be utilized for subsequent procedures performed on the same day as another procedure that is unrelated.

EXAMPLE

The patient has a cardiac pacemaker inserted in the morning and reduction of a distal radial fracture in the afternoon of the same day.

HCPCS modifier codes typically are utilized to identify a specific anatomical part of a specific location of services, such as follows:

E1–E4	Eyelid Modifiers
FA, F1–F9	Finger Modifiers
TA, T1–T9	Toe Modifiers
LC	Left Circumflex Artery
LD	Left Descending Artery
RC	Right Coronary Artery
RT	Right Side of Body
LT	Left Side of Body
SG	Ambulatory Surgical Center designation (ASC)
QM	Ambulance services provided under arrangement by hospital
QN	Ambulance services furnished directly by hospital

Those modifiers that indicate a specific location are known as "anatomical modifiers," such as "E1", "F1", or "T1." Anatomical modifiers should be appended only to CPT-4 codes and code descriptors that identify that specific anatomical site only.

Current Procedural Terminology (CPT) © 2005 American Medical Association. All Rights Reserved.

EXAMPLE OF CORRECT HCPCS MODIFIER USAGE: CODE 26750

As this code specifies "closed treatment distal phalangeal fracture," it would be appropriate to assign the "F" modifier to identify the specific finger.

However, Code 12002, simple repair of superficial wounds of scalp, neck, axillae, external genitalia, trunk and/or extremities (including hands/feet) 2.5 cm or less, as mentioned earlier, refers to multiple anatomical locations. Therefore, the use of an "F" modifier, even when the repair is being provided to a finger, would be inappropriate. Appropriate OCE (Outpatient Coding Edits) have been put into place that would deny this code assignment.

EXAMPLE

Code 12002 (no HCPCS modifier appropriate)

Specific Integumentary System Services Guidelines (10000–19999)

The integumentary system presents a number of distinct and unique procedures. Guidelines vary greatly within this section, so they are broken down by the specific types of procedures being performed.

Removal of Lesions   The removal of lesions, or any pathological change in tissue, is subcategorized based on the following breakdown:

First: Excision/Destruction/Curette
Second: Malignant/Benign
Third: Anatomical site
Fourth: Size (in cm)

Note that in order to be coded appropriately, this breakdown must be followed in the correct order.
Other coding considerations for the removal of lesions include:

- Because lipomas (fatty tumors) are not comprised of skin, they are not coded as lesion excisions, but as excisions from their specific anatomical site (such as shoulder or foot).
- Each lesion is coded separately—no lesion codes are combined
- Simple closure is included in the lesion excision code. Intermediate or complex closures are codable.
- The size of the lesion is measured in centimeters determined by the size of the lesion as well as the minimal margins.

EXAMPLE

1.0-cm lesion removed with 0.5-cm margins

Coded as 2.0-cm lesion removal

(1.0-cm lesion + 0.5-cm margin + 0.5-cm margin = 2.0 cm)

Current Procedural Terminology (CPT) © 2005 American Medical Association. All Rights Reserved.

Notes

Laceration/Wound Repairs   Codes for lacerations, open wounds, or wound repairs are assigned based on the following prioritization:

First:	Extent of wound (Simple, Intermediate, Complex)
Second:	Anatomical site
Third:	Size (in cm) of repair

In addition to the coding sequence, other important guidelines in the assignment of codes for laceration or wound repairs include:

- Code G0168 should be utilized for wound closure with tissue adhesive.
- Combine wound repair codes when extent of wound repair and anatomical grouping are the same.

EXAMPLE

Laceration Repair of Arm, Simple, 1.0 cm

Laceration Repair of Leg, Simple, 1.0 cm

Laceration Repair of Face, Simple, 1.0 cm

Laceration Repair of Leg, Intermediate, 1.0 cm

Lacerations, Simple of Arm and Leg

> Same anatomical grouping/simple extent—Coded as 2.0 cm Simple, Arm/Leg.

Laceration of Face, Simple

> Cannot be combined as not same anatomical grouping.

Laceration of Leg, Intermediate

> Cannot be combined as not same extent (intermediate vs simple).

- Extent of repair is defined as follows:

Simple:	One-layer closure
Intermediate:	Two-layer closure OR
	One layer with extensive debridement
Complex:	More than a layered closure;
	reconstructive work as well as closure is included

Skin Grafts   Skin grafts are assigned codes based on:

First:	Type of graft (Adjacent Tissue/Free)
Second:	Anatomical location of recipient site
Third:	Size (in sq cm)

Skin graft coding involves the application of several additional coding guidelines, including:

- Adjacent tissue transfer codes are utilized for grafts transferred or moved (not completely separated).

Current Procedural Terminology (CPT) © 2005 American Medical Association. All Rights Reserved.

Notes
_____
_____
_____
_____
_____
_____
_____
_____
_____
_____
_____
_____
_____
_____
_____
_____
_____
_____
_____
_____

- Free graft codes are utilized for grafts transferred completely from one location to another.
- Size (in sq cm) is determined by multiplying width times length.
- "Each additional" codes are available for additional sq cm of grafting.
- Graft size is determined by size of recipient site, not donor site.
- Muscle, myocutaneous and fasciocutaneous flaps are described in terms of the donor site (this is the only exception to the rule above.)
- Split-Thickness grafts are defined as top layer of skin only.
- Full-Thickness grafts contain the full thickness of epidermis and dermis.
- Autografts are obtained from a patient's body.
- Allografts are obtained from similar species (also referred to as homografts).
- Xenografts are defined as grafts obtained from a different species.

Breast Procedures Code assignment for breast procedures is subcategorized based on:

First:	Approach of procedure (Incision/Excision)
Second:	Extent of procedure (Excision Cyst/Lesion, Mastectomy)

The coding of procedures performed on the breast also includes a number of other guidelines. Keep in mind the following:

- Breast biopsy can be performed via percutaneous needle or incision.
- Operative reports may indicate "excisional biopsy"; however, if total lesion removed, utilize excision cyst/lesion code(s).
- Lesion may be excised with or without placement of radiological marker. Watch appropriate code assignment.
- Mastectomy codes are based on extent of procedure (e.g., lymph nodes, muscles).

Specific Musculoskeletal System Services Guidelines (20000–29999)

The musculoskeletal system is perhaps the largest subsection in the CPT-4 code book. While it is voluminous, it is quite organized, and the types of procedures are repeated through the subsection. The most common codes assigned in these sections include:

Fracture/Dislocation Repair Codes Fractures and dislocations codes are subcategorized based on the following:

First:	Fracture vs dislocation
Second:	Anatomical part
Third:	Method of repair (Closed, Open, Percutaneous Fixation)

Current Procedural Terminology (CPT) © 2005 American Medical Association. All Rights Reserved.

Notes

_____

_____

_____

_____

_____

_____

_____

_____

_____

_____

_____

_____

_____

_____

_____

_____

_____

_____

_____

_____

Fourth:	Manipulation involved (With Manipulation/Without)
Fifth:	Fixation Involved (Internal/External/Without)

In addition to proper sequencing of codes, additional guidelines for fractures/dislocations are:

- When fracture requires remanipulation on the same day, modifier 76 or 77 should be appended to the subsequent procedure.
- When closed repair requires additional open procedures, modifier 58 should be appended to the subsequent procedure.
- "Open treatment" requires fractures that are surgically opened and the bone ends visualized.
- "Closed treatment" involves fractures that do not require an incision.
- Percutaneous skeletal fixation involves placement of fixation device(s) across fracture site to stabilize (fracture is typically not visualized).
- Casts/splints applied as the immobilization for fracture care are included.

Cast/Splint Application Codes   Codes related to the application or removal of cast and splints are located at the end of the Musculoskeletal section. Codes are assigned based on the location of the splint or cast application, and are not for the materials and supplies, but the actual "application" of the immobilization device. Additional guidelines include:

- Initial cast/splint included in fracture care.
- Cast/splint code assigned when surgical repair of fracture care not provided.
- Subsequent or replacement casts and/or splints are codable.

Arthroscopic Procedures   Codes performed through an arthroscope inserted into the joint are assigned codes based on the following series:

First:	Approach (Arthroscopic or Surgical)
Second:	Anatomical site
Third:	Extent of procedure(s) performed

Use of the arthroscopic technique in the performance of surgical procedures on joints has become quite common. Guidelines for assignment of appropriate codes for this section include:

- Diagnostic arthroscopic procedures are incidental when surgical arthroscopy is performed on the same anatomical site.
- Arthroscopic procedures on different anatomical parts requires the use of modifier 59 to identify distinct components.
- Modifiers RT/LT are often utilized for identifying anatomical parts repaired arthroscopically.

Current Procedural Terminology (CPT) © 2005 American Medical Association. All Rights Reserved.

Notes

Specific Respiratory System Services Guidelines (30000–32999)

The respiratory section includes surgical codes assigned based on the following prioritization:

First: Anatomical part
Second: Approach (Incision/Excision/Scopy)
Third: Extent Procedure

Other guidelines that would be appropriate for the correct assignment of codes for procedures of the respiratory system include:

- Diagnostic endoscopic procedures are incidental when surgical endoscopic procedures are performed on the same anatomical site(s).
- The use of modifier 50 is appropriate for those respiratory anatomical sites where bilateral procedures are performed.
- The use of modifiers RT (Right) and LT (Left) are appropriate when the anatomical site indicated in CPT is specific to an anatomical site with only two sites and only one of those sites is involved.
- The accessory sinuses include:
  - Maxillary Sinuses
  - Frontal Sinuses
  - Ethmoid Sinuses
  - Sphenoid Sinuses
- The respiratory system is comprised of all organs that involve inspiration of air and expiration of carbon dioxide, including:
  - Nose
  - Accessory Sinuses
  - Larynx
  - Trachea/Bronchi
  - Lungs/Pleura
- Thoracentesis Code 32000 involves removal or air or fluid from the pleural space, while 32002 also involves insertion of a tube or catheter as well.

Specific Cardiovascular System Guidelines (33010–37799)

Cardiovascular surgery services involve invasive and/or definitive procedures on the heart, veins, arteries and blood. Noninvasive cardiovascular procedures such as cardiac catheterization are found in the Medicine section of CPT.

Pacemakers/Defibrillators Codes for this section are assigned based on:

First: Equipment involved (Pacemaker/Defibrillator/Electrodes)
Second: Procedure (Insertion/Replacement/Repositioning)
Third: Single/Dual Chamber (when appropriate)

Current Procedural Terminology (CPT) © 2005 American Medical Association. All Rights Reserved.

Notes

Other guidelines for assigning codes for the insertion, replacement, or removal of pacemakers and/or defibrillators include:

- Pacemakers are implanted for abnormal heart rhythms, while defibrillators are utilized for the purpose of defibrillating or restarting heart rhythm.
- Replacement of the battery of a pacemaker or defibrillator is actually the replacement of the pulse generator.
- When replacement of the pulse generator in an existing pacemaker is necessary, code for both the removal of the old pulse generator and the insertion of the new one.

Grafting for Coronary Artery Bypass Grafts   Codes assigned for CABG (Coronary Artery Bypass Graft) procedures are based on the following sequence:

First:	Grafting location (Venous, Arterial, or Combined Arterial-Venous)
Second:	Number of grafts performed
Third:	Additional codes for procurement of vein graft when: Upper Extremity Vein (35500) or Femoropopliteal Vein (35572)

In order to assign codes for CABGs appropriately, these additional guidelines must also be followed:

- When reporting arterial-venous grafts, it is necessary to report code for the appropriate arterial graft (range 33533–33536) as well as the combined arterial-venous graft code (range 335177–33523).
- When "redo" of previously performed coronary bypass graft is necessary more than one month after original surgery, Code 33530 should be utilized in addition to the primary procedure.

Ventricle Assist Device Insertions (Codes 33975–33980)   When ventricle assist devices are inserted, codes should be selected based on the following guidelines:

First:	Insertion vs removal
Second:	Single ventricle or biventricular

Repair of Aneurysms   Aneurysms or ballooned or weakened sections of a vessel are assigned codes based on the following criteria:

First:	Type of aneurysm (Abdominal Aortic/Iliac/Other)
Second:	Type of repair (placement of occlusion device, placement of prosthetic graft/open repair)

Current Procedural Terminology (CPT) © 2005 American Medical Association. All Rights Reserved.

Notes

Aneurysm repairs must also incorporate the following guidelines for appropriate code assignment:

- Fluoroscopic guidance should be coded in addition to the repair (Codes 75952–55953).
- Other interventions performed at the same time should be coded in addition to the aneurysm repair (such as angioplasty or embolization).

Vascular Injection Procedures   Injections into the vessels are assigned codes based on:

First: Intravenous, intra-arterial, venous approach
Second: Specific vessel

The coding of vascular injections can be quite involved. A medical illustration of the vascular system can be helpful in determining the extent of catheterization, as this will be essential in the correct assignment of codes as follows:

- Additional first-order or higher catheterization within the same vascular family supplied by a first-order vessel different from a previously selected and coded family should be coded separately.
- The procedure (s)hould be coded to include introduction and all lesser order selective catherizations.

Central Venous Catheters   Central venous catheters are commonly placed for prolonged intravenous therapy or chemotherapy. In many cases the patient has poor vascular access, or the treatment will be prolonged and compromise vascular access that may be needed in the future. Codes for central venous catheters are assigned based on the following categorization:

First: Centrally inserted/peripherally inserted
Second: Procedure (insertion, repair, replacement, removal)
Third: Tunneled/Nontunneled device
Fourth: Age (under 5/over 5 years of age)
Fifth: With/without subcutaneous port or pump

Key documentation information will be necessary in the correct assignment of codes for central venous catheters, as well as additional coding guidelines as follows:

- Centrally inserted catheters are placed in the central venous system, typically in the subclavian, iliac, inferior vena cava, superior vena cava, or right atrium.

Current Procedural Terminology (CPT) © 2005 American Medical Association. All Rights Reserved.

Notes
_____
_____
_____
_____
_____
_____
_____
_____
_____
_____
_____
_____
_____
_____
_____
_____
_____
_____
_____

- Centrally inserted catheters are utilized for short-term medications such as antibiotic therapy and are typically removed after treatment period (7–10 days).
- Venous access ports are implanted subcutaneously, usually in a surgically created skin pocket in the chest area, and are utilized for long-term care such as chemotherapy.

Specific Hemic and Lymphatic System Services Guidelines (38100–38999)

The hemic and lymphatic system primarily encompasses lymph node excision and bone marrow harvesting and transplantation. The section is somewhat small.

Lymph Node Excision   Unlike breast procedures, the excision or biopsy of lymph nodes is assigned codes from the same section. Categorization for these codes is based on:

First:	Method (needle, open)
Second:	Extent (superficial, deep)
Third:	Location (cervical, axillary)

Keep in mind these additional guidelines for appropriately coding lymph nodes:

- The same codes are assigned regardless of whether lymph nodes are biopsied or excised.
- One code only is assigned for lymph node biopsy or excision or multiple biopsies or excisions utilizing the same method, extent and location.

Specific Digestive System Guidelines (40490–49999)

The digestive system includes all organs and accessory organs necessary for the digestive process. These include the lips and mouth, dentoalveolar structures, palate, salivary glands, pharynx, adenoids, tonsils, esophagus, stomach, intestines, appendix, rectum, anus, liver, biliary tract, abdomen, peritoneum and omentum.

Some definitions are necessary in order to properly code services in this section:

Esophagoscopy	Visual examination via scope of the esophagus only.
Upper GI Endoscopy	Visual examination via scope of the esophagus, the stomach and either the duodenum or jejunum;

Current Procedural Terminology (CPT) © 2005 American Medical Association. All Rights Reserved.

	commonly referred to as an EGD (esophagogastroduodenoscopy).
Proctosigmoidoscopy	Visual examination via scope of the rectum and sigmoid colon.
Sigmoidoscopy	Visual examination via scope of the entire rectum, sigmoid colon and sometimes a portion of the descending colon.
Colonoscopy	Visual examination via scope of the entire colon, from the rectum to the cecum, sometimes including examination of the terminal ileum.

Codes for the digestive system are assigned based on the following categorizations:

First:	Anatomical site
Second:	Technique/procedure (incision/excision/endoscopy)
Third:	Procedure performed

There are a number of additional guidelines that must be followed closely in order to code correctly for the digestive system. They are as follows:

- Diagnostic endoscopic procedures are incidental when surgical endoscopic procedures are performed on the same anatomical site.
- Diagnostic endoscopies are assigned based on the definitive procedure performed for that site, (excision of polyp by hot biopsy forceps is attempted). However, converted to excision of polyp by snare technique would only be coded to the successful technique, Code 45385.
- Multiple endoscopic techniques to the same anatomical site will be subject to reduction based on the payment status indicator assigned for each procedure. Use of modifier 51 is not appropriate for outpatient hospital coding.
- Many procedures may be performed by either laparoscopic or open technique. Make certain to assign codes based on the definitive technique performed.
- Codes for endoscopic procedures are assigned based on the definitive procedures performed; therefore, each code would be assigned only once. These codes are defined as removal of tumor(s), polyp(s), lesion(s).
- Dilation codes should be assigned based on whether they are performed at the time of the endoscopy, or after the scope has been removed.

EXAMPLE

Upper GI endoscopy where dilation of esophagus over guide wire is performed at the time of the scope.

Use Code 43248 in addition to other definitive procedure(s).

Current Procedural Terminology (CPT) © 2005 American Medical Association. All Rights Reserved.

Notes

Upper GI endoscopy where scope is removed and dilation of esophagus is performed.

Use Code 43453 in addition to other definitive procedure(s).

- Hernia repairs are located at the end of the Digestive Surgery section. They are classified by type of hernia—initial vs recurrent—and by the age of the patient, as well as by whether the hernia is reducible or incarcerated or strangulated.

Specific Urinary System Guidelines (50010–53899)

The urinary system involves the kidneys, ureters, bladder, urethra and, in some instances, the prostate where it is attached to the neck of the bladder. The prostate is found in the Male Genital System section as well.

Codes are assigned based on:

First:	Anatomical part
Second:	Technique/procedure (incision/excision/scope)
Third:	Extent of Procedure

A number of additional guidelines are appropriate when assigning codes for the urinary system. Keep in mind the following:

- Urodynamics codes (51725–51798) typically involve multiple procedures during the same diagnostic session, and all these services should be assigned codes. The use of modifier 51 is NOT appropriate for outpatient hospital or facility coding purposes.
- Diagnostic endoscopies are incidental when surgical or interventional endoscopies are performed at the same surgical session.
- When multiple interventional or surgical endoscopies (cystoscopies, urethroscopies, or cystourethroscopies) are performed, endoscopic introduction and stent placement specefically to perform the definitive procedure are not assigned additional code(s).
- Watch the use of "ureteral" and "urethral" as they appear almost identical and are often miscoded due to lack of attention to these terms.

Specific Male Genital System Guidelines (54000–55899)

The male genital systems encompasses procedures performed on the male reproductive system. Keep in mind that the prostate is also included in this section. Codes are assigned from this section according to:

First:	Anatomical site
Second:	Approach (incision/destruction/excision/introduction)
Third:	Procedure performed

Current Procedural Terminology (CPT) © 2005 American Medical Association. All Rights Reserved.

Notes

Specific Female Genital System Guidelines (56405–58999)

Procedures performed on the female genital system are divided into two sections: nonmaternity and maternity-related procedures.

Codes for the Female Genital, nonmaternity section are subcategorized as follows:

First:	Anatomical site
Second:	Approach (incision/excision)
Third:	Procedure performed

When coding for female, nonmaternity procedures, the following guidelines must be considered:

- Hysterectomies can be performed either abdominally or vaginally. Assign codes accordingly.
- Abdominal hysterectomy codes include the incidental excision and removal of tubes and/or ovaries.
- Many procedures in this section may be performed utilizing various surgical techniques. For instance, tubal ligation may be performed:
    - Laparoscopically
        With fulguration of oviducts (58670)
        With occlusion of oviducts (58671)
    - Surgically
        Occlusion of tubes by device (58615)
        Ligation/transection (58600)
    - At time of another procedure
        Postpartum during same hospitalization (58605)
        During time of cesarean delivery or intra-abdominal surgery (58611)
- When laparoscopy involves visual examination and/or surgery of organs in addition to the female genital organs, the laparoscopic codes in the digestive system should be utilized.
- Codes exist for both hysteroscopies (visual examination via the uterus) and laparoscopies (visual examination via the abdomen).

Specific Maternity Care and Delivery Services Guidelines (59000–59899)

This section includes services performed during the course of pregnancy (antepartum, delivery and postpartum).

Codes for this section are subcategorized based on:

First:	Period of maternity care (antepartum, delivery, postpartum)
Second:	Procedure performed

Current Procedural Terminology (CPT) © 2005 American Medical Association. All Rights Reserved.

Notes

Additional maternity coding guidelines are necessary in order to code these procedures appropriately:

- Antepartum (before delivery) care includes initial and subsequent visits, recording weight, blood pressures, fetal heart tones, routine urinalysis and monthly visits to 28 weeks, biweekly to 36 weeks, and weekly visits until delivery.
- Delivery care includes hospitalization for delivery, management of uncomplicated labor and delivery.
- Postpartum includes follow-up services following delivery.
- Delivery may be accomplished via:
  - Vaginal delivery
  - Cesarean delivery
  - Delivery either vaginally or via cesarean section following previous cesarean section
- "Abortion" refers to the termination of pregnancy whether spontaneous or by induction.
- "Incomplete abortion" refers to spontaneous abortion where products of conception are retained.
- "Missed abortion" refers to spontaneous abortion where the demised fetus is retained.

Specific Endocrine System Services Guidelines (60000–60699)

Codes for the endocrine system are subcategorized as follows:

First:	Anatomical site
Second:	Approach (incision/excision)
Third:	Procedure performed

Specific Nervous System Services Guidelines (61000–64999)

The nervous system is comprised of services performed on the skull, meninges, brain, spine, spinal cord and nerves. Codes are assigned based on:

First:	Anatomical site
Second:	Approach (incision/excision)
Third:	Procedure performed

Note that the global guidelines we discussed in our General Coding section do not apply in the coding of procedures on the skull base. In addition to distinct

Current Procedural Terminology (CPT) © 2005 American Medical Association. All Rights Reserved.

coding differences for such procedures, these additional nervous system guidelines are appropriate as well:

- Skull base services are coded based on the approach, definitive and repair/reconstructive procedures performed. They are defined as follows:
  - Approach procedures necessary to obtain exposure
  - Definitive procedures necessary to treat
  - Repair/reconstructive procedures necessary to close defect
- Neurostimulator codes are utilized for placement of cranial neurostimulators (based on technique utilized for placement), while analysis and reprogramming are coded from the Medicine section of CPT-4.
- Spinal cord injections are separated based on:
  - Neurolytic substances (Codes 62280–62282)
  - Non-neurolytic substances (Codes 62310–62311)
  - Including catheter placement (Codes 62318–62319)
- Epidural catheter placement is coded with Codes 62350–62355 while pump implantation is coded with 62360–62368.
- Laminectomies are performed by excision or surgical removal of lamina, while laminotomies are incisions into the lamina.
- Implantation of neurostimulators (63650–63688) is coded based on placement location (epidural or subarachnoid) and approach for placement (laminectomy or percutaneous).

Specific Eye and Ocular Adnexa Services Guidelines (65091–68899)

Coding for the eye and ocular adnexa are subcategorized as follows:

First:	Anatomical site
Second:	Approach (removal/excision/incision)
Third:	Procedure performed

Other considerations for coding procedures in the Eye and Ocular Adnexa section are as follows:

- Cataract removal is performed on the lens of the eye. Codes are categorized by extracapsular or intracapsular. If not specified, assign a code from the extracapsular area.
- Cataract codes specify whether an intraocular lens (IOL) was placed at the time of the cataract removal (66982–66984) or at a time in the future (66985).
- Strabismus surgery (67311–67340) involves the adjustment of vertical or horizontal muscles of the ocular adnexa.

Current Procedural Terminology (CPT) © 2005 American Medical Association. All Rights Reserved.

Notes

Specific Auditory System Services Guidelines (69000–69979)

Coding of procedures on the ear and auditory system is subcategorized as follows:

> First: Location (external/middle/inner ear)
> Second: Procedure performed

Other considerations in assigning codes for the ear and auditory system include:

- Myringotomy involves incision into the middle ear, usually for drainage purposes.
- Tympanostomy involves the surgical creation of an artificial opening by incision into the middle ear and placement of a ventilating tube.
- When removal of exiting ventilating tube is necessary to replace or insert a new tube, the removal is included in the replacement procedure.
- Myringotomy and tympanostomy codes are unilateral and require the addition of RT/LT modifiers or 50 when performed bilaterally.

Operating Microscope Guidelines (69990)

When a surgical microscope is utilized as part of a surgical procedure, Code 69990 should be added. Some procedures already are inclusive of this procedure; they are listed in the CPT-4 manual.

ⓅRACTICE EXERCISE 6–5

Assign the appropriate codes to the following surgery exercises:

1. Patient presents for excision of multiple lesions of the back, face and arms. Several of these lesions are suspected to be malignant in nature, so we will biopsy them and send to pathology.
   Patient was prepped and draped in the usual sterile fashion. Excision of a 2-cm lesion was made from the lower back area with 0.5-cm margins, as it was suspected this lesion was malignant. Simple repair was made. Another lesion was excised from the face, 0.5 cm, which was also closed. Two lesions on the arm, both approximately 1.2 cm in size, were also excised and closed appropriately.
   Surgical pathology indicated that the lower back and both arm lesions were, in fact, malignant. The face lesion reported back as benign.

Current Procedural Terminology (CPT) © 2005 American Medical Association. All Rights Reserved.

<u>Notes</u>	CPT-4	ICD-9-CM Diagnosis	ICD-9-CM Procedures
_____	_____	_____	_____
_____	_____	_____	_____

Code Assignment: _____

_____

2. Patient presents for excisional breast biopsy. The patient is prepped and draped in the usual sterile manner. An incision is made around the whole lesion and the lesion is removed in toto. Lesion appears to be approximately 2 cm in diameter and it was sent to surgical pathology for evaluation. The wound was copiously irrigated and closed appropriately.

CPT-4	ICD-9-CM Diagnosis	ICD-9-CM Procedures
_____	_____	_____
_____	_____	_____

Code Assignment: _____

3. The patient presents with a lesion on the face area that is approximately 4.0 cm in size. Due to the size of the lesion and its locations, it was elected to perform this procedure under general anesthesia as a skin graft might be necessary for closure.

    The area was prepped and draped in the usual sterile fashion. Excision of the lesion was carried out in the usual fashion and sent to surgical pathology. In order to close the skin defect, a split-thickness skin graft approximately 2 × 2 was obtained from the thigh area and applied to the defect area on the cheek, which measured approximately 3.5 cm × 4.0 cm. Dressings were placed on both the donor site and the recipient site.

CPT-4	ICD-9-CM Diagnosis	ICD-9-CM Procedures
_____	_____	_____
_____	_____	_____
_____	_____	_____

Code Assignment: _____

4. Patient presents for closure of a 6.5 laceration to the forehead. Apparently the patient was involved in an automobile accident earlier in the day, and suffered a laceration to the forehead when her head hit the windshield. She was initially seen in the emergency room, and plastic surgery was called to close this head laceration. The patient was

Current Procedural Terminology (CPT) © 2005 American Medical Association. All Rights Reserved.

prepped in the usual sterile fashion and the wound was repaired in two layers. Dressing was applied and the patient was discharged in satisfactory condition.

CPT-4	ICD-9-CM Diagnosis	ICD-9-CM Procedures
_____	_____	_____
_____	_____	_____
_____	_____	

Code Assignment: _____

5. Patient presents for removal of splinter from finger. Patient was playing with a wooden broomstick and apparently ran their hand over the broom handle. On examination, there appears to be a small wooden splinter directly beneath the skin. An incision was made after probing and the splinter was removed. Wound was closed with Steri-strips and dressing was applied.

CPT-4	ICD-9-CM Diagnosis	ICD-9-CM Procedures
_____	_____	_____
_____	_____	_____

Code Assignment: _____

6. Patient presents with pain in the lower leg after falling from a ladder this morning while repairing their house. X-rays indicate a possible hairline fracture of the tib/fib area and the patient will be placed in a walking cast in the likelihood of a fracture and for convenience.

CPT-4	ICD-9-CM Diagnosis	ICD-9-CM Procedures
_____	_____	_____
_____	_____	_____

Code Assignment: _____

7. Patient presents for knee arthroscopy after several months of knee pain and "catching" knee joint. Patient is prepped and knee area is prepared in the usual sterile fashion. The arthroscope is introduced and the patellofemoral joint appears to be normal. The lateral compartment appears to be intact; however, the medial joint has some synovia that needs to be excised as well as meniscus that needs to be shaved. The patient is returned to the recovery room in satisfactory condition.

Current Procedural Terminology (CPT) © 2005 American Medical Association. All Rights Reserved.

Notes

CPT-4   ICD-9-CM Diagnosis   ICD-9-CM Procedures

Code Assignment: _____

8. Patient presents for status post pin removal following open reduction and internal fixation of a bimalleolar ankle fracture approximately 2 years ago. Apparently, one of the pins has dislodged and can be manipulated under the skin, and now the patient complains of pain and irritation in that area. The pin is removed, the area is closed with sutures and the patient is returned to the recovery room in satisfactory condition.

CPT-4   ICD-9-CM Diagnosis   ICD-9-CM Procedures

Code Assignment: _____

9. Patient presents for knee injection complaining of returning pain to the knee joint after strenuous exercise this weekend. We have treated with the patient conservatively with a knee joint injection in the past and that has been successful. The patient was prepped in the usual manner, Marcaine was used to inject the knee joint and the patient will return on a PRN basis.

CPT-4   ICD-9-CM Diagnosis   ICD-9-CM Procedures

Code Assignment: _____

10. Patient presents with painful wrist following an automobile accident. Range of motion is limited by pain and swelling, and x-rays reveal that the distal radius has been fractured in two locations. The patient is prepped and draped in the usual sterile manner. An incision is made and the distal radius is identified and manipulated into place. Two pins are placed for alignment purposes and the incision is closed appropriately. A short arm cast is applied and the patient is to follow up in 2 weeks.

CPT-4   ICD-9-CM Diagnosis   ICD-9-CM Procedures

Code Assignment: _____

Notes

11. Patient presents for admission for replacement of pacemaker for dysrythmia due to battery life. The patient has had satisfactory results from the pacemaker and the pulse generator needs to be replaced. An incision is made, the pacemaker pocket is entered, and the pulse generator is disconnected from the leads. Pulse generator is changed for a Serial #252XX, Model #Al-4465, leads are reconnected as they were intact and the pacemaker pocket is closed appropriately with sutures. The patient tolerated the procedure well.

CPT-4   ICD-9-CM Diagnosis   ICD-9-CM Procedures

_____   _____   _____

_____   _____   _____

                 Code Assignment: _____

12. This 45-year-old patient presents for placement of a central line for chemotherapy administration. Patient was recently diagnosed with breast carcinoma with poor venous access, so her physician has requested a central line be placed. The catheter was inserted into the subclavian and advanced appropriately. No tunneling was necessary. X-rays indicated the catheter was appropriately positioned in the subclavian and the patient was sent to the recovery area in satisfactory condition.

CPT-4   ICD-9-CM Diagnosis   ICD-9-CM Procedures

_____   _____   _____

_____   _____   _____

                 Code Assignment: _____

13. This 65-year-old patient presents for removal of a tunneled peripheral central venous catheter that was placed approximately 3 weeks ago for IV antibiotic therapy. The patient's condition has improved significantly and there is no longer a need for the central line. The patient is prepped and the catheter is removed with no problems encountered.

CPT-4   ICD-9-CM Diagnosis   ICD-9-CM Procedures

_____   _____   _____

_____   _____   _____

                 Code Assignment: _____

14. Patient presents for diagnostic bronchoscopy. Patient has been experiencing shortness of breath. Chest x-ray revealed an infiltrate or mass in the right upper lobe. Scope was introduced and advanced into the right upper lobe. The suspicious area was identified by fluoroscope

Current Procedural Terminology (CPT) © 2005 American Medical Association. All Rights Reserved.

and multiple biopsies were taken of the area. The patient tolerated the procedure well and was returned to the recovery room in satisfactory condition.

CPT-4   ICD-9-CM Diagnosis   ICD-9-CM Procedures

_____   _____   _____

_____   _____   _____

                                          Code Assignment: _____

15. Patient experiencing extreme shortness of breath with history of ascites. Patient prepped for procedure and catheter inserted with 1000 of bloody fluid removed. Catheter was left in place for further drainage.

CPT-4   ICD-9-CM Diagnosis   ICD-9-CM Procedures

_____   _____   _____

_____   _____   _____

                                          Code Assignment: _____

16. Patient fractured nose on multiple occasions as a youth and continues to have problems with breathing and obstructive sleep apnea as a result. Patient wishes to have deviated septum repaired in an effort to correct these problems. Patient was taken to the operating room and prepped in the usual sterile manner. The septum was identified, outfracture was necessary in order to correct the deviated septum. The nose was packed following the procedure and patient returned to the recovery room in satisfactory condition.

CPT-4   ICD-9-CM Diagnosis   ICD-9-CM Procedures

_____   _____   _____

_____   _____   _____

                                          Code Assignment: _____

17. Patient experienced several episodes of not being able to swallow foods, and was recommended for an EGD, upper GI, with the possibility of an esophageal dilation needed. The mouth was sprayed with anesthetic spray and the scope introduced and passed through the esophagus. One particular area was noted to be extremely narrow with scarring and the area was dilated. The scope was then advanced into the stomach and duodenum and no further abnormalities were noted. The patient tolerated the procedure well.

Current Procedural Terminology (CPT) © 2005 American Medical Association. All Rights Reserved.

Notes _____

CPT-4   ICD-9-CM Diagnosis   ICD-9-CM Procedures

_____   _____   _____

_____   _____   _____

Code Assignment: _____

18. Patient presented with complaints of black, tarry stools and a hemoccult was positive. Patient was recommended for a colonoscopy to determine pathology of presenting complaints. The patient was prepped and the scope was inserted into the rectum without difficulty. The scope was advanced all the way to the cecum. Two polyps were noted in the rectosigmoid junction, both were biopsied, and one of them subsequently removed in toto by snare as it appeared suspicious. Both were sent to surgical pathology and the results were carcinoma in situ of the colon. The procedure was terminated and the patient will follow up for further treatment and surgical intervention.

CPT-4   ICD-9-CM Diagnosis   ICD-9-CM Procedures

_____   _____   _____

_____   _____   _____

Code Assignment: _____

19. This 6-year-old patient has experienced multiple bouts of serous otitis media over the past few months. Despite months of antibiotic therapy, the patient presents today with chronic serous otitis media and the decision is made to place ventilation tubes. The patient is prepped in the usual sterile manner and the decision was made to perform the procedure with general anesthesia due to patient's age. An incision was made in the middle ear and a ventilating tube was placed. Corticosporin was applied and the patient left the operating room in satisfactory condition.

CPT-4   ICD-9-CM Diagnosis   ICD-9-CM Procedures

_____   _____   _____

_____   _____   _____

Code Assignment: _____

20. This 69-year-old patient with bilateral cataracts presents with removal of right cataract with intraocular lens implantation. The patient is prepped and given IV sedation. Upon entering the posterior capsule, the cataract was removed utilizing phacoemulsification technique. Following the removal, an intraocular lens, Model #2535xx, Serial #256346 was implanted. The patient tolerated the procedure well.

Current Procedural Terminology (CPT) © 2005 American Medical Association. All Rights Reserved.

<u>**Notes**</u>   CPT-4   ICD-9-CM Diagnosis   ICD-9-CM Procedures

_____   _____   _____   _____

_____   _____   _____   _____

_____   Code Assignment: _____

_____

21. This 8-year-old patient with chronic adenotonsillitis presents for
_____   tonsillectomy with possible adenoidectomy. Patient is prepped and
draped and the tonsils are examined. They are extremely large and
_____   erythematous. The tonsils are grasped and carefully excised along with
hypertrophic adenoidal tissue. The patient tolerated the procedure well.

_____   CPT-4   ICD-9-CM Diagnosis   ICD-9-CM Procedures

_____   _____   _____   _____

_____   _____   _____   _____

_____   Code Assignment: _____

22. Patient with urinary incontinence presents for diagnostic testing. After
_____   the insertion of a urinary catheter via the urethra, a cystometrogram
and uroflowmetry with the electronic uroflowmetric equipment is
_____   performed. Findings are consistent with stress incontinence and the
patient's PCP will be informed for treatment purposes.

_____   CPT-4   ICD-9-CM Diagnosis   ICD-9-CM Procedures

_____   _____   _____   _____

_____   _____   _____   _____

_____   Code Assignment: _____

23. Patient is presenting for cystourethroscopy due to lower abdominal
_____   pain and identification of a possible bladder tumor via ultrasound. The
patient was prepped in the usual manner and the cystoscope was
_____   inserted through the urethra. The tumor was identified and excised,
measuring approximately 3.0 cm. Surgical pathology verified the mass
_____   to be malignant and the patient will be sent for additional treatment.

_____   CPT-4   ICD-9-CM Diagnosis   ICD-9-CM Procedures

_____   _____   _____   _____

_____   _____   _____   _____

_____   Code Assignment: _____

24. Patient presents for tubal ligation. The patient is multiparity and wishes
_____   the tubal for contraceptive purposes. The patient was prepped and the

Current Procedural Terminology (CPT) © 2005 American Medical Association. All Rights Reserved.

Notes

laparoscope was introduced through a supraumbilical incision. The fallopian tubes were identified and banding was applied to both the right and left tube.

CPT-4	ICD-9-CM Diagnosis	ICD-9-CM Procedures
_____	_____	_____
_____	_____	_____

Code Assignment: _____

25. Patient presents for epidural injections for chronic low back pain. Injections are made at the C1/C2 and C3/4 interspaces with a combination of steroids. The patient tolerated the procedure well.

CPT-4	ICD-9-CM Diagnosis	ICD-9-CM Procedures
_____	_____	_____
_____	_____	_____

Code Assignment: _____

Outpatient Radiology Coding Guidelines (CPT-4 Codes 70000–79999)

The Radiology section is divided into four subcategories:

1. Diagnostic radiology (x-rays, CT and MRI scans)
2. Diagnostic ultrasounds
3. Radiation oncology
4. Nuclear medicine

Codes for the radiology section are subcategorized as follow:

First:	Subcategory (as outlined above)
Second:	Anatomical site
Third:	Extent of procedure (such as number of views)

Specific Radiology Coding Guidelines

Coding for radiological procedures involves a number of unique guidelines, many of which are at the front of the Radiology section. However, some guidelines to keep in mind when assigning codes for this section are:

• Use of RT/LT modifier or 50 (bilateral) is appropriate to designate site when CPT-4 code identifies one anatomical site (such as forearm).

Current Procedural Terminology (CPT) © 2005 American Medical Association. All Rights Reserved.

Notes
_____
_____
_____
_____
_____
_____
_____
_____
_____
_____
_____
_____
_____
_____
_____
_____
_____
_____
_____
_____
_____

- Number of views should be assigned based on radiology report. When not specified, the least significant number of views should be coded.
- CT/MRI codes often are categorized by:
  - Without contrast
  - With and without contrast
- "Contrast" is defined as materials utilized to enhance the radiological image, excluding oral and rectal contrast materials.
- Diagnostic ultrasounds are designated as limited or complete. In order for the ultrasonic image to be considered complete, all organs or body structures located in that area should be identified. (This rule will differ from carrier to carrier.)
- Pelvic ultrasound codes are categorized not only by limited and complete, but also by obstetrical and nonobstetrical.
- Ultrasonic guidance codes may be assigned when utilized in conjunction with surgical procedures. Keep in mind that these procedures should be coded only by those facilities and physicians that perform these services.
- Nuclear medicine radiologic codes include only the performance of the radiographic imaging. Codes for the radiopharmaceutical should also be assigned utilizing CPT-4 or HCPCS codes based on carrier specifications.

PRACTICE EXERCISE 6–6

Assign the appropriate codes to the following:

RADIOLOGY CASE 1

Date of Procedure:
Clinical Information: Rule out osteo right maxillary sinus

WATERS VIEW OF SINUS

The frontal sinuses are small but clear. There is mucosal thickening of the right maxillary sinus with a fluid level. The left maxillary sinus is clear. There is no definite bone destruction.

The findings are consistent with right maxillary sinusitis. Although there were no definite radiographic signs of osteomyelitis, this would be difficult to exclude on a single waters view. CT may be helpful for further evaluation.

Current Procedural Terminology (CPT) © 2005 American Medical Association. All Rights Reserved.

Notes

CONCLUSION:

Right Maxillary Sinusitis

CPT-4   ICD-9-CM Diagnosis   ICD-9-CM Procedures

_____   _____   _____

                                         Code Assignment: _____

RADIOLOGY CASE 2

Date of Procedure:
Clinical Information: Possible placenta previa

OB ULTRASOUND

Single intrauterine pregnancy with fetus in the cephalic position. Placenta is located posteriorly to the right in the uterus. No evidence of placenta previa. Amniotic fluid volume is within normal limits. Fetal anatomy appears normal on images provided.

   Average ultrasound age is estimated to be 33 weeks 2 days.

CPT-4   ICD-9-CM Diagnosis   ICD-9-CM Procedures

_____   _____   _____

                                         Code Assignment: _____

RADIOLOGY CASE 3

Date of Procedure:
Clinical Information: Fall three days ago; knee pain

THREE VIEW OF THE RIGHT KNEE

On the AP view, there is a 0.3-cm calcification or density projected over the central knee joint. Although this could be an artifact, a small avulsion fracture is a possibility. Recommend the AP view be repeated with a notch view to further evaluate. Otherwise negative evaluate; otherwise negative.

Current Procedural Terminology (CPT) © 2005 American Medical Association. All Rights Reserved.

Notes	CPT-4	ICD-9-CM Diagnosis	ICD-9-CM Procedures

Code Assignment: _____

RADIOLOGY CASE 4

Date of Procedure:
Clinical Information: Shortness of breath, cough

CHEST, PA AND LATERAL

Mild cardiomegaly. Interstitial markings in the right upper lung are mildly increased in density compared with previous films. This could represent early or localized active process such as pneumonia or possibly progressive fibrosis. There is a small amount of scattered fibrosis in the lower lungs. Also of note is a tortuous aorta.

CPT-4	ICD-9-CM Diagnosis	ICD-9-CM Procedures

Code Assignment: _____

RADIOLOGY CASE 5

Date of Procedure:
Clinical Information: Left-sided weakness, visual blurring, memory difficulty

CT SCAN OF THE HEAD

Exam is made without and with the use of IV contrast material.

Current Procedural Terminology (CPT) © 2005 American Medical Association. All Rights Reserved.

Notes

Mild generalized cerebral atrophy most evident in the frontal lobe area. No evidence of an expanding intracranial process. No evidence of acute inter-cerebral hemorrhage.

Demineralization of the bones of the calvarium.

CPT-4	ICD-9-CM Diagnosis	ICD-9-CM Procedures
_____	_____	_____
_____	_____	_____

Code Assignment: _____

RADIOLOGY CASE 6

Date of Procedure:
Clincial Information: 112.2 × 5.5-cm mass noted

CT OF THE ABDOMEN

Exam is made using oral and IV contrast. Noncontrast sections made of the kidneys and liver before introduction of contrast.

Caudad lobe of the liver is quite prominent and measures at least 7 cm in largest diameter. However, there is no definite evidence of a mass or lesion in this area with liver parenchyma uniform in density. Recommend repeat ultrasound be performed with special attention to the caudad of the liver. Gallbladder is generous in size. Kidneys, spleen and abdominal aorta are negative.

CPT-4	ICD-9-CM Diagnosis	ICD-9-CM Procedures
_____	_____	_____
_____	_____	_____

Code Assignment: _____

RADIOLOGY CASE 7

Date of Procedure:
Clinical Information: Low back pain

Current Procedural Terminology (CPT) © 2005 American Medical Association. All Rights Reserved.

FOUR VIEW OF THE LUMBAR SPINE

Approximately 1.0 cm of spondylolisthesis of L5 upon the sacrum. There is probably bilateral spondylolysis at this level, which should be checked with oblique views. Narrowing and degenerative changes at the lumbosacral interspace.

Minimal degenerative changes in the other lumbar interspaces. Surgical slips in the pelvis—probably related to tubal ligation.

CPT-4   ICD-9-CM Diagnosis   ICD-9-CM Procedures

_____   _____   _____

_____   _____

Code Assignment: _____

RADIOLOGY CASE 8

Date of Procedure:
Clinical Information: Renal calculus

RENAL ULTRASOUND

The exam demonstrates a small area of echogenicity with shadowing in the mid-left kidney that could represent a small calculus. No evidence of hydronephrosis. The left kidney measures approximately 11.7 cm in length and 5.4 cm in width.

Screening exam of the right kidney is negative, with measurements of 10.0 × 4.6 cm. The urinary bladder was not visualized.

CPT-4   ICD-9-CM Diagnosis   ICD-9-CM Procedures

_____   _____   _____

_____   _____

Code Assignment: _____

RADIOLOGY CASE 9

Date of Procedure:
Clinical Information:

Current Procedural Terminology (CPT) © 2005 American Medical Association. All Rights Reserved.

THREE VIEWS OF THE LEFT HAND

Negative left hand

CPT-4   ICD-9-CM Diagnosis   ICD-9-CM Procedures

_____   _____   _____

_____   _____   _____

Code Assignment: _____

RADIOLOGY CASE 10

Date of Procedure:
Clinical Information:

BARIUM ENEMA

Negative colon and terminal ileum

CPT-4   ICD-9-CM Diagnosis   ICD-9-CM Procedures

_____   _____   _____

_____   _____   _____

Code Assignment: _____

Outpatient Pathology Coding (CPT-4 Codes 80000–89999)

The Pathology section encompasses a variety of services performed on bodily fluids, such as blood, urine, saliva and cells. The codes from the Pathology section are categorized based on:

First: Category of service performed, such as:
          Organ- or disease-oriented panels
          Drug testing
          Therapeutic drug assays
          Evocative/suppression testing
          Clinical pathology consultations
          Urinalysis

Current Procedural Terminology (CPT) © 2005 American Medical Association. All Rights Reserved.

       Chemistry
       Hematology and coagulation
       Immunology
       Transfusion medicine
       Microbiology
       Anatomic pathology
       Cytopathology
       Cytogenetic studies
       Surgical pathology
    Second: Specific procedures performed, arranged alphabetically

Specific Pathology Coding Guidelines

The majority of pathology services provided or performed in the outpatient facility will be captured by the chargemaster CDM that we discussed in the overview of the hospital billing and coding systems. Thus the coder typically will not be required to assign CPT-4 procedure codes for these services. However, it is common for the diagnostic codes to be assigned by coding staff.

Some pathological coding guidelines that should be kept in mind are:

- When method performed is not specified, the order of significance is:
  - Dipstick (urinalysis)
  - Automated
  - Manual
- Modifiers are typically not required for lab services.
- Most outpatient hospital lab services will be captured, coded and billed through the chargemaster.
- Disease and organ panels should be coded only when all procedures have been ordered and performed. The facility should not perform all of the panel tests when a physician requests only some of these procedures.
- Tests listed separately, that are included in a disease or organ panel, should be coded and billed as a panel rather than separately.
- Make certain all laboratory services meet third-party carrier "medically necessary" guidelines.
- The unit of service for surgical pathology (Codes 88300–88399) is the specimen. For example: If 5 specimens are individually identified (whether in one container or 5), the appropriate code with 5 units should be assigned
- Should a frozen section be performed (Code 88331), this is for 1 specimen. If additional blocks are examined, assign 88332. These codes are in addition to the surgical pathology codes.

Current Procedural Terminology (CPT) © 2005 American Medical Association. All Rights Reserved.

Notes

Outpatient Medicine Service Coding Guidelines (CPT-4 Codes 90281–99602)

The Medicine section of CPT-4 contains services that are typically diagnostic or therapeutic in nature. In contrast to the Surgery section, the procedures coded from this section are typically not the definitive answer to the patient's medical problem. Again, as with the pathology CPT-4 services, a large majority of these servies will be captured.

Codes in the Medicine section are diverse, and categorized based on the following:

First: Type/specialty of procedure
Second: Specific procedure performed

Specific Medicine Coding Guidelines

Keep in mind the following when coding for procedures from the Medicine section:

- Most procedures performed from the Medicine section are captured, coded and billed by the facility chargemaster.
- Procedures are performed based on the technical (facility) and professional (physician/provider) portions. It is not necessary to indicate the facility vs professional component, as that information is encompassed in the assignment of revenue codes.

EXAMPLE

Facility performs technical portion of 94010.

Would be coded as CPT-4 Code 94010.

Facility bills for both technical and professional portions of 94010.

Would be coded as CPT-4 Code 94010 with Revenue Code for facility as well as CPT-4 Code 94010 with Revenue Code for professional.

In addition to the general guidelines above, specific guidelines for subsections in the Medicine section are:

- Injections, immunizations and vaccines require the use of two codes: one for the provision of the materials (e.g., toxoid or medications), and one for the administration of these materials.
- Intravenous and chemotherapy infusion codes are assigned by time: initial code for the first hour, subsequent code (multiple units may be required) for each additional hour.

Current Procedural Terminology (CPT) © 2005 American Medical Association. All Rights Reserved.

Notes

- ESRD (End Stage Renal Disease) service codes are based on whether the services performed are for the full month (90918–90921) or less than a full month (90922–90925), as well as the age of the patient.
- Proper coding of cardiac catheterizations requires the assignment of codes for:

Catheter placement:	Left/right/combined heart catheterization
Injection procedures:	Sites where dye injected for imaging
Imaging procedures:	Vessel where imaging occurs
Additional procedures:	

    All coded by the number of vessels:

        Angioplasty

        Stent

        Atherectomy

Cardiac catheterization procedures may be captured by the chargemaster or assigned codes by the coder, or a combination of both. Make certain all codes are captured and none are duplicated by both entitites.

- Allergy testing services are coded based on the technique for testing, such as percutaneous, intracutaneous, or patch tests. Multiple units are assigned when more than one test is performed.

PRACTICE EXERCISE 6–7

Take the following services, review the documentation and assign codes appropriately. Utilize the E & M acuity levels discussed earlier to assign the appropriate Evaluation and Management codes. Assign modifier codes as appropriate.

ER Case 1

Patient was eating hot dogs tonight and accidentally choked. He was administered the Heimlich maneuver and he then vomited up a lot of clear phlegm. He has no complaints now and denies any pain. He was given a drink of water and was able to drink without any difficulty.

Temperature 96, pulse 70, BP 146/86, O2 sats 99%. General: Alert, responsive, pleasant, cooperative, talkative, in no acute distress. Chest: lungs clear without any rales, rhonchi, wheezes. Breathing easy without retractions or use of other accessory muscles or respiration.

LAB: Chest x-ray is normal.
Dysphagia with esophageal obstruction.

Current Procedural Terminology (CPT) © 2005 American Medical Association. All Rights Reserved.

Notes	CPT-4	ICD-9-CM Diagnosis	ICD-9-CM Procedures
_____	_____	_____	_____
_____	_____	_____	_____
_____	_____	_____	_____
_____	_____	_____	_____
_____	_____	_____	

Code Assignment: _____

ER Case 2

Chief complaint: Possible hypoglycemic episode, severe hypertension

Patient with IDDM presented having gotten extremely woozy, weak and sweaty. No chest discomfort or shortness of breath. Felt she might be having a little low blood sugar reaction. She also has a history of hypertension and has had previous strokes.

No visual symptoms. Review of systems: No cardiac symptoms, breathing better. Family history noncontributory. Medications are Hyzaar, Humalog, Prozasin, Sular and Zoloft.

On exam her BP is initially high. That was monitored and it came down fine. She felt fine and felt ready to go after being watched in the ER for a half hour. She had no facial asymmetry. She had no palpable edema. She had a little bit of soreness of the left posterior neck muscle. I did not hear any carotid bruits. Lungs clear.

Probably hypoglycemia attached with reactive hypertensive episode, which is resolving.

CPT-4	ICD-9-CM Diagnosis	ICD-9-CM Procedures
_____	_____	_____
_____	_____	_____
_____	_____	_____
_____	_____	_____

Code Assignment: _____

ER Case 3

Patient presents with complaints of chest pain. He states he had a single-vessel bypass done approximately 5 years ago. He has been doing fairly well on his

Current Procedural Terminology (CPT) © 2005 American Medical Association. All Rights Reserved.

Notes
_____
_____
_____
_____
_____
_____
_____
_____
_____
_____
_____
_____
_____
_____
_____
_____
_____
_____
_____
_____

medical regimen until about 2 months ago, when he started having some twinges of chest pain with exertion. This has been gradually worsening over the last 2 months and now he gets chest pain when he is doing activities such as vacuuming. As soon as he rests, the pain goes away.

Chest clear, heart regular rate and rhythm without murmurs. EKG showed only some nonspecific STT wave changes, no evidence of acute MI. We did troponin and PTPTT; all within normal limits. Chest x-ray also appeared clear.

Chest pain, appears to be stable, worsening angina.

We will stop his Norvasc, start on Metoprolol 250 mg bid for now.

CPT-4	ICD-9-CM Diagnosis	ICD-9-CM Procedures
_____	_____	_____
_____	_____	_____
_____	_____	_____
_____	_____	_____

Code Assignment: _____

ER Case 4

This 65-year-old male noted onset of left lower quadrant pain yesterday. No nausea or vomiting. No past history of similar abdominal pain or GI problems. Two months ago he had a complete workup for microscopic hematuria, including an IVP and cystoscopy, which were normal. He has history of coronary artery disease with MI and angioplasty 6 months ago. Also has hypertension. His medications are listed. He is allergic to morphine.

He denies chest pain or palpitations. No cough or shortness of breath. No dysuria, increased urinary frequency, or nocturia.

Reveals an alert, pleasant gentleman. He is afebrile. Eyes are clear, TM appear normal. No nasal congestion. Mouth is moist, throat reveals no redness or swelling. Neck is supple with no adenopathy. Heart regular rate and rhythm. There is exquisite left lower quadrant tenderness. No masses, bowel tones are present. Rectal exam reveals good sphincter tone. No rectal masses or tenderness. No calf tenderness or ankle dema. Lab data includes a hemoglobin of 15.2, white count 10200, chemistry panel is entirely normal, urine contains 3–5 RBCs but otherwise unremarkable. Chest x-ray shows no active pulmonary disease. Abdominal x-ray shows stool in the right colon but otherwise unremarkable.

Given Augmentin 500 mg orally.

Diagnosis: Left lower quadrant pain, probably diverticulitis.

Current Procedural Terminology (CPT) © 2005 American Medical Association. All Rights Reserved.

Notes

Rest, stay on clear liquids today and progress his diet slowly. Continue Augmentin 500 tid. If he develops increased pain, vomiting, fever, or other problems, he is to return to ER.

CPT-4	ICD-9-CM Diagnosis	ICD-9-CM Procedures
_____	_____	_____
_____	_____	_____
_____	_____	_____
_____	_____	_____
	_____	_____

Code Assignment: _____

ER Case 5

Sixty-nine-year-old woman seen yesterday with an insect sting on the right foot. Today she is concerned that the redness is swelling. She is on Claritin and started on prednisone. There is no history of allergic reactions to bee stings. She does have respiratory allergies. Her medications are as listed. Her allergies are also listed. Her last tetanus was in 2000. She is afebrile. There is sting site visible on the lateral aspect of the right foot with surrounding erythema which does not appear to have spread significantly beyond skin marking which was applied yesterday.

Insect sting right foot with local reaction.

Continue resting and elevating foot with ice. She will continue her medication. If she develops increased swelling, pain, fever, or any problems, she is to return to the ER.

CPT-4	ICD-9-CM Diagnosis	ICD-9-CM Procedures
_____	_____	_____
_____	_____	_____
_____	_____	_____
_____	_____	_____
_____	_____	_____

Code Assignment: _____

Current Procedural Terminology (CPT) © 2005 American Medical Association. All Rights Reserved.

Surgery Chart 1

Surgeon:
Preoperative diagnosis: Abnormal calcifications left breast
Postoperative diagnosis: Same
Procedure: Left needle localization and breast biopsy
Anesthesia: Local with sedation
Blood loss: About 25 cc

Procedure:

The patient was placed in the supine position. The left breast was prepped
and draped in the usual fashion. An incision was made along the superior
aspect of the areola and dissection was carried down to the tip of the wire
incorporating 1 inch of breast tissue in each direction so as to incorporate all
calcifications. A second specimen had to be obtained in order to obtain the
most proximal one. The specimens were sent to radiology for confirmation
that all calcifications had been removed. Once confirmation was obtained,
the area was irrigated; hemostasis was obtained. The wound was approxi-
mated with a running 3–9 Monocryl. Benzoin, Steri-strips and Tegaderm
were applied and the patient was taken to the recovery room in satisfactory
condition.

CPT-4	ICD-9-CM Diagnosis	ICD-9-CM Procedures
_____	_____	_____
_____	_____	_____
_____	_____	_____
_____	_____	_____
_____	_____	_____

Code Assignment: _____

Surgery Chart 2

Surgeon:
Anesthetist:
Preoperative Diagnosis: Question of basal cell carcinoma of left nare
Postoperative Diagnosis: Basal cell carcinoma of left nare
Surgery:

Current Procedural Terminology (CPT) © 2005 American Medical Association. All Rights Reserved.

Notes

1. Wide excision basal cell carcinoma of left nare with frozen section.

2. Harvesting of split-thickness skin graft from the left neck and application of graft to site of excision of left nare.

Patient admitted for surgery today. She had seen me because of the lesion on the left nare. Because of the size, and the fact this could not be closed by primary repair, I advised wide excision and skin graft. She was admitted this morning for the same. On admission we took her to the x-ray department. We are going to do the procedure under IV sedation with monitored anesthesia.

Procedure:

In surgery the patient was properly positioned. The left nare was cleaned with Hibiclens and draped. The donor site for the left neck was cleaned with Hibiclens and draped. The operation was started. First, the graft was harvested. An appropriate skin segment was harvested from the left neck. This was a full-thickness skin segment. Following this the donor site was repaired primarily with interrupted sutures of 3–0 nylon. Next, the tumor site was marked out with a marking pen and infiltrated with 2% Xylocaine as was the donor site, and then excised adequately with margins. It was then submitted for frozen section exam, which showed it was basal cell carcinoma but all margins were free. Then the full-thickness skin was prepared for split-thickness skin graft portion, then sutured in place and held in place with sutures. Operation was terminated and the patient was then taken from surgery to the recovery room in satisfactory conditon.

CPT-4	ICD-9-CM Diagnosis	ICD-9-CM Procedures
_____	_____	_____
_____	_____	_____
_____	_____	_____
_____	_____	_____
_____	_____	_____

Code Assignment: _____

Surgery Chart 3

Surgeon:
Assistant:
Anesthesia:

Current Procedural Terminology (CPT) © 2005 American Medical Association. All Rights Reserved.

Preoperative diagnosis: Deflated right reconstructive breast implant
Postoperative diagnosis: Deflated right reconstructive breast implant
Procedure: Replacement of implant

This 69-year-old female had undergone a right breast reconstruction postmastectomy using a tissue expander and implant technique. Shortly after tattooing her nipple areolar complex, she noted that her implant was increasingly soft and smaller. On examination, it was apparent that her implant was deflating.

Findings:

A pinpoint hole on the posterior aspect of the implant was found. The only explanation for this is that it seems reasonable the implant may have flipped over at the time of the tattooing when local anesthetic was infiltrated beneath the areola. The new implant set in the existing pocket nicely and no further modifications to the pocket were necessary.

Procedure:

The patient was brought to the operating room, where uncomplicated general anesthesia was induced. The surgical site was prepped and Duraprep and routine sterile drapes applied. The existing inframammary incision was reopened sharply and extended to the implant capsule and the implant extracted. The only defect in the implant appeared to be a pinpoint hole on the posterior aspect of the implant. The wound was irrigated with dilute Betadine solution and a new breast implant was selected. This was a McGhann Style 363LF, saline-filled, textured breast implant, Serial #5364xx, Lot #583740xx. The implant was inspected and prepared and inserted using a no-touch technique and inflated with normal saline to 450 cc. The implant sat nicely in the existing pocket and the size seemed to be appropriate. Accordingly, the wound was closed with running 3–0 Vicryl for the implant capsule and muscular fascia. Buried interrupted 4–9 Biosyn for the buried dermal closure and running 5–0 plain gut for the skin. Steri-strips were used to cover the wound, followed by sterile dressing. The patient was moved to the recovery room in excellent condition.

CPT-4   ICD-9-CM Diagnosis   ICD-9-CM Procedures

_____   _____   _____

_____   _____   _____

_____   _____   _____

_____   _____   _____

_____   _____   _____

Code Assignment: _____

Current Procedural Terminology (CPT) © 2005 American Medical Association. All Rights Reserved.

Notes

Surgery Chart 4

Operative Report

Surgeon:

Anesthetist:

Procedure:	Excision lesion right forehead
Preoperative diagnosis:	Lesion right forehead
Postoperative diagnosis:	Same

The patient was admitted for excision of this lesion, which appeared suddenly over the past 2–3 weeks. We had planned to do this last week but the patient developed a temperature, which was aborted until today. The procedure was to be done under general anesthesia because it was clear we could not do this with local as the patient was very excitable.

The patient was brought to surgery, general anesthesia was administered. The right temple lesion was clearly evident, measuring 1 × 1 cm, pigmented, mole-type lesion. The reason we are excising it was because of the sudden history and sudden appearance. The area was cleaned with saline, infiltrated with 2% Xylocaine, then excised completely and submitted for pathology. Hemostasis was achieved using handheld cautery device. Wound was closed with sutures of 5–9 Prolene. Antibiotic ointment was applied. Patient was discharged back to parents for follow-up.

CPT-4	ICD-9-CM Diagnosis	ICD-9-CM Procedures
_____	_____	_____
_____	_____	_____
_____	_____	_____
_____	_____	_____
_____	_____	_____

Code Assignment: _____

Surgery Chart 5

Surgeon:

Anesthesia:	General
Preoperative diagnosis:	Impingement, right shoulder, with adhesive capsulitis and rotator cuff pathology
Postoperative diagnosis:	Same

Current Procedural Terminology (CPT) © 2005 American Medical Association. All Rights Reserved.

Notes

The patient was placed supine on the operating room table on the beach-chair attachment and general anesthesia was given. The right shoulder was prepped in the usual sterile manner. Arthroscope cannula was then introduced into the glenohumeral joint via the standard posterior portal followed by the arthroscope. The biceps anchor to the superior glenoid was intact with no evidence of tearing. The biceps tendon itself appeared intact with no evidence of stretching or tearing of its fibers. The anterior and posterior labral tissues appear intact without evidence of tearing or displacement. The articular surface of the humeral head and glenoid were intact without evidence of wearing or breakdown as well. The anterior ligamentous structures appeared intact as well.

The rotator cuff was viewed and showed some fibrillation and wear on its deep surface, mainly in the watershed area, but no evidence of tear or detachment of the rotator cuff was noted. The arthroscope was withdrawn and repositioned into the subacromial space where the subacromial bursa was noted to be markedly thickened and scarred. A probe was introduced via the lateral port followed by a shaver with attached suction. The bursal tissue was resected back to expose the whole undersurface of the acromion. A large bur was then applied with attached suction and an anterior-inferior acromioplasty was performed. The coracoacromial ligament was resected at the acromial-clavicular joint. Debris produced was removed via suction. An epidural-type catheter was placed into the site and taped to the patient's skin was sterile tape.

The arthroscope was withdrawn and each portal was closed with a single simple suture of 3–0 Ethilon. Dry, sterile dressings were applied in the incisional sites. Dressings were taped into place and the patient was transported to the recovery room in stable condition.

CPT-4	ICD-9-CM Diagnosis	ICD-9-CM Procedures
_____	_____	_____
_____	_____	_____
_____	_____	_____
_____	_____	_____
_____	_____	_____

Code Assignment: _____

HCPCS CODES

The second level of HCPCS codes was developed to incorporate medical services and supplies not included in CPT-4. These codes are alphanumeric,

Current Procedural Terminology (CPT) © 2005 American Medical Association. All Rights Reserved.

Notes

five-digit, with the first digit always alphabetic, and indicating the chapter or section in which services can be located.

A0000–A0999	Ambulatory/Transportation Services
A4000–A8999	Medical/Surgical Supplies
A9000–A9999	Admin/Misc/Investigational Supplies
B4000–B9999	Enteral/Parenteral Therapy
D0000–D9999	Dental Procedures
E0100–E9999	Durable Medical Equipment
J0000–J8999	Drugs Other Than Oral
J9000–J9999	Chemotherapy Drugs
L0000–L4999	Orthotics
L5000–L9999	Prosthetics
M0000–M0302	Medical Services
P0000–P9999	Pathology Services
R0000–R5999	Radiology Services
V0000–V2999	Vision Services
V5000–V5999	Hearing Services

Guidelines indicate that HCPCS Level II codes should be utilized in lieu of CPT-4 codes whenever possible; however, carrier guidelines may supersede this guideline.

HCPCS Level III codes are also five-digit alphanumeric codes and represent locally assigned codes. These codes are in the process of being eliminated due to the standardization of codes (sets) as mandated by the Health Insurance Portability and Accountability Act (HIPAA).

Specific HCPCS Coding Guidelines

The following represent guidelines specific to the Level II HCPCS codes:

- Identify the chapter or section the service was provided in.
- Identify the specific supply or item provided.
- Determine whether multiple units of service may be appropriate. Note that the codes for drugs in HCPCS Level II state "up to." Therefore, when more than the stated number of increments is administered, the next unit of service would be applicable.

EXAMPLE

730 mg of ampicillin sodium is administered.
Code Assignment:
J0290 × 2 units

Current Procedural Terminology (CPT) © 2005 American Medical Association. All Rights Reserved.

PRACTICE EXERCISE 6–8

Assign HCPCS Level II codes to the following:

HCPCS Code(s)

1. Syringe with needle, sterile 2 cc   _____

2. Collagen-based wound dressing   _____

3. Bedpan, plastic   _____

4. Heat lamp   _____

5. IV pole   _____

6. Colorectal cancer screening, fecal-occult blood test   _____

7. Injection ampicillin sodium, 450 mg   _____

8. Injection lidocaine HCl, 140 mg   _____

9. Leukocyte-poor blood, 3 units   _____

10. Screening Pap smear   _____

CONCLUSION

Outpatient facility coding encompasses a myriad of coding methods as well as a number of coding guidelines, all of which must be applied appropriately in order to ensure correct reimbursement. As with inpatient services, however, coding is only a part of the reimbursement process, as the appropriate codes and other information essential to reimbursement must be correctly placed on the UB-92/CMS 1450 in order for correct payment to occur.

Upon completing Chapter 6 and the accompanying practice exercises, the student should be able to differentiate between the guidelines for outpatient versus inpatient facility coding. In addition, the student should be able to apply these concepts by assigning appropriate HCPCS, CPT-4 and ICD-9-CM codes to outpatient facility services.

Chapter 7
Outpatient Billing

KEY TERMS

New Technology Services
Outpatient Code Editor (OCE)
Payment Status Indicators

Significant Procedures
Transitional Pass-through
   Allowances

LEARNING OBJECTIVES

- Discuss the basic concepts of the Outpatient Prospective System
- Describe the methodology of Ambulatory Payment Classifications
- Describe the various payment status indicators and their meanings
- Describe the revenue codes assigned for outpatient coding
- Discuss the purpose of the Outpatient Coding Editor
- Describe the proper completion of the CMS 1450/UB-92 as it relates to outpatient facility coding

GENERAL CONCEPTS OF OUTPATIENT PAYMENT PERSPECTIVE SYSTEM (OPPS)

Inpatient hospital reimbursement changed significantly under the Omnibus Budget Reconciliation Act of 1986. Services were no longer reimbursed individually, but as part of a "package" price. For instance: When patients were admitted for a specific diagnosis, or diagnostic testing for a specific diagnosis, an allowance was made for that admission. All resources the facility furnished in conjunction with that admission were reimbursed under that one allowance, known as a DRG or Diagnosis-Related Group. With the implementation of the Prospective Payment System (PPS) on the inpatient side of hospital reimbursement, hospitals were able to anticipate their reimbursement and control costs. This same legislation called for the

Notes

development of an outpatient prospective payment system (OPPS); however, that development and implementation did not occur until August, 2000.

The government aimed to accomplish the following under the OPPS system:

- Simplify the outpatient hospital payment system
- Ensure payments adequately compensate the facility for expenses incurred
- Implement the HCFA/CMS deficit reduction program for outpatient hospitals
- Reduce the beneficiary's share of payment by freezing coinsurance amounts until they are equal to 20 percent of total payment amounts

AMBULATORY PAYMENT CLASSIFICATIONS (APCs)

Following the original proposal by 3M Health Information Systems for an outpatient prospective payment system known as Ambulatory Payment Groups or APGs, HCFA/CMS proposed a modification of the plan, to be known as Ambulatory Payment Classifications or APCs. Under the Balanced Budget Act of 1997, the government proposed an OPPS implementation date of January 1999. This was delayed due to concerns regarding Y2K issues, and as a result, actual implementation did not take place until August 2000.

Guidelines for Assigning APCs

Unlike the prospective payment reimbursement system implemented for inpatient hospital services, a number of additional issues needed to be addressed under the outpatient prospective payment system. While the PPS/DRG system allows for reimbursement under one DRG only, it soon became evident that a similar methodology would not be possible on the outpatient facility side. As a result, the outpatient hospital facility encounter may consist of a number of CPT-4/HCPCS codes bundled into multiple APCs assignments. While some services or facility resources would be included in a packaged APC service, others would not be packaged, as the result of the varying services performed in the outpatient setting.

These issues are important to the outpatient facility because more than 25 percent of hospital revenue is generated from the outpatient perspective, while another 50 percent of that revenue is generated from outpatient surgery, emergency room and diagnostic services.

! **ALERT:** For more information regarding the Outpatient Prospective Payment System, and to learn the latest updates from Medicare about this reimbursement process, visit www.cms.hhs.gov or the Medlearn website (which is also maintained by the Center for Medicare Services) at www.cms.hhs.gov/medlearn.

Notes

Table 7–1 shows the services included and excluded under the OPPS/APC payment methodology.

TABLE 7–1   Services Included/Excluded Under OPPS/APC Methodology.

Included Services

Surgical Procedures

Radiology/Radiation Therapy

Clinic/Emergency Visits

Diagnostic Services/Tests

Partial Hospital/Mentally Ill

Psychiatric Services

Surgical Pathology

Chemotherapy Administration and Drugs

Areas of Hospital Excluded Under DRGs

Specified Inpatient Services Patients Exhausting Part A Benefits

Partial Hospitalization Community Mental Health Facilities

Skilled Nursing Facility (SNF) Services Provided to Inpatients

Certain Preventive Services

Antigens, Splints/Casts and Vaccines

Excluded Services

Outpatient Services in Critical Access Hospitals

Clinical Lab Services Paid Under Regular Fee Schedule

DME, Orthotics, Prosthetics, Other Devices Paid Under DME (Durable Medical Equipment) Fee Schedule

End Stage Renal Disease Services (Paid Under ESRD Fee Rate)

Hospital Outpatient Services Furnished to Inpatient Skilled Nursing Facility Patients When Covered Under SNF Payment System

Inpatient Services Payable Under Inpatient Prospective Payment System

Professional Services of Physicians/Nonphysicians Paid Under Medicare Physician

Physical, Occupational and Speech-Language Therapy (Paid Under Separate Fee Schedule)

Notes

Keep in mind that, as with DRGs, APCs are not assigned at the facility. They are utilized only for determining appropriate reimbursement and are assessed at the time the UB-92 claim is processed by the carrier. However, it is important to understand the reimbursement methodology so that the facility can determine their reimbursement prospectively, as the OPPS system was designed.

The following outpatient encounter illustrates the impact APC reimbursement methodology has on outpatient hospital services.

EXAMPLE

The following services were provided by the outpatient hospital facility:

Service	CPT Code	Actual Charge	APC	Estimated Allowance
Visit	99282-25	$125	610	Payment via APC
Supplies	—	$500	none	included in APC allowance
Pharmaceuticals	—	$800	none	included in APC allowance
Laceration Repair	12002	$400	0024	Payment via APC
X-Ray, Radius	73100	$250	0260	Payment via APC
X-Ray, Finger	73140	$200	0260	Payment via APC
Clinical Lab	various	$500	none	CPT-4 code assignment

! ALERT: While the methodology of OPPS and Ambulatory Payment Classifications remains relatively the same, code assignments, APC categories and reimbursements change on at least an annual basis. Updates to this information may be obtained by visiting the CMS website, www.cms.hhs.gov.

The following demonstrates one example of an APC and the CPT/HCPCS codes that are included in this APC grouping:

EXAMPLE

APC 0600—Low-Level Clinic Visits

99201	Office/Outpatient Visit, New, Level 1
99202	Office/Outpatient Visit, New, Level 2
99211	Office/Outpatient Visit, Established, Level 1
99212	Office/Outpatient Visit, Established, Level 2
99241	Office Consultation, Level 1
99242	Office Consultation, Level 2
99272	Confirmatory Consultation, Level 2
92012	Ophthalmological Exam, Established Patient, XXX Level

APCs are reimbursed on a predetermined, price-fixed payment based on services and the facility resources necessary to provide those services.

Notes _____

_____

_____

_____

_____

_____

All ambulatory patient types are included in reimbursements such as visits, outpatient surgeries, ancillary visits and any combinations of these services within the APC window of one day. The package basically includes anesthesia; recovery and/or treatment room charges; incidental services and/or procedures; specimen collection such as venipuncture, blood and blood products; drugs (except chemotherapy drugs); supplies and observation (except in a limited number of instances).

Specifically, medical visit codes will include supplies, drugs and incidental procedures, while surgical codes will include operating room, supplies, drugs, dressings, recovery room and other preoperative and postoperative charges.

APCs are assigned in the areas outlined in Table 7–2.

TABLE 7–2   APC Groupings Reimbursable Under APCs.

APC Grouping	*Included*	*Additional Payment*
Medical Visits	Packaged revenue center Incidental services Drugs, except chemo drugs Observation care (see exceptions)	Ancillary services

Diagnostic
  Ancillaries
	Packaged revenue center
	Incidental services
	Drugs, except chemo drugs
	Observation care (see
	  exceptions)
		Chemotherapy drugs
		Additional ancillaries
		Primary surgical services
		Secondary surgical services

Significant
  Procedures
	Packaged revenue center
	Drugs, except chemo drugs
	Anesthesia
	Observation care (see
	  exceptions)
		Additional significant procedures
		Additional surgical services
		Ancillary services
		Chemotherapy drugs

Surgical Services	Packaged revenue center Incidental services Drugs, except chemo drugs Observation care (see exceptions)	Accompanying significant procedures Additional surgical services Ancillary services Chemotherapy drugs

Partial
  Hospitalization
	Services performed at
	  Community Mental
	  Health Center	

(continued)

TABLE 7–2   *continued*

APC Grouping	Included	Additional Payment
Transitional Pass-through	Drugs/biologicals reimbursable before APCs Over and above usual services, costs exceed normal pricing	
New Technologies	New drugs, biologicals, supplies Not previously introduced Prior to APCs	

Notes

The number of APC groupings has grown to well over 1,120 APC categories. Every CPT-4/HCPCS procedure code is assigned an APC category, if appropriate. APC numbers are assigned for services that are similar in clinical services and resource costs.

Table 7–3 illustrates some of the most common outpatient hospital services and the assigned APC grouping for each code.

TABLE 7–3   Status Indicators for Ambulatory Payment Classifications.

Status Indicator	Services	Payment Methodology
A	Services Not Reimbursable Under OPPS:	
	Pulmonary Rehabilitation	Not Paid
	Durable Medical Equipment, Prosthetics/Orthotics	DME Fee Schedule
	Physical, Occupational, Speech Therapy	Rehab Fee Schedule
	Ambulance	Ambulance Fee Schedule
	Erythropoietin for End Stage Renal Disease	National Rate
	Diagnostic Laboratory Services	Lab Fee Schedule
	Screening Mammography	Lower of: Charge/National Rate

Notes

Status Indicator	Services	Payment Methodology
C	Inpatient Services	Bill under Inpatient PPS
E	Noncovered Services	Not Paid
F	Acquisition of Corneal Tissue	Reasonable Cost
G	Current Drug/Biological Pass Through	Additional Payment Consideration
H	Device Pass Through	Additional Payment Consideration
J	New Drug/Biological Pass-through	Additional Payment Consideration
K	Drug/Biological/Radiopharmaceutical Agents	Not Paid as Transitional Pass-through
L	Influenza/Pneumococcal Vaccines	Reasonable Cost
N	Incidental Services	Packaged In APC Rate
P	Partial Hospitalization Services	Paid Per Diem
S	Significant Procedures	Paid Under APC
T	Surgical Services	Paid Under APC Multiple Procedure Reduction Applies
V	Medical Visit	Paid Under APC
X	Ancillary Services	Paid Under APC

PRACTICE EXERCISE 7–1

Identify which services would be reimbursable under the outpatient OPPS/APC reimbursement methodology below:

	Yes	No
1. Chest X-Ray		
2. Urinalysis		
3. ER Visit Level 3		
4. Methotrexate 50 mg IV		
5. Inpatient Admission		
6. Outpatient Colonoscopy		
7. Inpatient Appendectomy		
8. Laceration Repair		
9. Electrocardiogram		
10. Screening Mammogram		

Payment Status Indicators Paid Under APC Reimbursement Methodology

With the implementation of APC reimbursement methodology, all APC categories have been assigned **payment status indicators.** These indicators identify how Medicare pays for various services that have been billed.

As illustrated in Table 7–3, there are only four categories that are reimbursable under the APC methodology. Note, however, that additional categories are reimbursable as well, not just the OPPS payment methods.

Payment Status Indicator S— Significant Procedures

Procedures for which the multiple-procedure reduction does not apply. (However, a 50% reduction does apply with the designation of modifier 73/52.)
Examples of services:

- Psychotherapy
- Dialysis
- Chemotherapy
- Pulmonary tests

Notes

Payment Status Indicator T—Surgical Services

Procedures performed in the surgical setting (where the multiple-procedure reduction DOES apply), such as:

- Incision/drainage
- Excision/biopsy
- Arthroplasty
- Arthroscopy
- Fracture repairs
- Endoscopy
- Procedures in the "Surgery" section of CPT-4

NOTE: Modifier 51 is not valid for outpatient hospital coding. In these cases, the payment status of the HCPCS code drives the reduction of multiple procedures.

Payment Status Indicator V—Medical Visits

Visits in the ambulatory, outpatient and/or emergency room setting.

Outpatient visit new visits	99201-99205	APCs 0600-0602
Outpatient visit established visits	99211-99215	APCs 0600-0602
Outpatient consultations	99241-99245	APCs 0600-0602
Emergency room visits	99281-99285	APCs 0610-0612
Critical care encounters	99291 only	APC 0620

Assignment of Evaluation and Management (E & M) codes is NOT based on the same criteria as physician assignment for these services. (This was discussed in Chapter 6, "Hospital Outpatient Coding.")

Multiple E & Ms are billable per day with the addition of applicable modifiers.

Observation Care is reimbursable only under specific circumstances and documentation for the following conditions:

- Chest pain
- Asthma
- Congestive heart failure

Again, the specific coding guidelines for observation care are covered in "Hospital Outpatient Coding," Chapter 6.

Notes

Payment Status Indicator X—Ancillary Services

Additional diagnostic testing services provided in the outpatient/ambulatory care setting such as:

- Radiology
- Electrocardiography (EKG)
- Immunizations
- Infusion therapy

NOTE: IV infusion therapy is reimbursable only when the infusion therapy is for diagnostic and/or therapeutic purposes. When it is for preventive or prophylactic therapy, it is not reimbursable under outpatient coding guidelines.

Reimbursable Payment Status Indicators Not Payable Under APC Methodology

Additional payments may be made for certain drugs and medical devices under the **transitional pass-through allowances** (Payment Status Indicators G, H and J). This allowance is allowed under two circumstances: Existing Drugs and Medical Devices, and New Drugs and Medical Devices.

Existing Drugs and Medical Devices

In order to qualify for reimbursement, these items must have been reimbursable under outpatient services at the time OPPS was implemented. They include such items as:

- Orphan drugs
- Cancer therapy drugs and biologicals
- Brachytherapy drug/seeds
- Radiopharmaceutical drugs

New Drugs and Medical Devices

In order to qualify as new drugs or medical devices, these items must not have been reimbursed prior to December 31, 1996, and the cost of the item must be significant in relationship to the procedure or service involved.

Payment for new drugs is calculated to be equal to 95 percent of the average wholesale price (AWP). Device payments are calculated by taking the hospital charges for each item, reducing to the cost by use of the hospitals' cost-to-charge ratio and subtracting the device cost.

Notes

In order to qualify as transitional pass-through services, the drugs or devices involved must meet specific requirements such as:

- Devices must be approved by the Food and Drug Administration
- Devices must be considered medically necessary for the condition for which they are being prescribed
- The device prescribed is integral to any procedure(s) performed
- They may not be materials utilized to replace human skin

Partial Hospitalization

Partial Hospitalization (Payment Status Indicator P) services are also reimbursable under the Outpatient Prospective Payment System. Since the unit of service for these services is one day, a per diem payment is the method for reimbursement under the partial hospitalization APCs.

Under OPPS, consideration was given for services that fall outside the norm. The Balanced Budget Act of 1999 defined outliers as those services where the calculated bill fell outside the APC payment by more than 2.5 times. In order to determine whether this threshold is met, all services for a specific outpatient encounter would need to be billed and/or accumulated.

In addition, OPPS also allows for a methodology for **new technology service** reimbursement as well. Unlike the other APC groups, these new technology services do not take into consideration the clinical aspect of the services they represent, only the cost of the items themselves.

Although OPPS introduced the concept of APCs, these categories only determine the reimbursement category of services provided in the outpatient setting. The completion of the UB-92 for outpatient hospital services still requires the assignment of revenue codes, ICD-9-CM codes and HCPCS codes as appropriate. With the implementation of OPPS in August 2000 came additional billing considerations for the outpatient hospital facility, including:

- Assignment of HCPCS/CPT codes (already discussed)
- Introduction of modifier code usage in the outpatient setting
- Implementation of CCI (Correct Coding Initiatives) in the outpatient hospital setting
- Additional coding edits for outpatient UB-92

A number of these new considerations relate directly to coding changes or additions, and have already been discussed in the previous sections devoted to outpatient coding concepts.

However, with the implementation of additional coding and code-edit restrictions on outpatient hospital services came the necessity of chargemaster review in the outpatient hospital setting as well.

PRACTICE EXERCISE 7–2

Take those services identified in Practice Exercise 7–1 as reimbursement under OPPS/APC reimbursement methodology and determine the appropriate Payment Status Indicator.

Payment Status Indicator

1. Chest X-Ray   _____

2. Urinalysis   _____

3. ER Visit Level 3   _____

4. Methotrexate 50 mg IV   _____

5. Inpatient Admission   _____

6. Outpatient Colonoscopy   _____

7. Inpatient Appendectomy   _____

8. Laceration Repair   _____

9. Electrocardiogram   _____

10. Screening Mammogram   _____

Outpatient Revenue Codes

Table 7–4 represents outpatient revenue codes represented on the chargemaster that will require CPT/HCPCS codes on the UB-92 billing form.

TABLE 7–4   **Outpatient Revenue Codes Requiring HCPCS/CPT Codes.**

Revenue Code	Service/Description
260	IV Therapy
261	Infusion Pump
274	Prosthetics and Orthotics
31x	Laboratory (Pathology)

Revenue Code	Service/Description
32x	Diagnostic Radiology
33x	Therapeutic Radiology
333	Radiation Therapy
34x	Nuclear Medicine
35x	CT Scan
36x	OR (Operating Room)
38x	Blood
40x	Other Not Specified Imaging Services
401	Diagnostic Mammograms
402	Screening Mammograms
41x	Respiratory Services
513	Hyperbaric Therapy
42x	Physical Therapy
43x	Occupational Therapy
44x	Speech/Language Therapy
45x	Emergency Room
46x	Pulmonary Function
47x	Audiology
471	Diagnostic Audiology

(continued)

Notes

TABLE 7–4 *continued*

Revenue Code	Service/Description
48x	Cardiovascular Therapeutic
480	Cardiology
481	Cardiac Catheterization
482	Stress Test
483	Echocardiography
49x	Ambulatory Surgery Center
51x	Clinic
61x	Magnetic Resonance Technology
623	Surgical Dressings
636	Drugs Requiring Additional Coding
70x	Cast Room
71x	Recovery Room
73x	EKG/ECG
731	Holter Monitor
732	Telemetry
74x	EKG/ECG
75x	Gastroenterology Service
76x	Treatment/Observation Room
77x	Preventive Care Services

Revenue Code	Service/Description
79x	Lithotripsy
900	Psychiatric/Psychological Treatment
901	Electroshock
904	Activity Therapy
91x	Psychiatric/Psychological Services
92x	Other Diagnostic Services
921	Peripheral Vascular Lab
922	Electromyography (EMG)
923	Allergy Testing
94x	Other Therapeutic Services
940	Therapeutic Phlebotomy
943	Cardiac Rehabilitation
949	Allergy Therapy

PRACTICE EXERCISE 7–3

Determine the appropriate revenue code range for each of the following services, and assign CPT/HCPCS codes where appropriate.

	CPT/HCPCS Code(s)	Revenue Code Range
1. Kenalog, 50 mg, IV	_____	_____
2. MRI, Brain, w/contrast	_____	_____
3. Electrocardiogram	_____	_____
4. Cardiac Catheterization	_____	_____
5. Blood Transfusion	_____	_____
6. Packed Red Cells	_____	_____

Notes		CPT/HCPCS Code(s)	Revenue Code Range
_____	**7.** ER Visit, Level II	_____	_____
_____	**8.** Spirometry	_____	_____
_____	**9.** CT Scan Head, with and without contrast	_____	_____
_____	**10.** X-Ray, Knee, 2 Views, RT	_____	_____
_____	**11.** EGD, w/polypectomy	_____	_____
_____	**12.** Cardiac Stress Test	_____	_____
_____	**13.** Allergy Testing, Scratch	_____	_____
_____	**14.** IV Infusion, Prophylactic	_____	_____
_____	**15.** Chemotherapy Infusion, 1 hr	_____	_____
_____	**16.** Outpatient Visit, New Pt Level III	_____	_____
_____	**17.** Complete Blood Count	_____	_____
_____	**18.** CABG, Venous Grafting 3 Vessels	_____	_____
_____	**19.** Temporary transcutaneous Pacing	_____	_____
_____	**20.** Excision 2.0-cm benign Lesion, Arm	_____	_____

In addition, certain services assigned to specific revenue codes will be considered included in the APC reimbursement for services. Table 7–5 outlines services bundled into APC reimbursement:

TABLE 7–5   Services Bundled in APC Assignments.

Revenue Code	Description	Surgery	Radiology	Diagnostic	Medical Visit	All Other
250	Pharmacy-General	I			I	I
251	Pharmacy-Generic	I			I	I
252	Pharmacy-Nongeneric	I			I	I
254	Incident to Other Diagnostic			I		
255	Incident to Radiology		I			

Revenue Code	Description	Surgery	Radiology	Diagnostic	Medical Visit	All Other
257	Nonprescription Drugs	I			I	I
258	IV Solutions	I			I	I
259	Other	I			I	I
260	IV Infusion Therapy, General	I				I
262	IV Therapy, Pharmacy Service	I				I
263	IV Drugs/Supplies	I				I
264	IV Therapy/Supplies	I				I
269	Other IV Therapy	I				I
270	Medical/Surgical General	I			I	I
271	Nonsterile Supplies	I			I	I
272	Sterile Supplies	I			I	I
276	Intraocular Lenses	I				
279	Other Medical/Surgical Supplies	I			I	I
370	Anesthesia					
371	Anesthesia Related to Radiology		I			
372	Incident to Diagnostics			I		
379	Other Anesthesia	I				
390	Blood Storage/Processing	I				
399	Other Blood Storage/Processing	I				
621	Supplies/Incident to Radiology		I			
622	Supplies/Incident to Other Diagnostics				I	
630	Pharmacy/Reserved	I			I	I
631	Single Source Drug	I			I	I
632	Multiple Source Drug	I			I	I
633	Restrictive Prescriptions	I			I	I
700	Cast Room/General	I			I	
709	Other Cast Room	I			I	
710	Recovery Room, General	I	I	I		
719	Recovery Room, Other	I	I	I		
720	Labor Room, General	I				

I–Included

(continued)

TABLE 7–5   *continued*

Revenue Code	Description	Surgery	Radiology	Diagnostic	Medical Visit	All Other
721	Labor	I				
722	Delivery	I				
723	Circumcision	I				
762	Observation Room	I	I	I	I	I
810	Organ Acquisition/General	I				
819	Organ Acquisition/Other	I				
890	Other Donor Bank	I				
891	Bone	I				
892	Organ	I				
893	Skin	I				
899	Other	I				

I–Included

Outpatient Code Editor

The **Outpatient Code Editor (OCE)** is a reimbursement tool developed by CMS and used by fiscal intermediaries (FI)—third-party entities employed to administer the CMS Medicare program—for editing claims data to identify errors and return edit flags related to diagnoses, procedure, demographic and other errors that result in nonpayment.

There are six general categories of claims edit through the OCE methodology:

1. Claim Rejection

These edits cause the claim to be rejected. The provider can correct and resubmit the claim; however, they cannot appeal the rejection.

2. Claim Denial

This type of edit also results in the claim being denied. The provider cannot resubmit the claim, but they can appeal the decision.

3. Claim Return to Provider (RTP)

This edit involves the claim simply being returned to the provider for necessary corrections. The provider may resubmit it once the corrections are made.

4. Claim Suspension

When errors result in the claim not being processed, the claim will be suspended. The claim cannot be processed until further information is obtained or a decision is made through review by the FI.

Notes

5. Line Item Rejection

When an individual line item is rejected, the provider can correct and resubmit the line item; however, they cannot appeal the rejection.

6. Line Item Denials

When edits cause individual line items to be denied, the provider cannot resubmit the claim, but they can appeal the decision.

Table 7–6 illustrates the most common OCE edits, how they will be processed and a suggested corrective action.

TABLE 7–6   Outpatient Coding Editor Edits.

OCE Edits	Disposition	Provider Action
Invalid Diagnosis	Return to Provider (RTP)	Review diagnosis for errors Review ICD-9-CM for assignment errors Correct and resubmit
Diagnosis and Age Conflict	RTP	Review diagnosis codes/age for errors Verify data billed against patient record Correct and resubmit
Diagnosis and Sex Conflict	RTP	Review diagnosis codes/sex for errors Verify data billed against patient record Correct and resubmit
Medicare Secondary Payer Alert	Suspend	If claim is RTP, review claim for correct coding of claim If liability, claim should be MSP claim with occurrence codes 01-04 or 06 If no liability, occurrence code 05
E Code as Primary Diagnosis	RTP	E code never primary diagnosis Review patient information for appropriate diagnosis Correct and resubmit
Invalid Procedure Code	RTP	Review codes for errors Refer to current CPT/HCPCS for possible coding assignment errors Correct and resubmit
Procedure and Age Conflict	RTP	Review procedure codes/age for errors Verify codes/age with patient record Correct and resubmit
Procedure and Sex Conflict	RTP	Review procedure codes/sex for errors Verify codes/sex with patient record Correct and resubmit

(continued)

TABLE 7–6   *continued*

OCE Edits	Disposition	Provider Action
Noncovered Service	Line Item Denial	Review claim for errors Resubmit claim with correct data
Noncovered Service Submitted for Verification of Denial	Claim Denial	No action indicated Condition Code 21

THE OUTPATIENT BILLING PROCESS

While the billing process typically occurs in the Business Office of the hospital facility, ICD-9-CM diagnostic codes and/or HCPCS codes are usually assigned in the Health Information or Coding Department. Responsibility for claims generation and processing, processing of remittance information, payment posting, appeals and other related reimbursement issues are usually Business Office functions. While facilities differ on work flow and the assignment of codes for services, Table 7–7 is representative of the typical outpatient facility:

TABLE 7–7   **Flow of Outpatient Billing in the Facility.**

Patient Arrives for Services
Medical Record Generated
Patient Information Obtained
Service Rendered
Physician Completes Appropriate Documentation
Non-HIM Staff Selects Codes for Services Rendered (Chargemaster/Encounter Form Services)
Charge Documents Forwarded to Health Information for Review, Additional Code Assignments
Data Entry Information Captured by Business Office for Submission to Carrier
Claims Submission
Adjudication of Claims Appeals, Reviews as Necessary

Payment for services under the APC grouping system would be based on a combination of APC groupings and services provided that are not traditionally grouped under the APC reimbursement methodology.

Notes

In order to properly understand the full methodology for reimbursement for hospital outpatient services, take a look at the following example:

EXAMPLE

EMERGENCY DEPARTMENT CHART

Seventy-seven-year-old male on antihypertensive medications. Patient took medications at approximately 8 AM. At approximately 9:45 AM patient began experiencing abdominal cramping and pain. Patient went to rest room and began diaphoretic, felt weak and experienced syncope. The patient struck his head and arm, resulting in a laceration to the wrist approximately 2 cm in length. At this time, the patient's wife called EMS.

Upon arrival, EMS took the patient's vitals, which were BP 70/40, Heart rate 55, Respiration 18.

Upon arrival at the emergency room, a comprehensive history and comprehensive exam are performed. CBC, C-Spine and EKG are performed, which are unremarkable. Laceration repair performed.

ASSESSMENT: Syncope
              Closed head injury with LOC
              Laceration, wrist
              Abdominal pain
              Hypertension
              Rheumatoid arthritis

ASSIGNMENT OF CODE would be as follows:

99285-25	Emergency Department, Level V	APC 0612
1313212001	Laceration Repair, 2 cm, Simple, Wrist	APC 0024
93005	EKG, Technical	APC 0366
CBC	CBC	Non-APC

Reimbursement for these services would be made as follows:
APC-assigned codes would be paid based upon the current APC rate, which is established by the facility and geographic location.

Non-APC assignments are paid under the fee schedule for the carrier during the current period.

Miscellaneous supplies and pharmaceuticals integral to performing the services during the encounter are not payable in addition to the actual services provided.

Table 7–8 represents the most common APC assignments we will be utilizing for our exercises. A complete listing is available from the Medicare/OPPS website.

TABLE 7–8   Common APC Code Assignments.

Description/Service Encounters	HCPCS/CPT	ICD-9-CM Procedure	APC	Comments
ER Level 1 Visit	99281	89.01	0610	Use of Modifier 25 When
ER Level 2 Visit	99282	89.01	0610	Status S/T Procedures
ER Level 3 Visit	99283	89.02	0611	Performed in Conjunction
ER Level 4 Visit	99284	89.03	0612	with ER Visit
ER Level 5 Visit	99285	89.03	0612	
Observation/Direct Admits	99281	89.01	0610	
Postoperative Checks	99281	89.01	0610	
Outpatient Level 1 Visit New	99201	89.01	0600	
Outpatient Level 1 Visit Established	99211	89.01	0600	
Outpatient Level 2 Visit New	99202	89.01	0600	
Outpatient Level 2 Visit Established	99212	89.01	0600	
Outpatient Level 3 Visit New	99203	89.01	0601	
Outpatient Level 3 Visit Established	99213	89.01	0601	
Outpatient Level 4 Visit New	99204	89.01	0602	
Outpatient Level 4 Visit Established	99214	89.01	0602	
Outpatient Level 5 Visit New	99205	89.01	0602	
Outpatient Level 5 Visit Established	99215	89.01	0602	
Diagnostic Radiology				
Abdomen (KUB), Single AP	74000	88.19	0260	
Abdomen (KUB), AP/Additional Oblique/Cone	74010	88.19	0260	
Ankle, AP and Lateral (2V)	73600	88.28	0260	Need RT/LT/50 Modifier
Ankle, 3 Views or More	73610	88.28	0260	Need RT/LT/50 Modifier
Chest, PA or AP View	71010	87.49	0260	
Chest, PA and Lateral	71020	87.49	0260	
Finger, 2 Views	73140	88.23	0260	Need HCPCS Finger Modifier
Foot, AP and Lateral	73620	88.28	0260	Need RT/LT/50 Modifier
Hand, 2 Views	73120	88.23	0260	Need RT/LT/50 Modifier
Mammogram, Screening	76092	87.37	None	Not Reimbursable Under APC
Mammogram, Unilateral	76090	87.37	0271	
Mammogram, Bilateral	76091	87.37	0271	

Description/Service Encounters	HCPCS/CPT	ICD-9-CM Procedure	APC	Comments
Ribs, Unilateral, 2 Views	71100	87.43	0260	
Spine, Cervical, 3 Views	72040	87.22	0260	
Upper GI	74240	87.62	0260	
Wrist, AP and Lateral	73100	88.23	0260	Need RT/LT/50 Modifier
Ultrasound				
Abdomen, Complete	76700	See Note	0266	ICD-9-CM Procedure Code:
Abdomen, Limited	76705	See Note	0266	88.75 Urinary
Retroperitoneal, Complete	76770	See Note	0266	88.76 Abdomen/
Retroperitoneal, Limited	76775	See Note	0266	Retroperitoneum
Transvaginal	76830	88.79	0266	
CT Scans				
Abdomen without contrast	74150	88.01	0283	
Abdomen with contrast	74160	88.01	0283	
Head/Brain without contrast	70450	87.03	0283	
Head/Brain with contrast	70460	87.03	0283	
Pelvis without contrast	72192	88.38	0283	
Pelvis with contrast	72193	88.38	0283	
MRI				
Brain without contrast	70551	88.91	0284	
Brain with contrast	70552	88.91	0284	
Extremity, Lower Joint	73721	88.94	0284	
Spine, Cervical, without contrast	72141	88.93	0284	
Spine, Cervical, with contrast	72142	88.93	0284	
Spine, Lumbar, without contrast	72148	88.93	0284	
Spine, Lumbar, with contrast	72149	88.93	0284	
Spine, Thoracic, without contrast	72146	88.93	0284	
Spine, Thoracic, with contrast	72147	88.93	0284	
Other				
Electrocardiogram	93005	89.52	0366	
Infusion Therapy	90780	99.29	0120	
Laceration Repair, Simple, Other Than Facial, <2.5 cm	12001	See Note	0024	ICD-9-CM Procedure Code: 08.81 Eyelid

(continued)

TABLE 7–8 *continued*

Description/Service Encounters	HCPCS/CPT	ICD-9-CM Procedure	APC	Comments
Laceration Repair, Simple, Facial <2.5 cm	12011	See Note	0024	27.51 Lip 27.52 Other Mouth 86.59 Other Skin
Pulmonary Function Spirometry	94010	89.37	0367	

Notes

OTHER OUTPATIENT BILLING CONSIDERATIONS

In addition to the introduction of OPPS, payment status indicators, outpatient coding editor and revenue code usage in the outpatient hospital, other billing procedures changed or were introduced to the outpatient hospital world as well.

Advance Beneficiary Notice

As with physician coding and billing, the outpatient facility must also conform to federal guidelines regarding patient notification of services. Under Medicare guidelines, any patient receiving services that the facility believes may not be covered under Medicare must be advised, in advance of such services, why they may not be considered for payment and their costs. The patient must sign a form called an Advance Beneficiary Notice (ABN) that describes those services, and acknowledge that, in the event Medicare does not pay for them, the patient will be fully responsible for payment. The ABN must be specific to services, not general; must be for a specific date, and should never be utilized for all services, or all services on a specific date.

An example of an Advance Beneficiary Notice was included in the Process Overview in Section I.

UB-92 Completion Guidelines

The completion of the UB-92 was changed significantly with the introduction of the OPPS/APC methodology. Table 7–9 (located at the end of this chapter) represents the fields on the UB-92/CMS 1450 necessary for the proper completion of claims for outpatient services.

Let's combine the knowledge from Chapter 6 on "Outpatient Coding" with the information we have learned about APC assignments. Take the same charts you assigned codes to in Chapter 6 and designate the proper APC for each chart. If you have already coded these charts, simply bring your diagnostic and procedures codes forward for this exercise, or utilize the charts in this chapter to code and assign APCs to practice the entire process.

Notes

PRACTICE EXERCISE 7–4

ER Case 1

Patient was eating hot dogs tonight and accidentally choked. He was administered the Heimlich maneuver and he then vomited up a lot of clear phlegm. He has no complaints now and denies any pain. He was given a drink of water and was able to drink without any difficulty.

Temperature 96, pulse 70, BP 146/86, O2 sats 99%. General: Alert, responsive, pleasant, cooperative, talkative, in no acute distress. Chest: lungs clear without any rales, rhonchi, wheezes. Breathing easy without retractions or use of other accessory muscles or respiration.

LAB: Chest x-ray is normal.

Dysphagia with esophageal obstruction.

CPT-4	ICD-9-CM Dx	ICD-9-CM Procedures	APC
_____	_____	_____	_____
_____	_____	_____	_____
_____	_____	_____	_____
_____	_____	_____	_____
_____	_____	_____	_____

Code Assignment(s): _____

ER Case 2

Chief complaint: Possible hypoglycemic episode, severe hypertension

Patient with IDDM presented having gotten extremely woozy, weak and sweaty. No chest discomfort or shortness of breath. Felt she might be having a little low blood sugar reaction. She also has a history of hypertension and has had previous strokes. No visual symptoms. Review of systems: No cardiac symptoms, breathing better. Family history noncontributory. Medications are Hyzaar, Humalog, Prozasin, Sular and Zoloft.

On exam her BP is initially high. That was monitored and it came down fine. She felt fine and felt ready to go after being watched in the ER for a half hour. She had no facial asymmetry. She had no palpable edema. She had a little bit of soreness of the left posterior neck muscle. I did not hear any carotid bruits. Lungs clear.

Probably hypoglycemia attached with reactive hypertensive episode, which is resolving.

Notes	CPT-4	ICD-9-CM Dx	ICD-9-CM Procedures	APC
_____	_____	_____	_____	_____
_____	_____	_____	_____	_____
_____	_____	_____	_____	_____
_____	_____	_____	_____	_____
_____	_____	_____	_____	_____

Code Assignment(s): _____

ER Case 3

_____

Patient presents with complaints of chest pain. He states he had a single-vessel bypass done approximately 5 years ago. He has been doing fairly well on his medical regimen until about 2 months ago, when he started having some twinges of chest pain with exertion. This has been gradually worsening over the last 2 months and now he gets chest pain when he is doing activities such as vacuuming. As soon as he rests, the pain goes away.

Chest clear, heart regular rate and rhythm without murmurs. EKG showed only some nonspecific STT wave changes, no evidence of acute MI. We did troponin and PT; all within normal limits. Chest x-ray also appeared clean.

Chest pain, appears to be stable, worsening angina.

We will stop his Norvasc, start on Metoprolol 250 mg bid for now.

	CPT-4	ICD-9-CM Dx	ICD-9-CM Procedures	APC
_____	_____	_____	_____	_____
_____	_____	_____	_____	_____
_____	_____	_____	_____	_____
_____	_____	_____	_____	_____
_____	_____	_____	_____	_____

Code Assignment(s): _____

ER Case 4

This 65-year-old male noted onset of left lower quadrant pain yesterday. No nausea or vomiting. No past history of similar abdominal pain or GI problems. Two months ago he had a complete workup for microscopic hematuria,

Notes

including an IVP and cystoscopy, which were normal. He has history of coronary artery disease with MI and angioplasty 6 months ago. Also has hypertension. His medications are listed. He is allergic to morphine.

He denies chest pain or palpitations. No cough or shortness of breath. No dysuria, increased urinary frequency, or nocturia.

Reveals an alert, pleasant gentleman. He is afebrile. Eyes are clear, TM appear normal. No nasal congestion. Mouth is moist, throat reveals no redness or swelling. Neck is supple with no adenopathy. Heart regular rate and rhythm. There is exquisite left lower quadrant tenderness. No masses, bowel tones are present. Rectal exam reveals good sphincter tone. No rectal masses or tenderness. No calf tenderness or ankle dema. Lab data includes a hemoglobin of 15.2, white count 10200, chemistry panel is entirely normal, urine contains 3–5 RBCs but otherwise unremarkable. Chest x-ray shows no active pulmonary disease. Abdominal x-ray shows stool in the right colon but otherwise unremarkable.

Given Augmentin 500 mg orally.

Diagnosis: Left lower quadrant pain, probably diverticulitis.

Rest, stay on clear liquids today and progress his diet slowly. Continue Augmentin 500 tid. If he develops increased pain, vomiting, fever, or other problems, he is to return to ER.

CPT-4	ICD-9-CM Dx	ICD-9-CM Procedures	APC

Code Assignment(s): _____

ER Case 5

Sixty-nine-year-old woman seen yesterday with an insect sting on the right foot. Today she is concerned that the redness is swelling. She is on Claritin and started on prednisone. There is no history of allergic reactions to bee stings. She does have respiratory allergies. Her medications are as listed. Her allergies are also listed. Her last tetanus was in 2000. She is afebrile. There is sting site visible on the lateral aspect of the right foot with surrounding erythema which does not appear to have spread significantly beyond skin marking which was applied yesterday.

Insect sting right foot with local reaction.

Continue resting and elevating foot with ice. She will continue her medication. If she develops increased swelling, pain, fever, or any problems, she is to return to the ER.

Notes	CPT-4	ICD-9-CM Dx	ICD-9-CM Procedures	APC
_____	_____	_____	_____	_____
_____	_____	_____	_____	_____
_____	_____	_____	_____	_____
_____	_____	_____	_____	_____
_____	_____	_____	_____	_____

Code Assignment(s): _____

Surgery Chart 1

Surgeon:

Preoperative diagnosis: Generator Exchange

Postoperative diagnosis: Same

Procedure: Dual chamber permanent pacemaker exchange

Anesthesia: Local with sedation

Blood loss: About 25 cc

Procedure:

Patient was brought to the cardiac cath lab and placed in the supine position. Procedure was performed under localized sedation. The patient was administered intravenous antibiotics. The anterior chest wall was cleaned and prepped and the leads were tested by a Medical representative and found to have adequate pacing and threshold values. Sufficient slack was placed in the leads and they were sutured to the base of the pocket. The pocket was irrigated and the pacemaker was then placed in the subcutaneous pocket and sutured with 2-0 silk. The pocket was then closed in layers with Vicryl sutures. The skin was closed with staples. The wound was dressing. The explanted generator was Model #88383 SUNGISI and was end of life.

CPT-4	ICD-9-CM Dx	ICD-9-CM Procedures	APC
_____	_____	_____	_____
_____	_____	_____	_____
_____	_____	_____	_____
_____	_____	_____	_____
_____	_____	_____	_____

Code Assignment(s): _____

Notes

Surgery Chart 2

Surgeon:

Anesthetist:

Preoperative Diagnosis: Fx right patella

Postoperative Diagnosis: Fx right patella with displacement

Surgery:

1. Open reduction, internal fixation, patella with repair of medial lateral reteinaculum

Patient was placed supined and a satisfactory general anesthetic was administered. Leg was prepped and dual traction was applied to the upper pole of the patella. The patella fracture was opened and the fracture site and knee joint was copiously irrigated with normal saline via pulse lavage. The distal fracture fragment was an approximately 1.5-cm cube with no articular surface. It was not comminuted and fit quite well into the proximal fracture fragment. Two drill holes were placed into the distal fracture fragment as well as into the proximal fracture fragment. A suture was placed through each drill hole and tied, allowing an anatomic reduction to the fracture itself. The retinaculum, both medially and laterally, was then reapproximated with interrupted figure-of-eight sutures.

The wound was irrigated, and dry sterile dressings were applied followed by sterile circumferential cast padding.

CPT-4	ICD-9-CM Dx	ICD-9-CM Procedures	APC
_____	_____	_____	_____
_____	_____	_____	_____
_____	_____	_____	_____
_____	_____	_____	_____
_____	_____	_____	_____

Code Assignment(s): _____

Surgery Chart 3

Surgeon:

Assistant:

Anesthesia:

Preoperative diagnosis: Chondromalacia patella

Postoperative diagnosis: Chondromalacia patella, lateral patellar tilt and lateral retinacular tightness

Procedure: Right knee arthroscopy and chondroplasty patella
               Right knee arthroscopic lateral release

After suitable general anesthesia was achieved, patient's right knee was prepped and daped. A thigh tourniquet was applied and an inflow cannula was inserted into the suprapatellar pouch on the medial side. The arthroscope was inserted through an anterior lateral portal. The medial compartment was examined first. There was noted to be intact stable medial meniscus and intact articular surfaces. Exam of the patellofemoral joint revealed localized chondromalacia at the lateral aspect of the inferior pole of the patella that was smoothed with a shaver and Oratec Probe. The patient also had a small medial synovial plica that was trimmed with a shaver as well. Following this, an arthroscopic lateral release was performed, the arthroscope was removed, patellar tracking reassessed. Knee joint was irrigated and dressings were applied.

CPT-4	ICD-9-CM Dx	ICD-9-CM Procedures	APC

Code Assignment(s): _____

Surgery Chart 4

Operative Report

Surgeon:

Anesthetist:

Procedure: Trigger finger

Preoperative diagnosis: Right middle trigger finger

Postoperative diagnosis: Same

Patient was placed in the supine position, tourniquet was placed about the right upper extremity and extremity was prepped and draped in the usual sterile fashion. Middle finger was incised over the proximal edge of the A-1 pulley and a transverse fashion. The incision was carried down through the soft tissue and the proximal edge of the A-1 pulley was identified and transected under

Notes

direct visualization from proximal to distal. At this point the wound was closed using a running 4-0 Prolene suture. A compression dressing was applied. Patient was taken to the recovery room in satisfactory condition.

CPT-4	ICD-9-CM Dx	ICD-9-CM Procedures	APC
_____	_____	_____	_____
_____	_____	_____	_____
_____	_____	_____	_____
_____	_____	_____	_____
_____	_____	_____	_____

Code Assignment(s): _____

Surgery Chart 5

Surgeon:

Anesthesia: General

Preoperative diagnosis: Avulsed laceration to ringer finger and gaping laceration in the fourth/fifth webspace, requiring closure

Postoperative diagnosis: Same

This patient is an 18 year old who has been on the job for two weeks as a welder. He was standing in front of a palette to move in onto the fork plates when his co-worker accidentally moved the forklift catching his right hand between the corner of the palette and the work. The fork went into his hand.

He presents for suturing. The hand was prepped and draped. Two 4-0 Ethilon suture were placed without difficulty. The avulsed tissue was debrided from the ring finger and the wound left open. The wound was dressed with dressings and the fourth and fifth fingers taped in partial flexion.

CPT-4	ICD-9-CM Dx	ICD-9-CM Procedures	APC
_____	_____	_____	_____
_____	_____	_____	_____
_____	_____	_____	_____
_____	_____	_____	_____
_____	_____	_____	_____

Code Assignment(s): _____

CONCLUSION

Upon completing Chapter 7 and the accompanying practice exercises, the student should now be capable of completing the UB-92/CMS 1450 for outpatient facility purposes, utilizing appropriate revenue codes, occurrence codes and other conventions on the claim form. The student should also be knowledgeable about the methodology utilized for reimbursement for outpatient hospital coding and billing.

Now that we have completed a review of the outpatient coding and billing process, do the CMS 1450/UB-92 claim exercises located on the CD-ROM that accompanies this text. Keep in mind that the assignment of APCs is not completed within the text of the UB-92; however, the facility should know the appropriate APC assignment in order to determine appropriate reimbursement expected. You may still wish to assign APCs to each case study to identify the level of reimbursement that may be expected. Keep in mind, that, unlike inpatient/DRGs, multiple CPT-4 codes and multiple APCs are common on outpatient facility coding.

TABLE 7–9   Outpatient UB-92/CMS1450 Completion Details.

FL	Field Name	Specifics	# Digits	Digits (A)lpha (N)um	Medicare (R)eq (O)pt	Others (R)eq (O)pt
PROVIDER BILLING INFORMATION (FL 1-11)						
1	Line a - Name of Provider	Information on Provider Submitting Bill		AlphaNum	REQ	REQ
	Line b - Street Address, PO Box	Address Where Payment Should Be Sent		AlphaNum	REQ	REQ
	Line c - City, St Abbreviation, Zip		5/9 zip	AlphaNum	REQ	REQ
	Line d - Telephone and Fax # Country Code		10	Num Alpha	OPT	OPT
2	Unlabeled Field	Unlabeled Field				

TABLE 7–9   *continued*

FL	Field Name	Specifics	# Digits	Digits (A)lpha (N)um	Medicare (R)eq (O)pt	Others (R)eq (O)pt
3	Patient Control Number	Unique identification number assigned by provider to each patient Speeds up processing of checks, data entry	20	AlphaNum	REQ	REQ
4	Type of Bill	First digit - Type of Facility	1	Num	REQ	REQ
		Second digit - Billing Classification	1	Num	REQ	REQ
		Third digit - Frequency of Billing	1	Num	REQ	REQ
	Type of Bill	Except Clinics/Special Facilities				

First Digit	Second Digit	Third Digit
0 - Not Applicable	0 - Not Applicable	0 - Nonpayment/zero claim
1 - Hospital		1 - Admit thru discharge claim
2 - Skilled Nursing		2 - Interim-First Claim
3 - Home Health Facility	3 - Outpatient	3 - Interim-Continuing Claim
4 - Relig nonmedical health care hospital inpatient	4 - Other (Medicare Part B)	4 - Interim-Last Claim
5 - Relig nonmedical health care post-hospital extended care		5 - Late Charge(s) only claim
6 - Intermediate Care		6 - Adjustment prior claim
7 - Clinic/hospital-based renal dialysis facility		7 - Replacement prior claim
8 - Special facility/hospital ASC		8 - Void/cancel prior claim
9 - Reserved for national assignment	8 - Reserved for national assignment	9 - Final claim Home Health PPS episode
	9 - Other	

PROVIDER BILLING INFORMATION (FL 1-11)

Clinics Only

First Digit	Second Digit	Third Digit
0 - Not Applicable	0 - Not Applicable	0 - Nonpayment/zero claim
1 - Hospital	1 - Rural Health Clinic (RHC)	1 - Admit thru discharge claim
2 - Skilled Nursing	2 - Hospital-Based/Independent Renal Dialysis	2 - Interim-First Claim

(continued)

FL	Field Name	Specifics	# Digits	Digits (A)lpha (N)um	Medicare (R)eq (O)pt	Others (R)eq (O)pt
4 (con-tinued)	3 - Home Health Facility	3 - Freestanding provider-based fed qualified health centers (FQHC)			3 - Interim-Continuing Claim	
	4 - Relig nonmedical health care hospital inpatient	4 - Outpatient rehab (ORF)			4 - Interim-Last Claim	
	5 - Relig nonmedical health care post-hospital extended care	5 - Comprehensive outpatient			5 - Late Charge(s) only claim	
	6 - Intermediate Care	6 - Community mental health (CMHC)			6 - Adjustment prior claim	
	7 - Clinic/hospital-based renal dialysis facility	7 - Reserved for national assignment			7 - Replacement prior claim	
	8 - Special facility/hospital ASC	8 - Reserved for national assignment			8 - Void/cancel prior claim	
	9 - Reserved for national assignment	9 - Other			9 - Final claim Home Health PPS episode	

Special Facilities Only

First Digit	Second Digit	Third Digit
0 - Not Applicable	0 - Not Applicable	0 - Nonpayment/zero claim
1 - Hospital	1 - Hospice (Nonhosp Based)	1 - Admit thru discharge claim
2 - Skilled Nursing	2 - Hospital (Hospital-Based)	2 - Interim-First Claim
3 - Home Health Facility	3 - Ambulatory Surgery Center Services to hospital outpatients	3 - Interim-Continuing Claim
4 - Relig nonmedical health care hospital inpatient	4 - Freestanding birthing center	4 - Interim-Last Claim
5 - Relig nonmedical health care post-hospital extended care	5 - Critical access hospitals	5 - Late Charge(s) only claim
6 - Intermediate Care	6 - Residential facility (Non-Medicare)	6 - Adjustment prior claim
7 - Clinic/hospital-based renal dialysis facility	7 - Reserved for national assignment	7 - Replacement prior claim
8 - Special facility/hospital ASC	8 - Reserved for national assignment	8 - Void/cancel prior claim
9 - Reserved for national assignment	9 - Other	9 - Final claim Home Health PPS episode

TABLE 7–9   *continued*

FL	Field Name	Specifics	# Digits	Digits (A)lpha (N)um	Medicare (R)eq (O)pt	Others (R)eq (O)pt
PROVIDER BILLING INFORMATION (FL 1-11)						
5	Federal Tax ID Number	Federal TIN (Tax ID Number) OR EIN (Employer ID Number)	9	AlphaNum	OPT	REQ
6	Statement Covers Period Same-Day Services Inpatient Interim/ No Discharge Final Bill	From/Thru Dates From/Thru Identical Thru calculated as part of FL 7-10 Thru Date of Discharge or Death	8	Num	REQ	REQ
7	Covered Days	No dashes/no slashes Records total number inpatient days author- ized by primary carrier within claim billing period	3	Num	No Outpt	REQ Medi as carrier
8	Noncovered Days	Days not covered by primary carrier FL 7 + FL 8 = FL 6 days	4	Num	No Outpt	REQ Medi as carrier
9	Coinsurance Days	Inpatient hospital days occurring after 60th day and before 91st day in single benefit period of spell of illness # cannot exceed 30 hospital days	2	Num	No Outpt	REQ Medi as carrier
10	Lifetime Reserve Days	Medicare patient used 60 covered hospital days and 30 coinsurance days may elect to use a lifetime reserve of up to 60 days inpatient hospital services	2	Num	No Outpt carrier	REQ Medi as
11	Unlabeled Field					
Patient Information (FL 12-23)						
12	Patient Name	No apostrophes, hyphens Titles not used Medicare: must appear exactly as on Medicare card Last Name, First Name, MI		Alpha	REQ	REQ

(continued)

FL	Field Name	Specifics		# Digits	Digits (A)lpha (N)um	Medicare (R)eq (O)pt	Others (R)eq (O)pt
13	Patient Address	Street Name/PO Box City, State Abbreviation, Zip 5-9 digits 1st 3 zip digits must be valid		50	AlphaNum	REQ	REQ
14	Patient Birth Date	If cannot obtain after reasonable efforts, should fill with zeros Do not leave blank		8	Num	REQ	REQ
15	Patient Sex	M-Male F-Female U-Unknown		1	Alpha	REQ	REQ
16	Patient Marital Status	S-Single M-Married P-Life partner (domestic partner) D-Divorced W-Widowed X-Legally separated U-Unknown		1	Alpha	NO	NO
17	Admission/Start of Care Date	Admission Date ** Required for inpatient, home health, hospice, outpt rehab/facility		8	Num	No Outpt **	NO Outpt ***
18	Admission Hour	AM	PM	2	Num	NO	NO Outpt
	0	12:00 mid-12:59	12 12:00-12:59				
	1	1:00-1:59	13 1:00-1:59				
	2	2:00-2:59	14 2:00-2:59				
	3	3:00-3:59	15 3:00-3:59				
	4	4:00-4:59	16 4:00-4:59				
	5	5:00-5:59	17 5:00-5:59				
	6	6:00-6:59	18 6:00-6:59				
	7	7:00-7:59	19 7:00-7:59				
	8	8:00-8:59	20 8:00-8:59				
	9	9:00-9:59	21 9:00-9:59				
	10	10:00-10:59	22 10:00-10:59				
	11	11:00-11:59	23 11:00-11:59 99 Unknown				

TABLE 7–9   *continued*

FL	Field Name	Specifics	# Digits	Digits (A)lpha (N)um	Medicare (R)eq (O)pt	Others (R)eq (O)pt
Patient Information (FL 12-23)						
19	Type of Admission	Code for establishing level of urgency For admission	1	Num	No Outpt	NO Outpt
20	Source of Admission		1	AlphaNum	No Outpt	
21	Discharge Hour	Use Same Table for Discharge Hour as for Admission Hour	2	Num	NO	PREF
22	Patient Status	Patient's discharge status at the time of the "thru" date on the UB-92	2	Num	No	No
23	Medical Record Number		17	AlphaNum	REQ	REQ TRICARE
CONDITION CODES (FL 24-31)						
24-30	Condition Codes	Identifies special condition/unique circumstance. Assist carrier in determination of eligibility for coverage/ payment Up to seven (7) may be listed List in ascending order, numbers then letters, separated by comma	2	AlphaNum	REQ if applic	REQ if applic

24-30   **Condition Codes**

Insurance Codes

01 - Military Service
    Related
02 - Employment
    Related
03 - Covered by Insurance
    Not on Claim
04 - Pt HMO Enrollee
05 - Lien Filed
06 - ESRD Pt First

Patient Condition Codes

17 - Patient Homeless
18 - Maiden Name Retained
19 - Child Retains Mother's Name
20 - Beneficiary Requested Billing
21 - Billing for Denial Notice
22 - Patient Multiple Drug
    Regimen
23 - Home Care Giver Available
24 - Home IV Patient Receiving

Room Codes

36 - General Care Patient/
    Special Unit
40 - Same-Day Transfer
41 - Partial Hospitalization
42 - Continuing Care Not
    Rel to Inpt Adm
43 - Continuing Care Not Provided
    within Prescribed
    Postdischarge Window

(continued)

FL	Field Name	Specifics	# Digits	Digits (A)lpha (N)um	Medicare (R)eq (O)pt	Others (R)eq (O)pt
24-30 (continued)	19 Months Covered by Employer Plan 07 - Treatment Nonterminal Condition Hospice Patient 08 - Beneficiary Would Not Provide Other Insur Info 09 - Patient/Spouse Employed 10 - Pt/Spouse Employed but No Employer Coverage 11- Disabled Beneficiary No Employer Coverage 12-16 Payer Use Only	HHA Services 25 - Patient Non-US Resident 26 - VA-Elig Patient Chooses Medicare-Certified Facility 27 - Pt Referred Sole Community Hosp Dx Laboratory Test(s) 28 - Pt/Spouse Employer 2nd to Care 29 - Disabled Beneficiary/Family Member Health Plan 2nd to Care 30 - Qualifying Clinical Trials 31 - Full-Time Day Student 32 - Student (Coop/Work Study) 33 - Student (Full-Time Night) 34 - Student (Part-Time) 35 - Reserved for National Assignment		44-45 Reserved for National Assignment **TRICARE Codes** 46 - Nonavailability Statement NOF 47 - Reserved for TRICARE 48 - Psych Residential Treatment Center 49-54 Reserved for National Assignment 55 - SNF Bed Not Available 56 - Medical Appropriateness 57 - SNF Readmission 58 - Term Medicare + Choice Organization 59 - Reserved for National Assignment 60 - Day Outlier 61 - Cost Outlier 62-65 Payer Only Codes		

SPECIAL CODES

Other Special Codes

66 - Provider Does Not Wish Cost Outlier Payment
67 - Beneficiary Elects Not to Use Lifetime Reserve Days
68 - Beneficiary Elects to Use Lifetime Reserve Days
69 - Operating Indirect Medical Education Payment Only

77 - Provider Accepts/ Obligated to Accept Payment Primary Payer as Payment in Full
78 - New Coverage Not Implemented by HMO
79 - CORD Services Provided Off-Site
80-99 Reserved State assignment

Miscellaneous Codes

A6 - Medicare Pneumococcal Pneumonia Vaccine/Influenza
A7 - Induced Abortion-Danger to Life
A8 - Induced Abortion-Victim Rape/Incest
A9 - 2nd Opinion Surgery
B0 - Medicare Coordinated Care Demonstration claim
B1 - Beneficiary Inelig Demonstration Prog
B2 - Critical Access Hosp Ambulance Attestation
B3-B9 Reserved for National Assignment

TABLE 7–9   *continued*

FL	Field Name	Specifics	# Digits	Digits (A)lpha (N)um	Medicare (R)eq (O)pt	Others (R)eq (O)pt
24-30 (con-tinued)	**Renal Dialysis Setting Codes**	**Special Programs**				

70 - Self-Administered Epoetin	A0 - TRICARE External Partnership
71 - Full Care in Unit	A1 - EPSDT/CHAP
72 - Self-Care in Unit	A2 - Physically Handicapped Children's Program
73 - Self-Care Training	A3 - Special Federal Funding
74 - Home	A4 - Family Planning
75 - Home-100% Reimbursement	A5 - Disability
76 - Backup In-facility Dialysis	

QIO Approval Indicator Svcs   **Claim Change Reasons**

C0 - Reserved for National Assignment	D0 - Changes to Service Dates	E0 - Change in Patient Status
C1 - Approved as Billed	D1 - Changes to Charges	E1-E9 Reserved for National Assignment
C2 - Auto Approval as Billed Based on Focused Review	D2 - Changes in Revenue Codes/ HCPCS Codes	G0 - Distinct Medical Visit
C3 - Partial Approval	D3 - 2nd/Subsequent Interim PPS Bill	G1-G9 Reserved for National Assignment
C4 - Admission/Service Denied	D4 - Change in Grouper Input	H0 - Delayed Filing, Statement of Intent Submitted
C5 - Postpayment Review	D5 - Cancel to Correct Claim # or Provider ID Number	H1-H9 Reserved for National Assignment
C6 - Admission Preauthorization	D6 - Cancel only to Repay Duplicate or OIG Overpayment	M0-M2 Payer Only codes
C7 - Extended Authorization	D7 - Change to Make Medicare 2nd	M3-M9 Reserved for Payer Assignment
C8-C9 Reserved for National Assignment	D8 - Change to Make Medicare Primary	N0-W9 Reserved for National Assignment
	D9 - Any Other Change	X0-Z9 Reserved for State Assignment

FL	Field Name
31	Unlabeled Field

OCCURRENCE CODES/DATES (FL 32-38)

FL	Field Name	Specifics	# Digits	Digits (A)lpha (N)um	Medicare (R)eq (O)pt	Others (R)eq (O)pt
32-35	Occurrence Codes/Dates	Significant event/occurrence that occurred in connection with service	2	Alpha Num	REQ if applic	REQ if applic

(continued)

FL	Field Name	Specifics	# Digits	Digits (A)lpha (N)um	Medicare (R)eq (O)pt	Others (R)eq (O)pt
32-35 (continued)	**Accident-Related Codes** 01 - Auto Accident 02 - No-Fault/Auto/Other 03 - Accident/Tort Liability 04 - Accident/Employment 05 - Other Accident 06 - Crime Victim 07-08 Reserved for National Assignment **Medical Condition Codes** 09 - Start Infertility Treatment 10 - Last Menstrual Period 11 - Onset Symptoms/Illness 12 - Date Onset Chronically Dependent Individual 13-15 Reserved for National Assignment	**Insurance-Related Codes** 16 - Date of Last Therapy 17 - Date Outpt Occupational Therapy Plan Established/ Last Reviewed 18 - Date Retirement Pt/ Beneficiary 19 - Date Retirement Spouse 20 - Guarantee of Payment Began 21 - UR Notice Received 22 - Date Active Care Ended 23 - Date Cancellation Hospice Elective Period 24 - Date Insurance Denied 25 - Date Benefits Terminated Primary Payer 26 - Date SNF Bed Available 27 - Date Hospice Cert or Recert 28 - Date Comprehensive Outpt Rehab Facility Plan Est/ Reviewed 29 - Date Outpt Physical Therapy Plan Established/Last Reviewed 30 - Date Outpt Speech Path Plan Established/Last Reviewed 31 - Date Beneficiary Notified of Intent to Bill (Accommodations) 32 - Date Beneficiary Notified of Intent to Bill (Procedures/ Trmts) 33 - 1st Day Medicare Coordination Period for ESRD Beneficiaries Covered by Employ Group Plan 34 - Date Election of Extended Care	**Patient Service Codes** 40 - Scheduled Date Admission 41 - Date 1st Test Preadmission Testing 42 - Date of Discharge 43 - Schedule Surgery Date Cancelled 44 - Date Occupational Therapy Started 45 - Date Speech Therapy Started 46 - Date Cardiac Rehab Started 47 - Date Cost Outlier Status Began 48-49 Payer Codes 50-69 Reserved for State Assignment 70-99 Reserved Occurrence Span Codes A0 - Reserved for National Assignment A1 - Birth Date - Insured A A2 - Effective Date-Insured A Policy A3 - Benefits Exhausted A4-A9 Reserved for National Assignment B0 - Reserved for National Assignment B1 - Birth Date - Insured B B2 - Effective Date-Insured B Policy B3 - Benefits Exhausted B4-B9 Reserved for National Assignment C0 - Reserved for National Assignment C1 - Birth Date - Insured C				

TABLE 7–9   *continued*

FL	Field Name	Specifics	# Digits	Digits (A)lpha (N)um	Medicare (R)eq (O)pt	Others (R)eq (O)pt
32-35 (con- tinued)		35 - Date Treatment Started Phy Ther		C2 - Effective Date - Insured C Policy		
				C3 - Benefits Exhausted		
		38 - Date Treatment Start IV Home Therapy		C4-C9 Reserved for National Assignment		
		39 - Date Discharged Continuous Course IV Therapy		D0-D9 Reserved for National Assignment		
				E0-G9 Follow same assignment for Insured E, F, G		
				H0-I9 Reserved for National Assignment		
				J0-L9 Reserved for State Assignment		
36	Occurrence Span Codes/ Dates	Cannot be used in conjunction with Occurrence Codes If > 2 codes, may utilize occurrence code fields of additional listing(s)	2	Alpha Num	REQ if applic	REQ if applic
	70 - Qualifying Stay Dates	76 - Patient Liability		M0 - QIO/UR Approved Stay Dates		
	71 - Prior Stay Date	77 - Provider Liability Period		M1 - Provider Liability-No Utilization		
	72 - First/Last Visit	Utilization Charged		M2 - Dates Inpatient Respite Care		
	73 - Benefit Eligibility Period	78 - SNF Prior Stay Dates		M3-W9 Reserved for National Assignment		
	74 - Noncovered Level of Care/Leave of Absence LOA	79 - Payer Code 80-99 Reserved for State Assignment		X0-Z9 Reserved for State Assignment		
	75 - SNF Level of Care					
37	Internal Control Number (ICN) Document Control Number (DCN)	Found on remittance voucher of original claim Must be reported for Medicare adjustment claims Subdivided into three (3) lines A - Primary Payer B - Secondary Payer C - Tertiary Payer			REQ Resub- missions	REQ
38	Responsible Party Name and Address	Guarantor on account May also be used when claim involves payer primary to Medicare		Alpha- Num	NO	NO

(continued)

FL	Field Name	Specifics	# Digits	Digits (A)lpha (N)um	Medicare (R)eq (O)pt	Others (R)eq (O)pt
VALUE CODES AND AMOUNTS (FL 39-41)						
39-41	Value Code/Amount	Multiples should be reported in alphanumeric order Decimal points not keyed Nondollars reported with 2 zeros on end (EX: 45 = 45.00)	2/Code 8/Amts	Alpha-Num	REQ If Applic	REQ If Applic

		21 - Medicaid/Catastrophic	46 - Number of Grace Days	
		22 - Medicaid/Surplus	47 - Any Liability Insurance	
		23 - Medicaid/Recurring Monthly Income	48 - Hemoglobin Reading	
03 - Reserved for National Assignment		24 - Medicaid Rate Code	49 - Hematocrit Reading	
		25-29 Unassigned/Reserved for Medicaid National Assignment		
05 - Prof Component Inc in Charges/Billed Separately to Carrier		30 - Preadmission Testing	50 - Physical Therapy Visits	
06 - Medicare Blood Deductible		31 - Patient Liability Amount	51 - Occupational Therapy Visits	
07 - Reserved for National Assignment		32-36 - Reserved for National Assignment	52 - Speech Therapy Visits	
08 - Medicare Lifetime Reserve Amount in 1st Calendar Year		37 - Pints of Blood Furnished	53 - Cardiac Rehab Visits	
09 - Medicare Coinsurance Amount in 1st Calendar Year in Billing Period		38 - Blood Deductible Pints	54 - Newborn Birth Weight in Grams	
10 - Medicare Lifetime Reserve Amount in 2nd Calendar Year in Billing Period		39 - Pints of Blood Replaced	55 - Reserved for National Assignment	

Home Health Codes

11- Medicare Coinsurance Amt 2nd Calendar Year	40 - New Coverage Not Implemented by HMO (Inpt Only)	56 - Skilled Nurse-Home Visit Hrs (HHA)	
12 - Working Aged Beneficiary/Spouse with Employer Health Plan	41 - Black Lung	57 - Home Health Aid - Visit Hours	

TABLE 7–9 ***continued***

FL	*Field Name*	*Specifics*	*# Digits*	*Digits (A)lpha (N)um*	*Medicare (R)eq (O)pt*	*Others (R)eq (O)pt*
39-41 (con-tinued)	13 - ESRD Beneficiary in Medicare Coordination Period with Employer Group Health	42 - Veterans Affairs	58 - Arterial Blood Gas			
	14 - No-Fault/Inc Auto/Other 15 - Workers' Compensation	43 - Disabled Beneficiary Under Age 65 with Group Health Plan	59 - Oxygen Saturation			
	16 - Public Health Service or other Federal Agency 17-20 Reserved Payer Use	44 - Amount Provider Agreed to Accept Primary Insurer When Amount < Total Charges But > Primary Insured Payment	60 - HHA Branch MSA			
		45 - Accident Hour as follows:	61 - Location Where Service Furnished (HHA/Hospice)			
		AM PM				
		0 12:00-12:59 12 12:00-12:59	62-65 Reserved for Payer Use			
		1 1:00-1:59 13 1:00-1:59	66 - Reserved for National Assignment			
		2 2:00-2:59 14 2:00-2:59				
		3 3:00-3:59 15 3:00-3:59	67 - Peritoneal Dialysis			
		4 4:00-4:59 16 4:00-4:59	68 - EPO - Drug			
		5 5:00-5:59 17 5:00-5:59	69 - Reserved for National Assignment			
		6 6:00-6:59 18 6:00-6:59				
		7 7:00-7:59 19 7:00-7:59	70-79 - Reserved for Payer Use			
		8 8:00-8:59 20 8:00-8:59	80-99 - Reserved for State Assignment			
		9 9:00-9:59 21 9:00-9:59				
		10 10:00-10:59 22 10:00-10:59				
		11 11:00-11:59 23 11:00-11:50				
		99 Unknown				
		A1 - Deductible Payer A B1 - Deductible Payer B C1 - Deductible Payer C A2 - Coinsurance Payer A B2 - Coinsurance Payer B C2 - Coinsurance Payer C A3 - Estimated Responsibility Payer A B3 - Estimated Responsibility Payer B C3 - Estimated Responsibility Payer C				

(continued)

FL	Field Name	Specifics	# Digits	Digits (A)lpha (N)um	Medicare (R)eq (O)pt	Others (R)eq (O)pt

REVENUE DESCRIPTIONS, CODES, CHARGES (FL 42-49)

FL	Field Name	Specifics	# Digits	Digits (A)lpha (N)um	Medicare (R)eq (O)pt	Others (R)eq (O)pt
42-43	Revenue Code/Description	Revenue code identifies specific service being billed	3	Num	REQ	REQ
		Last digit 0 = general code				
		Last digit 9 = Other				
		Detailed revenue codes (not ending in 0 required for following:				
		29X, 304, 33X, 367, 42X, 52X, 55-59X				
		624, 636, 80-85X				
		23 lines available				
		Up to 9 pages (450 lines) acceptable on one claim				
		List in ascending order by DOS except 001 Total Charges (last)				
	Revenue Code (Subcategory)	Standard Abbreviation				

42 Revenue Code   **43 Revenue Description**
01X Reserved
02X Health Insurance PPS
    0 Reserved
    1 Reserved
    2 SNF PPS System   SNF PPS (RUG)
    3 Rehab Facility PPS   HH PPS
    5-9 Reserved
03X - 09X Reserved

Accommodation Codes
10X All-Inclusive Rate
18X Leave of Absence (LOA)
    0 General   LOA OR LEAVE OF ABSENCE
    1 Reserved
    2 Pt Convenience-Billable   LOA/PT CONV CHGS BILLABLE
    3 Therapeutic Leave   LOA/THERAP
    9 Other LOA   LOA/OTHER

Ancillary Services
22X Special Charges
    0 General   SPECIAL CHARGES
    1 Admission Charge   ADMIT CHARGE
    2 Tech Support Charge   TECH SUPPT CHG
    3 UR Service Charge   UR CHARGE

TABLE 7–9   *continued*

FL	Field Name	Specifics	# Digits	Digits (A)lpha (N)um	Medicare (R)eq (O)pt	Others (R)eq (O)pt
42-43 (continued)	4 Late Discharge/ Med Necessity	LATE DISCH/MED NEC				
	9 Other Special Charges	OTHER SPEC CHG				
	25X Pharmacy					
	0 General	PHARMACY				
	1 Generic Drugs	DRUGS/GENERIC				
	2 Nongeneric Drugs	DRUGS/NONGENERIC				
	3 Take-Home Drugs	DRUGS/TAKEHOME				
	4 Drugs incident to Dx Serv	DRUGS/INCIDENT ODX				
	5 Drugs incident to Radiology	DRUGS/INCIDENT RAD				
	6 Experimental Drugs	DRUGS/EXPERIMT				
	7 Nonprescription Drugs	DRUGS/NONPSCRPT				
	8 IV Solutions	IV SOLUTIONS				
	9 Other Pharmacy	DRUGS/OTHER				
	26X IV Therapy	**Usually requires HCPCS code(s)**				
	0 General	IV THERAPY				
	1 Infusion Pump	IV THER/INFSN PUMP				
	2 IV Therapy/Pharmacy	IV THER/PHARM/SVC				
	3 IV Therapy/Drug/Supply/ Delivery	IV THER/DRUG/SUPPLY DELV				
	4 IV Therapy/Supplies	IV THER/SUPPLIES				
	9 Other IV Therapy	IV THERAPY/OTHER				
	27X Med/Surg Supplies/ Devices	**Only Nonroutine Billed with This RC**				
	0 General	MED-SUR SUPPLIES				
	1 Nonsterile Supply	NONSTER SUPPLY				
	2 Sterile Supply	STERILE SUPPLY				
	3 Take-Home Supplies	TAKEHOME SUPPLY				
	4 Prosthetic/Orthotic Devices	PROSTH/ORTH DEV				
	5 Pacemaker	PACEMAKER				
	6 Intraocular Lenses	INTRO OC LENS				
	7 Oxygen-Take Home	02/TAKEHOME				
	8 Other Implants	SUPPLY/IMPLANTS				
	9 Other Supplies/Devices	SUPPLY/OTHER				
	28X Oncology					
	0 General	ONCOLOGY				
	9 Other Oncology	ONCOLOGY/OTHER				
	29X DME (Other Than Renal)					
	0 General	MED EQUIP/DURAB				
	1 Rental	MED EQUIP/RENT				

(continued)

FL	Field Name	Specifics	# Digits	Digits (A)lpha (N)um	Medicare (R)eq (O)pt	Others (R)eq (O)pt
42-43 (con-tinued)	2 Purchase of new DME	MED EQUIP/NEW				
	3 Purchase of used DME	MED EQUIP/USED				
	4 Supplies/Drugs for DME Effectiveness (HHA)	MED EQUIP/SUPPLIES/DRUGS				
	9 Other Equipment	MED EQUIP/OTHER				
	30X Laboratory					
	0 General	LABORATORY OR LAB				
	1 Chemistry	LAB/CHEMISTRY				
	2 Immunology	LAB/IMMUNOLOGY				
	3 Renal Patient (Home)	LAB/RENAL HOME				
	4 Nonroutine Dialysis	LAB/NR DIALYSIS				
	5 Hematology	LAB/HEMATOLOGY				
	6 Bacteriology/Microbiology	LAB/BACT-MICRO				
	7 Urology	LAB/UROLOGY				
	9 Other Laboratory	LAB/OTHER				
	31X Laboratory Pathological					
	0 General	PATHOLOGY LAB OR PATH LAB				
	1 Cytology	PATHOL/CYTOLOGY				
	2 Histology	PATHOL/HISTOLOGY				
	4 Biopsy	PATHOL/BIOPSY				
	9 Other	PATHOL/OTHER				
	32X Radiology-Diagnostic					
	0 General	DX X-RAY				
	1 Angiocardiography	DX X-RAY/ANGIO				
	2 Arthrography	DX X-RAY/ARTH				
	3 Arteriography	DX X-RAY/ARTER				
	4 Chest X-Ray	DX X-RAY/CHEST				
	9 Other	DX X-RAY/OTHER				
	33X Radiology-Therapeutic					
	0 General	RX X-RAY				
	1 Chemotherapy-Injected	CHEMOTHER/INJ				
	2 Chemotherapy-Oral	CHEMOTHER/ORAL				
	3 Radiation Therapy	RADIATION RX				
	5 Chemotherapy/IV	CHEMOTHERAP-IV				
	9 Other	RX X-RAY/OTHER				
	34X Nuclear Medicine					
	0 General	NUCLEAR MEDICINE OR NUC MED				
	1 Diagnostic	NUC MED/DX				
	2 Therapeutic	NUC MED/RX				
	9 Other	NUC MED/OTHER				

TABLE 7–9 *continued*

FL	Field Name	Specifics	# Digits	Digits (A)lpha (N)um	Medicare (R)eq (O)pt	Others (R)eq (O)pt
42-43 (con- tinued)	**34X CT Scan**					
	0 General	CT SCAN				
	1 Head Scan	CT SCAN/HEAD				
	2 Body Scan	CT SCAN/BODY				
	9 Other CT Scans	CT SCAN/OTHER				
	36X Operating Room Services					
	0 General	OR SERVICES				
	1 Minor Surgery	OR/MINOR				
	2 Organ Transplant/Not Kidney	OR/ORGAN TRANS				
	7 Kidney Transplant	OR/KIDNEY TSRANS				
	9 Other	OR/OTHER				
	37X Anesthesia					
	0 General	ANESTHESIA				
	1 Anes Incident to RAD	ANESTHE/INCIDENT RAD				
	2 Anes Incident to Other Dx	ANESTHE/INCIDENT ODX				
	4 Acupuncture	ANESTHE/ACUPUNC				
	9 Other	ANESTHE/OTHER				
	38X Blood					
	0 General	BLOOD				
	1 Packed Red Cells	BLOOD/PKD RED				
	2 Whole Blood	BLOOD/WHOLE				
	3 Plasma	BLOOD/PLASMA				
	4 Platelets	BLOOD/PLATELETS				
	5 Leukocytes	BLOOD/LEUKOCYTES				
	6 Other Components	BLOOD/COMPONENTS				
	7 Other Derivatives	BLOOD/DERIVATIVES				
	9 Other Blood	BLOOD/OTHER				
	39X Blood Storage/Processing					
	0 General	BLOOD/STOR-PROC				
	1 Blood Administration	BLOOD/ADMI				
	9 Other	BLOOD/OTHER STOR				
	40X Other Imaging					
	0 General	IMAGE SERVICE				
	1 Dx Mammography	MAMMOGRAPHY				
	2 Ultrasound	ULTRASOUND				
	3 Screen Mammography	SCR MAMMOGRAPHY/GEN MAMMO				
	4 Positron Emission Tomography	PET SCAN				
	9 Other	OTHER IMAG SVS				

(continued)

FL	Field Name	Specifics	# Digits	Digits (A)lpha (N)um	Medicare (R)eq (O)pt	Others (R)eq (O)pt
42-43 (con-tinued)	**41X Respiratory**					
	0 General	RESPIRATORY SVC				
	2 Inhalation Services	INHALATION SVC				
	3 Hyperbaric Oxygen Therapy	HYPERBARIC 02				
	9 Other	OTHER RESPIR SVS				
	42X Physical Therapy					
	0 General	PHYSICAL THERP				
	1 Visit Charge	PHYS THERAP/VISIT				
	2 Hourly Charge	PHYS THERP/HOUR				
	3 Group Rate	PHYS THERP/GROUP				
	4 Evaluation/Reevaluation	PHYS THERP/EVAL				
	9 Other	OTHER PHYS THERP				
	43X Occupational Therapy					
	0 General	OCCUPATION THER				
	1 Visit Charge	OCCUP THERP/VISIT				
	2 Hourly Charge	OCCUP THERP/HOUR				
	3 Group Rate	OCCUP THERP/GROUP				
	4 Evaluation/Reevaluation	OCCUP THERP/EVAL				
	9 Other	OTHER OCCUP THERP				
	44X Speech-Language Pathology					
	0 General	SPEECH PATHOL				
	1 Visit Charge	SPEECH PATH/VISIT				
	2 Hourly Charge	SPEECH PATH/HOUR				
	3 Group Rate	SPEECH PATH/GROUP				
	4 Evaluation/Reevaluation	SPEECH PATH/EVAL				
	9 Other	OTHER SPEECH PATH				
	45X Emergency Room	450 Not to Be Used with Any Other Code from Series				
	0 General	EMERG ROOM				
	1 EMTALA Med Screen Services	ER/EMTALA				
	2 ER beyond EMTALA Screen	ER/BEYOND EMTALA				
	6 Urgent Care	URGENT CARE				
	9 Other	OTHER EMER ROOM				
	46X Pulmonary Function					
	0 General	PULMONARY FUNC				
	9 Other	OTHER PULMON FUNC				
	47X Audiology					
	0 General	AUDIOLOGY				
	1 Diagnostic	AUDIOLOGY/DX				
	2 Treatment	AUDIOLOGY/RX				
	9 Other	OTHER AUDIOL				

TABLE 7–9 *continued*

FL	Field Name	Specifics	# Digits	Digits (A)lpha (N)um	Medicare (R)eq (O)pt	Others (R)eq (O)pt
42-43 (con-tinued)	**48X Cardiology**					
	0 General	CARDIOLOGY				
	1 Cardiac Cath Lab	CARDIAC CATH LAB				
	2 Stress Test	STRESS TEST				
	3 Echocardiography	ECHOCARDIOLOGY				
	9 Other	OTHER CARDIOL				
	49X Ambulatory Surgical Care					
	0 General	AMBUL SURG				
	9 Other	OTHER AMBL SURG				
	50X Outpatient Services					
	0 General	OUTPATIENT SVS				
	9 Other	OUTPATIENT/OTHER				
	51X Clinic					
	0 General	CLINIC				
	1 Chronic Pain Center	CHRONIC PAIN CL				
	2 Dental Clinic	DENTAL CLINIC				
	3 Psychiatric Clinic	PSYCH CLINIC				
	4 Ob-Gyn Clinic	OB-GYN CLINIC				
	5 Pediatric Clinic	PEDS CLINIC				
	6 Urgent Care Clinic	URGENT CLINIC				
	7 Family Practice Clinic	FAMILY CLINIC				
	9 Other	OTHER CLINIC				
	52X Free-Standing Clinic					
	0 General	FREESTAND CLINIC				
	1 Rural Health-Clinic	RURAL/CLINIC				
	2 Rural Health-Home	RURAL/HOME				
	3 Family Practice Clinic	FR/STD FAMILY CLINIC				
	6 Urgent Care Clinic	FR/STD URGENT CLINIC				
	9 Other	OTHER FR/STD CLINIC				
	53X Osteopathic Services					
	0 General	OSTEOPATH SVS				
	1 Osteopathic Therapy	OSTEOPATH RX				
	9 Other	OTHER OSTEOPATH				
	54X Ambulance					
	0 General	AMBULANCE				
	1 Supplies	AMBUL/SUPPLY				
	2 Medical Transport	AMBUL/MED TRANS				
	3 Heart Mobile	AMBUL/HEARTMOBL				
	4 Oxygen	AMBUL/OXY				
	5 Air Ambulance	AIR AMBULANCE				

(continued)

FL	Field Name	Specifics	# Digits	Digits (A)lpha (N)um	Medicare (R)eq (O)pt	Others (R)eq (O)pt
42-43 (con-tinued)	6 Neonatal Ambulance	AMBUL/NEONATAL				
	7 Pharmacy	AMBUL/PHARMACY				
	8 Telephone Transmission EKG	AMBUL/TELEPHONIC EKG				
	9 Other	OTHER AMBULANCE				
	55X Skilled Nursing					
	0 General	SKILLED NURSING				
	1 Visit Charge	SKILLED NURS/VISIT				
	2 Hourly Charge	SKILLED NURS/HOUR				
	9 Other	SKILLED NURS/OTHER				
	56X Medical Social Services					
	0 General	SOCIAL SVS				
	1 Visit Charge	MED SOC SERV/VISIT				
	2 Hourly Charge	MED SOC SERV/HOUR				
	9 Other	MED SOC SERV/OTHER				
	57X Home Health Aid					
	0 General	AIDE/HOME HEALTH				
	1 Visit Charge	AIDE/HOME HLTH/VISIT				
	2 Hourly Charge	AIDE/HOME HLTH/HOUR				
	9 Other	AIDE/HOME HLTH/OTHER				
	58X Other Visits (Home Health)					
	0 General	VISIT/HOME HEALTH				
	1 Visit Charge	VISIT/HOME HLTH/VISIT				
	2 Hourly Charge	VISIT/HOME HLTH/HOUR				
	9 Other	VISIT/HOME HLTH/OTHER				
	59X Units of Service (Home Health)					
	0 General	UNIT/HOME HEALTH				
	9 Other	UNIT/HOME HLTH/OTHER				
	60X Oxygen (Home Health)					
	0 General	02/HOME HEALTH				
	1 Oxygen-Stat/Equip/Supp/or Contents	02/EQUIP/SUPPL/CONT				
	2 Oxygen-Stat/Equip/Supp Under 1 LPM	02/STAT EQUIP/UNDER 1 LPM				
	3 Oxygen-Stat/Equip/over 4 LPM	O2/STAT EQUIP/OVER 4 LPM				
	4 Oxygen-Portable Add-On	02/STAT EQUIP/PORT ADD-ON				
	61X Magnetic Resonance					
	0 General	MRI				
	1 Brain (inc brain stem)	MRI-BRAIN				
	2 Spinal Cord (inc spine)	MRI-SPINE				

TABLE 7–9   *continued*

FL	Field Name	Specifics	# Digits	Digits (A)lpha (N)um	Medicare (R)eq (O)pt	Others (R)eq (O)pt
42-43 (con-tinued)	3 Reserved					
	4 MRI-Other	MRI-OTHER				
	5 MRA-Head/Neck	MRA-HEAD AND NECK				
	6 MRA-Lower Extremities	MRA-LOWER EXTREMITIES				
	7 Reserved					
	8 MRA-Other	MRA-OTHER				
	9 Other	MRI-OTHER				
	62X Med/Surg/Supp **Extension of 27X**					
	1 Supplies incident Radiology	MED-SUR SUPP/INCIDNT RAD				
	2 Supplies incident Other Dx	MED-SUR SUPP INCIDNT ODX				
	3 Surgical Dressings	SURG DRESSING				
	4 FDA Investigation Devices	IDE				
	63X Pharmacy					
	0 Reserved					
	1 Single Source Drug	DRUG/SINGLE				
	2 Multiple Source Drug	DRUG/MULT				
	3 Restrictive Prescription	DRUG/RSTR				
	4 EPO $<$ 10,000 units	DRUG/EPO/$<$10,000 UNITS				
	5 EPO $>$10,000 units	DRUG/EPO/$>$10,000 UNITS				
	6 Drugs Req Detailed Coding	DRUGS/DETAIL CODE				
	7 Self-Admin Drugs	DRUGS/SELFADMIN				
	64X Home IV Therapy Services					
	0 General	IV THERAPY SVC				
	1 Nonroutine Nursing, Central Line	NONRT NURSING/CENTRAL				
	2 IV Site Care, Central Line	IV SITE CARE/CENTRAL				
	3 IV Start/Change, Peripheral Line	IV STRT/CHNG/PERIPHRL				
	4 Nonroutine Nursing, Peripheral Line	NONRT NURSING/PERIPHRL				
	5 Training Patient/Caregiver, Central Line	TRNG/PT/CARGVR/CENTRAL				
	6 Training, Disabled Patient, Central Line	TRNG DSBLPT/CENTRAL				
	7 Training Patient/Caregiver, Peripheral Line	TRNG/PT/CARGVR/PERIPHRL				
	8 Training, Disabled Patient, Peripheral Line	TRNG/DSBLPAT/PERIPHRL				
	9 Other IV Therapy Services	OTHER IV THERAPY SVC				

(continued)

FL	Field Name	Specifics	# Digits	Digits (A)lpha (N)um	Medicare (R)eq (O)pt	Others (R)eq (O)pt
42-43 (con-tinued)	**65X Hospice Services**					
	0 General	HOSPICE				
	1 Routine Home Care	HOSPICE/RTN HOME				
	2 Continuous Home Care	HOSPICE/CTNS HOME				
	3 Reserved					
	4 Reserved					
	5 Inpt Respite Care	HOSPICE/IP RESPITE				
	6 General Inpt Care (Nonrespite)	HOSPICE/IP NONRESPITE				
	7 Physician Services	HOSPICE/PHYSICIAN				
	9 Other Hospice	HOSPICE/OTHER				
	66X Respite Care (HHA Only)					
	0 General	RESPITE CARE				
	1 Hourly Chg/Skilled Nursing	RESPITE/SKILLED NURSE				
	2 Hourly Chg/HHA/ Homemaker	RESPITE/HMEAID/HMEMKE				
	9 Other Respite Care	RESPITE/CARE				
	67X Outpatient Special Residence					
	0 General	OP SPEC RES				
	1 Hospital-Based	OP SPEC RES/HOSP BASED				
	2 Contracted	OP SPEC RES/CONTRACTED				
	9 Other Special Residence	OP SPEC RES/OTHER				
	68X Not Assigned					
	69X Not Assigned					
	70X Cast Room					
	0 General	CAST ROOM				
	9 Other Cast Room	OTHER CAST ROOM				
	71X Recovery Room					
	0 General	RECOVERY ROOM				
	9 Other Recovery Room	OTHER RECOV RM				
	73X EKG/ECG					
	0 General	EKG/ECG				
	1 Holter Monitor	HOLTER MONT				
	2 Telemetry	TELEMETRY				
	9 Other EKG/ECG	OTHER EKG/ECG				
	74X EEG					
	0 General	EEG				
	9 Other EEG	OTHER EEG				
	75X Gastro-Intestinal Services					
	0 General	GASTRO-INTS SVS				
	9 Other Gastrointestinal	OTHER GASTRO-INTS				

TABLE 7–9   *continued*

FL	Field Name	Specifics	# Digits	Digits (A)lpha (N)um	Medicare (R)eq (O)pt	Others (R)eq (O)pt
42-43 (continued)	**76X Treatment/Observation Rm**					
	0 General	TREATMENT/OBSERVATION RM				
	1 Treatment Room	TREATMENT ROOM				
	2 Observation Room	OBSERVATION RM				
	9 Other Treatment Room	OTHER TREATMENT RM				
	77X Preventative Care Services					
	0 General	PREVENT CARE SVS				
	1 Vaccine Administration	VACCINE ADMIN				
	9 Other Prev Care Services	OTHER PREVENT				
	78X Telemedicine					
	0 General	TELEMEDICINE				
	9 Other Telemedicine	TELEMEDICINE/OTHER				
	79X Lithotripsy					
	0 General	LITHOTRIPSY				
	9 Other Lithotripsy	LITHOTRIPSY/OTHER				
	82X Hemodialysis-Outpatient/Home					
	0 General	HEMO/OP OR HOME				
	1 Hemodialysis/Composite or Other Rate	HEMO/COMPOSITE				
	2 Home Supplies	HEMO/HOME/SUPPL				
	3 Home Equipment	HEMO/HOME/EQUIP				
	4 Maintenance/100%	HEMO/HOME/100%				
	5 Support Services	HEMO/HOME/SUPSERV				
	9 Other Outpt Hemodialysis	HEMO/HOME/OTHER				
	83X Peritoneal Dialysis-Outpatient/Home					
	0 General	PERITONEAL/OP OR HOME				
	1 Peritoneal/Composite or Other Rate	PERTNL/COMPOSISTE				
	2 Home Supplies	PERTNL/HOME/SUPPL				
	3 Home Equipment	PERTNL/HOME/EQUIP				
	4 Maintenance/100%	PERTNL/HOME/100%				
	5 Support Services	PERTNL/HOME/SUPSERV				
	9 Other Peritoneal Dialysis	PERTNL/HOME/OTHER				
	84X Continuous Ambulatory Peritoneal Dialysis (CAPD) Outpatient/Home					
	0 General	CAPD/OP OR HOME				
	1 CAPD/Composite or Other Rate	CAPD/COMPOSITE				

(continued)

FL	Field Name	Specifics	# Digits	Digits (A)lpha (N)um	Medicare (R)eq (O)pt	Others (R)eq (O)pt
42-43 (con- tinued)	2 Home Supplies	CAPD/HOME/SUPPL				
	3 Home Equipment	CAPD/HOME/EQUIP				
	4 Maintenance/100%	CAPD/HOME/100%				
	5 Support Services	CAPD/HOME/SUPSERV				
	9 Other CAPD Dialysis	CAPD/HOME/OTHER				
	85X Continuous Cycling **Peritoneal Dialysis (CCPD)** **Outpatient/Home**					
	0 General	CCPD/OP OR HOME				
	1 CCPD/Composite or Other Rate	CCPD/COMPOSITE				
	2 Home Supplies	CCPD/HOME/SUPPL				
	3 Home Equipment	CCPD/HOME/EQUIP				
	4 Maintenance/100%	CCPD/HOME/100%				
	5 Support Services	CCPD/HOME/SUPSERV				
	9 Other CCPD Dialysis	CCPD/HOME/OTHER				
	86X Reserved Dialysis **National Assignment**					
	87X Reserved Dialysis State Assignment					
	88X Miscellaneous Dialysis					
	0 General	DIALY/MISC				
	1 Ultrafiltration	DIALY/ULTRAFILT				
	2 Home Dialysis Aid Visit	HOME DIALYSIS AID VISIT				
	9 Misc Dialysis Other	DIALY/MISC/OTHER				
	89X Reserved Natl Assignment					
	90X Psychiatric/Psychological **Treatments**					
	0 General	PSTAY TREATMENT				
	1 Electroshock Treatment	ELECTROSHOCK				
	2 Milieu Therapy	MILIEU THERAPY				
	3 Play Therapy	PLAY THERAPY				
	4 Activity Therapy	ACTIVITY THERAPY				
	9 Other	OTHER PSYCH RX				
	91X Psychiatric/Psychological **Services**					
	0 General	PSYCH/SERVICES				
	1 Rehabilitation	PSYCH/REHAB				
	2 Partial Hosp-Less Intensive	PSYCH/PARTIAL HOSP				
	3 Partial Hosp-Intensive	PSYCH/PARTIAL INTENSIVE				
	4 Individual Therapy	PSYCH/INDIV RX				

TABLE 7–9   *continued*

FL	Field Name	Specifics	# Digits	Digits (A)lpha (N)um	Medicare (R)eq (O)pt	Others (R)eq (O)pt
42-43 (con-tinued)	5 Group Therapy	PSYCH/GROUP RX				
	6 Family Therapy	PSYCH/FAMILY RX				
	7 Biofeedback	PSYCH/BIOFEED				
	8 Testing	PSYCH/TESTING				
	9 Other	PSYCH/OTHER				
	92X Other Dx Services					
	0 General	OTHER DX SVS				
	1 Peripheral Vascular Lab	PERI VASCUL LAB				
	2 Electromyelogram	EMG				
	3 Pap Smear	PAP SMEAR				
	4 Allergy Test	ALLERGY TEST				
	5 Pregnancy Test	PREG TEST				
	9 Other Dx Service	ADDITIONAL DX SVS				
	93X Med Rehab Day Program					
	1 Half Day	HALF DAY				
	2 Full Day	FULL DAY				
	94X Other Ther Services					
	0 General	OTHE RX SVS				
	1 Recreational Therapy	RECREATION RX				
	2 Education/Training	EDUC/TRAINING				
	3 Cardiac Rehab	CARDIAC REHAB				
	4 Drug Rehab	DRUG REHAB				
	5 Alcohol Rehab	ALCOHOL REHAB				
	6 Complex Med Equip-Routine	RTN COMPLX MED EQUIP-ROUT				
	7 Complex Med Equip-Ancillary	COMPLX MED EQUIP-ANX				
	9 Other Ther Services	ADDITIONAL RX SVS				
	95X Other Ther Services Extension of 94X					
	0 Reserved					
	1 Athletic Training	ATHLETIC TRAINING				
	2 Kinesiotherapy	KINESIOTHERAPY				
	96X Professional Fees					
	0 General	PRO FEE				
	1 Psychiatry	PRO FEE/PSYCH				
	2 Ophthalmology	PRO FEE/EYE				
	3 Anesthesiologist (MD)	PRO FEE/ANES MD				
	4 Anesthetist (CRNA)	PRO FEE/ANES CRNA				
	9 Other Prof Fees	OTHER PRO FEE				

(continued)

FL	Field Name	Specifics	# Digits	Digits (A)lpha (N)um	Medicare (R)eq (O)pt	Others (R)eq (O)pt
42-43 (con-tinued)	**97X Prof Fees continued**					
	1 Laboratory	PRO FEE/LAB				
	2 Radiology-Dx	PRO FEE/RAD/DX				
	3 Radiology-Therapeutic	PRO FEE/RAD/RX				
	4 Radiology-Nuclear Med	PRO FEE/NUC MED				
	5 Operating Room	PRO FEE/OR				
	6 Respiratory Therapy	PRO FEE/RESPIR				
	7 Physical Therapy	PRO FEE/PHYSI				
	8 Occupational Therapy	PRO FEE/OCUPA				
	9 Speech Pathology	PRO FEE/SPEECH				
	98X Prof Fees continued					
	1 Emergency Room	PRO FEE/ER				
	2 Outpatient Services	PRO FEE/OUTPT				
	3 Clinic	PRO FEE/CLINIC				
	4 Medical Social Services	PRO FEE/SOC SVC				
	5 EKG	PRO FEE/EKG				
	6 EEG	PRO FEE/EEG				
	7 Hospital Visit	PRO FEE/HOS VIS				
	8 Consultation	PRO FEE/CONSULT				
	9 Private Duty Nurse	PEE/PVT NURSE				
	99X Patient Convenience Items					
	0 General	PT CONVENIENCE				
	1 Cafeteria/Guest Tray	CAFETERIA				
	2 Private Linen Service	LINEN				
	3 Telephone/Telegraph	TELEPHONE				
	4 TV/Radio	TV/RADIO				
	5 Nonpatient Room Rentals	NONPT ROOM RENT				
	6 Late Discharge Charge	LATE DISCHARGE				
	7 Admission Kits	ADMIT KITS				
	8 Beauty Shop/Barber	BARBER/BEAUTY				
	9 Other Pt Convenience Items	PT CONVENCE/OTHER				
	100X – 209X Reserved for National Assignment					
	210X Alternative Therapy Svcs					
	0 General					
	1 Acupuncture					
	2 Acupressure					
	3 Massage					
	4 Reflexology					
	5 Biofeedback					

TABLE 7–9   *continued*

FL	Field Name	Specifics	# Digits	Digits (A)lpha (N)um	Medicare (R)eq (O)pt	Others (R)eq (O)pt
42-43 (con-tinued)	6 Hypnosis 9 Other Alternative Ther Svcs					
44	HCPCS/Rates/HIPPS Rate Codes	Accommodation Code or HCPCS Code Outpatient claims Accommodation Code Inpatient Claims Supplies/ESRD Services/ Drugs NO HCPCS Code Req Outpt Claim Multiple Codes List in Revenue Code Sequence Rates - Dollar value whole numbers decimal point/cents	2/ Codes 8/Amts	Alpha-Num	REQ	REQ
45	Service Date	Line item dates of service required where HCPCS code required Dates must fall within dates in FL 6	8	Num	REQ Outpt	REQ Outpt
46	Service Units	Required for following revenue code groups: 10X-15X 636 20X-21X 274 38X 30X-31X 51X, 52X 410/420/430/440 80X 480/910/943 29X 60X 450/452/459 32X/333/34X 35X/40X/61X	7 per line	Num	REQ Outpt	REQ Outpt
47	Total Charges	Units X Line Item Service Grand Total Listed as last line item Revenue Code 01 Includes Covered/Noncovered Chgs EXCEPT Medicare (only covered)	9	Num	REQ	REQ
48	Noncovered Charges	Utilized when noncovered days are indicated in FL 8		Num	REQ if applic	REQ if applic
49	Unlabeled Field					

(continued)

FL	Field Name	Specifics	# Digits	Digits (A)lpha (N)um	Medicare (R)eq (O)pt	Others (R)eq (O)pt
PAYER/INSURED/EMPLOYER INFO (FL 50-66)						

50	Payer Identification	A Primary Payer
		B Secondary Payer
		C Tertiary Payer
		Electronic must include
		  Payer ID #
		Paper must include Carrier
		  Code # and Name
		  (Available from FI)
			25	Alpha Num	REQ	REQ

51	Provider Number	Assigned by Payer Listed in 50		Alpha Num	REQ	REQ most
52	Release of Information Certification Indicator	Y - Yes (On File) N - No (Not on File) R - Restricted (limited authority)	1	Alpha	REQ	REQ most

53	Assignment of Benefits Certification Indicator	Y - Yes/Benefits Assigned
		   Payment to Provider
		N - No/Benefits Not Assigned
		   Payment to Insured
			1	Alpha	REQ	REQ

54	Prior Payments-Payers and Pt	All services other than
		  Medicare Inpt
		7 positions - dollars
		2 positions - cents
		1 position - character space for
		   credit if applicable
			10	Num	REQ Outpt	REQ

55	Estimated Amount Due	Estimated Due from Payer - Any Payments 10 positions in each line (A-D) 7 positions - dollars 2 positions - cents 1 position - character space for credit if applicable	10	Num	NO	NO
56-57	Unlabeled Fields					

58	Insured's Name	Patient or Policyholder
		25 characters Line A-D
		Must be exactly as on
		  insurance card
		Use comma to separate
		  names
		No titles
			25	Alpha Num	REQ	REQ

TABLE 7–9   *continued*

FL	Field Name	Specifics	# Digits	Digits (A)lpha (N)um	Medicare (R)eq (O)pt	Others (R)eq (O)pt
59	Patient's Relationship to Insured		2	Num	REQ Care 2nd	REQ
		01 - Patient Insured				
		02 - Spouse				
		03 - Natural Child				
		04 - Natural Child/Insured Not Responsible				
		05 - Stepchild				
		06 - Foster Child				
		07 - Ward of Court				
		08 - Employee				
		09 - Unknown				
		10 - Handicapped Dependent				
		11 - Organ Donor				
		12 - Cadaver Donor				
		13 - Grandchild				
		14 - Niece/Nephew				
		15 - Insured Plaintiff				
		16 - Sponsored Dependent				
		17 - Minor Dependent of a Minor Dependent				
		18 - Parent				
		19 - Grandparent				
		20 - Life Partner				
		21-99 Reserved for National Assignment				
60	Certificate/Social Security #/Health Insurance Claim #	No spaces/hyphens/characters	19	Alpha Num	REQ	REQ
61	Insured Group Name		14	Alpha Num	REQ	REQ if applic
62	Insured Group Number		17	Alpha Num	NO	NO
63	Treatment Authorization Codes		18	Alpha Num	REQ	NO
64	Employment Status Code of the Insured			Num	REQ MSP	NO
		1 - Employed Full-Time				
		2 - Employed Part-Time				

(continued)

FL	Field Name	Specifics	# Digits	Digits (A)lpha (N)um	Medicare (R)eq (O)pt	Others (R)eq (O)pt
64 (continued)		3 - Not Employed 4 - Self-Employed 5 - Retired 6 - Active Military Duty 7-8 Reserved for National Assignment				
65	Employer Name of the Insured		24	Alpha Num	REQ	REQ
66	Employer Location of the Insured	Can be specific city, employer, location 35 AlphaNum per Line (A-C)	35	Alpha Num	REQ	

DIAGNOSIS/PROCEDURE CODES (FL 67-81)

FL	Field Name	Specifics	# Digits	Digits (A)lpha (N)um	Medicare (R)eq (O)pt	Others (R)eq (O)pt
67	Principal Diagnosis Code	Condition established after study chiefly responsible for resulting in hospital admission or hospital services Cannot be E code	6	Alpha Num	REQ	REQ
68-75	Other Diagnosis Codes	Patient condition(s) that co-exist at the time of admission/service or develop during the hospital stay or encounter	6	Alpha Num	REQ if applic	REQ if applic
76	Admitting Diagnosis/ Patient's Reason for Visit	ICD-9-CM that best describes the patient's diagnosis or reason for visit in the patient's words	6	Alpha Num	REQ	REQ
77	External Cause of Injury	External cause for injury, poisoning, adverse effect	6	Alpha Num	State Reg	State Reg
78	Unlabeled Field					
79	Procedure Coding Method Used	1-3 Reserved for State Assignment 4 CPT-4 5 HCPCS 6-8 Reserved for National Assignment 9 ICD-9-CM		Alpha Num	NO	REQ
80	Principal Procedure Code/Date	Inpatient principal procedure Required for outpt by some third-party carriers	7/Proc 8/Date	Alpha Num	REQ if applic	
81	Other Procedure Code/Date	Additional inpatient procedures or outpt procedures when applicable	7/Proc 8/Date	Alpha Num	REQ if applic	

TABLE 7–9   *continued*

FL	Field Name	Specifics	# Digits	Digits (A)lpha (N)um	Medicare (R)eq (O)pt	Others (R)eq (O)pt
ATTENDING PHYSICIAN INFORMATION (FL 82-83)						
82	Attending Physician ID	Physician primarily responsible for patient's medical care/treatment FORMAT: UPIN__LastName_First Name_MI	25	Alpha Num	REQ	REQ
83	Other Physician ID	Name of other than Attending Physician performing principal procedure First line optional exc Medicare Lower line required if procedure inpatient/outpatient claims	25/upper 32/lower	Alpha Num		
REMARKS (FL 84-86)						
84	Remarks	Explain reason for reporting non-covered days OR Overflow information FL 32-35, FL 36, FL 24-30 and FL 39-41 Format Ex: FL XX: Code, Date, Value	48	Alpha Num	REQ if applic	REQ
85	Provider Representative Signature	Signature certifies provider conforms with certifications on UB-92	22	Alpha Num	REQ	REQ
86	Date Bill Submitted	Date UB-92 Signed/Sent to Payer	10	Num	NO	REQ

Glossary

accounts receivable (A/R)   Unpaid accounts and uncollected balances.

acuity levels   An outpatient billing methodology that assigns levels of complexities based on history, examination and medical decision-making components.

add-on procedure   A procedure performed during the same session as another procedure or surgical code.

adjudication   Advisement of a patient by a third-party carrier regarding processing of the patient's claim.

admitting diagnosis   Information regarding patient status and medical services requested at the beginning of an encounter or admission provided by the admitting physician at the time of admission.

advance beneficiary notice (ABN)   A form that Medicare patients are requested to sign if services are believed not covered prior to provision.

allowance   The amount agreed upon by the carrier and the provider as payment in full.

ambulatory payment classifications (APCs)   A prospective payment system under Medicare for the facility component of ambulatory care rendered in hospital ambulatory surgery, emergency room and outpatient and ancillary department clinic settings.

appeal   A formal request for reconsideration when appropriate reimbursement has not been made or a request made to the insurance carrier for additional consideration and payment when payment does not appear to agree with the insurance carrier's contractual guidelines.

assignment of benefits   A document obtained during the admission/preadmission process indicating that the patient has "assigned" the right of payment directly to the facility, rather than monies for services being sent to the patient.

authorization number   A preassigned number issued by a third-party carrier designating preapproval of admission and procedures.

birthday rule   A rule that specifies that if a child has insurance coverage through both parents, the carrier of the parent whose birthday is closer to the child's birthday will be primary.

capitation plan   A form of HMO in which the patient is covered under a per member per month (PMPM).

center for medicare and medicaid services (CMS)   The government body that administers Medicare and Medicaid.

CHAMPUS   The Civilian Health and Medical Program of the Uniformed Services, a program to help active military personnel pay medical costs.

CHAMPVA   The Civilian Health and Medical Program of the Department of Veterans Affairs, a program to help retired military personnel pay medical costs.

charge capturing   The gathering of charge documents from all departments within a facility that have provided services to patients, the process by which a facility ensures that all services it performs have been coded and billed appropriately.

charge description master (CDM) or chargemaster   The part of a facility's computerized billing system that maintains all services, codes and charges provided by the facility.

charge ticket or encounter form   A form on which facility personnel record patient information, services performed and a diagnosis.

claims scrubber   Software that detects errors in electronic claims.

clean claim   A claim without errors or omissions that meets all predetermined specifications by the carrier.

CMS 1450   The Uniform Billing form, sometimes referred to as HCFA 1450 or UB-92.

CMS 1450/UB-92 claim form   A Uniform Billing form by which compensation is considered for inpatient and outpatient facilities.

coinsurance   A certain percentage of services sometimes required to be paid by the patient.

collection agency   An agency outside the facility contracted to tend to uncollected accounts.

collections   The department of a facility responsible for billing and collection of patient balances.

commercial insurance   Carriers that do not restrict their enrollees as to where their services may be provided.

complications and comorbidities (CCs)   Secondary diagnoses that can affect the assignment of the DRG and reimbursement.

condition codes   Codes that identify special circumstances, events, or conditions that surround the services provided on a claim.

consent to treat   An authorization for the provider and facility to provide those services that are considered medically necessary.

contractual write-off   The difference between the facility charge and the allowance.

co-payment   A set amount required to be paid by the patient.

CPT-4 (Current Procedural Terminology, 4ᵗʰ edition)   The official resource for procedural codes, rules and guidelines.

deductible   The amount a patient must pay out of pocket before their carrier begins payment for services.

diagnosis related group (DRG)   Codes assigned based on the diagnostic evaluation performed during the patient's inpatient stay.

diagnosis related groups (DRGs)   Categories of diagnosis and treatment into which patients are grouped under PPS methodology.

dirty claim   A claim with errors or omissions, or that does not meet all the carrier's specifications.

E & M (evaluation and management)   The process by which physician-patient encounters are translated into codes to facilitate billing.

E codes   Codes for External Cause. E codes are never utilized as a primary diagnosis, but only to provide additional information regarding the cause for the injury, illness, or condition that precipitated the encounter.

each, each additional, or **per**   Terms that indicate the possibility of multiple units of service.

electronic media claim (EMC)   The submission of a UB-92 electronically, via computer.

encoding software   Software used by many larger facilities that allows the coder to enter diagnoses and procedures and assists in assigning the correct ICD-9-CM diagnostic and procedural codes and applying coding principles correctly.

exclusive provider organization (EPO)   A carrier plan in which the provider typically performs services only for a specific third-party carrier that does not provide services outside the network.

explanation of benefits (EOB)   A document that details the amount charged for a service, the allowance and any reason(s) for the denial of payment or reduction in payment.

fee for service (FFS)   A methodology for inpatient reimbursement that uses the actual expenses incurred by the facility for providing the medically necessary services to the patient.

form locators (FL)   Data elements on the UB-92 that provide specific information necessary to process a claim.

form records   The equivalent of form locators in electronic claims.

global service   A term applying to surgical codes indicating that the reimbursement for surgical services is inclusive of all preoperative, postoperative and surgical services performed by the surgeon and/or provider.

guarantor   The individual responsible for paying for services.

HCPCS (HCFA Common Procedure Coding System)   Codes in addition to ICD-9-CM diagnostic and procedural coding that are assigned for specific services provided.

health information management (HIM)   The area of a facility in which the process of reviewing documentation for services provided and assigning the appropriate ICD-9-CM and CPT-4 codes as applicable is typically performed.

health maintenance organization (HMO)   A managed care plan that controls health insurance costs by assigning each participant a primary care physician.

hospital-based physicians   Physicians who provide services only in a hospital setting.

ICD-9-CM (International Classification of Diseases, 9th edition, Clinical Modification)   A guide to the international classification of diseases designed for hospital billers and coders and insurance claim examiners.

lifetime reserve days   A reserve of inpatient days that may be utilized by the Medicare beneficiary when covered hospital days and coinsurance days have been exceeded during a specific period of time.

major diagnostic categories (MDCs)   The primary breakdown of principal diagnoses, based on patients who are clinically similar and use similar hospital resources.

managed care plan   An insurance plan that implements methods for controlling health costs, such as co-payments, primary care physicians and insurance carrier networks.

Medicaid   Federal funds for medical costs administered by individual states, typically provided to low-income, indigent and/or disabled patients.

medically indigent   Patients ineligible both for any third-party coverage and for Medicaid.

Medicare   Federal insurance for patients over the age of 65 or the disabled.

Medicare HMO replacement   A product available in lieu of federal Medicare that may cover additional services such as prescriptions and eyeglasses.

medigap   Insurance carriers who supplement Medicare, usually covering the coinsurance amount not covered by Medicare.

modifier codes   Two-digit codes that are appended to CPT-4 codes to describe unusual circumstances.

NEC (Not Elsewhere Classified)   No specific diagnosis code for the condition, even though the physician may have been very specific in his diagnostic statement.

neoplasms   Literally, "new growths," which may be either benign or malignant in nature.

new technology services   APC groups that do not take into consideration the clinical aspect of the services they represent, only the cost of the items themselves.

nonavailability statement (NAS)   A statement preauthorizing inpatient care outside of a military treatment facility for military personnel with TRICARE benefits.

nonparticipating   A facility that requires the patient to be responsible for the difference between the charges for service and the amount their carrier allows and pays for.

NOS (Not Otherwise Specified)   Physician documentation does not include any specific information about the condition.

occurrence codes   Codes conveying information regarding events connected to a claim that affect how it will be processed.

outpatient code editor   A reimbursement tool developed by CMS and used by fiscal intermediaries to identify errors in claims data.

outpatient prospective payment system (OPPS)   A prospective payment system under Medicare for hospital outpatient services, certain Part B services furnished to hospital inpatients who have no Part A coverage, and partial hospitalization services furnished by community mental health centers.

participating   A facility that has contracted with a carrier to perform services for a predetermined fee.

payment status indicators   Elements of APC reimbursment methodology that identify how Medicare pays for various services that have been billed.

per diem   A methodology for inpatient reimbursement in which a fixed rate per day is paid for all services performed or provided by the facility.

per member per month (PMPM)   A set fee covering all services on a monthly basis regardless of the amount of services provided or not provided.

physician employees   Physicians employed by a hospital facility.

physician order   The document with which a physician requests specific services from a facility admitting a patient.

point of service (POS)   A "hybrid" carrier network plan that can function either like an HMO or a PPO, depending on the point of service.

preadmission certification   Authorization of services obtained from a third-party carrier during the admission/preadmission process.

preferred provider organization (PPO)   A carrier plan in which the participant is required to remain within a network of providers.

primary care physician (PCP)   A physician assigned to participants in a Health Maintenance Organization (HMO) who must approve all their health care in advance.

principal diagnosis   Chief reason for admission following services.

prospective payment system (PPS)   A methodology for inpatient reimbursement in which payment rates to hospitals are set before services are rendered, based on a reimbursement rate in which patients are categorized according to diagnosis and treatment that entails similar lengths of stay.

query process   Requests from the coder to the physician for additional clarification.

revenue codes   Four-digit codes on the UB-92/CMS-1450, the first two digits of which designate the revenue code category.

revenue codes   Three-digit codes that identify the department and/or sub-department a facility's services are supplied from.

separate procedure   A surgical procedure that is performed alone, for a specific reason at the time of that surgical session, as an integral part of another procedure, or incidental to another procedure.

share of cost   An amount the patient must pay before Medicaid will pay for services.

significant procedures   Procedures for which the multiple-procedure reduction does not apply.

table of drugs and chemicals   A table found in the ICD-9-CM diagnosis code book that is utilized for locating codes relating to encounters that are the result of adverse effects from drugs and chemicals.

third-party contract   An agreement among the three parties involved in a contract for medical services: the facility or provider, the patient and the insurance carrier.

transitional pass-through allowances   Payment service indicators under which additional payments may be made for certain drugs and medical devices.

TRICARE   A program offering military personnel and their dependents three plans to help pay medical costs: TRICARE standard, TRICARE prime and TRICARE extra.

TRICARE extra   TRICARE's PPO product.

TRICARE prime   TRICARE's HMO product.

TRICARE standard   Formerly CHAMPUS, a commercial/indemnity product to help military personnel and their dependents pay medical costs.

UB-92   Uniform Billing form 1992, the universal claim form accepted by Medicare and Medical fiscal intermediaries as well as other insurance carriers for services provided by a facility. Also known as the CMS-1450.

unlisted procedure   A code that should be utilized only when a procedure or surgery is performed for which there is no specific CPT-4 code.

UPIN   Unique Physician Identification Number, a number assigned by the Center for Medicare and Medicaid Services to every physician in the nation as a unique identifier.

V codes   Codes utilized for circumstances other than signs, symptoms, illness, or diagnosis of a condition.

volume 3 ICD-9-CM Procedural Codes   Procedural coding that describes what services were performed during an encounter.

workers' compensation   Insurance covering an employee's injury or illness resulting from their job.

working aged   Medicare-eligible patients who also possess group health insurance coverage through an employer.

Instructions for Appendix I and II Case Scenarios

The following inpatient (Appendix I) and outpatient (Appendix II) case scenarios represent actual medical records from inpatient and outpatient facilities. While a number of records would normally be reviewed for complete information, some of those documents utilized in the review process have been omitted here for length. For the purposes of these case scenarios, information normally included in nursing notes, individual note pages, and other documentation are included here in the progress notes and admission history and physicals.

These inpatient and outpatient case scenarios may be utilized at the completion of the appropriate sections of the textbook, or utilized when only inpatient and/or outpatient coding or inpatient/outpatient billing are being reviewed in class. Refer to the UB-92 completion information in the inpatient and outpatient billing chapters of this textbook for reference when completing this information. Utilize the current edition of ICD-9-CM (Volumes I, II, and III) and CPT-4 to complete the coding portions of the forms as appropriate.

The UB-92s for these cases may be completed manually with the use of a blank UB-92 form, or completed electronically on the CD-ROM included with this textbook. For instructions on how to complete the case scenarios on the CD-ROM, please refer to the Tutorial section on the CD menu.

While DRGs and APCs are not assigned by the coder on the UB-92 form, the student may be instructed to complete the DRG or APC assignment. This information is utilized by the facility in pre-determination of expected reimbursement. Should the student be required to assign DRG codes, refer to the DRG listing in the Inpatient section of the textbook. As the APC listing is extensive, only a portion was included in the textbook. For a complete and current APC listing, refer to the www.cms.org website.

The following information applies to all case scenarios in Appendix I and II:

Payer Information

Payer #, Name
007   Medicare/Aetna
642   Blue Cross/Blue Shield of ZA
700   Medicaid

899 Federated Care of ZA
937 Medicare
998 Self-Pay
5271 BCBS of ZA

Attending Physician

Elizabeth Diamond, MD
UPIN # 1134711

Appendix I

Inpatient Scenarios

CODING REGIONAL HOSPITAL
123 MAIN STREET, ANYWHERE, USA

HOSPITAL ADMISSION FORM

ACCOUNT NUMBER	MEDICAL RECORD NUMBER
	334357

PATIENT INFORMATION

PATIENT LAST NAME	FIRST NAME	MI	DOB	ADMIT DATE/TIME
WHITE	BLANCHE	J	02/18/1934	04/26/20XX 11:00PM

STREET ADDRESS	CITY/STATE/ZIP	AREA CODE/PHONE NUMBER
4566 SYCAMORE DRIVE	ANYWHERE, ZA 10000	111-344-84XX

SEX		RACE	AGE	RELIGIOUS PREFERENCE	OCCUPATION	FT	PT
M	F X						

PATIENT'S EMPLOYER	STREET ADDRESS	CITY/STATE/ZIP	AREA CODE/PHONE NUMBER
RETIRED			

EMERGENCY CONTACT

#1 LAST NAME	FIRST NAME	MI	AREA CODE/PHONE NUMBER	RELATIONSHIP
WHITE	RICHARD	W	111-344-84XX	Husband
#2 LAST NAME	FIRST NAME	MI	AREA CODE/PHONE NUMBER	RELATIONSHIP

GUARANTOR

#1 LAST NAME	FIRST NAME	MI	AREA CODE/PHONE NUMBER	RELATIONSHIP
WHITE	BLANCHE	J	111-344-84XX	
#2 LAST NAME	FIRST NAME	MI	AREA CODE/PHONE NUMBER	RELATIONSHIP

ADMISSION INFORMATION

ADMISSION STATUS	PATIENT TYPE	UNIT	ROOM	ATTENDING MD	UPIN #
INPATIENT	MED SURG	SURG	356	ELIZABETH DIAMOND MD	1134711

ADMITTING DIAGNOSIS
Abdominal Pain

INSURANCE INFORMATION

#1 PAYOR NAME	STREET ADDRESS	CITY/STATE/ZIP	PHONE NUMBER
MEDICARE/AETNA	PO BOX 1440	ANYWHERE, ZA 10000	888-332-55XX

POLICY NUMBER	GROUP NUMBER	GROUP NAME
3824597XXA		

SUBSCRIBER NAME	DOB	AUTHORIZATION NUMBER	DEDUCTIBLE
Patient			Inpatient $50

#2 PAYOR NAME	STREET ADDRESS	CITY/STATE/ZIP	PHONE NUMBER
BC BS OF ZA	PO BOX 1492	ANYWHERE, ZA 10000	888-325-52XX

POLICY NUMBER	GROUP NUMBER	GROUP NAME
3824597XX	INDIVIDUAL	

SUBSCRIBER NAME	DOB	AUTHORIZATION NUMBER	DEDUCTIBLE
SAME	SAME		Inpatient $100

PROVIDER NUMBER	PROCEDURES/SERVICES	
	Semi Private Visit	$550.00
	X-Ray, Abdomen	$175.00
Medicare Provider #005437	Abdomen US	$280.00
BCBS # 77374	IV Supplies (5)	$150.00
	IV Meds	$2,500.00
Admitted 04/26/xx Through ER	IV Solutions (5)	$100.00
	Lab Urol	$150.00
	Lab Chemistry	$1,500.00

CONTROL NUMBER
0010001

ATTENDING PHYSICIAN _____ DATE _____

PATIENT RECORD   ORIGINAL

Inpatient Case 1

CODING REGIONAL HOSPITAL
123 MAIN STREET, ANYWHERE, USA

HISTORY AND PHYSICAL EXAMINATION

WHITE, BLANCHE   Joseph Smith, MD

ADMITTED: 04/26/20XX

MEDICAL RECORD NUMBER: 334357

Patient is an 89-year-old female who presents with abdominal pain, nausea, vomiting and weakness. She also has had a fairly substantial weight loss over the last year or so. Symptoms started getting worse yesterday. She denies fever or chills. Bowels have moved, although not substantially; she says she really has not eaten enough to have a bowel movement at this time. She denied any blood in her emesis. No blood in her stool. The pain seems to be in the epigastric area, although it seems to radiate a little bit to the right side. Denies pain into the back at all. She also denies chest pain. She has become weak, enough that she has fallen. Falling has been a problem for her in the past, but she has not had a fall for quite some time.

PAST MEDICAL HISTORY: Hypertension, cholelithiasis, depression, osteoarthritis, and CHF. She also has cholelithiasis but no cholecystitis. She reports the recent onset of Type II diabetes mellitus. She reports an allergy to penicillin and amoxicillin.

FAMILY AND SOCIAL HISTORY: Noncontributory except she does smoke.

REVIEW OF SYSTEMS: Denies dysuria or any difficulty urinating. She denies fever, chills or any swelling in her upper or lower extremities. No difficulties reported in breathing, joint pain, specifically knee pain she has reported in the past.

PHYSICAL EXAM

General:	Alert, oriented, in no obvious distress.
Vital Signs:	Temperature 98.4, respiration 20, BP 117/43.
HEENT:	Negative.
Neck:	Supple, no thyromegaly.
Chest:	Clear.
Heart:	Regular rate and rhythm, normal S1, S2, no gallops, rubs or murmurs.
Abdomen:	Soft, epigastric tenderness. No mass or organomegaly. No guarding, rebound or rigidity noted.
Back:	No pain or spinal tenderness is noted on exam.
Extremities:	No swelling or edema noted.
Neurological:	She appears a little less alert and oriented than she has in the past.

LABORATORY/RADIOLOGY: Lab tests include WBC of 13,200, hemoglobin 11.8, platelet count 220,000. Differential appears within normal range. Panel 20 shows a decreased sodium of 133, potassium 3.3, BUN and creatinine are 34 and 1.4. Calcium is 8.1, bilirubin 1.1. Proteins normal, liver functions normal and TSH is 2.2. Urinalysis is normal.

Inpatient Case 1

WHITE, BLANCHE

ADMITTED: 04/26/20XX

Joseph Smith, MD

MEDICAL RECORD NUMBER: 334357

Page Two (continued)

X-RAY: Flat and upright of her abdomen are pending at this time.

ASSESSMENT: Patient with abdominal pain, nausea, and weakness. This would be recurrent cholelithiasis or gastroenteritis.

PLAN: Admit to hospital, and will give her medications for her nausea. IV fluids for rehydration and watch for fever, chills. If things do not improve, will order ultrasound or CT.

Joseph Smith, M.D.

Inpatient Case 1

CODING REGIONAL HOSPITAL
123 MAIN STREET, ANYWHERE, USA

PROGRESS NOTE

DATE: 04/27/20XX

TIME:

S: Patient is feeling a little better, and she is not having as much abdominal pain. She is still experiencing some trouble with confusion and loose stools. She appears to have lapsing periods of confusion, even seeing people that are not actually there. Otherwise she indicates she feels somewhat better. Denies chest pain, but reports she still feels a little weak.

O: Afebrile, vital signs normal. Chest clear, heart regular rhythm, extremities show no appearance of edema.

A: Abdominal pain with diarrhea, improved. Confusion that may be related to infection.

P: Will get blood cultures and start her on IV medications. If her confusion continues, may determine CT scan or ultrasound would be appropriate.

Joseph Smith, M.D.

PATIENT ID

WHITE, BLANCHE

Admit: 04/26/20XX

MR #334357

PROGRESS NOTE   **Coding Regional Hospital**

Inpatient Case 1

CODING REGIONAL HOSPITAL
123 MAIN STREET, ANYWHERE, USA

PROGRESS NOTE

DATE: 04/28/20XX

TIME:

S: Patient is noticeably more alert this morning. She ate breakfast and indicates she is having little or no abdominal pain today. She is tolerating her Levaquin and experiencing no chest pain or SOB.

O: Afebrile, vital signs normal, chest clear, heart regular rhythm. Abdomen is soft, has positive bowel sounds with no masses or organomegaly noted.

A: Abdominal pain. Certainly would consider cholelithiasis or diverticulitis. With her significant weight loss, would also consider other causes, including the possibility of cancer.

P: Will set up abdominal ultrasound. Will continue IV medications. She also needs a colonoscopy for her diarrhea; however, we will wait until she is stable and order on an outpatient basis. Seems to be tolerating Amaryl well.

Joseph Smith, M.D.

PATIENT ID
WHITE, BLANCHE
Admit: 04/26/20XX
MR #334357

PROGRESS NOTE   **Coding Regional Hospital**

Inpatient Case 1

CODING REGIONAL HOSPITAL
123 MAIN STREET, ANYWHERE, USA

PROGRESS NOTE

DATE: 04/29/20XX

TIME:

S: Patient doing OK. Her diarrhea has resolved and she indicates her abdominal pain has resolved. Appetite has improved. Sugars are just a bit low this morning.

O: Patient remains afebrile with chest clear, heart normal. Abdomen is soft, no masses or organomegaly.

Laboratory blood work is improved.

A: Abdominal pain with fever, possible diverticulitis or cholelithiasis

P: Will await results of ultrasound and then make decision regarding future care.

Joseph Smith, M.D.

PATIENT ID

WHITE, BLANCHE

Admit: 04/26/20XX

MR #334357

PROGRESS NOTE   **Coding Regional Hospital**

Inpatient Case 1

CODING REGIONAL HOSPITAL
123 MAIN STREET, ANYWHERE, USA

PROGRESS NOTE

DATE: 04/30/20XX

TIME:

S: Patient seems to be improving daily. She has had no abdominal pain, fever, chills, and her blood sugar is stable.

O: Afebrile, vital signs stable, chest clear. Heart is normal, extremities no edema.

A: Abdominal pain, possible diverticulitis vs cholelithiasis, she certainly has the classic symptoms for gallbladder disease.

P: Switch to oral Levaquin, continue the Amaryl and arrange for OT/PT in order to stabilize her strength when walking. Will schedule in the next week to 10 days for a colonoscopy on an outpatient basis.

Joseph Smith, M.D.

PATIENT ID
WHITE, BLANCHE
Admit: 04/26/20XX
MR #334357

PROGRESS NOTE   **Coding Regional Hospital**

Inpatient Case 1

CODING REGIONAL HOSPITAL
123 MAIN STREET, ANYWHERE, USA

RADIOLOGY REPORT

MR#: 334357
PATIENT NAME: WHITE, BLANCHE
DOB: 02/18/1934

Dr. Joseph Smith

CLINICAL SUMMARY: Abdominal pain, R/O cholelithiasis

ABDOMEN: Supine and upright views were obtained. No free air was seen. Degenerative changes through the lumbar spine. There is calcification in the right upper quadrant, probably a gallstone. No evidence of bowel obstruction or masses.

CONCLUSION: Degenerative changes.
Probable gallstone.
No acute abnormalities seen.

Ddt/mm

D: 04/30/20XX
T: 04/30/20XX

Dr. Joseph Smith	Date

Inpatient Case 1

CODING REGIONAL HOSPITAL
123 MAIN STREET, ANYWHERE, USA

RADIOLOGY REPORT

MR#: 334357
PATIENT NAME: WHITE, BLANCHE
DOB: 02/18/1934

Dr. Joseph Smith

CLINICAL SUMMARY: Abdominal pain, R/O cholelithiasis

ABDOMINAL SONOGRAM

Transverse and longitudinal images were obtained. They confirm a single large stone in the lumen of the gallbladder. No gallbladder wall thickening or biliary duct dilatation seems to have taken place.

The visualized portions of the liver and kidneys appear normal.

CONCLUSION: Cholelithiasis.

Ddt/mm

D: 04/30/20XX
T: 04/30/20XX

Dr. Joseph Smith   Date

Inpatient Case 1

CODING REGIONAL HOSPITAL
123 MAIN STREET, ANYWHERE, USA

DISCHARGE SUMMARY

PATIENT NAME: WHITE, BLANCHE #334357
DOB: 02/18/1934

ADMITTED: 04/26/20XX
DISCHARGED: 04/30/20XX

DISCHARGE DIAGNOSES:
1. Abdominal pain with fever
2. Cholelithiasis
3. Confusion
4. Hypertension
5. Depression
6. Osteoarthritis
7. Congestive heart failure
8. Diabetes mellitus type II

HISTORY: Patient is an 89-year-old female who presented with abdominal pain, nausea and vomiting. She was also weak. She had lost some weight, mostly, I think, because of dietary measures to control her newly diagnosed diabetes. She had no fever or chills. Her BMs had been fairly regular although not substantial. I do not feel that she is eating enough because of her recent symptoms to make bowel movements. There was no diarrhea. There has been no blood in the stool. She did have an emesis earlier that had no blood in it. Pain seemed to be over the epigastrium and left side, sometimes would radiate to the right side.

On exam, temperature was 98.4, respiratory rate 20, blood pressure 117/43. HEENT examination was negative. Chest was clear. Heart had a regular rhythm, normal S1, S2, no gallops, rubs or murmurs. The abdomen was soft, there was epigastric tenderness. No mass or organomegaly. There was no guarding, rebound or rigidity. Extremities had no edema.

LABORATORY AND RADIOLOGY STUDIES: Lab tests included a CBC showing a white count of 15,200, hemoglobin 11.8, platelet count 220,000. Follow-ups remained stable with an improving white count of 7,600. Hemoglobin had dropped to 10.8 with hydration.

On admission her sodium was 133, potassium 3.3, BUN was elevated at 34, blood sugar 193. Calcium was low at 8.1. Bilirubin was up to 1.1 and her TSH was 2.2. Her sugars were followed in the hospital and they ranged fairly stable with a high being noted at 195, low of 75. Her potassium did respond to supplementation and was 3.9 on discharge. Her sodium also improved to 137 by discharge. BUN was back to normal, as was the creatinine. Liver function testing was normal by discharge.

Inpatient Case 1

CODING REGIONAL HOSPITAL
123 MAIN STREET, ANYWHERE, USA

DISCHARGE SUMMARY

PATIENT NAME: WHITE, BLANCHE #334357
DOB: 05/17/20XX

ADMITTED: 04/26/20XX
DISCHARGED: 04/30/20XX

Page Two (continued)

Urinalysis was remarkable for 2-3 WBCs per hpf. Blood cultures were negative.

Flat and upright of abdomen showed degenerative changes and a probable gallstone.

Abdominal ultrasound showed cholelithiasis.

HOSPITAL COURSE: Patient was admitted to the hospital because of her abdominal symptoms. She was started on Protonix 40 mg IV as well as Demerol for pain. Her pre-hospital medications were continued. Blood cultures were obtained and she was placed on Levaquin 500 mg every 24 hours. Amaryl was also started for her blood sugars, which remained stable except for a low of 56. She was a little symptomatic with this and so sugar was given. Her potassium was supplemented with cocktails in addition to the IV fluids. Over the course of her hospitalization she did feel better with her stomach. She did have some trouble with confusion on occasion, but mostly with the initial episode of her illness and during the time she had a fever. Over the course of her stay, however, she was still weak, and we needed to watch her blood sugars closely. She was switched to oral Levaquin, told to monitor her blood sugars closely, continue the Amaryl. She will be started on OT and PT to help in strengthening her gait.

Joseph Smith, MD

D: 04/30/20XX
T: 05/02/20XX

Inpatient Case 1

CODING REGIONAL HOSPITAL
123 MAIN STREET, ANYWHERE, USA

HOSPITAL ADMISSION FORM

ACCOUNT NUMBER	MEDICAL RECORD NUMBER
	694171

PATIENT INFORMATION

PATIENT LAST NAME	FIRST NAME	MI	DOB	ADMIT DATE/TIME
GREENE	ROBERT	J	03/01/56	05/07/20XX 5:30AM

STREET ADDRESS	CITY/STATE/ZIP	AREA CODE/PHONE NUMBER
34 BROAD AVENUE	ANYWHERE, ZA 10000	111-324-84XX

SEX	RACE	AGE	RELIGIOUS PREFERENCE	OCCUPATION	
M [X] F [ ]				SALES	FT[ ] PT[ ]

PATIENT'S EMPLOYER	STREET ADDRESS	CITY/STATE/ZIP	AREA CODE/PHONE NUMBER
AUTOMOTIVE INDUST.	134 MAIN ST	ANYWHERE, ZA 10000	111-342-53XX

EMERGENCY CONTACT

#1 LAST NAME	FIRST NAME	MI	AREA CODE/PHONE NUMBER	RELATIONSHIP
GREENE	MABEL	L	111-324-84XX	
#2 LAST NAME	FIRST NAME	MI	AREA CODE/PHONE NUMBER	RELATIONSHIP

GUARANTOR

#1 LAST NAME	FIRST NAME	MI	AREA CODE/PHONE NUMBER	RELATIONSHIP
GREENE	ROBERT	J	111-324-84XX	
#2 LAST NAME	FIRST NAME	MI	AREA CODE/PHONE NUMBER	RELATIONSHIP

ADMISSION INFORMATION

ADMISSION STATUS	PATIENT TYPE	UNIT	ROOM	ATTENDING MD	UPIN #
INPATIENT	SURG	SURG	367	ELIZABETH DIAMOND MD	1134711

ADMITTING DIAGNOSIS
Pain, swelling, left thigh

INSURANCE INFORMATION

#1 PAYOR NAME	STREET ADDRESS	CITY/STATE/ZIP	PHONE NUMBER
BC BS OF ZA	PO BOX 1492	ANYWHERE, ZA 10000	888-325-52XX

POLICY NUMBER	GROUP NUMBER	GROUP NAME
257-81-12XX	ZA113	AUTOMOTIVE INDUSTRIES, INC

SUBSCRIBER NAME	DOB	AUTHORIZATION NUMBER	DEDUCTIBLE
GREENE, ROBERT	SAME		

#2 PAYOR NAME	STREET ADDRESS	CITY/STATE/ZIP	PHONE NUMBER
POLICY NUMBER	GROUP NUMBER	GROUP NAME	
SUBSCRIBER NAME	DOB	AUTHORIZATION NUMBER	DEDUCTIBLE

PROVIDER NUMBER

BC BS #005437
Admitted through ER

PROCEDURES/SERVICES	
Semi Private Room	$550.00
X-Ray, Diagnostic	$200.00
OR	$1,000.00
Anesthesia	$1,000.00
Surgical Supplies	$1,000.00

CONTROL NUMBER
0010002

ATTENDING PHYSICIAN _____ DATE _____

PATIENT RECORD ORIGINAL

Inpatient Case 1

CODING REGIONAL HOSPITAL
123 MAIN STREET, ANYWHERE, USA

HISTORY AND PHYSICAL EXAMINATION

GREENE, ROBERT J.   James Jones, MD

ADMITTED: 05/07/20XX

MEDICAL RECORD NUMBER: 694171

CHIEF COMPLAINT: Pain, swelling, left thigh

HISTORY OF PRESENT ILLNESS: Male patient who fell off a ladder earlier today sustaining blunt trauma to his left thigh. He is having significant pain with ambulation and range of motion of the leg. Aspiration was attempted; however, it was too solidified.

ALLERGIES: None.

MEDICATIONS: None.

MEDICAL HISTORY: Seasonal allergies, arthritis and headaches.

SOCIAL HISTORY: Nondrinker, nonsmoker.

REVIEW OF SYSTEMS: Leg swelling, history of depression.

PREVIOUS SURGERIES: Includes knee surgery.

PHYSICAL EXAM:

General:	Well-developed, well-nourished male.
HEENT:	Normocephalic, atraumatic.
Neck:	Soft, supple.
Lungs:	Clear.
Heart:	Regular rate and rhythm.
Abdomen:	Soft and nontender.
Extremities:	Overall, symmetric. Negative clubbing, cyanosis, edema. Fairly large hematoma on the midlateral thigh on the left. Extremely tender to palpation. No sign of infection; however, hematoma appears to need to be relieved.
Neurological:	Patient appears to be somewhat disoriented, with possible minimal neurological deficit.

X-rays show no bony abnormality.

IMPRESSION: Hematoma, left thigh.
Possible neurological deficit due to concussion from fall.

Inpatient Case 2

GREENE, ROBERT J.   James Jones, MD

ADMITTED: 05/07/20XX

MEDICAL RECORD NUMBER: 694171

Page Two (continued)

PLAN: Will admit to observe for possible concussion and will schedule
                   evacuation of hematoma while inpatient.

Inpatient Case 2

CODING REGIONAL HOSPITAL
123 MAIN STREET, ANYWHERE, USA

PROGRESS NOTE

DATE: 05/08/20XX

TIME:

Patient appears stable, had good evening with no neurological deficit noted. Patient appears alert and oriented times four. Hematoma site is clean and dry. Dressings are changed. Patient will be discharged with instructions to follow up in 48 hours with primary care physician. Patient cautioned to watch for neurological changes, and head sheet is given for cautions. Cautioned patient to stay with another individual and be observed for any signs of confusion, irritability and be returned immediately if they appear.

Elizabeth Diamond, MD

PATIENT ID
GREENE, ROBERT J.
Admit: 05/07/20XX
MR #694171

PROGRESS NOTE   **Coding Regional Hospital**

Inpatient Case 2

CODING REGIONAL HOSPITAL
123 MAIN STREET, ANYWHERE, USA

OPERATIVE REPORT

PREOPERATIVE DIAGNOSIS: Left thigh hematoma.

POSTOPERATIVE DIAGNOSIS: Left thigh hematoma with iliotibial band rupture.

OPERATIVE PROCEDURE: Evacuation of left thigh hematoma with iliotibial band repair.

The patient was taken to the operating room and, after IV sedation was administered, his left lower extremity was prepped and draped in a sterile fashion. A mixture of 1% lidocaine and .5% Marcaine was used for local anesthesia. A 6 cm skin incision was made and sharp dissection down to the ITB was performed. It was found to be partially ruptured longitudinally. This was split further and approximately 400 cc of clotted blood was expressed. This appeared to track both proximally and distally under the iliotibial band. This was irrigated copiously and the area was inspected for arterial or venous bleeding. The ITB was repaired with 0 Vicryl, subcutaneous with 2-0 Vicryl and the skin with Biosyn and steri-strips. The patient was taken to the recovery room in stable condition.

Elizabeth Diamond, MD

Inpatient Case 2

CODING REGIONAL HOSPITAL
123 MAIN STREET, ANYWHERE, USA

HOSPITAL ADMISSION FORM	ACCOUNT NUMBER			MEDICAL RECORD NUMBER 873496

PATIENT INFORMATION

PATIENT LAST NAME WILSON	FIRST NAME THOMAS	MI W	DOB 04/17/1953	ADMIT DATE/TIME 08/11/20XX

STREET ADDRESS 841 BROAD AVE	CITY/STATE/ZIP ANYWHERE, ZA 10000	AREA CODE/PHONE NUMBER 111-842-88XX

SEX M [X] F [ ]	RACE	AGE	RELIGIOUS PREFERENCE	OCCUPATION SALES	FT [X] PT [ ]

PATIENT'S EMPLOYER ACME MEDICAL	STREET ADDRESS 4320 MAIN ST	CITY/STATE/ZIP ANYWHERE, ZA 10000	AREA CODE/PHONE NUMBER 111-843-81XX

EMERGENCY CONTACT

#1 LAST NAME WILSON	FIRST NAME NATALIE	MI	AREA CODE/PHONE NUMBER 111-842-88XX	RELATIONSHIP Wife
#2 LAST NAME	FIRST NAME	MI	AREA CODE/PHONE NUMBER	RELATIONSHIP

GUARANTOR

#1 LAST NAME WILSON	FIRST NAME THOMAS	MI W	AREA CODE/PHONE NUMBER 111-842-88XX	RELATIONSHIP
#2 LAST NAME	FIRST NAME	MI	AREA CODE/PHONE NUMBER	RELATIONSHIP

ADMISSION INFORMATION

ADMISSION STATUS INPATIENT	PATIENT TYPE MED/SURG	UNIT SURG	ROOM 231	ATTENDING MD ELIZABETH DIAMOND MD	UPIN # 1134711

ADMITTING DIAGNOSIS
Fever

INSURANCE INFORMATION

#1 PAYOR NAME FEDERATED CARE OF ZA	STREET ADDRESS 123 MAPLE ST	CITY/STATE/ZIP ANYWHERE, ZA 10000	PHONE NUMBER 800-338-90XX
POLICY NUMBER 3525078XX	GROUP NUMBER 247ZA	GROUP NAME ACME MEDICAL	
SUBSCRIBER NAME SAME	DOB SAME	AUTHORIZATION NUMBER	DEDUCTIBLE $1,000 Inpt
#2 PAYOR NAME	STREET ADDRESS	CITY/STATE/ZIP	PHONE NUMBER
POLICY NUMBER	GROUP NUMBER	GROUP NAME	
SUBSCRIBER NAME	DOB	AUTHORIZATION NUMBER	DEDUCTIBLE

PROVIDER NUMBER Provider #5255	PROCEDURES/SERVICES	
	Semi Private Room(4)	$800.00
	IV Drugs	$200.00
Admitted through ER	IV Solutions (4)	$800.00
08/11/20XX	IV Supplies (4)	$400.00
	Chest X-Ray	$100.00
	Lab Chemistry	$200.00

CONTROL NUMBER
0010002

ATTENDING PHYSICIAN _____   DATE _____

PATIENT RECORD   ORIGINAL

Inpatient Case 3

CODING REGIONAL HOSPITAL
123 MAIN STREET, ANYWHERE, USA

HISTORY AND PHYSICAL EXAMINATION

WILSON, THOMAS	**Elizabeth Diamond, MD**
ADMITTED: 08/11/20XX	
MEDICAL RECORD NUMBER: 873496	

HPI: Patient is a male who presents with about 1 1/2 hours of severe chills. Patient has been hospitalized in the past for pneumonia on several occasions. He has been treated in the past when he experienced extreme respiratory difficulties and required steroids and antibiotics. Patient states he had been feeling well under sometime early this afternoon. Denies nausea or vomiting, denies diarrhea, cough, but does complain of some burning with urination.

PREVIOUS MEDICAL HISTORY: Significant for CAD, hyperlipidemia, anxiety/depression, HTN, GERD, renal insufficiency, history of right BBB, OA/OP, S/P CABG, knee replacement, cholecystectomy and appendectomy. Patient was hospitalized approximately 4 weeks ago for pneumonia.

CURRENT MEDICATIONS:
1. Vitamin E 400 U q am
2. Centrum Silver q day
3. Calcium with vitamin D, 600 mg BID
4. Tylenol 1000 mg BID
5. Lipitor 10 mg q HS
6. Elavil 50 mg q HS
7. Protonix 40 mg q HS
8. ASA 81 mg po q day
9. Lasix 40 mg BID
10. Nitroglycerin .4 mg SL prn
11. Potassium chloride 20 mEq po q am

ALLERGIES: Codeine, Zithromax, penicillin

SOCIAL HISTORY: Patient is married. Lives at home with wife. Has a lot of stress with family issues. Denies tobacco or alcohol use.

REVIEW OF SYSTEMS: Patient denies any visual changes, cough cold, chest pain. Denies nausea, vomiting, diarrhea. His only complaints are dysuria and chills. BP 149/56, Pulse 97, respirations 20. Temperature 99.8. Patient does not appear well and is chilling despite his normal temperature.

Inpatient Case 3

WILSON, THOMAS   **Elizabeth Diamond, MD**

ADMITTED: 08/11/20XX

MEDICAL RECORD NUMBER: 873496

Page Two (continued)

EXAM:

HEENT:	Pupils equal, round, reactive to light. Tympanic membranes clear, oral pharynx clear.
Neck:	Supple, no adenopathy, no JVD or carotid bruits.
Lungs:	Clear to auscultation.
Heart:	Regular rate and rhythm, slight systolic murmur.
Abdomen:	Obese, bowel sounds are present, abdomen soft, non-tender.
Extremities:	Trace to 1+ bipedal edema. No clubbing, cyanosis noted. Peripheral pulses are intact.
Neurological:	Shows cranial nerves 2-12 intact.

LABORATORY/X-RAYS: Chest x-ray essentially clear. May be mild cardiomegaly but no definite infiltrates. White count 12.8 with 81% segs, 12% lymphs. Hemoglobin of 14.9. Hematocrit of 43.9. Glucose is slightly elevated at 114. BUN 16, Creatinine 1.3, Sodium 139, Potassium 4.2, Chloride is 98. Carbon dioxide 31, calcium 8.1, total protein 8.6, albumin 4.1, AST is 21, ALT 4, Alk Phos 158, Total bili is 7. Urinalysis shows clear yellow with a specific gravity of 1.010 and no evidence of leukocytes or bacteria. Glucose is negative, last WBC is 5.8.

ASSESSMENT/PLAN: Will admit patient with fever of unknown origin. Will start IV fluids and IV Claforan. If temperature becomes elevated above 101, will draw blood cultures. Will also repeat WBC in the AM.

Elizabeth Diamond, MD

Inpatient Case 3

CODING REGIONAL HOSPITAL
123 MAIN STREET, ANYWHERE, USA

PROGRESS NOTE

DATE: 08/12/20XX

TIME:

Patient states feeling quite tired, but no more chills. Denies cough, nausea or vomiting. Still complaining of dysuria.

Lungs, clear. Temperature up to 102. Abdomen soft with bowel signs.

WBC 16.7, 85.8% seg,

ASSESSMENT/PLAN:
Fever of unknown origin, cultures pending
Continue IV fluids and IV antibiotics; will repeat UA due to symptoms

Elizabeth Diamond, MD

PATIENT ID
WILSON, THOMAS
Admit: 08/11/20XX
MR #873496

PROGRESS NOTE   **Coding Regional Hospital**

Inpatient Case 3

CODING REGIONAL HOSPITAL
123 MAIN STREET, ANYWHERE, USA

PROGRESS NOTE

DATE: 08/13/20XX

TIME:

Patient feels much better, not as fatigued, denies chest pain, SOB, denies any further symptoms of dysuria.

Vital signs stable, afebrile. Lungs, clear. Heart, regular rate and rhythm.

ASSESSMENT/PLAN:
Fever of unknown origin. Will recheck CBC and repeat CXR. Switch to oral antibiotics this afternoon with possible discharge tomorrow if stable.

Elizabeth Diamond, MD

PATIENT ID
WILSON, THOMAS
Admit: 08/11/20XX
MR #873496

PROGRESS NOTE   **Coding Regional Hospital**

Inpatient Case 3

CODING REGIONAL HOSPITAL
123 MAIN STREET, ANYWHERE, USA

PROGRESS NOTE

DATE: 08/14/20XX

TIME:

Patient feeling well without complaints, ready for discharge. No symptoms, fever, chills, chest pain, SOB.

Lungs, clear; abdomen, positive bowel sounds; vital signs stable.

ASSESSMENT/PLAN:
Fever of unknown origin which has resolved. Patient has remained afebrile since switching to oral antibiotics over 24 hours ago. Discharge to home and follow-up in one week.

Elizabeth Diamond, MD

PATIENT ID
WILSON, THOMAS
Admit: 08/11/20XX
MR #873496

PROGRESS NOTE   **Coding Regional Hospital**

Inpatient Case 3

CODING REGIONAL HOSPITAL
123 MAIN STREET, ANYWHERE, USA

RADIOLOGY REPORT

MR# 873496
PATIENT NAME: WILSON, THOMAS
DOB: 04/17/1953

Dr. Elizabeth Diamond

PA AND LATERAL CHEST, 08/11/20XX

FINDINGS: Lung markings are prominent without definite infiltrate identified. No change from x-ray taken 07/04/20XX. Heart and pulmonary vessels are normal.

Thomas O'Toole, MD

D: 08/11/20XX
T: 08/11/20XX

Thomas O'Toole, MD   Date

Inpatient Case 3

CODING REGIONAL HOSPITAL
123 MAIN STREET, ANYWHERE, USA
RADIOLOGY REPORT

MR# 873496
PATIENT NAME: WILSON, THOMAS
DOB: 04/17/1953

Dr. Elizabeth Diamond

PA AND LATERAL CHEST, 08/13/20XX

FINDINGS: Pulmonary markings are prominent without definite infiltrate identified. No change from 08/11/20XX. Heart size is normal.

Thomas OToole, MD
Radiologist

D: 08/13/20XX
T: 08/13/20XX

Thomas O'Toole, MD   Date

Inpatient Case 3

CODING REGIONAL HOSPITAL
123 MAIN STREET, ANYWHERE, USA
DISCHARGE SUMMARY

PATIENT NAME: WILSON, THOMAS W #873496
DOB: 04/17/1953

ADMITTED: 08/11/20XX
DISCHARGED: 08/14/20XX

ADMITTING DIAGNOSIS: Fever of unknown origin

DISCHARGE DIAGNOSES:
1. Bronchitis
2. Coronary artery disease
3. Hyperlipidemia
4. Anxiety/depression
5. Hypertension
6. Gastroesophageal reflux disease
7. Renal insufficiency
8. History of right bundle branch block
9. Osteoarthritis/osteoporosis
10. S/P CABG
11. Bilateral knee replacements 1981
12. S/P cholecystectomy
13. S/P appendectomy

Patient presented to the ER with acute onset of fever and chills. Patient was admitted. He had a white count of 12.8 on admission, which went up to 16.7 the following day. It subsequently resolved on the next day. Blood cultures were obtained as the patient was running temps of 103. These showed no growth over the period of 7 days. Chest x-ray revealed prominent lung markings without definite infiltrate. Patient was given IV fluids and IV antibiotics. He showed gradual improvement with his energy level coming back as well as his appetite. Fever resolved in about 24 hours. Patient was switched on oral antiobiotics 24 hours before being discharged in preparation for discharge.

DISCHARGE MEDICATIONS:
1. Cefzil 250 mg 1 po BID X 7 days
2. Potassium chloride 20 mEq po q am
3. Lipitor 10 mg po q day
4. Elavil 50 mg po q hs
5. Protonix 40 mg po q day
6. Aspirin 81 mg po q day
7. Lasix 40 mg po q day
8. Univasc 7.5 mg po q day
9. Nitroglycerin .4 mg L SL q 5 minutes X 3, chest pain
10. Tylenol, 325 mg 1-2 po q 4-6 hours for fever, pain

Elizabeth Diamond, MD

Inpatient Case 3

CODING REGIONAL HOSPITAL
123 MAIN STREET, ANYWHERE, USA

| **HOSPITAL ADMISSION FORM** | ACCOUNT NUMBER | MEDICAL RECORD NUMBER 873496 |

PATIENT INFORMATION

| PATIENT LAST NAME WILSON | FIRST NAME THOMAS | MI W | DOB 04/17/1953 | ADMIT DATE/TIME 08/23/20XX 10:00 PM |
| STREET ADDRESS 841 BROAD AVE | | CITY/STATE/ZIP ANYWHERE, ZA 10000 | | AREA CODE/PHONE NUMBER 111-842-88XX |

| SEX M [X] F | RACE | AGE | RELIGIOUS PREFERENCE | OCCUPATION SALES | FT [X] PT |
| PATIENT'S EMPLOYER ACME MEDICAL | STREET ADDRESS 4320 MAIN ST | CITY/STATE/ZIP ANYWHERE, ZA 10000 | | AREA CODE/PHONE NUMBER 111-843-81XX |

EMERGENCY CONTACT

| #1 LAST NAME WILSON | FIRST NAME NATALIE | MI | AREA CODE/PHONE NUMBER 111-842-88XX | RELATIONSHIP Wife |
| #2 LAST NAME | FIRST NAME | MI | AREA CODE/PHONE NUMBER | RELATIONSHIP |

GUARANTOR

| #1 LAST NAME WILSON | FIRST NAME THOMAS | MI W | AREA CODE/PHONE NUMBER 111-842-88XX | RELATIONSHIP |
| #2 LAST NAME | FIRST NAME | MI | AREA CODE/PHONE NUMBER | RELATIONSHIP |

ADMISSION INFORMATION

| ADMISSION STATUS INPATIENT | PATIENT TYPE MED/SURG | UNIT SURG | ROOM 231 | ATTENDING MD ELIZABETH DIAMOND MD | UPIN # 1134711 |

ADMITTING DIAGNOSIS
Bilateral pedal edema, CHF, hypothyroidism

INSURANCE INFORMATION

#1 PAYOR NAME FEDERATED CARE OF ZA	STREET ADDRESS 123 MAPLE ST	CITY/STATE/ZIP ANYWHERE, ZA 10000	PHONE NUMBER 800-338-90XX
POLICY NUMBER 3525078XX	GROUP NUMBER 247ZA	GROUP NAME ACME MEDICAL	
SUBSCRIBER NAME SAME	DOB SAME	AUTHORIZATION NUMBER	DEDUCTIBLE $1,000 Inpt
#2 PAYOR NAME	STREET ADDRESS	CITY/STATE/ZIP	PHONE NUMBER
POLICY NUMBER	GROUP NUMBER	GROUP NAME	
SUBSCRIBER NAME	DOB	AUTHORIZATION NUMBER	DEDUCTIBLE

PROVIDER NUMBER Provider #005255	PROCEDURES/SERVICES	
	Semi Private Visits (5)	$2,750.00
	Drugs	$1,700.00
Admitted through ER	IV Solutions (5)	$500.00
	IV Supplies (5)	$250.00
	Lab Chemistry	$350.00
	Chest X-Ray	$250.00

CONTROL NUMBER
0052373

ATTENDING PHYSICIAN _____   DATE _____

PATIENT RECORD   ORIGINAL

Inpatient Case 3

CODING REGIONAL HOSPITAL
123 MAIN STREET, ANYWHERE, USA

HISTORY AND PHYSICAL EXAMINATION

WILSON, THOMAS   James Jones, MD

ADMITTED: 08/23/20XX

MEDICAL RECORD NUMBER: 873496

ADMISSION DATE: 08/23/20XX
DISCHARGE DATE: 08/27/20XX

HISTORY IDENTIFICATION: 52-year-old Caucasian male who initially appeared in the ER. Informant is patient who seems reliable and hospital records.

CC: Bilateral pedal edema.

HPI: Patient appeared in ER complaining of bilateral pedal edema that was getting increasingly worse. Patient states he has a prior history of heart failure and recently discontinued all of his medications on his own. He denies any chest pain or shortness of breath. Denies any upper respiratory symptoms or cough. Patient stated that he lives alone and would be willing to be hospitalized to get the edema under control. His edema does have him concerned.

PAST MEDICAL HISTORY: Medications: As stated above, patient is presently on no medications. According to medical records he has been on Levothyroxine 0.05 mg q am. Lasix 40 mg po q d, Peri-Colace 1 tablet bid and Darvocet 1-2 tablets po prn q 6 hours.

ALLERGIES: No known medical allergies.

PAST SURGICAL HISTORY: Bilateral hernia repair done approximately 20 years ago, gall bladder removal 1965, skin graft left and 12/2000.

TRANSFUSIONS: Patient feels he has been transfused before but cannot recall when.

CHRONIC ILLNESSES: CHF, hypothyroidism, cirrhosis of liver, osteomyelitis, PVD, COPD, ETOH abuse.

FAMILY HISTORY: Father with CHF.

SOCIAL HISTORY: Retired radiologist, also veteran U.S. Navy.
      States he quit tobacco products 20 years ago.
      Alcohol use is episodic. Does admit to drinking more recently, which might contribute to his problems.

Inpatient Case 4

WILSON, THOMAS W   James Jones, MD
ADMITTED: 08/23/20XX

MEDICAL RECORD NUMBER: 873496

Page Two (continued)

REVIEW OF SYSTEMS: Patient has dentures, wears glasses with bifocal corrective lenses.

PHYSICAL EXAM:

General:	Patient pleasant white Caucasian male sitting upright. Does not appear in any discomfort. T 96.3, P 92, R 22, BP 160/83 O2 sat 97% room air
HEENT:	Head normocephalic, eyes normal, clear. Ears, TMs pearly gray with cone of light and landmarks present. Nose symmetrical, sinuses nontender. Nasal mucosa pink and moist.
Neck:	Good range of motion without tenderness. No masses or lymphadenopathy. Carotids +2 out of 4 bilaterally.
Chest:	Symmetrical expansion.
Lungs:	Lung fields significant for very minimal crackles lower left and right lobe.
Heart:	Irregular rhythm, regular rate, no murmur, rubs, gallops.
Abdomen:	No tenderness to palpation, no guarding, no rebound.
M/S:	Good range of motion all joints. No erythema, tenderness, swelling, pedal edema +2 bilaterally.
Vascular:	Radial and dorsalis pedal pulses +2 our of 4 bilaterally.
Neurological:	Cranial nerves 2-12 intact, motor +4 out of 5.

LABORATORY FINDINGS: TSH elevated at 5.822. Panel 12 within normal limits. CBC within normal limits. Two chest x-rays significant for some cardiomegaly with small amount of fluid lower left lobe.

ASSESSMENT/PLAN:
1. Pedal edema
2. CHF
3. Hypothyroidism

PLAN: Patient admitted. Saline locked and placed and Lasix 40 mg IV tid ordered. Patient denies knowing he was hypothyroid. Patient is do not resuscitate status.

James Jones, MD

D: 08/23/20XX
T: 08/23/20XX

Inpatient Case 4

CODING REGIONAL HOSPITAL
123 MAIN STREET, ANYWHERE, USA

PROGRESS NOTE

DATE: 08/24/20XX

TIME:

Patient states feel very weak, denies cough, SOB, N/V/D. Feet are swollen and slightly tender.

BP 163/90, afebrile

Lungs: Scattered crackles throughout lower 1/3 of lungs.
CV: Irregular rhythm, 1+ bipedal edema with decreased pulses K+ 3.3.

ASSESSMENT/PLAN:
CHF, continue IV Lasix, will start potassium replacement and continue to monitor.

James Jones, MD

PATIENT ID
WILSON, THOMAS
Admit: 08/23/20XX
MR #873496

PROGRESS NOTE   **Coding Regional Hospital**

Inpatient Case 4

CODING REGIONAL HOSPITAL
123 MAIN STREET, ANYWHERE, USA

PROGRESS NOTE

DATE: 08/25/20XX

TIME:

Patient states still feeling weak, states breathing is better, ankles are much less edematous.
BP 155/75, T 96.3.
Lungs, bibasilar crackles.
BUN 1.3, Creatinine 1.1, Na+ 136, K= 3.3.

ASSESSMENT/PLAN:
CHF improving, will continue current therapies, probably will switch to PO tomorrow.

James Jones, MD

PATIENT ID
WILSON, THOMAS
Admit: 08/23/20XX
MR #873496

PROGRESS NOTE   **Coding Regional Hospital**

Inpatient Case 4

CODING REGIONAL HOSPITAL
123 MAIN STREET, ANYWHERE, USA

PROGRESS NOTE

DATE: 08/26/20XX

TIME:

Patient states he is feeling better, breathing improved, ankles much improved.
BP 147/73, P 81, R 20, Temp 96.8.
Lungs, clear.
No pedal edema.
Heart, regular, rate and rhythm.

ASSESSMENT/PLAN:
CHF, improving, switch to oral Lasix, increase potassium replacement. Continue to monitor on oral diuretics. If stable, discharge to home tomorrow.

James Jones, MD

PATIENT ID
WILSON, THOMAS
Admit: 08/23/20XX
MR #873496

PROGRESS NOTE   **Coding Regional Hospital**

Inpatient Case 4

CODING REGIONAL HOSPITAL
123 MAIN STREET, ANYWHERE, USA

PROGRESS NOTE

DATE: 08/27/20XX

TIME:

Patient feels good, didn't like saline lock so demanded it be removed.
Vital signs stable.
Lungs clear.
Heart, regular rate and rhythm.
No pedal edema.

ASSESSMENT:
CHF, tolerating oral meds, will discharge to home today.

James Jones, MD

PATIENT ID
WILSON, THOMAS
Admit: 08/23/20XX
MR #873496

PROGRESS NOTE   **Coding Regional Hospital**

Inpatient Case 4

CODING REGIONAL HOSPITAL
123 MAIN STREET, ANYWHERE, USA

RADIOLOGY REPORT

MR# 873496
PATIENT NAME: WILSON, THOMAS
DOB: 05/17/1953

Dr. James Jones

CLINICAL SUMMARY:

PA AND LATERAL CHEST, 08/23/20XX

Chest X-Ray, 08/23/20XX

CHEST, 08/23/20XX: PA and lateral views of chest compared with 06/23/XX revealed no significant interval change and no acute process.

Thomas O'Toole, MD

Ddt/mm

D: 08/23/20XX
T: 08/23/20XX

_____
Thomas O'Toole, MD   Date

Inpatient Case 4

CODING REGIONAL HOSPITAL
123 MAIN STREET, ANYWHERE, USA

RADIOLOGY REPORT

MR# 873496
PATIENT NAME: WILSON, THOMAS
DOB: 05/17/1953

Dr. James Jones

PA AND LATERAL CHEST, 08/25/20XX

CHEST, 08/25/20XX: PA and lateral views of chest compared with 08/23/20XX revealed a similar appearance between chest x-rays. No evidence of CHF, infiltrate or effusion noted. Findings compatible with COPD are minimal. Aorta is calcified and minimally tortuous. Moderate degenerative changes are noted in the spine. Healed curbstone fractures are noted.

IMPRESSION: No acute process. No significant interval changes.

Thomas O'Toole, MD

Ddt/mm

D: 08/25/20XX
T: 08/25/20XX

Thomas O'Toole, MD   Date

Inpatient Case 4

CODING REGIONAL HOSPITAL
123 MAIN STREET, ANYWHERE, USA

HOSPITAL ADMISSION FORM	ACCOUNT NUMBER				MEDICAL RECORD NUMBER 694171

PATIENT INFORMATION

PATIENT LAST NAME GREENE	FIRST NAME ROBERT	MI J	DOB 03/01/56	ADMIT DATE/TIME 02/17/20XX 11:30 PM

STREET ADDRESS 34 BROAD AVENUE	CITY/STATE/ZIP ANYWHERE, ZA 10000	AREA CODE/PHONE NUMBER 111-324-84XX

SEX M [X] F [ ]	RACE	AGE	RELIGIOUS PREFERENCE	OCCUPATION SALES	FT [X] PT [ ]

PATIENT'S EMPLOYER AUTOMOTIVE INDUST.	STREET ADDRESS 134 MAIN ST	CITY/STATE/ZIP ANYWHERE, ZA 10000	AREA CODE/PHONE NUMBER 111-342-53XX

EMERGENCY CONTACT

#1 LAST NAME GREENE	FIRST NAME MABEL	MI L	AREA CODE/PHONE NUMBER 111-324-84XX	RELATIONSHIP Wife
#2 LAST NAME	FIRST NAME	MI	AREA CODE/PHONE NUMBER	RELATIONSHIP

GUARANTOR

#1 LAST NAME GREENE	FIRST NAME ROBERT	MI J	AREA CODE/PHONE NUMBER 222-324-84XX	RELATIONSHIP
#2 LAST NAME	FIRST NAME	MI	AREA CODE/PHONE NUMBER	RELATIONSHIP

ADMISSION INFORMATION

ADMISSION STATUS INPATIENT	PATIENT TYPE SURG	UNIT SURG	ROOM 367	ATTENDING MD ELIZABETH DIAMOND MD	UPIN # 1134711

ADMITTING DIAGNOSIS LRI, Diabetes, A Fib

INSURANCE INFORMATION

#1 PAYOR NAME BCBS OF PA	STREET ADDRESS PO BOX 1492	CITY/STATE/ZIP ANYWHERE PA 10000	PHONE NUMBER 888-325-52XX

POLICY NUMBER 257-81-12XX	GROUP NUMBER ZA113	GROUP NAME AUTOMOTIVE INDUSTRIES, INC

SUBSCRIBER NAME GREENE, ROBERT	DOB SAME	AUTHORIZATION NUMBER	DEDUCTIBLE $500

#2 PAYOR NAME	STREET ADDRESS	CITY/STATE/ZIP	PHONE NUMBER
POLICY NUMBER	GROUP NUMBER	GROUP NAME	
SUBSCRIBER NAME	DOB	AUTHORIZATION NUMBER	DEDUCTIBLE

PROVIDER NUMBER BCBS #005437 Admitted through ER	PROCEDURES/SERVICES	
	Semi Private Visits (3)	$600.00
	X-Ray, Diagnostic	$100.00
	Respiratory Therapy (4)	$200.00
	IV Meds	$200.00
	IV Supplies (4)	$200.00
	IV Solutions (4)	$200.00

CONTROL NUMBER 0010014

ATTENDING PHYSICIAN _____ DATE _____

PATIENT RECORD   ORIGINAL

Inpatient Case 5

CODING REGIONAL HOSPITAL
123 MAIN STREET, ANYWHERE, USA

HISTORY AND PHYSICAL EXAMINATION

GREENE, Robert J	**James Jones, MD**
ADMITTED: 02/17/20XX	
MEDICAL RECORD NUMBER: 694171	

CHIEF COMPLAINT: Weakness

HISTORY OF PRESENT ILLNESS: Patient is a 44-year-old male who is known non-insulin dependent diabetic who is living at home. Apparently he developed cough and increasing weakness about 48 hours prior to admission. It is uncertain whether he had any fever at home, but because of the increasing weakness he was unable to get out of bed. He was brought to the emergency room and found to be in significant respiratory distress and fairly unresponsive. He was a very poor historian because he really did not answer many questions at all. He was found to be in atrial fibrillation with a blood sugar over 500. He was given Digoxin IV in the emergency room as well as put on a diltiazem drip which improved his rate somewhat, however, his blood pressure came down to around only 100 systolic. He was somewhat improved, however, and was admitted to the coronary care unit.

PAST MEDICAL HISTORY: History of NIDDM, peptic ulcer disease, degenerative arthritis. Previous surgeries: 1998 right lung lobectomy, 1983 TURP, 1994 cholecystectomy. Other hospitalizations for hepatitis secondary to sulfa reaction.

Allergies to sulfa.

CURRENT MEDICATIONS: Glucophage 500 mg two with breakfast, one with lunch, two with supper, Glipizide 10 mg pot id.

SOCIAL HISTORY: Does not smoke or drink alcohol. Caffeine occasionally.

FAMILY HISTORY: He had a sister, brother and cousin with diabetes. He also had a brother with multiple myeloma. He has one brother with CHF, No family history of atherosclerotic heart disease.

REVIEW OF SYSTEMS: Not obtainable at this time.

Inpatient Case 5

GREENE, Robert J.   **James Jones, MD**
ADMITTED: 02/17/20XX

MEDICAL RECORD NUMBER: 694171

Page Two (continued)

PHYSICAL EXAMINATION:

General: Male who is pale, diaphoretic, occasionally mumbles, but no intelligible responses with verbal stimuli.

Head: Normalcephalic. Eyes, pupils not related secondary to cataracts. No obvious fundoscopic changes. TMs clear, mucuous membranes are tacky.

Neck: Supple, No adenopathy or thyromegaly.

Chest: Decreased breath sounds on the right where he had surgery. The left side reveals scattered rhonchi as well as transmited upper airway sounds. No rales, labored breathing.

Cardio: Distant heart sounds. Irregular rhythm. SI and S2, no murmurs. No JVD. No carotid bruits. Carotid pulses +1 bilaterally, no abdominal bruits.

Rectal: Not done.

Extremities: No peripheral edema. Pedal pulses 2+ bilaterally.

Neurological: Difficult to assess due to his marked somnolence.

IMPRESSION:

1. Lower respiratory infection, probable influenza with fairly significant respiratory distress.
2. Insulin-dependent diabetes, poor control with blood sugar over 500. Recommend insulin sliding scale.
3. Atrial fibrillation. Rate is better controlled. He is on diltizem drop which we will taper. He is given IV nitroglycerin. We will also continue his 100% oxygen and plan on treating him while in the hospital with medical and supportive therapy.

Patient is DNR, DNI.

James Jones, MD

D: 02/17/20XX
T: 02/17/20XX

Inpatient Case 5

CODING REGIONAL HOSPITAL
123 MAIN STREET, ANYWHERE, USA

PROGRESS NOTE

DATE: 02/17/20XX

TIME:

TREATMENT NOTE

02/17/XX Respiratory

Patient seen for 2.5 mg Albuterol nebulizer treatment. Tolerated passively. Treatment done with mask. Breath sounds absent on the right, decreased on the left with rales in base. Slight increase in aeration with nebulizer. No cough.

James Taylor, RRT

PATIENT ID
  GREENE, ROBERT J.
  Admit: 02/17/20XX
  MR# 694171

PROGRESS NOTE   **Coding Regional Hospital**

Inpatient Case 5

CODING REGIONAL HOSPITAL
123 MAIN STREET, ANYWHERE, USA
PROGRESS NOTE

DATE: 02/18/20XX

TIME:

Patient really not improving. Given IV Lasix 80 mg IV for poor output. Has developed hypotension 73.43 now and coarse crackles are heard throughout the lung fields.

We will attempt to control with a "renal dose" of dopamine and see if his condition improves.

James Jones, MD

PATIENT ID
 GREENE, ROBERT J.
 Admit: 02/17/20XX
 MR# 694171

PROGRESS NOTE   **Coding Regional Hospital**

Inpatient Case 5

CODING REGIONAL HOSPITAL
123 MAIN STREET, ANYWHERE, USA

PROGRESS NOTE

DATE: 02/19/20XX

TIME:

PROGRESS NOTE:

02/19/20XX

Patient continues to deteriorate. Prognosis poor. Virtually no response to dopamine. Remains unresponsive, more difficult to arouse. Severe dehydration. Spoke with family regarding status and they wish to abide by his DNR, DNI orders.

We will continue supportive measures and see how patient does.

NURSE NOTE:

02/19/XX

Patient experiencing severe respiratory distress. DNR, DNI order in place. Will continue to support patient. Physician advised.

Time of death 02/19/20XX   11:35 PM

PATIENT ID
 GREENE, ROBERT J.
 Admit: 02/17/20XX
 MR# 694171

PROGRESS NOTE   **Coding Regional Hospital**

Inpatient Case 5

CODING REGIONAL HOSPITAL
123 MAIN STREET, ANYWHERE, USA

PROGRESS NOTE

DATE: 02/18/20XX

TIME:

TREATMENT NOTE

02/18/20XX Respiratory

Patient seen at 1450 for nebulizer with 2.5 mg Albuterol unit dose. Tolerated passively. Breath sounds increasingly coarse with rales and crackles heard throughout. Patient has deteriorated since treatment on 01/17/20XX. Physician advised.

James Taylor, RRT

PATIENT ID
GREENE, ROBERT J.
Admit: 02/17/20XX
MR# 694171

PROGRESS NOTE   **Coding Regional Hospital**

Inpatient Case 5

CODING REGIONAL HOSPITAL
123 MAIN STREET, ANYWHERE, USA

RADIOLOGY REPORT

MR# 694171
PATIENT NAME: GREENE, ROBERT J.
DOB: 03/01/1956

Dr. James Jones

CLINICAL SUMMARY: Patient unresponsive. Low O2 saturation.

PA AND LATERAL CHEST, 02/18/20XX

FINDINGS: Comparison with study of 02/02/20XX. There has been no change in appearance of the chest. Patient apparently had a right pneumonectomy with complete opacification of the right hemothorax and the heart and mediastinal structures deviate into the right chest. Pleural calcifications are seen in the right hemothorax. The left lung remains clear and fully expanded, although there are some patchy areas of atelectasis at the left lung base. There is considerable motion artifact. I cannot totally exclude the possibility of an early infiltrative process at the left lower lobe and if clinical symptoms persist, I would suggest an attempted follow-up study.

IMPRESSION: The residual left lung appears clear. The questionable findings at the left lung base may be related to motion artifact. If clinically indicated, follow-up exam should be performed.

Thomas O'Toole, MD

D: 02/18/20XX
T: 02/18/20XX

Thomas O'Toole, MD	Date

Inpatient Case 5

CODING REGIONAL HOSPITAL
123 MAIN STREET, ANYWHERE, USA

HOSPITAL ADMISSION FORM	ACCOUNT NUMBER		MEDICAL RECORD NUMBER 779464

PATIENT INFORMATION

PATIENT LAST NAME JOHNSON	FIRST NAME MARLENE	MI	DOB 05/17/53	ADMIT DATE/TIME 03/01/20XX 7:20 AM IP

STREET ADDRESS 3277 MAIN STREET	CITY/STATE/ZIP ANYWHERE, ZA 10000	AREA CODE/PHONE NUMBER 111-328-45XX

SEX M ☐ F ☒	RACE	AGE	RELIGIOUS PREFERENCE	OCCUPATION	FT ☐ PT ☐

PATIENT'S EMPLOYER UNEMPLOYED	STREET ADDRESS	CITY/STATE/ZIP	AREA CODE/PHONE NUMBER

EMERGENCY CONTACT

#1 LAST NAME JOHNSON	FIRST NAME MAUREEN	MI	AREA CODE/PHONE NUMBER 111-328-45XX	RELATIONSHIP
#2 LAST NAME	FIRST NAME	MI	AREA CODE/PHONE NUMBER	RELATIONSHIP

GUARANTOR

#1 LAST NAME JOHNSON	FIRST NAME MARLENE	MI	AREA CODE/PHONE NUMBER 111-328-45XX	RELATIONSHIP
#2 LAST NAME	FIRST NAME	MI	AREA CODE/PHONE NUMBER	RELATIONSHIP

ADMISSION INFORMATION

ADMISSION STATUS INPATIENT	PATIENT TYPE MED/SURG	UNIT SURG	ROOM 342	ATTENDING MD ELIZABETH DIAMOND MD	UPIN # 1134711

ADMITTING DIAGNOSIS
03/01/20XX Shortness of breath

INSURANCE INFORMATION

#1 PAYOR NAME MEDICAID	STREET ADDRESS PO BOX 4444	CITY/STATE/ZIP ANYWHERE, ZA 10000	PHONE NUMBER 800-123-45XX

POLICY NUMBER 3728432XX	GROUP NUMBER	GROUP NAME

SUBSCRIBER NAME	DOB	AUTHORIZATION NUMBER	DEDUCTIBLE

#2 PAYOR NAME	STREET ADDRESS	CITY/STATE/ZIP	PHONE NUMBER

POLICY NUMBER	GROUP NUMBER	GROUP NAME

SUBSCRIBER NAME	DOB	AUTHORIZATION NUMBER	DEDUCTIBLE

PROVIDER NUMBER Medicaid Provider #0041367	PROCEDURES/SERVICES	
	Semi-Private Room (4)	$800.00
	Chest X-Ray	$100.00
	Laboratory-Chemistry	$200.00
	Respiratory Treatment	$200.00
	IV Solutions	$200.00
	IV Meds	$200.00
	IV Supplies	$400.00

CONTROL NUMBER
0100091 - 03/01/20XX

ATTENDING PHYSICIAN _____   DATE _____

PATIENT RECORD   ORIGINAL

Inpatient Case 5

CODING REGIONAL HOSPITAL
123 MAIN STREET, ANYWHERE, USA

HISTORY AND PHYSICAL EXAMINATION

JOHNSON, MARLENE	**James Jones, MD**
ADMITTED: 03/01/20XX	

MEDICAL RECORD NUMBER: 779464

CHIEF COMPLAINT: Shortness of breath

HISTORY OF PRESENT ILLNESS: This 52-year-old lady with a long history of steroid-dependent COPD started feeling sick yesterday with some fevers and chills, started becoming increasingly short of breath today with some cough productive of whitish sputum. The patient did have one emesis earlier prior to arrival.

PAST MEDICAL HISTORY:
1.   COPD which has lately become steroid-dependent.
2.   History of hypertension; currently off medications.
3.   History of renal failure now resolved.
4.   History of cholelithiasis S/P cholecystectomy in 10/2000.
5.   History of peptic ulcer disease.
6.   Status post abdominal hysterectomy
7.   Patient reports history of "small heart attack" in 2000 although I could find no record in her chart at this facility.

FAMILY HISTORY: Patient's father died of an MI in upper 80s. Patient's mother died in her 70s of unknown causes. Mother did have hypertension. No family history of diabetes.

HABITS: Patient smokes 1 pack of cigarettes per day but states she quit last night. Does have a history of 3 to 4 alcoholic beverages per day but quit and reportedly has not drunk alcohol in the past 2 years.

REVIEW OF SYSTEMS:

General:	Fever and chills as listed in HPI.
HEENT:	No complaints.
Cardiac:	No complaints.
GI/GU:	No complaints.
Hema:	Complaints of easy bruising.

Inpatient Case 6

JOHNSON, MARLENE   James Jones, MD
ADMITTED: 03/01/20XX

MEDICAL RECORD NUMBER: 779464

Page Two (continued)

PHYSICAL EXAMINATION:
General: Pleasant lady in mild respiratory distress.
Vitals: Temperature 102.5, pulse 145, BP 192/113 O2 Sat 89% of room air
HEENT: Exam PERRLA, EOMI, TMs clear. Pharynx clear.
Neck: Supple without lymphadenopathy.
Heart: Regular rate and rhythm, S1, S2 no murmurs noted
Lungs: Markedly decreased air movement bilaterally, right more than left. No
               wheezes; however, patient not moving enough air for wheezes.
Abdomen: Soft, nontender, with positive bowel sounds.
Extremities: Without clubbing, cyanosis, edema. Peripheral pulses 2+.

Chem 7 and troponin within normal limits. CBC shows WBC is elevated at 11 with an
elevated absolute neutrophil count of 8.0.

ASSESSMENT AND PLAN:
COPD exacerbation. Will admit, give Albuterol nebs and place on SoluMedrol 125 mg IV
q8h. Will also cover her with Ceftriaxone 1 mg IV q24h.

James Jones, MD

D: 03/01/20XX
T: 03/01/20XX

Inpatient Case 6

CODING REGIONAL HOSPITAL
123 MAIN STREET, ANYWHERE, USA

PROGRESS NOTE

DATE: 03/01/20XX

TIME:

Patient continues to experience SOB and weakness especially with exertion. O2 sats 93% at rest. Neb treatments given X2 in past 24 hours with minimal Improvement.

James Jones, MD

PATIENT ID
JOHNSON, MARLENE
Admit: 03/01/20XX
MR #779464

PROGRESS NOTE   **Coding Regional Hospital**

Inpatient Case 6

CODING REGIONAL HOSPITAL
123 MAIN STREET, ANYWHERE, USA

PROGRESS NOTE

DATE: 03/02/20XX

TIME:

Patient feeling better. Continued O2. Patient is still moving air poorly; however, feel it is improved slightly since yesterday. Will continue treatments. Cough productive. Watch for fever, edema.

COPD exacerbation

James Jones, MD

PATIENT ID
JOHNSON, MARLENE
Admit: 03/01/20XX
MR #779464

PROGRESS NOTE   **Coding Regional Hospital**

Inpatient Case 6

```
┌─────────────────────────────────────────────────────────────┐
│                 CODING REGIONAL HOSPITAL                       │
│                 123 MAIN STREET, ANYWHERE, USA                 │
├───────────────────────────────────────────────────────────────┤
│                      PROGRESS NOTE                             │
├───────────────────────────────────────────────────────────────┤
```

DATE: 03/03/20XX

TIME:

Patient much improved in past 24 hours. Air moving through fields, significantly less exertion with breathing. No rales, crackles or wheezes heard. Will convert patient to oral meds for next 24 hours in preparation for discharge.

James Jones, MD

PATIENT ID
 JOHNSON, MARLENE
 Admit: 03/01/20XX
 MR #779464

PROGRESS NOTE   **Coding Regional Hospital**

Inpatient Case 6

CODING REGIONAL HOSPITAL
123 MAIN STREET, ANYWHERE, USA

RADIOLOGY REPORT

MR# 779464
PATIENT NAME: JOHNSON, MARLENE
DOB: 05/17/1953

Dr. James Jones

CLINICAL SUMMARY: Shortness of Breath

PORTABLE CHEST, 03/01/20XX

FINDINGS: Lungs are hyperexpanded likely due to COPD. No acute infiltrate or congestion is seen.

IMPRESSION: No significant acute abnormality is seen in the chest.

Thomas O'Toole, MD

Ddt/mm

D: 03/01/20XX
T: 03/01/20XX

Thomas O'Toole, MD   Date

Inpatient Case 6

CODING REGIONAL HOSPITAL
123 MAIN STREET, ANYWHERE, USA

DISCHARGE SUMMARY

PATIENT NAME: JOHNSON, MARLENE #779464
DOB: 05/17/1953

ADMITTED: 03/01/20XX
DISCHARGED: 03/04/20XX

Patient being discharged with the following meds:
Albuterol nebs every 4 hours as needed
Atrovent nebs as needed
Patient to continue home meds as well.

At discharge the patient indicates she is significantly improved and back to her usual level of SOB.

DISCHARGE DIAGNOSES:
1.   COPD which has lately become steroid dependent.
2.   Hypertension currently off medications

James Jones, MD

D: 03/04/20XX
T: 03/04/20XX

Inpatient Case 6

CODING REGIONAL HOSPITAL
123 MAIN STREET, ANYWHERE, USA

HOSPITAL ADMISSION FORM

ACCOUNT NUMBER		MEDICAL RECORD NUMBER
		873496

PATIENT LAST NAME	FIRST NAME	MI	DOB	ADMIT DATE/TIME
WILSON	THOMAS	W	04/17/1953	01/12/20XX

STREET ADDRESS	CITY/STATE/ZIP	AREA CODE/PHONE NUMBER
841 BROAD AVE	ANYWHERE, ZA 10000	111-842-88XX

SEX		RACE	AGE	RELIGIOUS PREFERENCE	OCCUPATION		
M [X] F [ ]					SALES	FT [X]	PT [ ]

PATIENT'S EMPLOYER	STREET ADDRESS	CITY/STATE/ZIP	AREA CODE/PHONE NUMBER
ACME MEDICAL	4320 MAIN ST	ANYWHERE, ZA 10000	111-843-81XX

EMERGENCY CONTACT

#1 LAST NAME	FIRST NAME	MI	AREA CODE/PHONE NUMBER	RELATIONSHIP
WILSON	NATALIE		111-842-88XX	Wife
#2 LAST NAME	FIRST NAME	MI	AREA CODE/PHONE NUMBER	RELATIONSHIP

GUARANTOR

#1 LAST NAME	FIRST NAME	MI	AREA CODE/PHONE NUMBER	RELATIONSHIP
WILSON	THOMAS	W	111-842-88XX	
#2 LAST NAME	FIRST NAME	MI	AREA CODE/PHONE NUMBER	RELATIONSHIP

ADMISSION INFORMATION

ADMISSION STATUS	PATIENT TYPE	UNIT	ROOM	ATTENDING MD	UPIN #
INPATIENT	MED/SURG	SURG	231	ELIZABETH DIAMOND MD	1134711

ADMITTING DIAGNOSIS
Chest Pain

INSURANCE INFORMATION

#1 PAYOR NAME	STREET ADDRESS	CITY/STATE/ZIP	PHONE NUMBER
FEDERATED CARE OF ZA	123 MAPLE ST	ANYWHERE, ZA 10000	800-338-48XX

POLICY NUMBER	GROUP NUMBER	GROUP NAME
3525078XX	247ZA	ACME MEDICAL

SUBSCRIBER NAME	DOB	AUTHORIZATION NUMBER	DEDUCTIBLE
SAME	SAME		$1,000 Inpt

#2 PAYOR NAME	STREET ADDRESS	CITY/STATE/ZIP	PHONE NUMBER

POLICY NUMBER	GROUP NUMBER	GROUP NAME

SUBSCRIBER NAME	DOB	AUTHORIZATION NUMBER	DEDUCTIBLE

PROVIDER NUMBER	PROCEDURES/SERVICES	
Provider #005255	Semi Private Room (6)	$600.00
Admitted through ER	Drugs	$1,500.00
	IV Solutions (6)	$600.00
	Lab Chemistry	$350.00
	Lab/Urinalysis	$100.00
	Chest X-Ray	$125.00
	Electrocardiogram	$200.00

CONTROL NUMBER
0804396

ATTENDING PHYSICIAN _____   DATE _____

PATIENT RECORD   ORIGINAL

Inpatient Case 7

CODING REGIONAL HOSPITAL
123 MAIN STREET, ANYWHERE, USA

HISTORY AND PHYSICAL EXAMINATION

WILSON, THOMAS   James Jones, MD

ADMITTED: 01/12/20XX

MEDICAL RECORD NUMBER: 873496

CHIEF COMPLAINT: Chest pain

HPI: This man has an extensive history of coronary artery disease. He had coronary artery bypass grafting in 1982, with subsequent redo. He had a PTCA on three or four occasions. He obtained his primary cardiac care down at the VA Medical Center. He has had myocardial infarctions. Just about a month ago, he had chest pain, and was hospitalized there. Had workup and was told, in his words, "that he had mild heart attack, but no muscle damage." He had a cardiac catheterization there, had multiple areas of involvement, was told that medical management was the best option, with the other option being a repeat bypass grafting, though, of course, that would be complicated by his history of two bypasses already. Thus, he was managed medically. Also, a couple of months ago he went to the VA for routine visit, had been having trouble with increasing shortness of breath, edema, and orthopnea. They told him he was "full of fluid," admitted him for eight days, and he dropped his weight from 254 to 212 pounds during that time, and he felt markedly improved, "a total makeover" since then. They increased his Lasix to 100 mg bid and added Metolazone 5 mg every other day. He was a smoker, but has quit within the past few years. He also has a history of cerebrovascular disease with mild stroke when he was visiting about 2 years ago. Had transient left-sided weakness, but has no residual.

PMH: Is as noted above. He also had dual-chamber pacemaker that has been replaced once. He is a Type II diabetic on oral therapy. He does home blood sugars, and they have been excellent. He was baffled when it was over 300 here in the emergency room, but I presume that is associated with the stress of his current presentation.

He was feeling fine when he went to bed last night. He got up at about 2:15 to void and had some precordial chest pressure possibly radiating a little bit to the left arm. He sat on the edge of the bed; the pain got worse, got to about a 6/10 in intensity. He took a nitroglycerin. The first one helped promptly. Then the pain got worse. He took another, and 10 minutes later there was no improvement, so he took a third, which, as well, did not help. Therefore, he presented to the hospital for evaluation. There was no shortness of breath or diaphoresis associated with this chest pain; possibly he felt a little lightheaded, but no nausea or vomiting. On presentation to the emergency room, he tells me his pain was 6/10. There, Dr. Smith evaluated him. He received another sublingual nitroglycerin, O2 was placed. His pain resolved, and he is entirely pain-free at this time.

Inpatient Case 7

WILSON, THOMAS W   James Jones, MD

ADMITTED: 01/12/20XX

MEDICAL RECORD NUMBER: 873496

Page Two (continued)

PMH (continued): His SA 02 were noted to be 96 percent on room air. He was noted to be hypokalemic with potassium level of 2.7 and therefore we added 40 mEq of potassium per liter of IV fluids, and he did not tolerate that due to a lot of burning pain in the arm, so the attempt is being made to replace it orally. Currently, is without chest pain or pressure, no dyspnea or orthopnea.

SURGERIES: He has had bilateral cataract extraction. He recently had some sort of last procedure to the left eye. He is being fitted for glasses. He had a right inguinal hernia repaired in 1999. TURP in the past. He does have hyperlipidemia. Allergy noted to Lisinopril.

HABITS: Nonsmoker.

CURRENT MEDICATIONS: Isosorbide 40 mg tid, furosemide 100 mg bid, glyburide 5 mg daily, lansoprazole (Prevacid) 15 mg daily, metolazone 5 mg every other day, metoprolol 50 mg bid, simvastatin 10 mg q pm, Plavix 75 mg daily, diazepam 5 mg prn, quinine sulfate 250 mg at hs prn for leg cramps, nitroglycerin .4 mg sublingually prn, and potassium chloride is 8 mEq tablets 2 taken tid.

FAMILY HISTORY: Father died in age 82 of coronary artery disease, having had first MI at approximately age 60. Mother had hardening of the arteries. Sister has some sort of cancer.

SOCIAL HISTORY: Apparently on SSD for coronary artery disease and takes primary medical care at the VA. Lives with his wife.

REVIEW OF SYSTEMS: Otherwise negative.

PHYSICAL EXAMINATION: Pleasant man. He had been given some Valium in the ER because of pain in his arm and was resting comfortably with snoring when I came in. I awakened him. He is in absolutely no distress. He is pain-free. Vital signs are stable with temp 98.3, pulse 61 and regular, respirations 20 and unlabored, blood pressure 115/63. Skin is clear, warm and dry. No cyanosis. HEENT: Normocephalic, atraumatic. PERRL. EOMI. He has had bilateral cataract extractions. TMs are fine. Pharynx is clear. Upper and lower dentures. Neck is supple. Carotids normal, symmetrical. I do not hear bruits, and there is no JVD or HJR. Lungs are clear throughout. Heart is regular, distant heart sounds with very soft Grade I/VI rumbly low-pitched systolic murmur. Abdomen is soft and nontender without hepatosplenomegaly or other masses. Normal bowel sounds. I hear no bruits. Extremities: He has no edema. He has an easily palpable right dorsalis pedis pulse, none palpable on the left, though feet are warm. Neurological: Cranial nerves 2-12 are intact. Motor and sensory are normal.

Inpatient Case 7

WILSON, THOMAS W   **James Jones, MD**

ADMITTED: 01/12/20XX

MEDICAL RECORD NUMBER: 873496

Page Three (continued)

PHYSICAL EXAMINATION (continued): Electrocardiogram, paced rhythm. Chemistries show glucose of 363, sodium 138, potassium 2.7, chloride 88, bicarb 38. His LDH and CK are normal and the troponin is normal at 0.3. BUN 46, creatinine 1.4.

ASSESSMENT:
1.   72-year-old man with extensive history of coronary artery disease with previous bypass X2, several angioplasties, recent angiogram, the specifics of which I do not have, but recommendation, apparently, at that time of medical management with possibility of redo bypass consideration if not controlled, presents with nocturnal onset of chest pain, somewhat prolonged. Resolved at present. Unstable angina, rule out infarction.
2.   CHF, controlled.
3.   Hypokalemia, secondary to diuretics.
4.   Hyperlipidemia
5.   Type II diabetes mellitus.
6.   PUD/GERD
7.   History of cerebrovascular disease with previous CVA

PLAN:
At this point he is stable and comfortable. He is admitted to the coronary care unit. I think it would be wise to put him on IV heparin infusion. Will follow his cardiograms and enzymes closely. From a medical management standpoint, he is on fairly maximal therapies. We could increase his beta blocker somewhat, but will need to watch his pulse and blood pressure. We need to replace his potassium, which we will try to do orally. I am simply going to follow his glucose for now. I would like to avoid giving any insulin, as this is simply going to drop his potassium further by forcing it intracellularly. I have discussed all this with the patient.

James Jones, MD

D: 01/12/20XX
T: 01/12/20XX

Inpatient Case 7

CODING REGIONAL HOSPITAL
123 MAIN STREET, ANYWHERE, USA

PROGRESS NOTE

DATE: 01/13/20XX

TIME:

S: No chest pain, no SOB. Feels good. "I thought I could go home today."

O: All vital signs normal. Color good, no JVD or edema. Lungs clear, heart regular, abdomen nontender. Extremities show no edema.

Potassium level now 3.0. EKG paced rhythm, PTT 51.4.

A: Unstable angina in setting of severe CAD.
Hypokalemia.
Diabetes mellitus - poor control.

P: Continue in CCU today.
Continue heparin, PO KCL.
Arrange for patient and patient's wife to meet with diabetic nurse for counseling.

James Jones, MD

PATIENT ID
WILSON, THOMAS
Admit: 01/12/20XX
MR #873496

PROGRESS NOTE   **Coding Regional Hospital**

Inpatient Case 7

CODING REGIONAL HOSPITAL
123 MAIN STREET, ANYWHERE, USA

PROGRESS NOTE

DATE: 01/14/20XX

TIME:

S: Feels fine, but with closer questioning did have chills and felt feverish. Denies cough, SOB, chest pain or UTI symptoms.

O: Alert and oriented, temperature 100.3, lungs clear.

A: Stable angina, now with fever.

P: Continue previous treatment, add Tylenol for fever.

James Jones, MD

PATIENT ID

WILSON, THOMAS

Admit: 01/12/20XX

MR #873496

PROGRESS NOTE   **Coding Regional Hospital**

Inpatient Case 7

CODING REGIONAL HOSPITAL
123 MAIN STREET, ANYWHERE, USA

PROGRESS NOTE

DATE: 01/15/20XX

TIME:

S: Patient complaining of not feeling well and feeling worn out. Temperature 103.4. Will draw blood cultures and continue treating with Tylenol and Keflex IV.

O: Alert, oriented, pale. Fever continues despite Tylenol so will start IV antibiotics. Other vital signs stable. Lungs clear, few rales in right base. Cardiovascular, regular rate and rhythm.

A: Improving, except for problems with fever.

P: Continue Rx.

James Jones, MD

PATIENT ID

WILSON, THOMAS

Admit: 01/12/20XX

MR #873496

PROGRESS NOTE   **Coding Regional Hospital**

Inpatient Case 7

CODING REGIONAL HOSPITAL
123 MAIN STREET, ANYWHERE, USA

PROGRESS NOTE

DATE: 01/16/20XX

TIME:

S: Patient feels "100%" better today and "ready to go home."

O: All vital signs are normal including temperature at 98.3. Input and output appear normal as well.

A: Improving, fever resolved.

P: Start patient on oral antibiotics for consideration for discharge tomorrow.

James Jones, MD

PATIENT ID
WILSON, THOMAS
Admit: 01/12/20XX
MR #873496

PROGRESS NOTE   **Coding Regional Hospital**

Inpatient Case 7

CODING REGIONAL HOSPITAL
123 MAIN STREET, ANYWHERE, USA

RADIOLOGY REPORT

MR# 876496
PATIENT NAME: WILSON, THOMAS
DOB: 04/17/1953

Dr. James Jones

CLINICAL SUMMARY: Chest pain

PORTABLE CHEST, 01/12/20XX

FINDINGS: Comparison made to study performed 10/05/20XX. There has been no change apparent in the chest. As noted previously, there is evidence of open heart surgery with cardiac pacemaker in place. The heart remains mildly enlarged, but unchanged from prior studies. The pulmonary vascularity is normal in appearance. Calcified granulomas and fibrotic changes are seen with no new infiltrates identified.

IMPRESSION: Stable appearing postoperative chest with no evidence of active or acute disease.

Thomas O'Toole, MD

Ddt/mm

D: 08/11/20XX
T: 08/11/20XX

Thomas O'Toole, MD   Date

Inpatient Case 7

CODING REGIONAL HOSPITAL
123 MAIN STREET, ANYWHERE, USA

RADIOLOGY REPORT

MR# 876496
PATIENT NAME: WILSON, THOMAS
DOB: 04/17/1953

Dr. James Jones

CLINICAL SUMMARY: Angina

PA AND LATERAL CHEST, 01/15/20XX

FINDINGS: The heart is borderline in size. Pacemaker is seen with wires extending into the right atrium and ventricle. Pulmonary vasculature is within normal limits. Severe degenerative changes are seen in the spine.

IMPRESSION: No significant acute abnormality seen in the chest.

Thomas O'Toole, MD

Ddt/mm

D: 01/15/20XX
T: 01/15/20XX

_____
Thomas O'Toole, MD   Date

Inpatient Case 7

CODING REGIONAL HOSPITAL
123 MAIN STREET, ANYWHERE, USA

DISCHARGE SUMMARY

PATIENT NAME: WILSON, THOMAS #873496
DOB: 04/17/1953

ADMITTED: 01/12/20XX
DISCHARGED: 01/17/20XX

ADMITTING DIAGNOSIS: Chest pain

DISCHARGE DIAGNOSES:
1.	Unstable angina, rule out infarction.
2.	CHF, controlled.
3.	Hypokalemia, secondary to diuretics.
4.	Hyperlipidemia.
5.	Type II diabetes mellitus.
6.	PUD/GERD
7.	History of cerebrovascular disease with previous CVA.

Patient's course was unremarkable except for fever that spiked on the third day of admission. Blood cultures were performed, and the patient was started on IV Keflex and given Tylenol for fever control.

The fever resolved within 24 hours after Tylenol and IV antibiotics were given, and the patient was switched to oral antibiotics for discharge.

Discharge Medications:
Cipro 500 mg bid 7 days
Continue present medications as well.

Patient should follow up within one week with cardiologist.

James Jones, MD

D: 01/17/20XX
T: 01/17/20XX

Inpatient Case 7

CODING REGIONAL HOSPITAL
123 MAIN STREET, ANYWHERE, USA

HOSPITAL ADMISSION FORM	ACCOUNT NUMBER		MEDICAL RECORD NUMBER 417991

PATIENT INFORMATION

PATIENT LAST NAME JEFFERSON	FIRST NAME WANDA	MI M	DOB 01/12/1932	ADMIT DATE/TIME 03/17/20XX 1:35 AM INPT

STREET ADDRESS 347 MAPLE ST	CITY/STATE/ZIP ANYWHERE, ZA 10000	AREA CODE/PHONE NUMBER 111-332-84XX

SEX M ☐ F ☒	RACE	AGE	RELIGIOUS PREFERENCE	OCCUPATION RETIRED	FT ☐ PT ☐

PATIENT'S EMPLOYER	STREET ADDRESS	CITY/STATE/ZIP	AREA CODE/PHONE NUMBER

EMERGENCY CONTACT

#1 LAST NAME JEFFERSON	FIRST NAME RONALD	MI W	AREA CODE/PHONE NUMBER 111-332-84XX	RELATIONSHIP
#2 LAST NAME	FIRST NAME	MI	AREA CODE/PHONE NUMBER	RELATIONSHIP

GUARANTOR

#1 LAST NAME JEFFERSON	FIRST NAME WANDA	MI M	AREA CODE/PHONE NUMBER 111-332-84XX	RELATIONSHIP
#2 LAST NAME	FIRST NAME	MI	AREA CODE/PHONE NUMBER	RELATIONSHIP

ADMISSION INFORMATION

ADMISSION STATUS INPATIENT	PATIENT TYPE MED/SURG	UNIT SURG	ROOM 124	ATTENDING MD ELIZABETH DIAMOND MD	UPIN # 1134711

ADMITTING DIAGNOSIS DJD right knee

INSURANCE INFORMATION

#1 PAYOR NAME MEDICARE/AETNA	STREET ADDRESS PO BOX 1440	CITY/STATE/ZIP ANYWHERE, ZA 10000	PHONE NUMBER 888-332-55XX

POLICY NUMBER 4578271XXB	GROUP NUMBER	GROUP NAME

SUBSCRIBER NAME SAME AS PT	DOB SAME AS PT	AUTHORIZATION NUMBER	DEDUCTIBLE Outpatient $100

#2 PAYOR NAME	STREET ADDRESS	CITY/STATE/ZIP	PHONE NUMBER

POLICY NUMBER	GROUP NUMBER	GROUP NAME

SUBSCRIBER NAME	DOB	AUTHORIZATION NUMBER	DEDUCTIBLE

PROVIDER NUMBER Medicare Provider #005437	PROCEDURES/SERVICES	
	Semi-Private (4) $200.00	$800.00
	OR	$1,500.00
	Surgical Supplies	$1,500.00
	Knee Replacement	$4,500.00
	Knee Joint	$2,400.00
	IV Supplies (4)	$1,000.00
	IV Solutions (4)	$1,000.00
	Anesthesia	$1,000.00
	IV Meds	$500.00

CONTROL NUMBER #00400970 - 03/17/20XX

ATTENDING PHYSICIAN _____	DATE _____

PATIENT RECORD   ORIGINAL

Inpatient Case 8

CODING REGIONAL HOSPITAL
123 MAIN STREET, ANYWHERE, USA

PRE-OP HISTORY AND PHYSICAL EXAMINATION

JEFFERSON, WANDA   **James Jones, MD**

ADMITTED: 03/17/20XX

MEDICAL RECORD NUMBER: 417991

The patient is scheduled for a right total arthroplasty today.

CHIEF COMPLAINT: Bilateral knee pain, right greater than left.

HISTORY OF PRESENT ILLNESS: The patient is a married female. She has always been extremely active. She has rather severe DJD, particularly involving the right knee, and has a lot of associated pain. It is limiting her significantly and she is scheduled for total knee arthroplasty on the right.

PAST MEDICAL HISTORY: She has had several surgeries. In January 2002 she had fusion for right bunion, in August 2003 she had vaginal hysterectomy with A & P repair, cystourethroscopy for uterine prolapse and urinary incontinence.

She has had normal spontaneous vaginal deliveries x 5. Medical problems include her DJD, hypertension and hyperlipidemia. No history of heart disease, diabetes or cancer. No history of anesthesia or bleeding complications.

HABITS: Nonsmoker, nondrinker.

CURRENT MEDICATIONS: Lipitor 10 mg daily, lisinopril 20 mg daily, hydrochlorothiazide 25 mg daily. She also takes some over-the-counter ibuprofen and a baby aspirin daily but has held those prior to the surgery as directed by her physician.

FAMILY HISTORY: Mother died at age 96 of "old age, her heart gave out." Father died at an advanced age of old age as well. Nine siblings, one with diabetes, one sister who died of "bone cancer" and a brother with throat cancer. She is married, has 5 children, one died at age 3 months apparently of a congenital abnormality. The others are living and well.

SOCIAL HISTORY: Currently retired. She had her own catering business and her own bakery that was in her home. She is very socially active and lives with her husband. Her husband has been having some problems with renal failure.

Inpatient Case 8

JEFFERSON, WANDA   James Jones, MD
ADMITTED: 03/17/20XX

MEDICAL RECORD NUMBER: 417991

Page Two (continued)

REVIEW OF SYSTEMS:
General: No fevers, chills or night sweats. Her weight is stable.
Neurological: No complaints.
Psychiatric: Negative.
EENT: No complaints.
Cardio: No chest pain, orthopnea, PND, claudication or edema.
Respiratory: No symptoms.
GI: No symptoms.
GU: Has had some history of UTI but none in the past year or so. She has chronic stress incontinence, always wears a pad.
M/S: As noted above.
Hema/Lymph: Negative. No history of blood transfusion.
Allergies: Garlic.
Skin: No complaints.

PHYSICAL EXAMINATION:
General: Very pleasant, vigorous, healthy-appearing woman appearing her stated age of 72 and in no distress.
                Weight 165, temperature 97.7, pulse 76, BP 160/64.
Skin: Clear. No adenopathy.
HEENT: Normocephalic, atraumatic. PERRL, EOMI. TMs normal.Pharynx clear.
Neck: Supple, carotids normal, no bruits, no JVD, no masses, trachea midline.
Back: Straight, no spinal or CVA tenderness.
Chest: Lungs are clear to auscultation and percussion.
Heart: Regular, slightly bradycardiac in the mid 50s. No murmurs, no gallops or rubs. Peripheral pulses are good throughout, including dorsalis pedis bilaterally. No dependent edema.
Abdomen: Overweight. Soft, nontender. Well healed lower abdominal surgical scar. No masses, normal bowel sounds, no bruits.
Pelvic: Not done.
Extremities: Significant DJD particularly on the right knee, probably some on the left as well. She has some varicosities left lower extremity without edema. No calf tenderness.
Neurological: Cranial nerves II through XII intact.
Motor: Deep tendon reflexes are normal and symmetrical.

Inpatient Case 8

Page Three (continued)

ELECTROCARDIOGRAM: Mild sinus bradycardia with a rate in the 50s, otherwise normal.

CHEST X-RAY: Not repeated as she had one less than 30 days ago that was normal.

LABS: Pending.
She will actually come in early in the day for these, fasting; that will include CBC, chem-7, urinalysis.

ASSESSMENT:
1.   DJD, particularly the right knee.
2.   Hypertension.
3.   Varicose veins left lower extremity.
4.   Hyperlipidemia.

PLAN: Assuming her labs are OK, I see no contraindications to anesthesia and surgery. We want to be careful with DVD prophylactics postoperatively, and support stocking should be worn on the left lower extremity as well.

James Jones, MD

Inpatient Case 8

CODING REGIONAL HOSPITAL
123 MAIN STREET, ANYWHERE, USA

OPERATIVE REPORT

PATIENT NAME: JEFFERSON, WANDA
DATE OF SURGERY: 03/17/20XX

PREOPERATIVE DIAGNOSIS: Severe degenerative arthrosis, right knee.

POSTOPERATIVE DIAGNOSIS: Same.

PROCEDURE: Johnson and Johnson cemented right total knee arthroplasty.

ANESTHESIA: Epidural.

ESTIMATED BLOOD LOSS: 50cc.

TOURNIQUET TIME: Approximately 50 minutes at 300 mg Hg.

COMPLICATIONS: None apparent.

INDICATION: Patient is female with a long-standing history of severe arthrosis of the right knee. Patient failed conservative treatment and other alternatives and risks, possible complications were very carefully discussed, the patient desired surgery and consent was obtained.

DESCRIPTION OF PROCEDURE: The patient was brought to the main operating room and after spinal anesthesia was adequately obtained she was positioned supine. Tourniquet was placed around the right proximal thigh, 1g Ancef was given intravenously, right lower extremity was prepped and draped in the usual sterile fashion. Limb was elevated and tourniquet inflated.

Linear longitudinal incision was made centered over the patella. Subcutaneous tissue was divided sharply. Paramedian arthrotomy was performed in the standard fashion, patella was everted and knee brought into flexion. Distal femur was cut utilizing the intermedullary guide to fit a #3 component. Following demonstration of complete range of motion, the incision was closed appropriately and the patient was returned to the recovery area in satisfactory condition.

James Jones, MD

D: 03/17/20XX
T: 03/17/20XX

Inpatient Case 8

CODING REGIONAL HOSPITAL
123 MAIN STREET, ANYWHERE, USA

DISCHARGE SUMMARY

PATIENT NAME: JEFFERSON, WANDA
DOB: 01/12/20XX

ADMITTED: 03/17/20XX
DISCHARGED: 03/20/20XX

ADMITTING DIAGNOSIS: Degenerative arthritis, right knee.

DISCHARGE DIAGNOSES: Severe degenerative arthrosis of right knee.

ADDITIONAL DIAGNOSES: 1. Hypertension; 2. Hyperlipidemia; 3. Varicose veins, left lower extremity.

PROCEDURES: Johnson and Johnson cemented right total knee arthroplasty under epidural anesthesia on 03/17/20XX.

COMPLICATIONS: None.

HISTORY: Female with knee pain, right greater than left. Preoperative history and physical examination were unremarkable. Please see H & P for further details. She did have significant DJD of both knees, particularly on the right with some varicosities left lower extremity, no edema.

LABORATORY DATA: Preoperative hemoglobin 12.3. White count, 4,500, normal platelets. Glucose 95, BUN 29, creatinine 0.8, potassium 4.1, sodium 144. UA showed 2+ leukocytes but on microscopic only 1-3 per high-powered field. Nonetheless, as a precaution she was placed on three days of trimenthoprim methox prior to surgery. EKG was normal.
Postoperatively, her hemoglobin dropped to low of 9.2. She was asymptomatic. Placed on iron. INR was monitored. She was treated with Coumadin.

HOSPITAL COURSE: She underwent above noted procedure without complication. Postoperatively, things were very uncomplicated. She had epidural anesthesia and then epidural analgesia. She did have some vomiting initially. Resolved. Therapy went extremely well. Had no complications. She will continue with outpatient physical therapy here in town and that was arranged. Activity as tolerated. She is on low cholesterol, no added salt diet. Medications at discharge include enteric coated aspirin, one po daily, FESO4, 325 mg po bid for one month, at which time hemoglobin will be rechecked. Vicodin 1 po q4-6 prn pain #20, no refills. She of course will use plain acetaminophen as well if that is adequate. Lipitor 10 mg daily. Lisinopril 20 mg daily. Hydrochlorothiazide 25 mg daily. To follow up with orthopedist in approximately 2 weeks, when hemoglobin will be repeated.
Discharge instructions reviewed with patient.

James Jones, MD
D: 03/20/20XX
T: 03/20/20XX

Inpatient Case 8

CODING REGIONAL HOSPITAL
123 MAIN STREET, ANYWHERE, USA

HOSPITAL ADMISSION FORM

ACCOUNT NUMBER		MEDICAL RECORD NUMBER
		873496

PATIENT INFORMATION

PATIENT LAST NAME	FIRST NAME	MI	DOB	ADMIT DATE/TIME
WILSON	THOMAS	W	04/17/1953	01/10/20XX

STREET ADDRESS	CITY/STATE/ZIP	AREA CODE/PHONE NUMBER
841 BROAD AVE	ANYWHERE, ZA 10000	111-842-88XX

SEX	RACE	AGE	RELIGIOUS PREFERENCE	OCCUPATION	
M [X] F [ ]				SALES	FT [X] PT [ ]

PATIENT'S EMPLOYER	STREET ADDRESS	CITY/STATE/ZIP	AREA CODE/PHONE NUMBER
ACME MEDICAL	4320 MAIN ST	ANYWHERE, ZA 10000	111-843-81XX

EMERGENCY CONTACT

#1 LAST NAME	FIRST NAME	MI	AREA CODE/PHONE NUMBER	RELATIONSHIP
WILSON	NATALIE		111-842-88XX	Wife
#2 LAST NAME	FIRST NAME	MI	AREA CODE/PHONE NUMBER	RELATIONSHIP

GUARANTOR

#1 LAST NAME	FIRST NAME	MI	AREA CODE/PHONE NUMBER	RELATIONSHIP
WILSON	THOMAS	W	111-842-88XX	
#2 LAST NAME	FIRST NAME	MI	AREA CODE/PHONE NUMBER	RELATIONSHIP

ADMISSION INFORMATION

ADMISSION STATUS	PATIENT TYPE	UNIT	ROOM	ATTENDING MD	UPIN #
INPATIENT	MED/SURG	SURG	231	ELIZABETH DIAMOND MD	1134711

ADMITTING DIAGNOSIS
Shortness of breath

INSURANCE INFORMATION

#1 PAYOR NAME	STREET ADDRESS	CITY/STATE/ZIP	PHONE NUMBER
FEDERATED CARE OF ZA	123 MAPLE ST	ANYWHERE, ZA 10000	800-338-48XX

POLICY NUMBER	GROUP NUMBER	GROUP NAME	
3525078XX	247ZA	ACME MEDICAL	

SUBSCRIBER NAME	DOB	AUTHORIZATION NUMBER	DEDUCTIBLE
SAME	SAME		$1,000 Inpt

#2 PAYOR NAME	STREET ADDRESS	CITY/STATE/ZIP	PHONE NUMBER

POLICY NUMBER	GROUP NUMBER	GROUP NAME	

SUBSCRIBER NAME	DOB	AUTHORIZATION NUMBER	DEDUCTIBLE

PROVIDER NUMBER	PROCEDURES/SERVICES	
Provider #005255	ICU (3) @ $1,000	$3,000.00
	Semi Private Room (3) $200	$600.00
	Drugs	$1,500.00
	IV Solutions (6) $100	$600.00
	IV Supplies (6) $100	$600.00
	Lab Chemistry	$350.00
	Chest X-Ray	$175.00

CONTROL NUMBER
0833074

ATTENDING PHYSICIAN _____   DATE _____

PATIENT RECORD   ORIGINAL

Inpatient Case 9

CODING REGIONAL HOSPITAL
123 MAIN STREET, ANYWHERE, USA

HISTORY AND PHYSICAL EXAMINATION

WILSON, THOMAS	James Jones, MD
ADMITTED: 01/10/20XX	
MEDICAL RECORD NUMBER: 873496	

CHIEF COMPLAINT: Shortness of breath

HISTORY OF PRESENT ILLNESS: This smoker has had an approximately 1-month history of cough and congestion and was treated for pneumonia back in November and never really improved. He was seen in the ER two days ago. At that time he was placed on Biaxin 500 mg bid and told to return if shortness of breath ensued and he has become progressively short of breath. He has been drinking fluids the last day or so, but prior to that was not drinking well at all. He has had fevers in the 102-103 range and just seems to be progressively worse. He presented again complaining of shortness of breath and O2 sats on admission were 83% on room air. He does require occasional use of oxygen at home.

PAST MEDICAL HISTORY: Includes a history of carotid endardectomy. He is a smoker and has severe COPD, coronary artery disease, and also has had a history of bladder cancer.

CURRENT MEDICATIONS: Include diltiazem CD 120 mg once/day, lovastatin 20 mg once/day, sublingual nitroglycerin 0.4 mg prn. Atrovent and albuterol nebulizers, 325 mg of aspirin per day, calcium and vitamin D, vitamin E, Lasix 20 mg bid prn and occasional home oxygen.

FAMILY HISTORY: Reviewed. Quite a bit of heart disease in the family, he is not sure who, but he had a couple brothers die of an MI. Father died of duodenal ulcer rupture but also had heart disease. Mother died of breast cancer.

REVIEW OF SYSTEMS: Positive for shortness of breath and cough. He does have dentures, upper and lower. HEENT: Hearing is normal, vision somewhat impaired, he wears glasses. GU and GI negative other than for GU; he does have frequency but that has been fairly normal and long-standing for him.

Inpatient Case 9

WILSON, THOMAS   James Jones, MD

ADMITTED: 01/10/20XX

MEDICAL RECORD NUMBER: 873496

Page Two (continued)

PHYSICAL EXAMINATION: Temperature 101.2, BP 120/60, respirations 30, O2 sats 83% on room air Does not appear to be dyspneic at this point.

HEENT:	Normal
Skin:	Turgor is fairly normal, although her eyes seem a little sunken so she may be slightly dehydrated. No evidence of jaundice. Pupils are equal, round, reactive to light and accommodation. Extraocular movements are full and intact. Mouth clear.
Neck:	Supple, no bruits.
Lungs:	Decreased breath sounds bilaterally. Some rales present bilaterally, as well as some wheezing
Heart:	Distant. No murmurs.
Breasts:	Normal, no masses.
Abdomen:	Soft, nontender, and no masses or organomegaly. Bowel sounds normal.
Extremities:	Without edema.
Neurological:	Alert and oriented X 3. Deep tendon reflexes are 2+ and symmetrical.

ASSESSMENT: Pneumonia, gradually worsening.

PLAN: Will admit, get him on oxygen, nebulizers, chest x-ray, CBC and electrolytes. Start Timentin 3.1 grams q 8 h and continue Biaxin 500 mg bid, IV fluids with potassium.

James Jones, MD

D: 01/10/20XX
T: 01/10/20XX

Inpatient Case 9

CODING REGIONAL HOSPITAL
123 MAIN STREET, ANYWHERE, USA

PROGRESS NOTE

DATE: 01/11/20XX

TIME:

Patient very SOB, face dusty, fine crackles bases, expiratory wheezes throughout. Will order ABGs. Suspect mucous plug. Discussed with daughter possible need to intubate. Anesthesia called for intubation. Will transfer to ICU.

James Jones, MD

PATIENT ID
WILSON, THOMAS
Admit: 01/10/20XX
MR #873496

PROGRESS NOTE   **Coding Regional Hospital**

Inpatient Case 9

CODING REGIONAL HOSPITAL
123 MAIN STREET, ANYWHERE, USA

PROGRESS NOTE

DATE: 01/12/20XX

TIME:

ICU NOTE

Patient intubated yesterday before transfer to ICU. ABGs performed and patient breathing less labored. Chest x-ray still shows infiltrate same as previous. Will continue to treat with IV antibiotics, IV potassium.

James Jones, MD

ICU NOTE
01/13/20XX

Patient responding to IV antibiotics. Chest x-ray shows some clearing of infiltrate. If patient continues to improve we will transfer to medical floor tomorrow.

Continue meds and treatment.

James Jones, MD

PATIENT ID
WILSON, THOMAS
Admit: 01/10/20XX
MR #873496

PROGRESS NOTE   **Coding Regional Hospital**

Inpatient Case 9

CODING REGIONAL HOSPITAL
123 MAIN STREET, ANYWHERE, USA

PROGRESS NOTE

DATE: 01/14/20XX

TIME:

ICU NOTE

Patient responding to IV antibiotics, improved chest x-ray. Intubation tube removed and patient to be removed to medical floor. Switch to oral antibiotics, and if stable tomorrow, will discharge.

James Jones, MD

PATIENT ID
WILSON, THOMAS
Admit: 01/10/20XX
MR #873496

PROGRESS NOTE   **Coding Regional Hospital**

Inpatient Case 9

CODING REGIONAL HOSPITAL
123 MAIN STREET, ANYWHERE, USA

PROGRESS NOTE

DATE: 01/15/20XX

TIME:

PROGRESS NOTE

Patient remains afebrile without SOB. No wheezing, rales or crackles. Patient will be discharged on oral antibiotics with follow-up visit to PCP in 1-2 days.

James Jones, MD

PATIENT ID

WILSON, THOMAS

Admit: 01/10/20XX

MR #873496

PROGRESS NOTE   **Coding Regional Hospital**

Inpatient Case 9

CODING REGIONAL HOSPITAL
123 MAIN STREET, ANYWHERE, USA

RADIOLOGY REPORT

MR#: 873496
PATIENT NAME: WILSON, THOMAS
DOB: 04/17/1953

Dr. James Jones

CLINICAL SUMMARY: Cough and congestion
PA AND LATERAL CHEST, 12/14/20XX

FINDINGS: Comparison is made to the most recent study of 12/01/20XX. The infiltrate previously described in the medial segment of the right middle lobe is more prominent on today's study and this would be consistent with an active process superimposed on a chronic middle lobe process. The heart and pulmonary vessels are normal in size and appearance and lungs otherwise are clear.

CONCLUSION: Infiltrate medial segment of right middle lobe which has increased in size and density since 12/01/20XX and is consistent with an active process.

Thomas O'Toole, MD

Ddt/mm

D: 08/11/20XX
T: 08/11/20XX

_____
Thomas O'Toole, MD   Date

Inpatient Case 9

CODING REGIONAL HOSPITAL
123 MAIN STREET, ANYWHERE, USA

HOSPITAL ADMISSION FORM	ACCOUNT NUMBER		MEDICAL RECORD NUMBER 374242

PATIENT INFORMATION

PATIENT LAST NAME MARTIN	FIRST NAME ROBERT	MI J	DOB 01/25/1931	ADMIT DATE/TIME 06/01/20XX 2:30 AM

STREET ADDRESS 3462 BROAD AVENUE	CITY/STATE/ZIP ANYWHERE, ZA 10000	AREA CODE/PHONE NUMBER 111-382-45XX

SEX M [X] F	RACE	AGE	RELIGIOUS PREFERENCE	OCCUPATION	FT [ ] PT [ ]

PATIENT'S EMPLOYER RETIRED	STREET ADDRESS	CITY/STATE/ZIP	AREA CODE/PHONE NUMBER

EMERGENCY CONTACT

#1 LAST NAME MARTIN	FIRST NAME MILDRED	MI J	AREA CODE/PHONE NUMBER 111-382-45XX	RELATIONSHIP
#2 LAST NAME	FIRST NAME	MI	AREA CODE/PHONE NUMBER	RELATIONSHIP

GUARANTOR

#1 LAST NAME MARTIN	FIRST NAME ROBERT	MI J	AREA CODE/PHONE NUMBER 111-382-45XX	RELATIONSHIP
#2 LAST NAME	FIRST NAME	MI	AREA CODE/PHONE NUMBER	RELATIONSHIP

ADMISSION INFORMATION

ADMISSION STATUS INPATIENT	PATIENT TYPE MED/SURG	UNIT SURG	ROOM 223	ATTENDING MD ELIZABETH DIAMOND MD	UPIN # 1134711

ADMITTING DIAGNOSIS Confusion, disorientation

INSURANCE INFORMATION

#1 PAYOR NAME MEDICARE	STREET ADDRESS PO BOX 1440	CITY/STATE/ZIP ANYWHERE, ZA 10000	PHONE NUMBER 888-332-55XX
POLICY NUMBER 2359681XXA	GROUP NUMBER	GROUP NAME	
SUBSCRIBER NAME SAME	DOB SAME	AUTHORIZATION NUMBER	DEDUCTIBLE
#2 PAYOR NAME	STREET ADDRESS	CITY/STATE/ZIP	PHONE NUMBER
POLICY NUMBER	GROUP NUMBER	GROUP NAME	
SUBSCRIBER NAME	DOB	AUTHORIZATION NUMBER	DEDUCTIBLE

PROVIDER NUMBER #032571	PROCEDURES/SERVICES	
	Semi-Private Room (3) $600	$1,800.00
	CT	$1,500.00
	Lab-Chemistry	$400.00
	Medical Supplies	$200.00
	IV Supplies (3) $200	$600.00
	IV Medications (3)	$300.00
	IV Solutions (3) $100	$300.00

CONTROL NUMBER 0830793

ATTENDING PHYSICIAN _____	DATE _____

PATIENT RECORD   ORIGINAL

Inpatient Case 10

CODING REGIONAL HOSPITAL
123 MAIN STREET, ANYWHERE, USA

DISCHARGE SUMMARY

PATIENT NAME: MARTIN, ROBERT
DOB: 01/25/1931

ADMITTED: 06/01/20XX
DISCHARGED: 06/03/20XX

ADMITTING DIAGNOSIS: Confusion, disorientation

DISCHARGE DIAGNOSES: Cerebrovascular accident with residual right-sided weakness
   Speech difficulty
   Chronic ischemic heart disease
   Hypertension
   S/P cardiac pacemaker placement, status stable

Patient is a 76-year-old male who presented to the Emergency Room with confusion, disorientation, incoordination and generalized weakness affecting ability to stand or sit. Patient has previous history of chronic ischemic heart disease, hypertension and previously had cardiac pacemaker placed for arrhythmia. Patient has longtime history of cardiac disease and has been treated in the past with angioplasty X 2, CABG, 2 vessels in 2002, and was told he had a cerebrovascular accident in 2003 with left-sided weakness, but had no residual.

Patient's current symptoms began approximately 4 hours ago, when the patient was watching television with his wife. His wife noticed her husband in the reclining chair, attempted to stand up, appeared disoriented, and then fell to the ground. He did not appear to lose consciousness, however was confused, disoriented and unable to stand or sit up. Patient's wife called 911. Upon arrival at the scene, the patient was conscious; however, still unable to recall the events, weak, disoriented and was transported to the hospital at that time.

Upon admission, he was not oriented to time, place or person. Pulse was 70, BP 140/80 and his jugular veins were not distended. Carotids were normal with no viable bruits.

His physical examination upon admission showed no significant murmurs, good air entry on both sides, abdomen soft, nontender. His extremities showed good pulses with no ankle swelling or calf tenderness. Neurologically, cranial nerves appeared intact, fundal exam was deferred, and he was moving all extremities. Babinski was negative on the left, positive on the right and he demonstrated appreciable weakness on the right side.

CT scan was negative. Initial blood tests revealed normal values, including ABGs, BUN and creatinine were normal. Electrolytes normal, troponin normal, blood sugar was elevated at 154.

Patient was admitted with clinical diagnosis of recent cerebrovascular accident.

Inpatient Case 10

CODING REGIONAL HOSPITAL
123 MAIN STREET, ANYWHERE, USA

DISCHARGE SUMMARY

PATIENT NAME: MARTIN, ROBERT
DOB: 01/25/1931

ADMITTED: 06/01/20XX
DISCHARGED: 06/03/20XX

Page Two (continued)

Patient improved in regards to ambulation by day 3; however, remained confused, although oriented to time and place. Speech is affected and the patient remained unable to communicate clearly.

Clinically, the patient was stable, and the wife and patient were anxious for him to return home. It was felt, after consultation with social services, that the patient and wife could care for the patient at home with the assistance of Home Health and Speech Therapy.

The patient was discharged home on 06/03/20XX.

James Jones, MD

D: 06/03/20XX
T: 06/03/20XX

Inpatient Case 10

Appendix II

Outpatient Scenarios

CODING REGIONAL HOSPITAL
123 MAIN STREET, ANYWHERE, USA

HOSPITAL ADMISSION FORM

ACCOUNT NUMBER	MEDICAL RECORD NUMBER
	355676

PATIENT INFORMATION

PATIENT LAST NAME	FIRST NAME	MI	DOB	ADMIT DATE/TIME
DAVIS	PAMELA	R	03/01/2001	02/17/20XX 5:30 PM

STREET ADDRESS	CITY/STATE/ZIP	AREA CODE/PHONE NUMBER
841 BEDFORD ST	ANYWHERE, ZA 10000	111-372-84XX

SEX		RACE	AGE	RELIGIOUS PREFERENCE	OCCUPATION	FT	PT
M ☐ F ☒							

PATIENT'S EMPLOYER	STREET ADDRESS	CITY/STATE/ZIP	AREA CODE/PHONE NUMBER

EMERGENCY CONTACT

#1 LAST NAME	FIRST NAME	MI	AREA CODE/PHONE NUMBER	RELATIONSHIP
DAVIS	RHONDA	J	111-372-84XX	
#2 LAST NAME	FIRST NAME	MI	AREA CODE/PHONE NUMBER	RELATIONSHIP

GUARANTOR

#1 LAST NAME	FIRST NAME	MI	AREA CODE/PHONE NUMBER	RELATIONSHIP
DAVIS	ROGER	P	111-372-84XX	
#2 LAST NAME	FIRST NAME	MI	AREA CODE/PHONE NUMBER	RELATIONSHIP

ADMISSION INFORMATION

ADMISSION STATUS	PATIENT TYPE	UNIT	ROOM	ATTENDING MD	UPIN #
OUTPATIENT	ER	ER	1	ELIZABETH DIAMOND MD	1134711

ADMITTING DIAGNOSIS
02/17 Injury, Arm Lacerations, eyebrow

INSURANCE INFORMATION

#1 PAYOR NAME	STREET ADDRESS	CITY/STATE/ZIP	PHONE NUMBER
FEDERATED CARE OF ZA	123 MAPLE ST	ANYWHERE, ZA 10000	888-833-23XX

POLICY NUMBER	GROUP NUMBER	GROUP NAME
2643511XX	GX1134	ACME MEDICAL

SUBSCRIBER NAME	DOB	AUTHORIZATION NUMBER	DEDUCTIBLE
DAVIS, RHONDA	05/16/1973		$100/Outpatient

#2 PAYOR NAME	STREET ADDRESS	CITY/STATE/ZIP	PHONE NUMBER
BC BS OF ZA	PO BOX 1492	ANYWHERE, ZA 10000	888-325-52XX

POLICY NUMBER	GROUP NUMBER	GROUP NAME
8112632XX	BC 2253	BROWN SUPPLY COMPANY

SUBSCRIBER NAME	DOB	AUTHORIZATION NUMBER	DEDUCTIBLE
DAVIS, ROGER P	10/10/1975		

PROVIDER NUMBER	PROCEDURES/SERVICES	
005255 Federated	99283 ER Level 3	$175.00
77374 BC BS	73100 X-Ray Wrist	$125.00
Admitted through ER 02/17	12011 Laceration Repairs	$275.00
	25600 Distal Radial Fx	$590.00
	99070 Casting Supplies	$380.00

CONTROL NUMBER
0100061

ATTENDING PHYSICIAN _____   DATE _____

PATIENT RECORD   ORIGINAL

Outpatient Case 1

CODING REGIONAL HOSPITAL
123 MAIN STREET, ANYWHERE, USA

EMERGENCY ROOM RECORD

PATIENT NAME: DAVIS, PAMELA
DOB: 03/01/2001
ER PHYSICIAN: Elizabeth Diamond, MD

INITIAL ASSESSMENT: Patient presents with laceration to eyelid/eyebrow.

PHYSICIAN COURSE OF TREATMENT: This female was at the park this afternoon and tripped over a tree stump and fell into a row of hedges. Examination revealed that the patient had a 2.6 cm laceration to the right lower eyelid and a 2.0 cm laceration to the right eyebrow area as well as an obvious dislocation/fracture of the right radial area.

X-ray revealed a non-displaced radial fracture and the fracture was casted appropriately. The skin around the lacerations was scrubbed and draped in a sterile fashion. The right lower eyelid laceration was then re-opposed and sutured with six 5-0 Vicryl deep sutures to re-oppose the subcutaneous tissue. The skin was then re-opposed and sutured with one running 6-0 Nylon suture. The eyebrow laceration was then re-opposed and sutured with four 5-0 Vicryl deep sutures and the skin closed with 6-0 Nylon sutures. Gentamicin ointment was placed around the eye area.

DIAGNOSIS: Lacerations of the eyebrow and eyelid, repaired.
Non-displaced radial fracture
Return in 7 days for suture removal. Keep dry and bandaged.

Elizabeth Diamond, MD

D: 02/17/20XX
T: 02/17/20XX

Outpatient Case 1

CODING REGIONAL HOSPITAL
123 MAIN STREET, ANYWHERE, USA

HOSPITAL ADMISSION FORM	ACCOUNT NUMBER		MEDICAL RECORD NUMBER 779464

PATIENT INFORMATION

PATIENT LAST NAME JOHNSON	FIRST NAME MARLENE	MI	DOB 05/17/53	ADMIT DATE/TIME 06/01/20XX 7:20 AM OP

STREET ADDRESS 3277 MAIN STREET	CITY/STATE/ZIP ANYWHERE, ZA 10000	AREA CODE/PHONE NUMBER 111-328-45XX

SEX M☐ F☒	RACE	AGE	RELIGIOUS PREFERENCE	OCCUPATION	FT☐ PT☐

PATIENT'S EMPLOYER UNEMPLOYED	STREET ADDRESS	CITY/STATE/ZIP	AREA CODE/PHONE NUMBER

EMERGENCY CONTACT

#1 LAST NAME JOHNSON	FIRST NAME MAUREEN	MI	AREA CODE/PHONE NUMBER 111-328-45XX	RELATIONSHIP
#2 LAST NAME	FIRST NAME	MI	AREA CODE/PHONE NUMBER	RELATIONSHIP

GUARANTOR

#1 LAST NAME JOHNSON	FIRST NAME MARLENE	MI	AREA CODE/PHONE NUMBER 111-328-45XX	RELATIONSHIP
#2 LAST NAME	FIRST NAME	MI	AREA CODE/PHONE NUMBER	RELATIONSHIP

ADMISSION INFORMATION

ADMISSION STATUS OUTPATIENT	PATIENT TYPE MED/SURG	UNIT SURG	ROOM 342	ATTENDING MD ELIZABETH DIAMOND MD	UPIN # 1134711

ADMITTING DIAGNOSIS 06/01/20XX Old torn medial meniscus, posterior horn, torn ACL

INSURANCE INFORMATION

#1 PAYOR NAME MEDICAID	STREET ADDRESS PO BOX 4444	CITY/STATE/ZIP ANYWHERE, ZA 10000	PHONE NUMBER 800-123-45XX
POLICY NUMBER 3728432XX	GROUP NUMBER	GROUP NAME	
SUBSCRIBER NAME	DOB	AUTHORIZATION NUMBER	DEDUCTIBLE
#2 PAYOR NAME	STREET ADDRESS	CITY/STATE/ZIP	PHONE NUMBER
POLICY NUMBER	GROUP NUMBER	GROUP NAME	
SUBSCRIBER NAME	DOB	AUTHORIZATION NUMBER	DEDUCTIBLE

PROVIDER NUMBER Medicaid Provider #0041367	PROCEDURES/SERVICES	
	Arthroscopic: Medial Meniscectomy	$2,500
	Chondroplasty	$1,100
	ACL Repair	$1,500
	Splint	$275
	Surgical Supplies	$1,750
	OR Room	$1,900

CONTROL NUMBER 0100071	

ATTENDING PHYSICIAN _____ DATE _____

PATIENT RECORD   ORIGINAL

Outpatient Case 2

CODING REGIONAL HOSPITAL
123 MAIN STREET, ANYWHERE, USA

OPERATIVE REPORT

PATIENT NAME: JOHNSON, MARLENE
DATE OF SURGERY: 06/01/20XX
MEDICAL RECORD: 779464

PREOPERATIVE DIAGNOSIS: Knee injury

POSTOPERATIVE DIAGNOSIS: Torn ACL, older posterior horn meniscus tear

PROCEDURE PERFORMED: Arthroscopic medial meniscectomy with ACL repair

ANESTHESIA: General sedation

DESCRIPTION OF PROCEDURE: This female was involved in a fall during a ski accident approximately 10 months ago, sustaining a twisting injury to the knee. Conservative treatment and management failed to correct her pain, and she is admitted for outpatient knee arthroscopy.

OPERATIVE REPORT: Arthroscope was inserted and, upon exploration, the medial meniscus revealed a small, old posterior horn meniscus tear. A medial meniscectomy was performed. In addition, a chondroplasty was performed with shaving of the articular cartilage of the knee. Upon further exploration, it was also noted that the patient had a torn anterior cruciate ligament from the accident, which was also repaired through the arthroscope.

The patient tolerated the procedure well.

Elizabeth Diamond, MD

D: 06/01/20XX
T: 06/01/20XX

Outpatient Case 2

CODING REGIONAL HOSPITAL
123 MAIN STREET, ANYWHERE, USA

HOSPITAL ADMISSION FORM	ACCOUNT NUMBER		MEDICAL RECORD NUMBER 779464

PATIENT INFORMATION

PATIENT LAST NAME JOHNSON	FIRST NAME MARLENE	MI	DOB 05/17/53	ADMIT DATE/TIME 08/01/20XX 6:00 AM OP

STREET ADDRESS: 3277 MAIN STREET CITY/STATE/ZIP: ANYWHERE, ZA 10000 AREA CODE/PHONE NUMBER: 111-328-45XX

SEX: M [ ] F [X] RACE AGE RELIGIOUS PREFERENCE OCCUPATION FT [ ] PT [ ]

PATIENT'S EMPLOYER: UNEMPLOYED STREET ADDRESS CITY/STATE/ZIP AREA CODE/PHONE NUMBER

EMERGENCY CONTACT

#1 LAST NAME JOHNSON FIRST NAME MAUREEN MI AREA CODE/PHONE NUMBER 111-328-45XX RELATIONSHIP

#2 LAST NAME FIRST NAME MI AREA CODE/PHONE NUMBER RELATIONSHIP

GUARANTOR

#1 LAST NAME JOHNSON FIRST NAME MARLENE MI AREA CODE/PHONE NUMBER 111-328-45XX RELATIONSHIP

#2 LAST NAME FIRST NAME MI AREA CODE/PHONE NUMBER RELATIONSHIP

ADMISSION INFORMATION

ADMISSION STATUS: OUTPATIENT PATIENT TYPE: MED/SURG UNIT: SURG ROOM: 342 ATTENDING MD: ELIZABETH DIAMOND MD UPIN #: 1134711

ADMITTING DIAGNOSIS: 08/01/20XX Stress Incontinence, UTI

INSURANCE INFORMATION

#1 PAYOR NAME MEDICAID STREET ADDRESS PO BOX 4444 CITY/STATE/ZIP ANYWHERE, ZA 10000 PHONE NUMBER 800-123-45XX

POLICY NUMBER 3728432XX GROUP NUMBER GROUP NAME

SUBSCRIBER NAME DOB AUTHORIZATION NUMBER DEDUCTIBLE

#2 PAYOR NAME STREET ADDRESS CITY/STATE/ZIP PHONE NUMBER

POLICY NUMBER GROUP NUMBER GROUP NAME

SUBSCRIBER NAME DOB AUTHORIZATION NUMBER DEDUCTIBLE

PROVIDER NUMBER: Medicaid Provider #0041367

PROCEDURES/SERVICES

Cystourethroscopy w/dilation of bladder	$3,500
Cysto Catheter	$175
OR Room	$1,100
Surigcal Supplies	$1,900

CONTROL NUMBER: 0100072 - 08/01/20XX

ATTENDING PHYSICIAN _____ DATE ___

PATIENT RECORD ORIGINAL

Outpatient Case 3

CODING REGIONAL HOSPITAL
123 MAIN STREET, ANYWHERE, USA

OPERATIVE REPORT

PATIENT NAME: JOHNSON, MARLENE
DATE OF SURGERY: 08/01/20XX
MEDICAL RECORD: 779464

PREOPERATIVE DIAGNOSIS: Stress incontinence; Chronic cystitis

POSTOPERATIVE DIAGNOSIS: Same

PROCEDURE PERFORMED: Cystoscopy with dilation

ANESTHESIA: General sedation

DESCRIPTION OF PROCEDURE: 52-year-old female is admitted to the outpatient surgery area for cytoscopy to evaluate her stress incontinence and repeated urinary tract infections.

OPERATIVE REPORT: The patient was prepped and the cystoscope inserted. Visualization revealed some areas of chronic cystitis. Catheter was inserted and the bladder was dilated for additional evaluation. No lesions, tumors or masses were observed and the scope was removed without incident. The patient tolerated the procedure well.

Joseph Smith, MD

D: 08/01/20XX
T: 08/01/20XX

Outpatient Case 3

CODING REGIONAL HOSPITAL
123 MAIN STREET, ANYWHERE, USA

HOSPITAL ADMISSION FORM	ACCOUNT NUMBER			MEDICAL RECORD NUMBER 417991

PATIENT INFORMATION

PATIENT LAST NAME JEFFERSON	FIRST NAME WANDA	MI M	DOB 01/12/1932	ADMIT DATE/TIME 04/18/20XX 02:45 PM OP

STREET ADDRESS 347 MAPLE ST	CITY/STATE/ZIP ANYWHERE, ZA 10000	AREA CODE/PHONE NUMBER 111-332-84XX

SEX M ☐ F ☒	RACE	AGE	RELIGIOUS PREFERENCE	OCCUPATION	FT ☐ PT ☐

PATIENT'S EMPLOYER RETIRED	STREET ADDRESS	CITY/STATE/ZIP	AREA CODE/PHONE NUMBER

EMERGENCY CONTACT

#1 LAST NAME JEFFERSON	FIRST NAME RONALD	MI W	AREA CODE/PHONE NUMBER 111-332-84XX	RELATIONSHIP
#2 LAST NAME	FIRST NAME	MI	AREA CODE/PHONE NUMBER	RELATIONSHIP

GUARANTOR

#1 LAST NAME JEFFERSON	FIRST NAME WANDA	MI M	AREA CODE/PHONE NUMBER 111-332-84XX	RELATIONSHIP
#2 LAST NAME	FIRST NAME	MI	AREA CODE/PHONE NUMBER	RELATIONSHIP

ADMISSION INFORMATION

ADMISSION STATUS OUTPATIENT	PATIENT TYPE MED/SURG	UNIT SURG	ROOM 334	ATTENDING MD ELIZABETH DIAMOND MD	UPIN # 1134711

ADMITTING DIAGNOSIS Cataract, Right Eye

INSURANCE INFORMATION

#1 PAYOR NAME MEDICARE/AETNA	STREET ADDRESS PO BOX 1440	CITY/STATE/ZIP ANYWHERE, ZA 10000	PHONE NUMBER 888-332-55XX
POLICY NUMBER 4578271XXB	GROUP NUMBER	GROUP NAME	
SUBSCRIBER NAME SAME	DOB SAME	AUTHORIZATION NUMBER	DEDUCTIBLE Outpt $100
#2 PAYOR NAME	STREET ADDRESS	CITY/STATE/ZIP	PHONE NUMBER
POLICY NUMBER	GROUP NUMBER	GROUP NAME	
SUBSCRIBER NAME	DOB	AUTHORIZATION NUMBER	DEDUCTIBLE

PROVIDER NUMBER Medicare #005437 Admitted OP thru ER	PROCEDURES/SERVICES	
	OR	$1,100
	Surgical Supplies	$1,500
	Cataract Extraction	$3,500
	IOL	$1,100
	IV Supplies	$1,000
	IV Solutions	$1,000

CONTROL NUMBER 0010081 - 04/18/20XX

ATTENDING PHYSICIAN _____ DATE _____

PATIENT RECORD ORIGINAL

Outpatient Case 4

CODING REGIONAL HOSPITAL
123 MAIN STREET, ANYWHERE, USA

OPERATIVE REPORT

PATIENT NAME: JEFFERSON, WANDA
DATE OF SURGERY: 04/18/20XX
MEDICAL RECORD: 417991

PREOPERATIVE DIAGNOSIS: Cataract, right eye

POSTOPERATIVE DIAGNOSIS: Cataract, right eye

PROCEDURE PERFORMED: Phacoemulsification of lens of the right eye, with posterior chamber intraocular lens implant

ANESTHESIA: Topical

Admitted to outpatient surgery area for cataract extraction with intraocular lens implantation.

DESCRIPTION OF PROCEDURE: The patient was brought to the anesthesia waiting room and administered drop of tetracaine in the eye. The patient was then taken into the operating room and placed in the supine position. Two drops of viscous lidocaine were placed in the conjunctival cul-de-sac of the eye. The patient was administered a mild sedative intravenously. The patient was then prepared and draped in the usual sterile fashion.

A 15-degree blade was used to make a stab incision approximately 2 o'clock hours to the left of the temporal median. One-half cc of unpreserved 1% lidocaine was then irrigated into the anterior chamber. The anterior chamber was filled with Vitrax. A 2.65 keratome was advanced through the temporal limbus into the anterior chamber. A stab capsulotomy was then made with a 25-gauge bent tip cystotome. Forceps were used to complete the circular capsulorrhexis.

The nucleus of the lens was hydrodissected with balanced salt solution. Phacoemulsification of the nucleus of the lens was carried out using a phaco chop method in 20 seconds with an EPT of 6 seconds. The residual cortex was aspirated from the cul-de-sac. The posterior capsule was polished. The capsular bag was filled with Biolon. An Allergan model AR 40, 14-diopter posterior chamber lens was then introduced into the capsular bag. The residual Biolon was removed from the eye.

The wound was hydrated with balanced salt solution. The wound was stable without leakage. Drops of Ocuflox, Pred Forte and Timoptic 0.5% were placed in the eye.

Patient was taken to the recovery area in stable condition.

Elizabeth Diamond, MD

D: 04/18/20XX
T: 04/18/20XX

Outpatient Case 4

CODING REGIONAL HOSPITAL
123 MAIN STREET, ANYWHERE, USA

ACCOUNT NUMBER	MEDICAL RECORD NUMBER
HOSPITAL ADMISSION FORM	779464

PATIENT INFORMATION

PATIENT LAST NAME	FIRST NAME	MI	DOB	ADMIT DATE/TIME
JOHNSON	MARLENE		05/17/53	12/01/20XX 05:30 AM OP

STREET ADDRESS	CITY/STATE/ZIP	AREA CODE/PHONE NUMBER
3277 MAIN STREET	ANYWHERE, ZA 10000	111-328-45XX

SEX	RACE	AGE	RELIGIOUS PREFERENCE	OCCUPATION	FT	PT
M ☐ F ☒						

PATIENT'S EMPLOYER	STREET ADDRESS	CITY/STATE/ZIP	AREA CODE/PHONE NUMBER
UNEMPLOYED			

EMERGENCY CONTACT

#1 LAST NAME	FIRST NAME	MI	AREA CODE/PHONE NUMBER	RELATIONSHIP
JOHNSON	MAUREEN		111-328-45XX	
#2 LAST NAME	FIRST NAME	MI	AREA CODE/PHONE NUMBER	RELATIONSHIP

GUARANTOR

#1 LAST NAME	FIRST NAME	MI	AREA CODE/PHONE NUMBER	RELATIONSHIP
JOHNSON	MARLENE		111-328-45XX	
#2 LAST NAME	FIRST NAME	MI	AREA CODE/PHONE NUMBER	RELATIONSHIP

ADMISSION INFORMATION

ADMISSION STATUS	PATIENT TYPE	UNIT	ROOM	ATTENDING MD	UPIN #
OUTPATIENT	MED/SURG	SURG	342	ELIZABETH DIAMOND MD	1134711

ADMITTING DIAGNOSIS
12/01/20XX Sigmoid Polyp; Diverticulosis of Colon
Internal Hemorrhoids

INSURANCE INFORMATION

#1 PAYOR NAME	STREET ADDRESS	CITY/STATE/ZIP	PHONE NUMBER
MEDICAID	PO BOX 4444	ANYWHERE, ZA 10000	800-123-45XX

POLICY NUMBER	GROUP NUMBER	GROUP NAME
3728432XX		

SUBSCRIBER NAME	DOB	AUTHORIZATION NUMBER	DEDUCTIBLE

#2 PAYOR NAME	STREET ADDRESS	CITY/STATE/ZIP	PHONE NUMBER

POLICY NUMBER	GROUP NUMBER	GROUP NAME

SUBSCRIBER NAME	DOB	AUTHORIZATION NUMBER	DEDUCTIBLE

PROVIDER NUMBER	PROCEDURES/SERVICES	
Medicaid Provider #0041367	Surgical Pathology	$900
	Polypectomy	$3,300
	Colonoscopy Tip	$175
	OR Room	$1,100
	Surgical Supplies	$1,700
	IV Supplies	$1,100
	IV Solutions	$1,000
	IV Meds	$975
	Local Anesthetic	$200

CONTROL NUMBER
0100073 - 12/01/20XX

ATTENDING PHYSICIAN _____	DATE
PATIENT RECORD	ORIGINAL

Outpatient Case 5

CODING REGIONAL HOSPITAL
123 MAIN STREET, ANYWHERE, USA

OPERATIVE REPORT

PATIENT NAME: JOHNSON, MARLENE
DATE OF SURGERY: 12/01/20XX
MEDICAL RECORD: 779464

PREOPERATIVE DIAGNOSIS: Screening colonoscopy

POSTOPERATIVE DIAGNOSIS: Diverticulosis of colon
     Sigmoid polyps
     Internal hemorrhoids
     Small fibroepithelial polyp on hemorrhoids

PROCEDURE PERFORMED: Colonoscopy and polypectomy

ANESTHESIA: RN sedation

The patient is here for a screening colonoscopy.

DESCRIPTION OF PROCEDURE: The patient was brought to the endoscopy suite and placed in the left lateral position. After she was connected to the EKG, blood pressure and pulse oximeter, they were found to be within reasonable limits. IV sedation was given initially by IV Demerol and then IV Versed. After adequate sedation was obtained, Xylocaine cream was used in the perirectal area. Rectal examination was performed and the patient was found to have a very small, fibroepithelial polyp on her internal hemorrhoids.

The colonoscope was inserted and passed through all the flexures to the cecum. Position in the cecum was identified by the ileocecal valve, and transillumination. The patient had a few diverticuloses in the sigmoid colon, none of which were acutely inflamed. The patient had a small sessile polyp measuring 2 to 3 mm in diameter in the distal sigmoid that was removed. The scope was then retroflexed in the rectum. The scope was withdrawn.

The patient tolerated the procedure well and was transferred to the Same Day Surgery area in stable condition.

Elizabeth Diamond, MD

D: 12/01/20XX
T: 12/01/20XX

Outpatient Case 5

CODING REGIONAL HOSPITAL
123 MAIN STREET, ANYWHERE, USA

SURGICAL PATHOLOGY REPORT

PATIENT NAME: JOHNSON, MARLENE
DATE OF SURGERY: 12/01/20XX
MEDICAL RECORD: 779464

FINAL DIAGNOSIS: Sigmoid colon

BIOPSY: hyperplastic polyp

PREOPERATIVE DIAGNOSIS: Screening colonoscopy, small polyp

POSTOPERATIVE DIAGNOSIS: Diverticulosis, sigmoid polyp and internal hemorrhoids

GROSS DESCRIPTION: The specimen is received in formalin. It is labeled with the above patient's name and "sigmoid polyp." The specimen consists of a small, flat strip of pale tan membrane. It measures 0.3 X 0.1 X 0.1 cm. The specimen is totally embedded in one cassette.

MICROSCOPIC DESCRIPTION: The tubules of the colon are enlarged. Their surfaces are slightly serrated, created by crowding of the epithelium. Lymphocytes, plasma cells and eosinophils are present.

Andrew Berry, MD
Pathologist

D: 12/01/20XX
T: 12/01/20XX

Outpatient Case 5

CODING REGIONAL HOSPITAL
123 MAIN STREET, ANYWHERE, USA

HOSPITAL ADMISSION FORM	ACCOUNT NUMBER		MEDICAL RECORD NUMBER 274939

PATIENT INFORMATION

PATIENT LAST NAME HARLAND	FIRST NAME JOHN	MI J	DOB 08/01/1960	ADMIT DATE/TIME 08/17/20XX 11:00 PM OUT

STREET ADDRESS 8423 BROAD ST	CITY/STATE/ZIP ANYWHERE, ZA 10000	AREA CODE/PHONE NUMBER 111-324-32XX

SEX M [X] F	RACE	AGE	RELIGIOUS PREFERENCE	OCCUPATION	FT [ ] PT [ ]

PATIENT'S EMPLOYER UNEMPLOYED	STREET ADDRESS	CITY/STATE/ZIP	AREA CODE/PHONE NUMBER

EMERGENCY CONTACT

#1 LAST NAME HARLAND	FIRST NAME MELVIN	MI	AREA CODE/PHONE NUMBER 111-382-11XX	RELATIONSHIP
#2 LAST NAME	FIRST NAME	MI	AREA CODE/PHONE NUMBER	RELATIONSHIP

GUARANTOR

#1 LAST NAME HARLAND	FIRST NAME JOHN	MI J	AREA CODE/PHONE NUMBER 111-324-32XX	RELATIONSHIP
#2 LAST NAME	FIRST NAME	MI	AREA CODE/PHONE NUMBER	RELATIONSHIP

ADMISSION INFORMATION

ADMISSION STATUS OUTPATIENT	PATIENT TYPE MED/SURG	UNIT SURG	ROOM 111	ATTENDING MD ELIZABETH DIAMOND, MD	UPIN # 1134711

ADMITTING DIAGNOSIS Esophageal Bleeding

INSURANCE INFORMATION

#1 PAYOR NAME NO INSURANCE/SELF PAY	STREET ADDRESS	CITY/STATE/ZIP	PHONE NUMBER
POLICY NUMBER	GROUP NUMBER	GROUP NAME	
SUBSCRIBER NAME	DOB	AUTHORIZATION NUMBER	DEDUCTIBLE
#2 PAYOR NAME	STREET ADDRESS	CITY/STATE/ZIP	PHONE NUMBER
POLICY NUMBER	GROUP NUMBER	GROUP NAME	
SUBSCRIBER NAME	DOB	AUTHORIZATION NUMBER	DEDUCTIBLE

PROVIDER NUMBER	PROCEDURES/SERVICES	
	Esophagogastroduodenoscopy	$800.00
	EGD Tip	$200.00
	OR Room	$1,000.00
	Surgical Supplies	$1,500.00
	IV Supplies	$500.00
	IV Solutions	$500.00
	IV Meds	$250.00

CONTROL NUMBER 02000073 - 08/17/20XX

ATTENDING PHYSICIAN _____	DATE _____

PATIENT RECORD	ORIGINAL

Outpatient Case 6

CODING REGIONAL HOSPITAL
123 MAIN STREET, ANYWHERE, USA

OPERATIVE REPORT

PATIENT NAME: HARLAND, JOHN
DATE OF SURGERY: 08/17/20XX
MEDICAL RECORD: 274939

POSTOPERATIVE DIAGNOSIS:
1.   Evidence of distal esophageal narrowing with bleeding post passage of the scope and successful subsequent dilatation of distal esophagus.
2.   Evidence of bleeding in the stomach, likely from the GE junction with suspicious pyloric ulcerative area.
3.   Normal duodenum and second part of duodenum.

ANESTHESIA: By CRNA with 1 mg Versed, 1 1/2 cc fentanyl, 25 mg propofol

OPERATION: Esophagogastroduodenoscopy with dilatation of the stricture of GE junction.

This patient is well-known to me from when he had some meat catch in the distal esophagus approximately 2 years ago. At that time we pushed the meat through and did an esophageal dilatation. He is having recurrent pressure after each meal. He has been on some protonics earlier in the year without successful resolution. His other medications include Ditropan XL, which is helping his urinary incontinence, furosemide, Accupril, and oxygen for his underlying COPD. He has a history of hiatal hernia. We were concerned he had recurrence of the stricture at the esophagus based on his symptoms.

DESCRIPTION OF PROCEDURE: Using the Olympus EGD scope, the scope was inserted to about 38, at which time we encountered what appeared to be the GE junction. We proceeded through the GE junction with the scope and immediately saw strands of dark material that appeared to be old clotted blood in the stomach. Looking back up the scope we saw what appeared to be some bleeding in the GE junction and we dilated the stricture with the scope. Via a guide wire, a catheter-type esophageal dilator was utilized and the GE junction was dilated for 5 minutes on a pressure gauge of 7. He tolerated the procedure well. We then completed the EGD to the second part of the duodenum, looking at the pylorus and into the duodenal bulb. We saw some areas of ulceration around the pylorus and several biopsies were obtained around the site.

We then went back and looked at our bleeding sites and they appeared well-controlled and then withdrew the scope.

Patient will be released home when stable in PAR.

Elizabeth Diamond, MD

D: 08/17/20XX
T: 08/17/20XX

Outpatient Case 6

CODING REGIONAL HOSPITAL
123 MAIN STREET, ANYWHERE, USA

| **HOSPITAL ADMISSION FORM** | ACCOUNT NUMBER | | | | MEDICAL RECORD NUMBER 694171 |

PATIENT INFORMATION

| PATIENT LAST NAME GREENE | FIRST NAME ROBERT | MI J | DOB 03/01/56 | ADMIT DATE/TIME 08/17/20XX 11:30PM |
| STREET ADDRESS 34 BROAD AVENUE | | CITY/STATE/ZIP ANYWHERE, ZA 10000 | | AREA CODE/PHONE NUMBER 111-324-84XX |

SEX M [X] F [ ]   RACE   AGE   RELIGIOUS PREFERENCE   OCCUPATION SALES   FT [X] PT [ ]

| PATIENT'S EMPLOYER AUTOMOTIVE INDUST. | STREET ADDRESS 134 MAIN STRE | CITY/STATE/ZIP ANYWHERE, ZA 10000 | AREA CODE/PHONE NUMBER 111-342-53XX |

EMERGENCY CONTACT

| #1 LAST NAME GREENE | FIRST NAME MABEL | MI L | AREA CODE/PHONE NUMBER 111-324-84XX | RELATIONSHIP Wife |
| #2 LAST NAME | FIRST NAME | MI | AREA CODE/PHONE NUMBER | RELATIONSHIP |

GUARANTOR

| #1 LAST NAME GREENE | FIRST NAME ROBERT | MI J | AREA CODE/PHONE NUMBER 222-324-84XX | RELATIONSHIP |
| #2 LAST NAME | FIRST NAME | MI | AREA CODE/PHONE NUMBER | RELATIONSHIP |

ADMISSION INFORMATION

| ADMISSION STATUS OUTPATIENT | PATIENT TYPE SURG | UNIT SURG | ROOM 367 | ATTENDING MD ELIZABETH DIAMOND MD | UPIN # 1134711 |

ADMITTING DIAGNOSIS
08/17/20XX History of Bladder Cancer

INSURANCE INFORMATION

#1 PAYOR NAME BC BS OF ZA	STREET ADDRESS PO BOX 1492	CITY/STATE/ZIP ANYWHERE, ZA 10000	PHONE NUMBER 888-325-52XX
POLICY NUMBER 257-81-12XX	GROUP NUMBER ZA113	GROUP NAME AUTOMOTIVE INDUSTRIES, INC	
SUBSCRIBER NAME GREENE ROBERT	DOB SAME	AUTHORIZATION NUMBER	DEDUCTIBLE $500
#2 PAYOR NAME	STREET ADDRESS	CITY/STATE/ZIP	PHONE NUMBER
POLICY NUMBER	GROUP NUMBER	GROUP NAME	
SUBSCRIBER NAME	DOB	AUTHORIZATION NUMBER	DEDUCTIBLE

PROVIDER NUMBER BCBS #523711 Admitted through ER	PROCEDURES/SERVICES	
	OR	$1,000.00
	Anesthesia	$1,000.00
	Surgical Supplies	$1,000.00
	Cytoscopy	$1,500.00
	IV Supplies	$500.00
	IV Meds	$250.00

CONTROL NUMBER
08000738 - 08/17/20XX

ATTENDING PHYSICIAN _____   DATE _____

PATIENT RECORD   ORIGINAL

Outpatient Case 7

CODING REGIONAL HOSPITAL
123 MAIN STREET, ANYWHERE, USA

OPERATIVE REPORT

PATIENT NAME: GREENE, ROBERT
DATE OF SURGERY: 08/17/20XX
MEDICAL RECORD: 694171

PREOPERATIVE DIAGNOSIS: History of bladder cancer

POSTOPERATIVE DIAGNOSIS: History of bladder cancer

PROCEDURE: Cystoscopy

ANESTHESIA: Local

DESCRIPTION OF PROCEDURE: The patient was taken to the operating room and placed in the supine position. He was prepped and draped in the usual sterile fashion. Then 2% xylocaine jelly was placed in the urethra for local anesthesia. A 16-French flexible cystoscope was passed into the bladder for direct visualization. The anterior urethra was normal. The prostatic fossa was essentially normal and the bladder showed no evidence of tumor recurrence.

The patient tolerated the procedure well and returned to the recovery room in satisfactory condition.

Elizabeth Diamond, MD

D: 08/17/20XX
T: 08/17/20XX

Outpatient Case 7

CODING REGIONAL HOSPITAL
123 MAIN STREET, ANYWHERE, USA

HOSPITAL ADMISSION FORM

ACCOUNT NUMBER	MEDICAL RECORD NUMBER
	873496

PATIENT INFORMATION

PATIENT LAST NAME	FIRST NAME	MI	DOB	ADMIT DATE/TIME
WILSON	THOMAS	W	04/17/1953	03/17/20XX

STREET ADDRESS	CITY/STATE/ZIP	AREA CODE/PHONE NUMBER
841 BROAD AVE	ANYWHERE, ZA 10000	111-842-88XX

SEX	RACE	AGE	RELIGIOUS PREFERENCE	OCCUPATION	
M [X] F [ ]				SALES	FT [X] PT [ ]

PATIENT'S EMPLOYER	STREET ADDRESS	CITY/STATE/ZIP	AREA CODE/PHONE NUMBER
ACME MEDICAL	4320 MAIN ST	ANYWHERE, ZA 10000	111-843-81XX

EMERGENCY CONTACT

#1 LAST NAME	FIRST NAME	MI	AREA CODE/PHONE NUMBER	RELATIONSHIP
WILSON	NATALIE		111-842-88XX	WIFE
#2 LAST NAME	FIRST NAME	MI	AREA CODE/PHONE NUMBER	RELATIONSHIP

GUARANTOR

#1 LAST NAME	FIRST NAME	MI	AREA CODE/PHONE NUMBER	RELATIONSHIP
WILSON	THOMAS	W	111-842-88XX	
#2 LAST NAME	FIRST NAME	MI	AREA CODE/PHONE NUMBER	RELATIONSHIP

ADMISSION INFORMATION

ADMISSION STATUS	PATIENT TYPE	UNIT	ROOM	ATTENDING MD	UPIN #
OUTPATIENT	MED/SURG	SURG	231	ELIZABETH DIAMOND MD	1134711

ADMITTING DIAGNOSIS
Persistent Epigastric Pain

INSURANCE INFORMATION

#1 PAYOR NAME	STREET ADDRESS	CITY/STATE/ZIP	PHONE NUMBER
FEDERATED CARE OF ZA	123 MAPLE ST	ANYWHERE, ZA 10000	800-338-48XX

POLICY NUMBER	GROUP NUMBER	GROUP NAME
3525078XX	247ZA	ACME MEDICAL

SUBSCRIBER NAME	DOB	AUTHORIZATION NUMBER	DEDUCTIBLE
SAME	SAME		$1,000 Inpt

#2 PAYOR NAME	STREET ADDRESS	CITY/STATE/ZIP	PHONE NUMBER
POLICY NUMBER	GROUP NUMBER	GROUP NAME	
SUBSCRIBER NAME	DOB	AUTHORIZATION NUMBER	DEDUCTIBLE

PROVIDER NUMBER	PROCEDURES/SERVICES	
#327831	EGD with biopsy	$2,000.00
	IV Solutions (5)	$100.00
	IV Supplies (5)	$50.00
	Lab Chemistry	$350.00
	Scope Biopsy Tip	$100.00
	Surgical Supplies	$900.00
	IV Meds	$400.00

CONTROL NUMBER
0288837 - 03/17/20XX

ATTENDING PHYSICIAN _____ DATE _____

PATIENT RECORD   ORIGINAL

Outpatient Case 8

CODING REGIONAL HOSPITAL
123 MAIN STREET, ANYWHERE, USA

OPERATIVE REPORT

PATIENT NAME: WILSON, THOMAS
DATE OF SURGERY: 03/17/20XX
MEDICAL RECORD: 873496

PREOPERATIVE DIAGNOSIS: Persistent epigastric pain
      Loss of appetite
      Loss of weight

POSTOPERATIVE DIAGNOSIS: Prominent gastric folds in fundus
      Prominent folds on curvature/gastric mass
      Duodenal biopsy

OPERATION: Esophagogastroduodenoscopy with biopsy

ANESTHESIA: IV conscious sedation with 5 mg Versed, 50 mg Demerol

DESCRIPTION OF PROCEDURE: The gastroscope was introduced with ease all the way to the second part of the duodenum. The mucosa of the esophagus looked normal. The fundus on retroflexion revealed very prominent gastric folds in the fundus. On the lesser curvature in the proximal area there was a very prominent fold of tissue, almost like a gastric mass. It measured 4 X 4 cm, and multiple biopsies were taken from this area. Antrum looked normal, and the duodenal bulb and second part of the duodenum were unremarkable.

Two biopsies were also taken by hot biopsy forceps in the second part of the duodenum to rule out any malabsorption.

Follow-up biopsy results in one week.

Elizabeth Diamond, MD

D: 03/17/20XX
T: 03/17/20XX

Outpatient Case 8

CODING REGIONAL HOSPITAL
123 MAIN STREET, ANYWHERE, USA

HOSPITAL ADMISSION FORM

ACCOUNT NUMBER	MEDICAL RECORD NUMBER
	883434

PATIENT INFORMATION

PATIENT LAST NAME	FIRST NAME	MI	DOB	ADMIT DATE/TIME
SMITH	FELIX	W	03/18/1999	03/01/20XX 2:35

STREET ADDRESS	CITY/STATE/ZIP	AREA CODE/PHONE NUMBER
2342 LAFAYETTE CIRCLE	ANYWHERE, ZA 10000	111-280-53XX

SEX	RACE	AGE	RELIGIOUS PREFERENCE	OCCUPATION
M [X] F [ ]				OFFICE MGR FT [ ] PT [ ]

PATIENT'S EMPLOYER	STREET ADDRESS	CITY/STATE/ZIP	AREA CODE/PHONE NUMBER
FATHER-ABC SEC.			

EMERGENCY CONTACT

#1 LAST NAME	FIRST NAME	MI	AREA CODE/PHONE NUMBER	RELATIONSHIP
SMITH	ALBERT	J	111-280-53XX	
#2 LAST NAME	FIRST NAME	MI	AREA CODE/PHONE NUMBER	RELATIONSHIP

GUARANTOR

#1 LAST NAME	FIRST NAME	MI	AREA CODE/PHONE NUMBER	RELATIONSHIP
SMITH	ALBERT	J	111-280-53XX	
#2 LAST NAME	FIRST NAME	MI	AREA CODE/PHONE NUMBER	RELATIONSHIP

ADMISSION INFORMATION

ADMISSION STATUS	PATIENT TYPE	UNIT	ROOM	ATTENDING MD	UPIN #
OUTPATIENT	ER	ER	1	ELIZABETH DIAMOND MD	1134711

ADMITTING DIAGNOSIS
03/10/20XX Finger Laceration

INSURANCE INFORMATION

#1 PAYOR NAME	STREET ADDRESS	CITY/STATE/ZIP	PHONE NUMBER
BC BS OF ZA	PO BOX 1492	ANYWHERE, ZA 10000	888-325-52XX

POLICY NUMBER	GROUP NUMBER	GROUP NAME	
8118251XX	AX324	ABC SECRETARIAL	

SUBSCRIBER NAME	DOB	AUTHORIZATION NUMBER	DEDUCTIBLE
SMITH ALBERT J.	03/11/78		

#2 PAYOR NAME	STREET ADDRESS	CITY/STATE/ZIP	PHONE NUMBER

POLICY NUMBER	GROUP NUMBER	GROUP NAME	

SUBSCRIBER NAME	DOB	AUTHORIZATION NUMBER	DEDUCTIBLE

PROVIDER NUMBER	PROCEDURES/SERVICES	
523711	ER	$275.00
	Surgical Supplies	$325.00
	Sterile Tray	$50.00
	Local Anesthetic	$150.00
	Finger X-Ray	$150.00
	Oral Meds	$25.00

CONTROL NUMBER
01002073 - 03/01/20XX

ATTENDING PHYSICIAN _____ DATE _____

PATIENT RECORD   ORIGINAL

Outpatient Case 9

CODING REGIONAL HOSPITAL
123 MAIN STREET, ANYWHERE, USA

EMERGENCY ROOM RECORD

PATIENT NAME: SMITH, FELIX
DOS:
ER PHYSICIAN:

INTIAL ASSESSMENT:

PHYSICIAN COURSE OF TREATMENT:

CURRENT MEDICATIONS:

PROCEDURE:

D:
T:

Outpatient Case 9

CODING REGIONAL HOSPITAL
123 MAIN STREET, ANYWHERE, USA

RADIOLOGY REPORT

MR#: 883434
PATIENT NAME: SMITH, FELIX
DOS: 03/01/20XX

REQUESTING PHYSICIAN: James Smith, MD

Right Index Finger

There is a fracture off the proximal ulnar aspect of the distal phalanx. There is associated laceration in the soft tissue. These findings are compatible with a skill-saw injury. The small bone fragment is separated from the main body of the phalanx a few millimeters.

Thomas Johnson, MD
Radiologist

D: 03/01/20XX
T: 03/01/20XX

Thomas Johnson, MD	Date

Outpatient Case 9

CODING REGIONAL HOSPITAL
123 MAIN STREET, ANYWHERE, USA

| **HOSPITAL ADMISSION FORM** | ACCOUNT NUMBER | | MEDICAL RECORD NUMBER 417991 |

PATIENT INFORMATION

| PATIENT LAST NAME JEFFERSON | FIRST NAME WANDA | MI M | DOB 01/12/1932 | ADMIT DATE/TIME 12/11/20XX 11:20 AM OP |
| STREET ADDRESS 347 MAPLE ST | | CITY/STATE/ZIP ANYWHERE, ZA 10000 | AREA CODE/PHONE NUMBER 111-332-84XX |

SEX M ☐ F ☒   RACE ___   AGE ___   RELIGIOUS PREFERENCE ___   OCCUPATION ___   FT ☐ PT ☐

| PATIENT'S EMPLOYER RETIRED | STREET ADDRESS | CITY/STATE/ZIP | AREA CODE/PHONE NUMBER |

EMERGENCY CONTACT

| #1 LAST NAME JEFFERSON | FIRST NAME RONALD | MI W | AREA CODE/PHONE NUMBER 111-332-84XX | RELATIONSHIP |
| #2 LAST NAME | FIRST NAME | MI | AREA CODE/PHONE NUMBER | RELATIONSHIP |

GUARANTOR

| #1 LAST NAME JEFFERSON | FIRST NAME WANDA | MI M | AREA CODE/PHONE NUMBER 111-332-84XX | RELATIONSHIP |
| #2 LAST NAME | FIRST NAME | MI | AREA CODE/PHONE NUMBER | RELATIONSHIP |

ADMISSION INFORMATION

| ADMISSION STATUS OUTPATIENT | PATIENT TYPE MED/SURG | UNIT SURG | ROOM 334 | ATTENDING MD ELIZABETH DIAMOND MD | UPIN # 1134711 |

ADMITTING DIAGNOSIS
Right Breast Cancer

INSURANCE INFORMATION

#1 PAYOR NAME MEDICARE/AETNA	STREET ADDRESS PO BOX 1440	CITY/STATE/ZIP ANYWHERE, ZA 10000	PHONE NUMBER 888-332-55XX
POLICY NUMBER 4578271XXB	GROUP NUMBER		GROUP NAME
SUBSCRIBER NAME SAME AS PT	DOB SAME AS PT	AUTHORIZATION NUMBER	DEDUCTIBLE Outpt $100
#2 PAYOR NAME	STREET ADDRESS	CITY/STATE/ZIP	PHONE NUMBER
POLICY NUMBER	GROUP NUMBER		GROUP NAME
SUBSCRIBER NAME	DOB	AUTHORIZATION NUMBER	DEDUCTIBLE

PROVIDER NUMBER Medicare #337181 Admitted OP	PROCEDURES/SERVICES	
	OR	$1,100.00
	Surgical Supplies	$500.00
	Breast Surgery	$3,500.00
	IV Supplies	$500.00
	IV Solutions	$500.00
	Anesthesia	$1,500.00

CONTROL NUMBER
00200098 - 12/11/20XX

ATTENDING PHYSICIAN _____ DATE _____

PATIENT RECORD   ORIGINAL

Outpatient Case 10

CODING REGIONAL HOSPITAL
123 MAIN STREET, ANYWHERE, USA

OPERATIVE REPORT

PATIENT NAME: JEFFERSON, WANDA
DATE OF SURGERY: 12/11/20XX
MEDICAL RECORD: 417991

PREOPERATIVE DIAGNOSIS: Right-breast cancer

POSTOPERATIVE DIAGNOSIS: Same

OPERATION: Lumpectomy, right breast with axillary node dissection

ANESTHESIA: General

DESCRIPTION OF PROCEDURE: Patient was placed on the operating table in the supine position. After induction of general anesthesia and endotracheal intubation, the right breast and axilla were prepped and draped in the usual manner. The palpable mass in the upper right breast was marked. An elliptical incision was made above the tumor and the needle biopsy site. The incision was about 10-12 cms in length and a few cms above the areola. Incision was made shapely with a knife and carried superiorly to the infraclavicular area and inferiorly below the areola, removing the tumor down to the pectoralis fascia. The tumor was later sent to frozen section and showed the margins were clear. Axillary dissection was carried out. A Jackson-Pratt was placed in the axilla and secured to the skin with 2-0 silk. The breast incision was closed in layers with 2-0 Vicryl, 3-0 Vicryl and then staples to the skin.

Elizabeth Diamond, MD

D: 12/11/20XX
T: 12/11/20XX

Outpatient Case 11

CODING REGIONAL HOSPITAL
123 MAIN STREET, ANYWHERE, USA

SURGICAL PATHOLOGY REPORT

PATIENT NAME: JEFFERSON, WANDA
DATE OF SURGERY: 12/11/20XX
MEDICAL RECORD: 417991

REQUESTING PHYSICIAN: Elizabeth Diamond, MD

DIAGNOSIS: Invasive ductal carcinoma, grade III.
Surgical margin is free of tumor.
Twelve benign lymph nodes.

GROSS DESCRIPTION: The specimen is labeled as right breast. Received is a lumpectomy specimen with an axillary node dissection measuring 11 X 7 X 5 cm. An overlying skin ellipse measures 11 X 14 cm. Specimen is inked in black on its deep and lateral surfaced serially sectioned to reveal a 3 X 2 X 2.5 cm tumor mass located in the deep and superior portion of the specimen.

Andrew Berry, MD
Radiologist

D: 12/11/20XX
T: 12/11/20XX

Outpatient Case 11

CODING REGIONAL HOSPITAL
123 MAIN STREET, ANYWHERE, USA

HOSPITAL ADMISSION FORM

ACCOUNT NUMBER	MEDICAL RECORD NUMBER
	779464

PATIENT INFORMATION

PATIENT LAST NAME	FIRST NAME	MI	DOB	ADMIT DATE/TIME
JOHNSON	MARLENE		05/17/53	12/21/20XX 8:45 AM OP

STREET ADDRESS	CITY/STATE/ZIP	AREA CODE/PHONE NUMBER
3277 MAIN STREET	ANYWHERE, ZA 10000	111-328-45XX

SEX	RACE	AGE	RELIGIOUS PREFERENCE	OCCUPATION	
M ☐ F ☒					FT ☐ PT ☐

PATIENT'S EMPLOYER	STREET ADDRESS	CITY/STATE/ZIP	AREA CODE/PHONE NUMBER
UNEMPLOYED			

EMERGENCY CONTACT

#1 LAST NAME	FIRST NAME	MI	AREA CODE/PHONE NUMBER	RELATIONSHIP
JOHNSON	MAUREEN		111-328-45XX	
#2 LAST NAME	FIRST NAME	MI	AREA CODE/PHONE NUMBER	RELATIONSHIP

GUARANTOR

#1 LAST NAME	FIRST NAME	MI	AREA CODE/PHONE NUMBER	RELATIONSHIP
JOHNSON	MARLENE		111-328-45XX	
#2 LAST NAME	FIRST NAME	MI	AREA CODE/PHONE NUMBER	RELATIONSHIP

ADMISSION INFORMATION

ADMISSION STATUS	PATIENT TYPE	UNIT	ROOM	ATTENDING MD	UPIN #
OUTPATIENT	MED/SURG	SURG	342	ELIZABETH DIAMOND MD	1134711

ADMITTING DIAGNOSIS

12/21/20XX Recurrent Endometriosis

Pelvic Adhesive Disease

INSURANCE INFORMATION

#1 PAYOR NAME	STREET ADDRESS	CITY/STATE/ZIP	PHONE NUMBER
MEDICAID	PO BOX 4444	ANYWHERE, ZA 10000	800-123-45XX

POLICY NUMBER	GROUP NUMBER	GROUP NAME
3728432XX		

SUBSCRIBER NAME	DOB	AUTHORIZATION NUMBER	DEDUCTIBLE

#2 PAYOR NAME	STREET ADDRESS	CITY/STATE/ZIP	PHONE NUMBER

POLICY NUMBER	GROUP NUMBER	GROUP NAME

SUBSCRIBER NAME	DOB	AUTHORIZATION NUMBER	DEDUCTIBLE

PROVIDER NUMBER	PROCEDURES/SERVICES	
0041367	General Anesthesia	$1,000.00
	Laparoscopy	$2,000.00
	Surgical Supplies	$1,750.00
	OR Room	$1,900.00
	IV Supplies	$800.00
	IV Solutions	$500.00
	IV Meds	$200.00

CONTROL NUMBER

0200089 - 12/21/20XX

ATTENDING PHYSICIAN _____ DATE _____

PATIENT RECORD   ORIGINAL

Outpatient Case 11

CODING REGIONAL HOSPITAL
123 MAIN STREET, ANYWHERE, USA

OPERATIVE REPORT

PATIENT NAME: JOHNSON, MARLENE
DATE OF SURGERY: 12/21/20XX
MEDICAL RECORD: 779464

PREOPERATIVE DIAGNOSIS: Recurrent endometriosis/pelvic adhesive disease

POSTOPERATIVE DIAGNOSIS: Same

PROCEDURE: Laparoscopy with fulguration of endometriosis
       Lysis of adhesions

ANESTHESIA: General by mask

DESCRIPTION OF PROCEDURE: The patient was placed under anesthesia and legs placed in the dorsal lithotomy position in the usual manner for laparoscopy. She was prepped and draped as usual. A cone cannula was placed at the cervix. A stab incision was made at the umbilicus. A direct Trocar insertion was made using the step introducer and then a second suprapublic 5 mm port was established. The bipolar coagulator was used to coagulate and bluntly take down adhesions, as was the bipolar scissors. The area of endometriosis was studied and all implants were fulgurated. Tubes looked normal and the patient does not appear to have PIP. After determining we had treated all the areas of endometriosis, the pneumoperitoneum was decompressed and all hardware removed. Incisions were closed with interrupted 4-0 Vicryl sutures. She was sent to the recovery room in satisfactory condition.

Elizabeth Diamond, MD

D: 12/21/20XX
T: 12/21/20XX

Outpatient Case 11

CODING REGIONAL HOSPITAL
123 MAIN STREET, ANYWHERE, USA

HOSPITAL ADMISSION FORM	ACCOUNT NUMBER		MEDICAL RECORD NUMBER 417991

PATIENT INFORMATION

PATIENT LAST NAME JEFFERSON	FIRST NAME WANDA	MI M	DOB 01/12/1932	ADMIT DATE/TIME 05/06/20XX 10:00 AM OP

STREET ADDRESS 347 MAPLE ST	CITY/STATE/ZIP ANYWHERE, ZA 10000	AREA CODE/PHONE NUMBER 111-332-84XX

SEX M☐ F☒	RACE	AGE	RELIGIOUS PREFERENCE	OCCUPATION	FT☐ PT☐

PATIENT'S EMPLOYER RETIRED	STREET ADDRESS	CITY/STATE/ZIP	AREA CODE/PHONE NUMBER

EMERGENCY CONTACT

#1 LAST NAME JEFFERSON	FIRST NAME RONALD	MI W	AREA CODE/PHONE NUMBER 111-332-84XX	RELATIONSHIP
#2 LAST NAME	FIRST NAME	MI	AREA CODE/PHONE NUMBER	RELATIONSHIP

GUARANTOR

#1 LAST NAME JEFFERSON	FIRST NAME WANDA	MI M	AREA CODE/PHONE NUMBER 111-332-84XX	RELATIONSHIP
#2 LAST NAME	FIRST NAME	MI	AREA CODE/PHONE NUMBER	RELATIONSHIP

ADMISSION INFORMATION

ADMISSION STATUS OUTPATIENT	PATIENT TYPE MED/SURG	UNIT SURG	ROOM 334	ATTENDING MD ELIZABETH DIAMOND MD	UPIN # 1134711

ADMITTING DIAGNOSIS Abdominal Pain

INSURANCE INFORMATION

#1 PAYOR NAME MEDICARE/AETNA	STREET ADDRESS PO BOX 1440	CITY/STATE/ZIP ANYWHERE, ZA 10000	PHONE NUMBER 888-332-55XX

POLICY NUMBER 4578271XXB	GROUP NUMBER	GROUP NAME

SUBSCRIBER NAME SAME AS PT	DOB SAME AS PT	AUTHORIZATION NUMBER	DEDUCTIBLE Outpatient $100

#2 PAYOR NAME	STREET ADDRESS	CITY/STATE/ZIP	PHONE NUMBER

POLICY NUMBER	GROUP NUMBER	GROUP NAME

SUBSCRIBER NAME	DOB	AUTHORIZATION NUMBER	DEDUCTIBLE

PROVIDER NUMBER 005437	PROCEDURES/SERVICES	
	OR	$1,500.00
	Surgical Supplies	$1,100.00
	EGD	$2,500.00
	Colonoscopy	$800.00
	IV Supplies	$1,000.00
	IV Solutions	$1,000.00
	IV Sedation	$200.00

CONTROL NUMBER 0010211 - 05/06/20XX

ATTENDING PHYSICIAN _____   DATE _____

PATIENT RECORD   ORIGINAL

Outpatient Case 12

CODING REGIONAL HOSPITAL
123 MAIN STREET, ANYWHERE, USA

OPERATIVE REPORT

PATIENT NAME: JEFFERSON, WANDA
DATE OF SURGERY: 05/06/20XX
MEDICAL RECORD: 417991

PREOPERATIVE DIAGNOSIS: Weight loss
     Abdominal pain
     Occult positive stool
     Nausea

POSTOPERATIVE DIAGNOSIS: Same

OPERATION: EGD and attempted colonoscopy

This patient was referred for evaluation of weight loss, chronic abdominal pain, occult positive stool and continual nausea.

After adequate preparation, a gastroscope was inserted under direct vision into the esophagus. This was passed down the EG junction, stomach and first and second part of the duodenum.

A colonoscope was then inserted into the rectum. However, the scope could not be advanced, so the procedure was terminated.

Elizabeth Diamond, MD

D: 05/06/20XX
T: 05/06/20XX

Outpatient Case 12

CODING REGIONAL HOSPITAL
123 MAIN STREET, ANYWHERE, USA

HOSPITAL ADMISSION FORM	ACCOUNT NUMBER		MEDICAL RECORD NUMBER 830701

PATIENT INFORMATION

PATIENT LAST NAME JONES	FIRST NAME REBECCA	MI M	DOB 05/18/2004	ADMIT DATE/TIME 04/28/20XX 10:30 AM

STREET ADDRESS 6523 MAPLE DR	CITY/STATE/ZIP ANYWHERE, ZA 10000	AREA CODE/PHONE NUMBER 111-234-84XX

SEX M ☐ F ☒	RACE	AGE	RELIGIOUS PREFERENCE	OCCUPATION	FT ☐ PT ☐

PATIENT'S EMPLOYER CHILD	STREET ADDRESS	CITY/STATE/ZIP	AREA CODE/PHONE NUMBER

EMERGENCY CONTACT

#1 LAST NAME JONES	FIRST NAME ROBERT	MI E	AREA CODE/PHONE NUMBER 111-234-84XX	RELATIONSHIP
#2 LAST NAME	FIRST NAME	MI	AREA CODE/PHONE NUMBER	RELATIONSHIP

GUARANTOR

#1 LAST NAME JONES	FIRST NAME ROBERT	MI E	AREA CODE/PHONE NUMBER 111-234-84XX	RELATIONSHIP
#2 LAST NAME	FIRST NAME	MI	AREA CODE/PHONE NUMBER	RELATIONSHIP

ADMISSION INFORMATION

ADMISSION STATUS OUTPATIENT	PATIENT TYPE ER	UNIT ER	ROOM 3	ATTENDING MD ELIZABETH DIAMOND MD	UPIN # 1134711

ADMITTING DIAGNOSIS Finger Injury

INSURANCE INFORMATION

#1 PAYOR NAME MEDICAID	STREET ADDRESS PO BOX 4444	CITY/STATE/ZIP ANYWHERE, ZA 10000	PHONE NUMBER 800-123-45XX
POLICY NUMBER 3422484XX	GROUP NUMBER	GROUP NAME	
SUBSCRIBER NAME JONES REBECCA M	DOB 05/18/2004	AUTHORIZATION NUMBER	DEDUCTIBLE
#2 PAYOR NAME	STREET ADDRESS	CITY/STATE/ZIP	PHONE NUMBER
POLICY NUMBER	GROUP NUMBER	GROUP NAME	
SUBSCRIBER NAME	DOB	AUTHORIZATION NUMBER	DEDUCTIBLE

PROVIDER NUMBER 0041367	PROCEDURES/SERVICES	
	ER VISIT	$300.00
	Surgical Supplies	$200.00
	Finger X-Ray	$125.00

CONTROL NUMBER 0030050

ATTENDING PHYSICIAN _____ DATE _____

PATIENT RECORD   ORIGINAL

Outpatient Case 13

CODING REGIONAL HOSPITAL
123 MAIN STREET, ANYWHERE, USA

EMERGENCY ROOM RECORD

PATIENT NAME: JONES, REBECCA
DOS: 04/28/20XX
MEDICAL RECORD: 830701
ER PHYSICIAN: Elizabeth Diamond, MD

INITIAL ASSESSMENT: Injured finger

PHYSICIAN COURSE OF TREATMENT: A female fell from a ladder at home, fracturing her fourth distal phalanx. She presented to the emergency room for evaluation. The emergency room physician assessed that the fracture was minimal and treated it by application of a static finger splint.

The patient was discharged, to be followed up by her family physician if needed.

Elizabeth Diamond, MD

D: 04/28/20XX
T: 04/28/20XX

Outpatient Case 13

CODING REGIONAL HOSPITAL
123 MAIN STREET, ANYWHERE, USA

HOSPITAL ADMISSION FORM	ACCOUNT NUMBER		MEDICAL RECORD NUMBER 830701

PATIENT INFORMATION

PATIENT LAST NAME JONES	FIRST NAME REBECCA	MI M	DOB 05/18/2004	ADMIT DATE/TIME 10/03/20XX 9:00 AM

STREET ADDRESS 6523 MAPLE DR	CITY/STATE/ZIP ANYWHERE, ZA 10000	AREA CODE/PHONE NUMBER 111-234-84XX

SEX M☐ F☒	RACE	AGE	RELIGIOUS PREFERENCE	OCCUPATION	FT☐ PT☐

PATIENT'S EMPLOYER CHILD	STREET ADDRESS	CITY/STATE/ZIP	AREA CODE/PHONE NUMBER

EMERGENCY CONTACT

#1 LAST NAME JONES	FIRST NAME ROBERT	MI E	AREA CODE/PHONE NUMBER 111-234-84XX	RELATIONSHIP
#2 LAST NAME	FIRST NAME	MI	AREA CODE/PHONE NUMBER	RELATIONSHIP

GUARANTOR

#1 LAST NAME JONES	FIRST NAME ROBERT	MI E	AREA CODE/PHONE NUMBER 111-234-84XX	RELATIONSHIP
#2 LAST NAME	FIRST NAME	MI	AREA CODE/PHONE NUMBER	RELATIONSHIP

ADMISSION INFORMATION

ADMISSION STATUS ER	PATIENT TYPE ER	UNIT ER	ROOM 6	ATTENDING MD ELIZABETH DIAMOND MD	UPIN # 1134711

ADMITTING DIAGNOSIS Nausea and Vomiting

INSURANCE INFORMATION

#1 PAYOR NAME MEDICAID	STREET ADDRESS PO BOX 4444	CITY/STATE/ZIP ANYWHERE, ZA 10000	PHONE NUMBER 800-123-45XX

POLICY NUMBER 3422484XX	GROUP NUMBER	GROUP NAME	

SUBSCRIBER NAME JONES REBECCA M	DOB 05/18/2004	AUTHORIZATION NUMBER	DEDUCTIBLE

#2 PAYOR NAME	STREET ADDRESS	CITY/STATE/ZIP	PHONE NUMBER

POLICY NUMBER	GROUP NUMBER	GROUP NAME	

SUBSCRIBER NAME	DOB	AUTHORIZATION NUMBER	DEDUCTIBLE

PROVIDER NUMBER 0041367	PROCEDURES/SERVICES	
	ER VISIT	$400.00
	IV Solutions	$200.00
	IV Meds	$200.00
	IV Supplies	$200.00

CONTROL NUMBER 00300782 - 10/03/20XX

ATTENDING PHYSICIAN _____   DATE _____

PATIENT RECORD   ORIGINAL

Outpatient Case 14

CODING REGIONAL HOSPITAL
123 MAIN STREET, ANYWHERE, USA

EMERGENCY ROOM RECORD

PATIENT NAME: JONES, REBECCA
DOS: 10/03/20XX
MEDICAL RECORD: 830701
ER PHYSICIAN: Elizabeth Diamond, MD

INITIAL ASSESSMENT: Nausea and vomiting

PHYSICIAN COURSE OF TREATMENT: Patient presented to the emergency room with approximately 4-6 hour history of nausea and vomiting. Denies abdominal pain. Other members of the family reported similar symptoms following picnic yesterday. Patient was observed in the emergency room and given IV saline for rehydration with no further episodes of nausea or vomiting.

Patient was discharged to follow up if necessary with her family physician.

DIAGNOSIS: Acute nausea and vomiting, probably viral gastritis or food poisoning.

Elizabeth Diamond, MD

D: 10/03/20XX
T: 10/03/20XX

Outpatient Case 14

CODING REGIONAL HOSPITAL
123 MAIN STREET, ANYWHERE, USA

HOSPITAL ADMISSION FORM

ACCOUNT NUMBER	MEDICAL RECORD NUMBER
	694171

PATIENT LAST NAME	FIRST NAME	MI	DOB	ADMIT DATE/TIME
GREENE	ROBERT	J	03/01/56	11/11/20XX 10:00AM

STREET ADDRESS	CITY/STATE/ZIP	AREA CODE/PHONE NUMBER
34 BROAD AVENUE	ANYWHERE, ZA 10000	111-324-84XX

PATIENT INFORMATION

SEX M [X] F [ ] RACE AGE RELIGIOUS PREFERENCE OCCUPATION SALES FT [X] PT [ ]

PATIENT'S EMPLOYER	STREET ADDRESS	CITY/STATE/ZIP	AREA CODE/PHONE NUMBER
AUTOMOTIVE INDUST.	134 MAIN STRE	ANYWHERE, ZA 10000	111-342-53XX

EMERGENCY CONTACT

#1 LAST NAME	FIRST NAME	MI	AREA CODE/PHONE NUMBER	RELATIONSHIP
GREENE	MABEL	L	111-324-84XX	WIFE
#2 LAST NAME	FIRST NAME	MI	AREA CODE/PHONE NUMBER	RELATIONSHIP

GUARANTOR

#1 LAST NAME	FIRST NAME	MI	AREA CODE/PHONE NUMBER	RELATIONSHIP
GREENE	ROBERT	J	222-324-84XX	
#2 LAST NAME	FIRST NAME	MI	AREA CODE/PHONE NUMBER	RELATIONSHIP

ADMISSION INFORMATION

ADMISSION STATUS	PATIENT TYPE	UNIT	ROOM	ATTENDING MD	UPIN #
OUTPATIENT	SURG	SURG	367	ELIZABETH DIAMOND MD	1134711

ADMITTING DIAGNOSIS
Hallux Abducto Valgus, Right Foot

INSURANCE INFORMATION

#1 PAYOR NAME	STREET ADDRESS	CITY/STATE/ZIP	PHONE NUMBER
BC BS OF ZA	PO BOX 1492	ANYWHERE, ZA 10000	888-325-52XX

POLICY NUMBER	GROUP NUMBER	GROUP NAME
257-81-12XX	ZA113	AUTOMOTIVE INDUSTRIES, INC

SUBSCRIBER NAME	DOB	AUTHORIZATION NUMBER	DEDUCTIBLE
GREENE ROBERT J	SAME		$500

#2 PAYOR NAME	STREET ADDRESS	CITY/STATE/ZIP	PHONE NUMBER
POLICY NUMBER	GROUP NUMBER	GROUP NAME	
SUBSCRIBER NAME	DOB	AUTHORIZATION NUMBER	DEDUCTIBLE

PROVIDER NUMBER
BCBS #52371

PROCEDURES/SERVICES	
OR	$1,000.00
Anesthesia	$700.00
Surgical Supplies	$500.00
Hallux Abducto Valgus	$1,000.00
IV Solutions	$400.00
IV Meds	$200.00
IV Supplies	$400.00

CONTROL NUMBER
0070043

ATTENDING PHYSICIAN _____ DATE _____

PATIENT RECORD   ORIGINAL

Outpatient Case 15

CODING REGIONAL HOSPITAL
123 MAIN STREET, ANYWHERE, USA

OPERATIVE REPORT

PATIENT NAME: GREENE, ROBERT
DATE OF SURGERY: 11/11/20XX
MEDICAL RECORD: 694171

PREOPERATIVE DIAGNOSIS: Hallux abducto valgus

POSTOPERATIVE DIAGNOSIS: Same

PROCEDURE PERFORMED: Austin bunionectomy

ANESTHESIA: General sedation

DESCRIPTION OF PROCEDURE: Male patient presents with hallux abducto valgus of the right foot that has developed over the past several years. Patient well-known as he has had several other foot procedures performed in the past, including bunionectomy of the left foot approximately 1 year ago.

The patient was prepped and draped in the usual sterile manner. An Austin bunionectomy with 0.050 K wire fixation and osteotomy was performed on the right foot.

The patient tolerated the procedure well and was discharged in satisfactory status.

Elizabeth Diamond, MD

D: 11/11/20XX
T: 11/11/20XX

Outpatient Case 15

Appendix III

Proposed UB-92 Revision (UB-04) Information

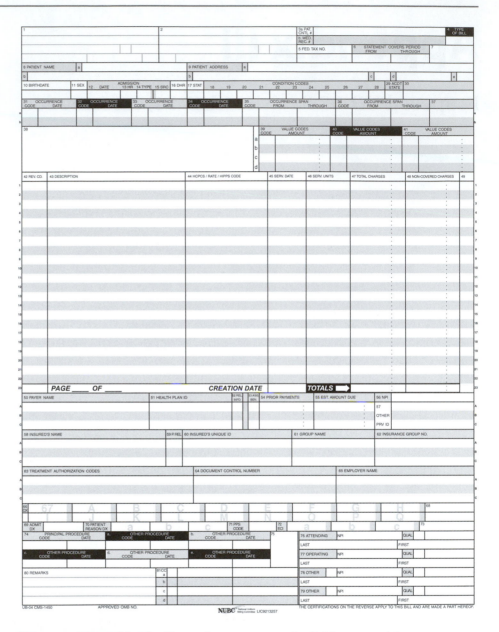

This material provided for illustrative purposes only. Subject to revisions by National Uniform Billing Committee (www.nubc.org).

UB-92 to UB-04 CROSSWALK

	UB-92						UB-04				* FL.68,75,80 Size Updated 6/21/05	
											Buffer	
FL	Description	Line	Type	Size		FL	Description	Line	Type	Size	Space	Notes
FL01	Provider Name	1	AN	25		FL01	Provider Name	1	AN	25		
FL01	Provider Street Address	2	AN	25		FL01	Provider Street Address	2	AN	25		
FL01	Provider City, State, Zip	3	AN	25		FL01	Provider City, State, Zip	3	AN	25		
FL01	Provider Telephone, Fax, Country Code	4	AN	25		FL01	Provider Telephone, Fax, Country Code	4	AN	25		
FL02	Unlabeled Fields	1	AN	20		FL02	Pay-to Name	1	AN	25		New
FL02	Unlabeled Fields	2	AN	30		FL02	Pay-to Address	2	AN	25		New
						FL02	Pay-to City, State	3	AN	25		New
						FL02	Pay-to ID	4	AN	25		New
FL03	Patient Control Number	1	AN	20		FL03a	Patient Control Number		AN	24		
						FL03b	Medical Record Number		AN	24		Moved/New
FL04	Type of Bill	1	AN	3		FL04	Type of Bill	1	AN	4	1	Expanded
FL05	Federal Tax Number	1	AN	4		FL05	Federal Tax Number	1	AN	4		
FL05	Federal Tax Number	2	AN	10		FL05	Federal Tax Number	2	AN	10		
FL06	Statement Covers Period - From/Through	1	N/N	6/6		FL06	Statement Covers Period - From/Through	1	N/N	6/6	1/1	
						FL07	Unlabeled	1	AN	8		
FL07	Covered Days	1	N	3			Eliminated - Substitute new Value Code					
FL08	Non-covered Days	1	N	4			Eliminated - Substitute new Value Code					
FL09	Coinsurance Days	1	N	3			Eliminated - Substitute new Value Code					
FL10	Lifetime Reserve Days	1	N	3			Eliminated - Substitute new Value Code					
FL11	Unlabeled	1		12			Eliminated					
FL11	Unlabeled	2		13			Eliminated					
FL12	Patient Name	1	AN	30		FL08	Patient Name - ID	1a	AN	19		New
						FL08	Patient Name	2b	AN	29		
FL13	Patient Address	1	AN	50		FL09	Patient Address - Street	1a	AN	40	1	Discrete
						FL09	Patient Address - City	2b	AN	30	2	Discrete
						FL09	Patient Address - State	2c	AN	2	1	Discrete
						FL09	Patient Address - ZIP	2d	AN	9	1	Discrete
						FL09	Patient Address - Country Code	2e	AN	3		Discrete
FL14	Patient Birthdate	1	N	8		FL10	Patient Birthdate	1	N	8	1	
FL15	Patient Sex	1	AN	1		FL11	Patient Sex	1	AN	1	2	
FL16	Patient Marital Status	1	AN	1			Eliminated					
FL17	Admission Date	1	N	6		FL12	Admission Date	1	N	6		
FL18	Admission Hour	1	AN	2		FL13	Admission Hour	1	AN	2	1	
FL19	Type of Admission/Visit	1	AN	1		FL14	Type of Admission/Visit	1	AN	1	2	
FL20	Source of Admission	1	AN	1		FL15	Source of Admission	1	AN	1	1	
FL21	Discharge Hour	1	AN	2		FL16	Discharge Hour	1	AN	2	2	
FL22	Patient Status/Discharge Code	1	AN	2		FL17	Patient Discharge Status	1	AN	2	2	
FL23	Medical/Health Record Number		AN	17			Moved to FL3b					
FL24	Condition Codes		AN	2		FL18	Condition Codes		AN	2	1	
FL25	Condition Codes		AN	2		FL19	Condition Codes		AN	2	1	
						FL20	Condition Codes		AN	2	1	

This material provided for illustrative purposes only. Subject to revisions by National Uniform Billing Committee (www.nubc.org).

UB-92 to UB-04 CROSSWALK

UB-92						UB-04						
											FL68,75,80 Size Updated 6/21/05	
											Buffer	
FL	Description	Line	Type	Size		FL	Description	Line	Type	Size	Space	Notes
FL26	Condition Codes		AN	2		FL21	Condition Codes		AN	2	1	
						FL22	Condition Codes		AN	2	1	
FL27	Condition Codes		AN	2		FL23	Condition Codes		AN	2	1	
						FL24	Condition Codes		AN	2	1	
FL28	Condition Codes		AN	2		FL25	Condition Codes		AN	2	1	
						FL26	Condition Codes		AN	2	1	New
FL29	Condition Codes		AN	2		FL27	Condition Codes		AN	2	1	New
						FL28	Condition Codes		AN	2	1	New
FL30	Condition Codes		AN	2								
						FL29	Accident State	1	AN	2	1	New
						FL30	Unlabeled	1	AN	12		
						FL30	Unlabeled	2	AN	13		
FL31	Unlabeled	1		5								
FL31	Unlabeled	2		6								
FL32	Occurrence Code/Date	a	AN/N	2/6		FL31	Occurrence Code/Date	a	AN/N	2/6	1/1	
FL32	Occurrence Code/Date	b	AN/N	2/6		FL31	Occurrence Code/Date	b	AN/N	2/6	1/1	
FL33	Occurrence Code/Date	a	AN	2/6		FL32	Occurrence Code/Date	a	AN/N	2/6	1/1	
FL33	Occurrence Code/Date	b	AN/N	2/6		FL32	Occurrence Code/Date	b	AN/N	2/6	1/1	
FL34	Occurrence Code/Date	a	AN	2/6		FL33	Occurrence Code/Date	a	AN/N	2/6	1/1	
FL34	Occurrence Code/Date	b	AN/N	2/6		FL33	Occurrence Code/Date	b	AN/N	2/6	1/1	
FL35	Occurrence Code/Date	a	AN	2/6		FL34	Occurrence Code/Date	a	AN/N	2/6	1/1	
FL35	Occurrence Code/Date	b	AN/N	2/6		FL34	Occurrence Code/Date	b	AN/N	2/6	1/1	
FL36	Occurrence Span Code/From/Through	a	AN/N/N	2/6/6		FL35	Occurrence Span Code/From/Through	a	AN/N/N	2/6/6	1/1/1	
FL36	Occurrence Span Code/From/Through	b	AN/N/N	2/6/6		FL35	Occurrence Span Code/From/Through	b	AN/N/N	2/6/6	1/1/1	
						FL36	Occurrence Span Code/From/Through	a	AN/N/N	2/6/6	1/1/1	New
						FL36	Occurrence Span Code/From/Through	b	AN/N/N	2/6/6	1/1/1	New
						FL37	Unlabeled	a	AN	8		
						FL37	Unlabeled	b	AN	8		
FL37	ICN/DCN	A	AN	23		*Moved to FL64*						Relocated
FL37	ICN/DCN	B	AN	23		*Moved to FL64*						
FL37	ICN/DCN	C	AN	23		*Moved to FL64*						
FL38	Responsible Party Name/Address	1	AN	40		FL38	Responsible Party Name/Address	1	AN	40	2	
FL38	Responsible Party Name/Address	2	AN	40		FL38	Responsible Party Name/Address	2	AN	40	2	
FL38	Responsible Party Name/Address	3	AN	40		FL38	Responsible Party Name/Address	3	AN	40	2	
FL38	Responsible Party Name/Address	4	AN	40		FL38	Responsible Party Name/Address	4	AN	40	2	
FL38	Responsible Party Name/Address	5	AN	40		FL38	Responsible Party Name/Address	5	AN	40	2	
FL39	Value Code - Code	a	AN	2		FL39	Value Code - Code	a	AN	2	1	
FL39	Value Code - Amount	a	N	9		FL39	Value Code - Amount	a	N	9	1	
FL39	Value Code - Code	b	AN	2		FL39	Value Code - Code	b	AN	2	1	
FL39	Value Code - Amount	b	N	9		FL39	Value Code - Amount	b	N	9	1	
FL39	Value Code - Code	c	AN	2		FL39	Value Code - Code	c	AN	2	1	
FL39	Value Code - Amount	c	N	9		FL39	Value Code - Amount	c	N	9	1	
FL39	Value Code - Code	d	AN	2		FL39	Value Code - Code	d	AN	2	1	
FL39	Value Code - Amount	d	N	9		FL39	Value Code - Amount	d	N	9	1	
FL40	Value Code - Code	a	AN	2		FL40	Value Code - Code	a	AN	2	1	
FL40	Value Code - Amount	a	N	9		FL40	Value Code - Amount	a	N	9	1	
FL40	Value Code - Code	b	AN	2		FL40	Value Code - Code	b	AN	2	1	
FL40	Value Code - Amount	b	N	9		FL40	Value Code - Amount	b	N	9	1	
FL40	Value Code - Code	c	AN	2		FL40	Value Code - Code	c	AN	2	1	
FL40	Value Code - Amount	c	N	9		FL40	Value Code - Amount	c	N	9	1	
FL40	Value Code - Code	d	AN	2		FL40	Value Code - Code	d	AN	2	1	
FL40	Value Code - Amount	d	N	9		FL40	Value Code - Amount	d	N	9	1	
FL41	Value Code - Code	a	AN	2		FL41	Value Code - Code	a	AN	2	1	
FL41	Value Code - Amount	a	N	9		FL41	Value Code - Amount	a	N	9	1	
FL41	Value Code - Code	b	AN	2		FL41	Value Code - Code	b	AN	2	1	

This material provided for illustrative purposes only. Subject to revisions
by National Uniform Billing Committee (www.nubc.org).

UB-92 to UB-04 CROSSWALK

	UB-92					UB-04				* FL68,75,80 Size Updated 6/21/05	
										Buffer	
FL	**Description**	**Line**	**Type**	**Size**	**FL**	**Description**	**Line**	**Type**	**Size**	**Space**	**Notes**
FL41	Value Code - Amount	b	N	9	FL41	Value Code - Amount	b	N	9	1	
FL41	Value Code - Code	c	AN	2	FL41	Value Code - Code	c	AN	2	1	
FL41	Value Code - Amount	c	N	9	FL41	Value Code - Amount	c	N	9	1	
FL41	Value Code - Code	d	AN	2	FL41	Value Code - Code	d	AN	2	1	
FL41	Value Code - Amount	d	N	9	FL41	Value Code - Amount	d	N	9	1	
FL42	Revenue Code	1-23	N	4	FL42	Revenue Code	1-23	N	4	0.5	
FL43	Revenue Code Description	1-23	AN	24	FL43	Revenue Code Description	1-22	AN	24	0.5	
					FL43-44	*PAGE ___ OF ___ CREATION DATE*	23	N/N	3/3	0.5	New
FL44	HCPCS/Rates/HIPPS Rate Codes	1-23	AN/N/AN	9	FL44	HCPCS/Rates/HIPPS Rate Codes	1-22	AN/N/AN	14	0.5	Expanded size
FL45	Service Date	1-23	N	6	FL45	Service Date	1-22	N	6	0.5	
					FL45	Creation Date	23	N	6	0.5	New
FL46	Units of Service	1-23	N	7	FL46	Units of Service	1-22	N	7	0.5	
FL47	Total Charges	1-23	N	10	FL47	Total Charges	1-23	N	9	0.5	Removed sign field
FL48	Non-Covered Charges	1-23	N	10	FL48	Non-Covered Charges	1-23	N	9	0.5	Removed sign field
FL49	Unlabeled	1-23	AN	4	FL49	Unlabeled	1-23	AN	2	0.5	
FL50	Payer - Primary	A	AN	25	FL50	Payer Name - Primary	A	AN	23		
FL50	Payer - Secondary	B	AN	25	FL50	Payer Name - Secondary	B	AN	23		
FL50	Payer - Tertiary	C	AN	25	FL50	Payer Name - Tertiary	C	AN	23		
FL51	Provider Number	A	AN	13	FL51	Health Plan ID	A	AN	15		
FL51	Provider Number	B	AN	13	FL51	Health Plan ID	B	AN	15		
FL51	Provider Number	C	AN	13	FL51	Health Plan ID	C	AN	15		
FL52	Release of Information - Primary	A	AN	1	FL52	Release of Information - Primary	A	AN	1	1	
FL52	Release of Information - Secondary	B	AN	1	FL52	Release of Information - Secondary	B	AN	1	1	
FL52	Release of Information - Tertiary	C	AN	1	FL52	Release of Information - Tertiary	C	AN	1	1	
FL53	Assignment of Benefits - Primary	A	AN	1	FL53	Assignment of Benefits - Primary	A	AN	1	1	
FL53	Assignment of Benefits - Secondary	B	AN	1	FL53	Assignment of Benefits - Secondary	B	AN	1	1	
FL53	Assignment of Benefits - Tertiary	C	AN	1	FL53	Assignment of Benefits - Tertiary	C	AN	1	1	
FL54	Prior Payments - Primary	A	N	10	FL54	Prior Payments - Primary	A	N	10	1	
FL54	Prior Payments - Secondary	B	N	10	FL54	Prior Payments - Secondary	B	N	10	1	
FL54	Prior Payments - Tertiary	C	N	10	FL54	Prior Payments - Tertiary	C	N	10	1	
FL54	Prior Payments - Patient	4	N	10		*Eliminated Patient Prior Payments*					
FL55	Estimated Amount Due - Primary	A	N	10	FL55	Estimated Amount Due - Primary	A	N	10	1	
FL55	Estimated Amount Due - Secondary	B	N	10	FL55	Estimated Amount Due - Secondary	B	N	10	1	
FL55	Estimated Amount Due - Tertiary	C	N	10	FL55	Estimated Amount Due - Tertiary	C	N	10	1	
FL55	Estimated Amount Due - Patient	4	N	10		*Eliminated Due from Patient*					
FL56	Unlabeled	1		13	FL56	NPI	1	AN	15		
FL56	Unlabeled	2		14	FL57	Other Provider ID - Primary	A	AN	15		
					FL57	Other Provider ID - Secondary	B	AN	15		
					FL57	Other Provider ID - Tertiary	C	AN	15		
FL57	Unlabeled	1		27		*Deleted from UB-04*					
FL58	Insured's Name - Primary	A	AN	25	FL58	Insured's Name - Primary	A	AN	25	1	
FL58	Insured's Name - Secondary	B	AN	25	FL58	Insured's Name - Secondary	B	AN	25	1	
FL58	Insured's Name - Tertiary	C	AN	25	FL58	Insured's Name - Tertiary	C	AN	25	1	
FL59	Patient's Relationship - Primary	A	AN	2	FL59	Patient's Relationship - Primary	A	AN	2	1	
FL59	Patient's Relationship - Secondary	B	AN	2	FL60	Patient's Relationship - Secondary	B	AN	2	1	
FL59	Patient's Relationship -Tertiary	C	AN	2	FL59	Patient's Relationship - Tertiary	C	AN	2	1	

This material provided for illustrative purposes only. Subject to revisions by National Uniform Billing Committee (www.nubc.org).

UB-92 to UB-04 CROSSWALK

											Buffer	

UB-92 | | | | | | UB-04 | | | | | * FL68,75,80 Size Updated 6/21/05

FL	Description	Line	Type	Size		FL	Description	Line	Type	Size	Buffer Space	Notes
FL60	CERT./ SSN/ HIC/ ID NO. - Primary	A	AN	19		FL60	Insured's Unique ID - Primary	A	AN	20		
FL60	CERT./ SSN/ HIC/ ID NO.- Secondary	B	AN	19		FL60	Insured's Unique ID - Secondary	B	AN	20		
FL60	CERT./ SSN/ HIC/ ID NO. - Tertiary	C	AN	19		FL60	Insured's Unique ID - Tertiary	C	AN	20		
FL61	Insurance Group Name - Primary	A	AN	14		FL61	Insurance Group Name - Primary	A	AN	14	1	
FL61	Insurance Group Name -Secondary	B	AN	14		FL61	Insurance Group Name -Secondary	B	AN	14	1	
FL61	Insurance Group Name - Tertiary	C	AN	14		FL61	Insurance Group Name - Tertiary	C	AN	14	1	
FL62	Insurance Group Number - Primary	A	AN	17		FL62	Insurance Group Number - Primary	A	AN	17	1	
FL62	Insurance Group Number - Secondary	B	AN	17		FL62	Insurance Group Number - Secondary	B	AN	17	1	
FL62	Insurance Group Number - Tertiary	C	AN	17		FL62	Insurance Group Number - Tertiary	C	AN	17	1	
FL63	Treatment Authorization Code - Primary	A	AN	18		FL63	Treatment Authorization Code - Primary	A	AN	30	1	
FL63	Treatment Authorization Code - Secondary	B	AN	18		FL63	Treatment Authorization Code - Secondary	B	AN	30	1	
FL63	Treatment Authorization Code - Tertiary	C	AN	18		FL63	Treatment Authorization Code - Tertiary	C	AN	30	1	
						FL64	Document Control Number	A	AN	26		
						FL64	Document Control Number	B	AN	26		
						FL64	Document Control Number	C	AN	26		
FL64	Employment Status Code - Primary	A	N	1			*Deleted from UB-04*					
FL64	Employment Status Code - Secondary	B	N	1			*Deleted from UB-04*					
FL64	Employment Status Code - Tertiary	C	N	1			*Deleted from UB-04*					
FL65	Employer Name - Primary	A	N	24		FL65	Employer Name - Primary	A	AN	25		
FL65	Employer Name - Secondary	B	N	24		FL65	Employer Name - Secondary	B	AN	25		
FL65	Employer Name - Tertiary	C	N	24		FL65	Employer Name - Tertiary	C	AN	25		
FL66	Employer Location - Primary	A	AN	35			*Deleted from UB-04*					
FL66	Employer Location - Secondary	B	AN	35			*Deleted from UB-04*					
FL66	Employer Locations -Tertiary	C	AN	35			*Deleted from UB-04*					
						FL66	DX Version Qualifier		AN	1		New Denotes ICD v.
FL67	Principal Diagnosis Code	1	AN	6		FL67	Principal Diagnosis Code		AN	8		Expanded field
FL68	Other Diagnoses	1	AN	6		FL67A	Other Diagnosis		AN	8		Expanded field
FL69	Other Diagnoses	1	AN	6		FL67B	Other Diagnosis		AN	8		Expanded field
FL70	Other Diagnoses	1	AN	6		FL67C	Other Diagnosis		AN	8		Expanded field
FL71	Other Diagnoses	1	AN	6		FL67D	Other Diagnosis		AN	8		Expanded field
FL72	Other Diagnoses	1	AN	6		FL67E	Other Diagnosis		AN	8		Expanded field
FL73	Other Diagnoses	1	AN	6		FL67F	Other Diagnosis		AN	8		Expanded field
FL74	Other Diagnoses	1	AN	6		FL67G	Other Diagnosis		AN	8		Expanded field
FL75	Other Diagnoses	1	AN	6		FL67H	Other Diagnosis		AN	8		Expanded field
						FL67I	Other Diagnosis		AN	8		New
						FL67J	Other Diagnosis		AN	8		New
						FL67K	Other Diagnosis		AN	8		New
						FL67L	Other Diagnosis		AN	8		New
						FL67M	Other Diagnosis		AN	8		New
						FL67N	Other Diagnosis		AN	8		New
						FL67O	Other Diagnosis		AN	8		New
						FL67P	Other Diagnosis		AN	8		New
						FL67Q	Other Diagnosis		AN	8		New
						FL68	Unlabeled	1a	AN	8*		
						FL68	Unlabeled	1b	AN	9*		
FL76	Admitting Diagnosis/Patient's Reason for Visit	1	AN	6		FL69	Admitting Diagnosis Code	1	AN	7		Expanded by 1
						FL70	Patient's Reason for Visit Code	A	AN	7		Distinct FL
						FL70	Patient's Reason for Visit Code	B	AN	7		Distinct FL
						FL70	Patient's Reason for Visit Code	C	AN	7		Distinct FL
						FL71	PPS Code	1	AN	3	2	New

This material provided for illustrative purposes only. Subject to revisions by National Uniform Billing Committee (www.nubc.org).

UB-92 to UB-04 CROSSWALK

UB-92						UB-04					* FL68,75,80 Size Updated 6/21/05
										Buffer	
FL	Description	Line	Type	Size		FL	Description	Line	Type	Size	Space Notes
FL77	External Cause of Injury Code	1	AN	6		FL72	External Cause of Injury Code	1a	AN	8	
						FL72	External Cause of Injury Code	1b	AN	8	New
						FL72	External Cause of Injury Code	1c	AN	8	New
FL78	Unlabeled					FL73	Unlabeled	1	AN	9	
FL79	Procedure Coding Method Used	1	N	1			*Deleted from UB-04*				Deleted
FL80	Principal Procedure Code/Date	1	N/N	6/6		FL74	Principal Procedure Code/Date		N/N	7/6	1/1 Expanded by 1
FL81	Other Procedure Code/Date	A	N/N	6/6		FL74a	Other Procedure Code/Date		N/N	7/6	1/1 Expanded by 1
FL81	Other Procedure Code/Date	B	N/N	6/6		FL74b	Other Procedure Code/Date		N/N	7/6	1/1 Expanded by 1
FL81	Other Procedure Code/Date	C	N/N	6/6		FL74c	Other Procedure Code/Date		N/N	7/6	1/1 Expanded by 1
FL81	Other Procedure Code/Date	D	N/N	6/6		FL74d	Other Procedure Code/Date		N/N	7/6	1/1 Expanded by 1
FL81	Other Procedure Code/Date	E	N/N	6/6		FL74e	Other Procedure Code/Date		N/N	7/6	1/1 Expanded by 1
						FL75	Unlabeled	1	AN	4*	0*
						FL75	Unlabeled	2	AN	4	1
						FL75	Unlabeled	3	AN	4	1
						FL75	Unlabeled	4	AN	4	1
FL82	Attending Physician ID	a	AN	23		FL76	Attending - NPI/QUAL/ID	1	AN/AN/AN	11/2/9	New Layout
FL82	Attending Physician ID	b	AN	32		FL76	Attending - Last/First	2	AN/AN	16/12	New Layout
FL83A	Other Physician ID	a	AN	25		FL77	Operating - NPI/QUAL/ID	1	AN/AN/AN	11/2/9	New Layout
FL83A	Other Physician ID	b	AN	32		FL77	Operating - Last/First	2	AN/AN	16/12	New Layout
FL83B	Other Physician ID	a	AN	25		FL78	Other ID - QUAL/NPI/QUAL/ID	1	AN/AN/ AN/AN	2/11/2/9	New Layout
FL83B	Other Physician ID	b	AN	32		FL78	Other ID - Last/First	2	AN/AN	16/12	New Layout
						FL79	Other ID - QUAL/NPI/QUAL/ID	1	AN/AN/ AN/AN	2/11/2/9	New
						FL79	Other ID - Last/First	2	AN/AN	16/12	New
FL84	Remarks	1	AN	43		FL80	Remarks	1	AN	19*	Reduced Field Size
FL84	Remarks	2	AN	48		FL80	Remarks	2	AN	24*	Reduced Field Size
FL84	Remarks	3	AN	48		FL80	Remarks	3	AN	24*	Reduced Field Size
FL84	Remarks	4	AN	48		FL80	Remarks	4	AN	24*	Reduced Field Size
						FL81	Code-Code - QUAL/CODE/VALUE	a	AN/AN/AN	2/10/12	New
						FL81	Code-Code - QUAL/CODE/VALUE	b	AN/AN/AN	2/10/12	New
						FL81	Code-Code - QUAL/CODE/VALUE	c	AN/AN/AN	2/10/12	New
						FL81	Code-Code - QUAL/CODE/VALUE	d	AN/AN/AN	2/10/12	New
FL85	Provider Rep. Signature	1	AN	22			*Deleted from UB-04*				
FL86	Date Bill Submitted	1	Date	6			*Deleted from UB-04; See FL45, line 23*				

This material provided for illustrative purposes only. Subject to revisions by National Uniform Billing Committee (www.nubc.org).

Index

IMPORTANT! READ CAREFULLY: This End User License Agreement ("Agreement") sets forth the conditions by which Thomson Delmar Learning, a division of Thomson Learning Inc. ("Thomson") will make electronic access to the Thomson Delmar Learning-owned licensed content and associated media, software, documentation, printed materials, and electronic documentation contained in this package and/or made available to you via this product (the "Licensed Content"), available to you (the "End User"). BY CLICKING THE "I ACCEPT" BUTTON AND/OR OPENING THIS PACKAGE, YOU ACKNOWLEDGE THAT YOU HAVE READ ALL OF THE TERMS AND CONDITIONS, AND THAT YOU AGREE TO BE BOUND BY ITS TERMS, CONDITIONS, AND ALL APPLICABLE LAWS AND REGULATIONS GOVERNING THE USE OF THE LICENSED CONTENT.

1.0 SCOPE OF LICENSE

1.1 Licensed Content. The Licensed Content may contain portions of modifiable content ("Modifiable Content") and content which may not be modified or otherwise altered by the End User ("Non-Modifiable Content"). For purposes of this Agreement, Modifiable Content and Non-Modifiable Content may be collectively referred to herein as the "Licensed Content." All Licensed Content shall be considered Non-Modifiable Content, unless such Licensed Content is presented to the End User in a modifiable format and it is clearly indicated that modification of the Licensed Content is permitted.

1.2 Subject to the End User's compliance with the terms and conditions of this Agreement, Thomson Delmar Learning hereby grants the End User, a nontransferable, nonexclusive, limited right to access and view a single copy of the Licensed Content on a single personal computer system for non-commercial, internal, personal use only. The End User shall not (i) reproduce, copy, modify (except in the case of Modifiable Content), distribute, display, transfer, sublicense, prepare derivative work(s) based on, sell, exchange, barter or transfer, rent, lease, loan, resell, or in any other manner exploit the Licensed Content; (ii) remove, obscure, or alter any notice of Thomson Delmar Learning's intellectual property rights present on or in the Licensed Content, including, but not limited to, copyright, trademark, and/or patent notices; or (iii) disassemble, decompile, translate, reverse engineer, or otherwise reduce the Licensed Content.

2.0 TERMINATION

2.1 Thomson Delmar Learning may at any time (without prejudice to its other rights or remedies) immediately terminate this Agreement and/or suspend access to some or all of the Licensed Content, in the event that the End User does not comply with any of the terms and conditions of this Agreement. In the event of such termination by Thomson Delmar Learning, the End User shall immediately return any and all copies of the Licensed Content to Thomson Delmar Learning.

3.0 PROPRIETARY RIGHTS

3.1 The End User acknowledges that Thomson Delmar Learning owns all rights, title and interest, including, but not limited to all copyright rights therein, in and to the Licensed Content, and that the End User shall not take any action inconsistent with such ownership. The Licensed Content is protected by U.S., Canadian and other applicable copyright laws and by international treaties, including the Berne Convention and the Universal Copyright Convention. Nothing contained in this Agreement shall be construed as granting the End User any ownership rights in or to the Licensed Content.

3.2   Thomson Delmar Learning reserves the right at any time to withdraw from the Licensed Content any item or part of an item for which it no longer retains the right to publish, or which it has reasonable grounds to believe infringes copyright or is defamatory, unlawful, or otherwise objectionable.

4.0   PROTECTION AND SECURITY

4.1   The End User shall use its best efforts and take all reasonable steps to safeguard its copy of the Licensed Content to ensure that no unauthorized reproduction, publication, disclosure, modification, or distribution of the Licensed Content, in whole or in part, is made. To the extent that the End User becomes aware of any such unauthorized use of the Licensed Content, the End User shall immediately notify Thomson Delmar Learning. Notification of such violations may be made by sending an e-mail to delmarhelp@thomson.com.

5.0   MISUSE OF THE LICENSED PRODUCT

5.1   In the event that the End User uses the Licensed Content in violation of this Agreement, Thomson Delmar Learning shall have the option of electing liquidated damages, which shall include all profits generated by the End User's use of the Licensed Content plus interest computed at the maximum rate permitted by law and all legal fees and other expenses incurred by Thomson Delmar Learning in enforcing its rights, plus penalties.

6.0   FEDERAL GOVERNMENT CLIENTS

6.1   Except as expressly authorized by Thomson Delmar Learning, Federal Government clients obtain only the rights specified in this Agreement and no other rights. The Government acknowledges that (i) all software and related documentation incorporated in the Licensed Content is existing commercial computer software within the meaning of FAR 27.405(b)(2); and (2) all other data delivered in whatever form, is limited rights data within the meaning of FAR 27.401. The restrictions in this section are acceptable as consistent with the Government's need for software and other data under this Agreement.

7.0   DISCLAIMER OF WARRANTIES AND LIABILITIES

7.1   Although Thomson Delmar Learning believes the Licensed Content to be reliable, Thomson Delmar Learning does not guarantee or warrant (i) any information or materials contained in or produced by the Licensed Content, (ii) the accuracy, completeness or reliability of the Licensed Content, or (iii) that the Licensed Content is free from errors or other material defects. THE LICENSED PRODUCT IS PROVIDED "AS IS," WITHOUT ANY WARRANTY OF ANY KIND AND THOMSON DELMAR LEARNING DISCLAIMS ANY AND ALL WARRANTIES, EXPRESSED OR IMPLIED, INCLUDING, WITHOUT LIMITATION, WARRANTIES OF MERCHANTABILITY OR FITNESS OR A PARTICULAR PURPOSE. IN NO EVENT SHALL THOMSON DELMAR LEARNING BE LIABLE FOR: INDIRECT, SPECIAL, PUNITIVE OR CONSEQUENTIAL DAMAGES INCLUDING FOR LOST PROFITS, LOST DATA, OR OTHERWISE. IN NO EVENT SHALL THOMSON DELMAR LEARNING'S AGGREGATE LIABILITY HEREUNDER, WHETHER ARISING IN CONTRACT, TORT, STRICT LIABILITY OR OTHERWISE, EXCEED THE AMOUNT OF FEES PAID BY THE END USER HEREUNDER FOR THE LICENSE OF THE LICENSED CONTENT.

8.0 GENERAL

8.1 <u>Entire Agreement</u>. This Agreement shall constitute the entire Agreement between the Parties and supercedes all prior Agreements and understandings oral or written relating to the subject matter hereof.

8.2 <u>Enhancements/Modifications of Licensed Content</u>. From time to time, and in Thomson Delmar Learning's sole discretion, Thomson Delmar Learning may advise the End User of updates, upgrades, enhancements and/or improvements to the Licensed Content, and may permit the End User to access and use, subject to the terms and conditions of this Agreement, such modifications, upon payment of prices as may be established by Thomson Delmar Learning.

8.3 <u>No Export</u>. The End User shall use the Licensed Content solely in the United States and shall not transfer or export, directly or indirectly, the Licensed Content outside the United States.

8.4 <u>Severability</u>. If any provision of this Agreement is invalid, illegal, or unenforceable under any applicable statute or rule of law, the provision shall be deemed omitted to the extent that it is invalid, illegal, or unenforceable. In such a case, the remainder of the Agreement shall be construed in a manner as to give greatest effect to the original intention of the parties hereto.

8.5 <u>Waiver</u>. The waiver of any right or failure of either party to exercise in any respect any right provided in this Agreement in any instance shall not be deemed to be a waiver of such right in the future or a waiver of any other right under this Agreement.

8.6 <u>Choice of Law/Venue</u>. This Agreement shall be interpreted, construed, and governed by and in accordance with the laws of the State of New York, applicable to contracts executed and to be wholly preformed therein, without regard to its principles governing conflicts of law. Each party agrees that any proceeding arising out of or relating to this Agreement or the breach or threatened breach of this Agreement may be commenced and prosecuted in a court in the State and County of New York. Each party consents and submits to the nonexclusive personal jurisdiction of any court in the State and County of New York in respect of any such proceeding.

8.7 <u>Acknowledgment</u>. By opening this package and/or by accessing the Licensed Content on this Web site, THE END USER ACKNOWLEDGES THAT IT HAS READ THIS AGREEMENT, UNDERSTANDS IT, AND AGREES TO BE BOUND BY ITS TERMS AND CONDITIONS. IF YOU DO NOT ACCEPT THESE TERMS AND CONDITIONS, YOU MUST NOT ACCESS THE LICENSED CONTENT AND RETURN THE LICENSED PRODUCT TO DELMAR LEARNING (WITHIN 30 CALENDAR DAYS OF THE END USER'S PURCHASE) WITH PROOF OF PAYMENT ACCEPTABLE TO THOMSON DELMAR LEARNING, FOR A CREDIT OR A REFUND. Should the End User have any questions/comments regarding this Agreement, please contact Thomson Delmar Learning at delmarhelp@thomson.com.

Minimum System Requirements:

- Operating System: Microsoft Windows 98 SE, Windows 2000 or Windows XP
- Processor: Pentium PC 500 MHz or higher (750Mhz recommended)
- RAM: 64 MB of RAM (128 MB recommended)
- 32 MB free hard drive space
- Monitor Screen Resolution: 800 × 600 pixels
- Color Depth: 16-bit color (thousands of colors)
- Mouse
- Printer: 16MB memory recommended

Installing the Student Practice Software on your computer:

1. Insert the CD-ROM into a CD-ROM drive.
2. Click **Start**, then click **Run**.
3. Enter d:/Setup and click **OK** (Note: replace d with your CD-ROM drive letter).
4. In a few moments, you will be welcomed to the installation program. Click **Next** to start the installation.
5. A dialog box will ask you for the drive and directory where you want the program installed. To install the program in the default directory at **c:\Program Files\Delmar\UHC**, click **Next.** If you want to change this, click Browse, and enter the directory and drive where you want the program to be installed.
6. Once the installation begins, it can be cancelled at any time by clicking **Cancel.**
7. An *Understanding Hospital Coding and Billing* icon will be added to the **Start** menu under **Programs | Delmar Applications.**
8. The install program will automatically complete the installation process. Click **OK** when you see the **Installation is Complete** message.